FUNDAMENTALS OF AUTOMOTIVE AIR CONDITIONING

TL 271.5 .D94 1990

Dwiggins, Boyce H.

Fundamentals of automotive air conditioning

NEW ENGLAND INSTITUTE
OF TECHNOLOGY
LEARNING RESOURCES CENTER

FUNDAMENTALS OF AUTOMOTIVE AIR CONDITIONING

Boyce H. Dwiggins

NEW ENGLAND INSTITUTE
OF TECHNOLOGY
LEARNING RESOURCES CENTER

DELMAR PUBLISHERS INC.®

NOTICE TO THE READER

Publisher does not warrant or guarantee any of the products described herein or perform any independent analysis in connection with any of the product information contained herein. Publisher does not assume, and expressly disclaims, any obligation to obtain and include information other than that provided to it by the manufacturer.

The reader is expressly warned to consider and adopt all safety precautions that might be indicated by the activities described herein and to avoid all potential hazards. By following the instructions contained herein, the reader willingly assumes all risks in connection with such instructions.

The publisher makes no representations or warranties of any kind, including but not limited to, the warranties of fitness for particular purpose or merchantability, nor are any such representations implied with respect to the material set forth herein, and the publisher takes no responsibility with respect to such material. The publisher shall not be liable for any special, consequential or exemplary damages resulting, in whole or in part, from the readers' use of, or reliance upon, this material.

Cover photo credits: Dashboard by Ford Motor Company; Gauges by Robinair Division, Sealed Power Corporation; Prototype car by Oldsmobile.

Delmar Staff

Administrative Editor: Joan Gill
Production Manager: Gerry East
Project Editor: Marlene McHugh Pratt
Production Coordinator: Sandra Woods
Design Coordinator: Susan C. Mathews

For information, address Delmar Publishers Inc.
2 Computer Drive West, Box 15-015
Albany, New York 12212

COPYRIGHT © 1990
BY DELMAR PUBLISHERS INC.

All rights reserved. No part of this work covered by the copyright hereon may be reproduced or used in any form or by any means—graphic, electronic, or mechanical, including photocopying, recording, or information storage and retrieval systems—without written permission of the publisher.

Printed in the United States of America
Published simultaneously in Canada by Nelson Canada
a division of The Thomson Corporation

10 9 8 7 6 5 4 3 2 1

Library of Congress Cataloging-in-Publication Data

Dwiggins, Boyce H.
    Fundamentals of automotive air conditioning/Boyce H. Dwiggins.
       p.cm.
    ISBN 0-8273-3944-5 (pbk.)
    ISBN 0-8273-3945-3 (instructor's guide)
    1. Automobiles—Air conditioning. 2. Automobiles—Air conditioning—Maintenance and repair. I. Title.
TL271.5.D94 1990
629.27'7—dc20   89-25977
                                                                            CIP

CONTENTS

ACKNOWLEDGMENTS — xii
PREFACE — xiii

CHAPTER 1: Theory — 1

Heat — 1
SENSIBLE HEAT — 1
LATENT HEAT — 1
SPECIFIC HEAT — 2
COLD—THE ABSENCE OF HEAT — 3

Body Comfort — 4
THE BODY REJECTS HEAT — 4
CONDITIONS THAT AFFECT BODY COMFORT — 5

Refrigerant and Refrigeration Oil — 5
TEMPERATURE AND PRESSURE RELATIONSHIP OF REFRIGERANT 12 — 6
HANDLING REFRIGERANT — 6
SPECIAL SAFETY PRECAUTIONS — 7
REFRIGERATION OIL — 8

The Refrigeration Circuit — 8

CHAPTER 2: Operation — 11

The Basic System — 11

Compressors — 12
FUNCTION — 12
DESIGN — 12
DRIVES — 14
RECIPROCATING OR PISTON-TYPE COMPRESSORS — 15
YORK VANE ROTARY COMPRESSOR — 19
VARIABLE DISPLACEMENT COMPRESSORS — 20
ELECTROMAGNETIC CLUTCH — 21

The Receiver/Dehydrator and Accumulator — 22
RECEIVER/DRIER COMPONENTS — 22
ACCUMULATOR — 23

The Thermostatic Expansion Valve and Orifice Tube — 24

- OPERATION OF THE THERMOSTATIC EXPANSION VALVE — 24
- THE THERMOSTATIC EXPANSION VALVE AS A CONTROL DEVICE — 26
- EQUALIZERS — 27
- FIXED ORIFICE TUBE — 28
- VALVES-IN-RECEIVER (VIR) — 28
- COMBINATION VALVE — 29
- OTHER VALVE TYPES — 30
- EVAPORATOR — 30
- BLOWER MOTOR — 31
- CONDENSER — 31
- HOSES — 32

CHAPTER 3: Controls — 33

- SUCTION PRESSURE REGULATORS — 33
- EVAPORATOR PRESSURE REGULATOR — 33
- SUCTION THROTTLING VALVE — 35
- VALVES-IN-RECEIVER — 36
- COMBINATION VALVE — 38
- MASTER CONTROL — 39
- THERMOSTAT — 40
- PRESSURE CUTOFF SWITCH — 40
- COMPRESSOR DISCHARGE PRESSURE SWITCH — 40
- TIME-DELAY RELAY — 41
- ELECTROVACUUM RELAY — 41
- AMBIENT SWITCH — 41
- THERMOSTATIC VACUUM VALVE — 41
- SUPERHEAT SWITCH — 42

CHAPTER 4: Basic Systems — 43

Types of Systems — 43

- CYCLING CLUTCH SYSTEM — 43
- EVAPORATOR PRESSURE REGULATOR — 44
- SUCTION THROTTLING VALVE — 44
- VALVES-IN-RECEIVER — 45
- SUMMARY — 45

CHAPTER 5: Automatic Temperature Controls — 46

- SENSORS — 48
- ELECTRONIC TEMPERATURE CONTROL SYSTEMS — 48
- CONTROL PANEL — 48

PROGRAMMER	49
BLOWER AND CLUTCH CONTROL	50
POWER MODULE	50
CLUTCH DIODE	50
HIGH-SIDE TEMPERATURE SWITCH	51
LOW-SIDE TEMPERATURE SWITCH	52
HIGH-PRESSURE SWITCH	52
LOW-PRESSURE SWITCH	52
PRESSURE CYCLING SWITCH	52
SUNLOAD SENSOR	52
OUTSIDE TEMPERATURE SENSOR	52
IN-CAR TEMPERATURE SENSOR	53
ASPIRATOR	53
COOLANT TEMPERATURE SENSOR	53
VEHICLE SPEED SENSOR	54
THROTTLE POSITION SENSOR	54
HEATER DELAY SWITCH	54
BRAKE BOOSTER VACUUM SWITCH	54
POWER STEERING CUTOFF SWITCH	54
MODE ACTUATOR	54
WATER VALVE ACTUATOR	54
SUMMARY	55

CHAPTER 6: Troubleshooting and Diagnosis   56

Service Procedure 1:
TROUBLESHOOTING THE AIR-CONDITIONING SYSTEM 56

System Diagnosis 1:
THE COMPRESSOR—CYCLING CLUTCH TXV OR FOT SYSTEM 61

System Diagnosis 2:
THE CONDENSER—CYCLING CLUTCH TXV OR FOT SYSTEM 62

System Diagnosis 3:
THE DEHYDRATOR—CYCLING CLUTCH TXV SYSTEM 63

System Diagnosis 4:
THE ACCUMULATOR—CYCLING CLUTCH FOT SYSTEM 64

System Diagnosis 5:
THE ACCUMULATOR—CYCLING CLUTCH FOT SYSTEM 65

System Diagnosis 6:
THERMOSTATIC EXPANSION VALVE—CYCLING CLUTCH TXV SYSTEM 66

System Diagnosis 7:
THERMOSTATIC EXPANSION VALVE–CYCLING CLUTCH TXV SYSTEM 67

System Diagnosis 8:
THE ORIFICE TUBE–CYCLING CLUTCH FOT SYSTEM 68

System Diagnosis 9:
THE THERMOSTAT–CYCLING CLUTCH TXV OR FOT SYSTEM 69

System Diagnosis 10:
THE THERMOSTAT–CYCLING CLUTCH TXV OR FOT SYSTEM 70

System Diagnosis 11:
THE SYSTEM–CYCLING CLUTCH TXV OR FOT SYSTEM 71

System Diagnosis 12:
THE SYSTEM–CYCLING CLUTCH TXV OR FOT SYSTEM 72

System Diagnosis 13:
THE SYSTEM–CYCLING CLUTCH TXV OR FOT SYSTEM 73

System Diagnosis 14:
THE SYSTEM–CYCLING CLUTCH TXV OR FOT SYSTEM 74

System Diagnosis 15:
THE SYSTEM–CYCLING CLUTCH TXV OR FOT SYSTEM 75

System Diagnosis 16:
THE SYSTEM–CYCLING CLUTCH TXV OR FOT SYSTEM 76

CHAPTER 7: Servicing   77

Safety   77

Manifold and Gauge Set   77
MANIFOLD 78
LOW-SIDE GAUGE (ENGLISH) 78
HIGH-SIDE GAUGE (ENGLISH) 79
GAUGE CALIBRATION AND SCALES 79
HOSES 80
THE THIRD GAUGE 80

Leak Detectors — 81
HALIDE LEAK DETECTOR — 81
LEAK DETECTION USING A SOAP SOLUTION — 81
LEAK DETECTION USING DYE — 82
ELECTRONIC LEAK DETECTORS — 82

Service Valves — 83
SCHRADER VALVE — 83
HAND SHUTOFF VALVE — 84
MOISTURE REMOVAL — 85
TRIPLE EVACUATION METHOD — 86

Service Procedure 1:
CONNECTING THE MANIFOLD AND GAUGE SET INTO THE SYSTEM — 87

Service Procedure 2:
LEAK TESTING THE SYSTEM — 89

Service Procedure 3:
EVACUATING THE SYSTEM — 93

Service Procedure 4:
ADDING DYE OR TRACE SOLUTION TO THE AIR-CONDITIONING SYSTEM — 94

Service Procedure 5:
PURGING THE AIR-CONDITIONING SYSTEM — 96

Service Procedure 6:
CHARGING THE SYSTEM — 98

CHAPTER 8: Repair — 102

Service Procedure 1:
ISOLATING THE COMPRESSOR FROM THE SYSTEM — 102

Service Procedure 2:
PERFORMING A VOLUMETRIC TEST OF THE AIR-CONDITIONING COMPRESSOR — 103

Service Procedure 3:
PERFORMANCE TESTING THE AIR-CONDITIONER — 105

Service Procedure 4:
SERVICING REFRIGERANT HOSES AND FITTINGS 107

Service Procedure 5:
TESTING THE PERFORMANCE OF THE VALVES-IN-RECEIVER (VIR) 111

Service Procedure 6:
REBUILDING THE VALVES-IN-RECEIVER (VIR) 112

Service Procedure 7:
TESTING AND/OR REPLACING THE FIXED ORIFICE TUBE (FOT) 116

Service Procedure 8:
CHECKING THE COMPRESSOR OIL LEVEL (AIR-TEMP, TECUMSEH, YORK COMPRESSORS) 120

Service Procedure 9:
CHECKING THE COMPRESSOR OIL LEVEL (SANKYO COMPRESSORS) 121

Service Procedure 10:
CHECKING AND ADDING OIL: DELCO AIR FOUR-CYLINDER COMPRESSORS (R-4) 122

Service Procedure 11:
CHECKING AND ADDING OIL: DELCO AIR SIX-CYLINDER COMPRESSORS (A-6 AND DA-6) 123

Service Procedure 12:
CHECKING AND/OR ADDING OIL: NIPPONDENSO COMPRESSOR (INCLUDES FORD FS-6 AND CHRYSLER C-171) 124

Service Procedure 13:
CHECKING AND ADDING OIL: TECUMSEH HR-980 COMPRESSOR SYSTEM 125

Service Procedure 14:
CHECKING AND ADDING OIL: YORK VANE ROTARY COMPRESSOR 126

CHAPTER 9: Compressor Repair
128

Safety
128

Service Procedure 1:
SERVICING THE NIPPONDENSO COMPRESSOR (INCLUDES CHRYSLER C-171 AND FORD FS-6) 129

Service Procedure 2:
SERVICING THE NIPPONDENSO TEN-CYLINDER COMPRESSOR, MODEL 10P15 136

Service Procedure 3:
SERVICING THE SANKYO COMPRESSOR 139

Service Procedure 4:
SERVICING THE TECUMSEH HR-980 COMPRESSOR 144

Service Procedure 5:
REPLACING THE COMPRESSOR SHAFT OIL SEAL (YORK AND TECUMSEH COMPRESSORS) 149

Service Procedure 6:
REPLACING THE COMPRESSOR SHAFT OIL SEAL (CHRYSLER AIR-TEMP) 152

Service Procedure 7:
SERVICING THE DELCO AIR FOUR-CYLINDER COMPRESSOR 154

Service Procedure 8:
SERVICING THE DELCO AIR SIX-CYLINDER COMPRESSOR (A-6) 161

Service Procedure 9:
SERVICING THE DELCO AIR DA-6 COMPRESSOR 166

Service Procedure 10:
SERVICING THE DELCO AIR V-5 COMPRESSOR 177

GLOSSARY 187

INDEX 197

ACKNOWLEDGMENTS

This text would not have been possible without the generous cooperation of the many manufacturers of automotive air-conditioning equipment and components. Their contributions over the past twenty-one years, since the first edition, have been most helpful in providing the latest information available.

Chrysler Motors Corporation

Controls Company of America

Everhot Products Company

Ford Motor Company

General Electric Company

General Motors Corporation:
    Buick Motor Division, Cadillac Motor Car Division, Chevrolet Motor Division, Delco Radio Division, Oldsmobile Division

Mapco

John E. Mitchell Company, Inc.

Murray Corporation

Robinair Manufacturing Company

Sankyo

Sears, Roebuck and Company

Tecumseh Products Company

Thermal Industries

T.I.F. Instruments, Inc.

Uniweld Products, Inc.

Warner Electric Brake and Clutch Company

York Corporation, Subsidiary of Borg-Warner Corporation

Thanks to the instructors who reviewed the revised manuscript.

Larry Adams, Portland Community College, Portland, Oregon

Edward Hester, Cedar Valley College, Lancaster, Texas

George Knebel, Northwestern Business College, Lima, Ohio

Mr. Gaff, ITT Technical Institute, Chelsea, Massachusetts

B. H. Dwiggins

PREFACE

The information given in this text is a balanced introduction to automotive air conditioning. The student will develop a basic understanding of the theory, diagnostic practices, safety practices, and service procedures essential to air conditioning. At the same time, the student will develop habits of sound practice and good judgment in the performance of all air-conditioning procedures. The instructional chapters can be regarded as entry level for those who immediately apply the basic skills developed in the class and shop. The chapters are preparatory for those who plan continued study in advanced phases of refrigeration and air conditioning, including systems not related to automotive applications.

In 1962, slightly more than eleven percent of all cars sold were equipped with air conditioners. This percent accounted for 756 781 units, including both factory-installed systems and those added after the purchase of the automobile. Just five years later, in 1967, the total number of installed air-conditioning units rose to 3 546 255. At the present time, nearly eighty percent of all automobiles sold are equipped with air-conditioning units. It is expected that the usage of these units will remain at approximately eighty percent. This means that eighty cars out of every one hundred cars on the road will be equipped with factory-installed or add-on air conditioning. When air conditioning was first used in automobiles, it was considered a luxury. Its usefulness soon made air conditioning a necessity.

At this point, the definition of air conditioning should be reviewed before tracing its history and its application to the automobile. *Air conditioning* is the process by which air is cooled, cleaned, and circulated. In addition, the quantity and quality of the conditioned air are controlled. This means that the temperature, humidity, and volume of air are controlled in any given situation. Under ideal conditions, air conditioning can be expected to accomplish all of these tasks at the same time. The student should recognize that the air-conditioning process includes the process of refrigeration (cooling by removing heat).

THE SERVICE TECHNICIAN

How does all this affect the student of automotive air conditioning? As the popularity of air conditioning in vehicles increases, it is obvious that the need for installation, maintenance, and service technicians will also increase. Many shops that just a few years ago added air-conditioning service as a sideline now find it to be their primary business.

The air-conditioning technician must have a thorough working knowledge and understanding of the operation and function of the vacuum, electrical, and refrigeration circuits and controls of the automotive air conditioner. A good knowledge of the equipment, special tools, techniques, and skills of the trade is also essential.

Air conditioning has made it possible for the Space Age to become part of the twentieth century. What was fiction at the turn of the century is commonplace today. The service technician's contribution to the industry may help make today's fiction commonplace by the twenty-first century.

SAFETY

It must be recognized that the procedures used by technicians performing automotive service vary greatly. It is not possible to anticipate all ways or conditions under which service may be performed. Therefore, it is not possible to provide precautions for every conceivable hazard that may result. The following precautions, then, are basic and apply to any type automotive service.

1. Wear safety glasses or goggles for eye protection.
2. Set the parking brake. Place the gear select in *park* (automatic transmissions) or *neutral* (manual transmissions).

3. Be sure the ignition switch is in the OFF position, unless otherwise required for the procedure.
4. When required for the procedure, operate the engine *only* in a well-ventilated area.
5. Keep clear of all moving parts when the engine is running. Remove rings, watches, and loose-hanging jewelry. Avoid loose clothing. Tie long hair securely behind the head.
6. Keep hands, clothing, tools, and test leads away from the radiator cooling fan. Electric cooling fans can start without warning even when the ignition switch is in the OFF position.
7. Avoid contact with hot parts such as radiator, exhaust manifold, and high-side refrigeration lines.

ABOUT THE AUTHOR

Boyce H. Dwiggins organized one of the first courses in vocational education for Automotive Air Conditioning. This course has run continuously since 1965. He was in charge of automotive classes as a county-level administrator and was a consultant for the writing of educational specifications for a five-shop automotive complex in an area vocational center.

Mr. Dwiggins has served as an examiner, administering the "Automotive Excellence" test for the International Garage Owner's Association (IGOA) for the certification of auto mechanics. He was invited to serve with a committee of the National Institute for Automotive Service Excellence (NIASE) to write the certification test for automotive air conditioning.

Mr. Dwiggins holds patents on teaching devices and copyrights on teaching material in the automotive and refrigeration fields. He has conducted workshops for automotive and refrigeration teachers throughout the eastern United States. He is currently Head of the Industrial Department of a vocational-technical center in Florida.

CHAPTER 1:

Theory

Heat

The word heat may be defined in many ways. The definition best suited for refrigeration service is that *heat* is a form of energy which can be transferred from one place to another. This transfer, however, cannot take place unless there is a difference in temperature between the two objects in which transfer is to take place.

Everything in nature contains heat. Some things contain more heat than others — but all contain heat. Heat cannot be created or destroyed, but it can be moved from one place to another or from one form of energy to another form of energy. Heat energy travels in one direction only: from a warmer object to a cooler object. This transfer of heat takes place in one of three ways: by conduction, convection, or radiation.

Conduction means that heat is being transferred through a solid. For example, when food is frying in a pan, heat from the burner is conducted through the pan and to the food.

Convection means that heat transfer is taking place as a result of the circulation of a fluid. The automobile cooling system is a good example of convection cooling. The coolant (a mixture of water and antifreeze) in the cooling system removes the heat created by the engine by carrying it from the engine block to the radiator. The heat is then dissipated into the surrounding air.

Radiation means that heat is being transmitted through a medium and the medium does not become hot. An example of this situation is the way in which people acquire sunburns at the beach. That is, part of the heat from the sun is transmitted to the skin through the air.

SENSIBLE HEAT

Sensible heat is any heat that can be felt and that can be measured on a thermometer.

One example of sensible heat is the heat in the surrounding air. This air is called *ambient air*. The temperature of this air is called the *ambient temperature*. When this temperature drops ten or fifteen degrees, one feels cool. An increase in the temperature causes one to feel warmer.

LATENT HEAT

Latent heat is the term applied to the heat required to cause a change of state of matter. This heat cannot be recorded on a thermometer, and it cannot be felt. The British thermal unit (Btu) is used as the standard measure for latent heat.

A change of state occurs when a solid changes to a liquid or a liquid changes to a gas or vice versa. Water at atmospheric pressure between 32°F (0°C) and 212°F (100°C) is called *subcooled liquid*. Water at 212°F (100°C) is called *saturated liquid*. That is, water at 212°F (100°C) contains all of the heat it can hold and still remain a liquid. Any additional heat will cause the water to vaporize.

To change the state of one pound (0.453 6 kg) of water at 212°F (100°C) to one pound (0.453 6 kg) of steam at 212°F (100°C) requires an amount of heat equal to 970 Btu (244.44 kg-cal). This heat is called the *latent heat of vaporization*. Remember that this latent heat cannot be measured on a thermometer and does not cause a change in the temperature of the water.

In addition, steam at 212°F (100°C) gives up 970 Btu (244.44 kg-cal) of heat per pound (0.453 6 kg) as it condenses into water at 212°F (100°C).

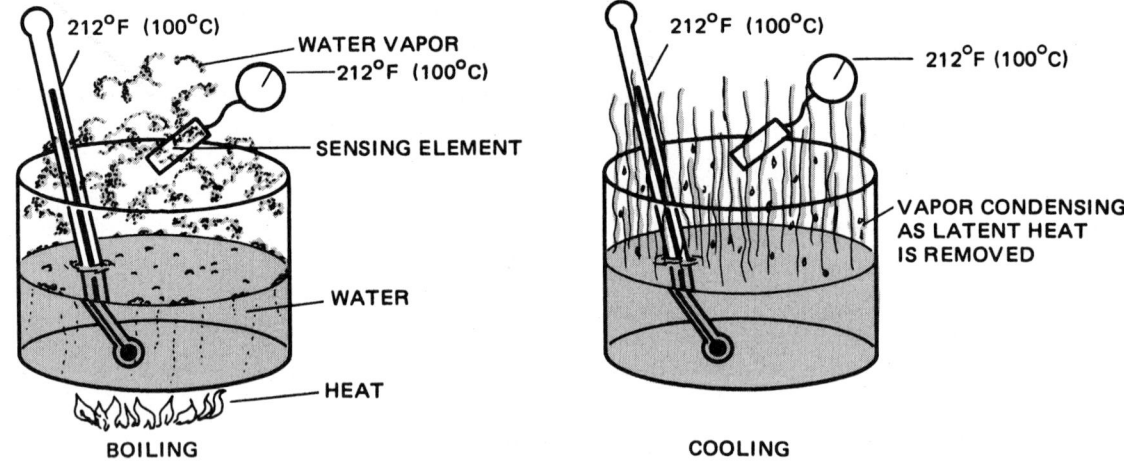

Fig. 1-1 Effect of latent heat.

The heat released in this process is called the *latent heat of condensation*.

The additional removal of heat at the rate of 1 Btu (0.252 kg-cal) per pound (0.453 6 kg) lowers the temperature of the water. This temperature decrease can be measured on the thermometer until 32°F (0°C) is reached. (A later section of this chapter covers the use of thermometers to make heat measurements.)

At 32°F (0°C), all of the heat that can be removed from the water without causing a change of state is removed. The heat that must be removed so that one pound (0.453 6 kg) of water at 32°F (0°C) can be changed to one pound (0.453 6 kg) of ice is 144 Btu (35.288 kg-cal). This value of heat energy is called the *latent heat of fusion*.

This principle governing the addition and removal of heat energy is the basis for refrigeration and air conditioning. A refrigerant is selected for its ability to absorb and to give up large quantities of heat rapidly.

Figure 1-3 illustrates the relative values of the latent heat of fusion and the latent heat of vaporization for water.

SPECIFIC HEAT

Every element or compound has its own heat characteristics. Every substance has a different capacity for accepting and emitting heat. All matter generates heat which is called "specific heat."

The capacity to accept (absorb) or emit (expel) heat is known as the *specific heat* or *thermal heat* of a substance. *Specific heat* is defined as

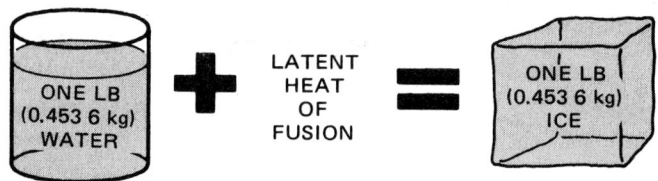

Fig. 1-2 Change from liquid to solid state.

the amount of heat that must be absorbed by a material if it is to undergo a temperature change of 1°F (0.556°C).

The following experiment can be performed with three small balls, each made of a different substance, such as copper, steel, and glass. Heat the balls in a container of hot oil until they all reach the same temperature. Now, place each of the three balls on a slab of paraffin and observe what happens. Each ball sinks to a different depth in the paraffin. The depth to which each ball sinks depends on the amount of heat emitted. This experiment illustrates that different materials, at the same temperature, absorb and emit different amounts of heat.

A scale is used to show the relationship of the abilities of various substances to absorb or emit heat. Water (H_2O) is used as a standard to which other substances are compared. The value of water is given as 1 or 1.000. When compared to water, most substances require less heat per unit of weight to cause an increase in their temperature. Two

Perspiration appearing as drops of moisture on the body indicates that the body is producing more heat than can be removed by convection, radiation, and normal evaporation.

CONDITIONS THAT AFFECT BODY COMFORT

The three main factors that affect body comfort are temperature, relative humidity, and air movement.

Temperature

Cool air increases the rate of convection; warm air slows it down. Cool air lowers the temperature of the surrounding surfaces. Therefore, the rate of radiation increases. Since warm air raises the surrounding surface temperature, the radiation rate decreases. In general, cool air increases the rate of evaporation and warm air slows it down. The evaporation rate also depends upon the amount of humidity already in the air and the amount of air movement.

Humidity

Moisture in the air is measured in terms of humidity. For example, 50% relative humidity means that the air contains half the amount of moisture that it is capable of holding at a given temperature.

A low relative humidity permits heat to be taken away from the body by evaporation. Because low humidity means the air is relatively *dry*, it can readily absorb moisture. A high relative humidity has the opposite effect. The evaporation process slows down in humid conditions; thus, the speed at which heat can be removed by evaporation decreases. An acceptable comfort range for the human body is 72° to 80°F (22.2°C to 26.6°C) at 45% to 50% relative humidity.

Air Movement

Another factor which affects the ability of the body to give off heat is the movement of air around the body. As the air movement increases, the following processes occur.

- The evaporation process of removing body heat speeds up because moisture in the air near the body is carried away at a faster rate.
- The convection process increases because the layer of warm air surrounding the body is carried away more rapidly.
- The radiation process increases because the heat on the surrounding surfaces is removed at a faster rate. As a result, heat radiates from the body at a faster rate.

As the air movement decreases, the processes of evaporation, convection, and radiation decrease.

Refrigerant and Refrigeration Oil

SAFETY CAUTION: Refrigerant must be handled with extreme care.

The term *refrigerant* refers to the fluid used in a refrigeration system to produce cold by removing heat. For automotive refrigeration systems, Refrigerant 12 is used. It has the highest safety factor of any refrigerant available that is capable of withstanding high pressures and temperatures without deteriorating or decomposing.

Refrigerant 12 is ideal for automotive use because of its relatively low operating pressures, as compared to other refrigerants. Its stability at high and low operating temperatures is also desirable. Refrigerant 12 (commonly abbreviated R-12) does not react with most metals such as iron, aluminum, copper, or steel.

R-12 is soluble in oil and does not react with rubber. Some synthetic rubber compositions, however, may deteriorate if used as refrigerant hose.

R-12 does not affect the taste, odor, or color of water or food. In normal use it is not harmful to animal or plant life. At the present time, however, pending federal legislation is considering restricting the sale of R-12 — perhaps by a form of rationing. The concern is due to some scientific investigation which claims that expended R-12 is contaminating the ozone.

Refrigerant 12 is odorless in concentrates of less than 20%. In greater concentrations, it can be detected by the faint odor of its original compound, carbon tetrachloride. The proper name for R-12 is dichlorodifluoromethane. Its chemical symbol is CCl_2F_2.

TEMPERATURE AND PRESSURE RELATIONSHIP OF REFRIGERANT 12

One of the characteristics of Refrigerant 12 which makes it a suitable refrigerant for automotive use is the fact that the temperature (on the Fahrenheit scale) and English system pressure values in the 20 to 80 psig range are very close.

The table in figure 1-5 shows that there is only a slight variation between the temperature and pressure values of the refrigerant in this range. These variations can be detected by sensitive thermometers and pressure gauges. In this range, the assumption is made that for every pound of pressure recorded, the temperature is the same. For example, for a pressure of 23.1 psig, the temperature is 23°F. This value is the temperature of the refrigerant itself. It is not the temperature of the outside surface of the container or the air passing over it.

HANDLING REFRIGERANT

SAFETY CAUTION: Liquid refrigerant should be properly stored and used since it can cause blindness if it splashes into the eyes. In addition, if refrigerant is allowed to contact the skin, frostbite may result.

A refrigerant container should never be exposed to excessive heat or be allowed to come into contact with a heating device. The increase in refrigerant pressure inside the container as a result of heating can become great enough to cause the container to explode.

Temp. °F	Press. psig	Temp. °F	Press. psig	Temp. °F	Press. psig	Temp. °F	Press. psig	Temp. °F	Press. psig
0	9.1	35	32.5	60	57.7	85	91.7	110	136.0
2	10.1	36	33.4	61	58.9	86	93.2	111	138.0
4	11.2	37	34.3	62	60.0	87	94.8	112	140.1
6	12.3	38	35.1	63	61.3	88	96.4	113	142.1
8	13.4	39	36.0	64	62.5	89	98.0	114	144.2
10	14.6	40	36.9	65	63.7	90	99.6	115	146.3
12	15.8	41	37.9	66	64.9	91	101.3	116	148.4
14	17.1	42	38.8	67	66.2	92	103.0	117	151.2
16	18.3	43	39.7	68	67.5	93	104.6	118	152.7
18	19.7	44	40.7	69	68.8	94	106.3	119	154.9
20	21.0	45	41.7	70	70.1	95	108.1	120	157.1
21	21.7	46	42.6	71	71.4	96	109.8	121	159.3
22	22.4	47	43.6	72	72.8	97	111.5	122	161.5
23	23.1	48	44.6	73	74.2	98	113.3	123	163.8
24	23.8	49	45.6	74	75.5	99	115.1	124	166.1
25	24.6	50	46.6	75	76.9	100	116.9	125	168.4
26	25.3	51	47.8	76	78.3	101	118.8	126	170.7
27	26.1	52	48.7	77	79.2	102	120.6	127	173.1
28	26.8	53	49.8	78	81.1	103	122.4	128	175.4
29	27.6	54	50.9	79	82.5	104	124.3	129	177.8
30	28.4	55	52.0	80	84.0	105	126.2	130	182.2
31	29.2	56	53.1	81	85.5	106	128.1	131	182.6
32	30.0	57	55.4	82	87.0	107	130.0	132	185.1
33	30.9	58	56.6	83	88.5	108	132.1	133	187.6
34	31.7	59	57.1	84	90.1	109	135.1	134	190.1

Fig. 1-5 Temperature-pressure chart for Refrigerant 12 (English system).

If refrigerant is allowed to come into contact with an open flame or heated metal, a poisonous gas is created. Anyone breathing this gas becomes violently ill. *Remember – refrigerant is not a toy.*

R-12 is commonly packaged in 14-ounce (396.9 g) cans, figure 1-6, which are called "pound" cans. This refrigerant is also available in 2-pound (0.907 2-kg) and 2-1/2-pound (1.134-kg) cans. These cans use a special adapter as a means of transferring the refrigerant to the system. No attempt should be made to remove the refrigerant by other means.

The pound cans of refrigerant are the most popular because of their convenience and the ease of measuring the proper amount of refrigerant into a system. However, bulk packaging of refrigerant (in cylinders or tanks) generally is the least expensive method of buying refrigerant.

R-12 drums and cylinders are painted white for easy identification. However, there is no standard system of refrigerant color codes. Some manufacturers may use different colors to designate the same refrigerant. Therefore, it is suggested that the contents of a cylinder be identified before the refrigerant is introduced into the system.

SPECIAL SAFETY PRECAUTIONS

Because it is important that the student be aware of the hazards involved in the use of Refrigerant 12, the following safety procedures must be observed.

1. Above 130°F (54.44°C), liquid refrigerant completely fills a container and hydrostatic pressure builds up rapidly with each degree of temperature rise. To provide for some margin of safety, *never heat a refrigerant cylinder above 125°F (51.66°C) or allow it to reach this temperature.*
2. *Never apply a direct flame to a refrigerant cylinder or container. Never place an electrical resistance heater near or in direct contact with a container of refrigerant.*
3. *Do not abuse a refrigerant cylinder or container.* To avoid damage, use an approved valve wrench for opening and closing the valves. Secure all cylinders in an upright position for storing and withdrawing refrigerant.
4. *Do not handle refrigerant without suitable eye protection.*
5. *Do not discharge refrigerant into an enclosed area having an open flame.*

Fig. 1-6 Typical "pound" can of Refrigerant 12 actually contains 14 ounces (397 grams).

6. When purging a system, discharge the refrigerant slowly.
7. *Do not discharge Refrigerant 12 into a confined space.* Discharge refrigerant only in a well-ventilated area.
8. For an automotive refrigeration system, do not introduce anything but pure Refrigerant 12 and approved refrigerant oil into the system.

R-12 is *dangerous* because of the damage it can do if it strikes the human eye or comes into contact with the skin. Since the evaporation temperature of R-12 is −21.6°F (−29.9°C), suitable eye protection should be worn by anyone handling R-12 to protect the eyes from splashing refrigerant. If R-12 does enter the eye, freezing of the eye can occur with resultant blindness. The following procedure is suggested if R-12 enters the eye(s).

1. Do not rub the eye.
2. Splash large quantities of cool water into the eye to increase the temperature.
3. Tape a sterile eye patch in place to prevent dirt from entering the eye.
4. Go immediately to a doctor or hospital for professional care.
5. *Do not attempt self-treatment.*

If liquid R-12 strikes the skin, frostbite can occur. The same procedure outlined for emergency eye care can be used to combat the effects of R-12 contact with the skin. Refrigerant 12 in air is harmless unless it is released in a confined space. Under this condition, Refrigerant 12 displaces oxygen in the air and may cause drowsiness or unconsciousness.

Refrigerant 12 must not be allowed to come into contact with an open flame or a very hot metal. Many texts state that Refrigerant 12 produces phosgene gas when exposed to hot metal or an open flame.

Tests by Underwriters' Laboratory, Inc. (UL) in recent years, using advanced technology equipment, prove that phosgene is not produced in this manner. Decomposition does, however, result in the formation of carbonyl fluoride (COF_2) and carbonyl chlorofluoride (COClF) with small amounts of free chlorine (Cl_2).

Though 20 to 50 times less toxic than phosgene, the decomposed gases of R-12 must be avoided. At high concentrations, the lack of oxygen (O), which results in asphyxiation, is the real hazard. A primary rule, then, is to *avoid breathing these fumes or any others.*

REFRIGERATION OIL

The moving parts of a compressor assembly must be lubricated to prevent damage during operation. Oil is used on these moving parts and on the seals and gaskets as well. In addition, a small amount of oil is added to the refrigerant which circulates through the system. This refrigerant/oil combination maintains the thermostatic expansion valve in the proper operating condition.

The oil which must be used in an automobile air-conditioning system is a nonfoaming sulfur-free grade specifically formulated for use in certain types of air-conditioning systems. This special oil is known as *refrigeration oil*, and it is available in several grades and types. The grade and type to be used is determined by the compressor manufacturer.

The properties of a good refrigeration oil are low wax content, good thermal and chemical stability, low viscosity, and a low pour point. A few simple rules are listed as follows for handling refrigeration oil:

DO
- Use only approved refrigeration oil.
- Make sure the cap is tight on the container when not in use.
- Replace oil if there is any doubt of its condition.
- Avoid contaminating the oil.

DO NOT
- Transfer oil from one container to another.
- Return used oil to the container.
- Leave the oil container uncapped.
- Use a grade of oil other than that recommended for the air conditioner.

The Refrigeration Circuit

The following description of the refrigeration part of the air-conditioning system is intended to familiarize the service technician with the general arrangement and function of the components in the system. A complete understanding of the overall operation of the system is necessary when working on air-conditioning units. Each component of the system will be examined in detail.

SAFETY CAUTION: It should be emphasized again that eye protection is recommended when servicing air-conditioning units.

Study the schematic diagram of the components of the refrigeration system, figure 1-7. The compressor (B) pumps heat-laden refrigerant vapor from the evaporator (A). The refrigerant is compressed at (B) and then is sent, under high pressure, to the condenser (C) as a superheated vapor.

Since this vapor is much hotter than the surrounding air, it gives up its heat to the outside air flowing through the condenser fins.

As the refrigerant vapor gives up its heat, it changes to a liquid. The condensed liquid refrigerant is filtered, dried, and temporarily stored, under pressure, in the receiver/drier (D) until it is needed by the evaporator.

Liquid refrigerant is metered from the receiver/drier into the evaporator by the thermostatic expansion valve (E). This valve controls the flow of refrigerant in this part of the system. The pressure of the refrigerant is lowered by the expansion valve. As a result, the refrigerant begins to boil and change to a vapor. During this process, the refrigerant picks up heat from the warm air passing through the fins of the evaporator. Thus, the process repeats as this heat is transmitted first to the compressor, and then to the condenser for dissipation.

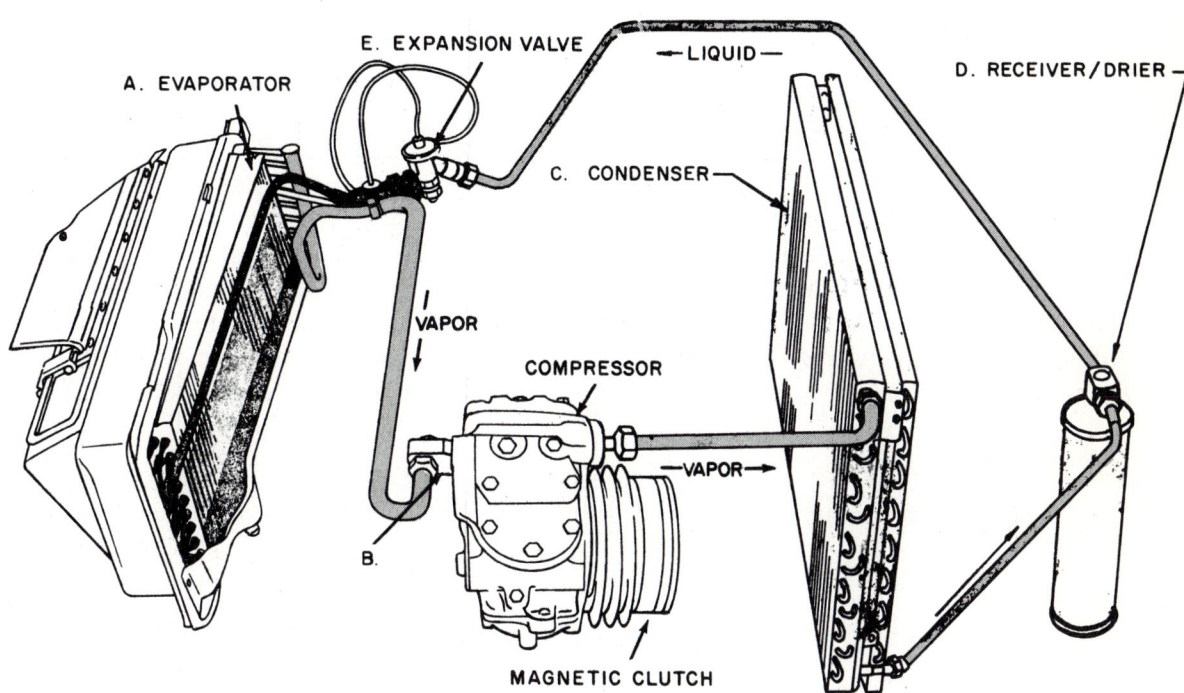

Fig. 1-7 Refrigeration system components (typical).

CHAPTER 2:

Operation

The Basic System

There are four major components in a basic automotive air-conditioning system. To understand how each component works in the system, think of the system as a circuit containing one continuous loop of tubing through which fluid (liquid or vapor) can move, figure 2-1.

A pump has been added in figure 2-2. The pump will move the fluid in a clockwise (cw) direction, as shown in the illustration. The air-conditioning pump, called a compressor, will only handle fluid in the vapor state. Also, there can be no exchange of heat if there is no change of state: liquid to vapor and/or vapor to liquid.

To meet the change-of-state requirement, a metering device has been added, figure 2-3. The metering device reduces the pressure of the fluid

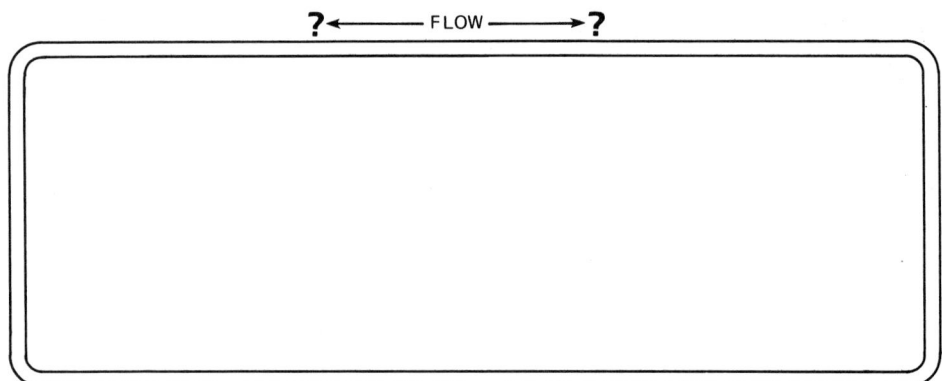

Fig. 2-1 A basic circuit. Continuous loop of tubing.

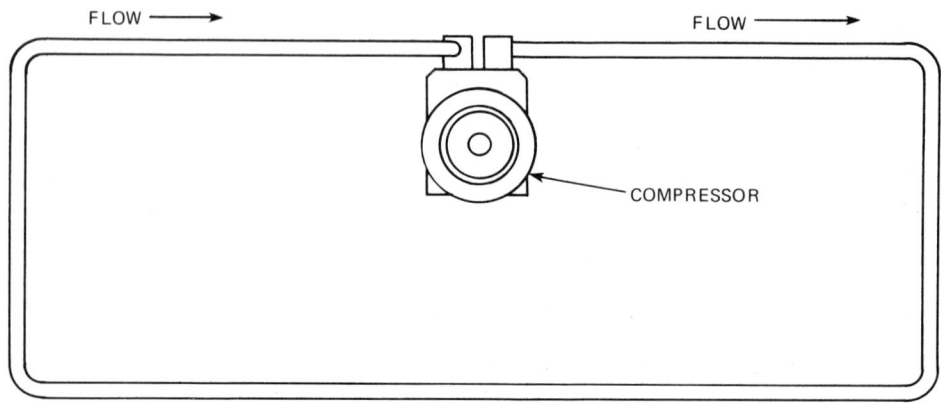

Fig. 2-2 A pump (compressor) has been added to the loop.

The Basic System 11

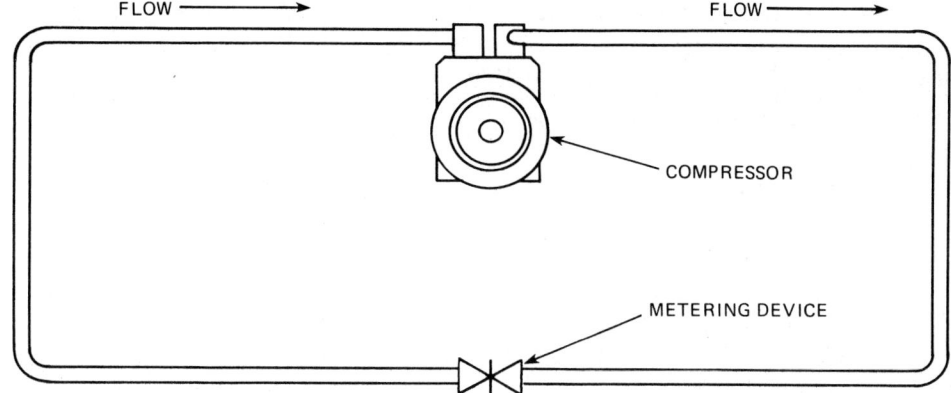

Fig. 2-3 A metering device has been added.

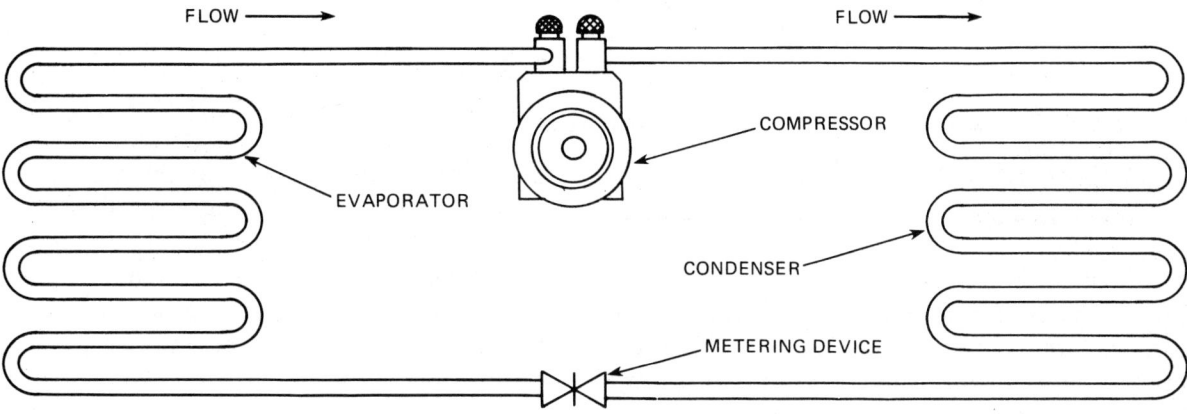

Fig. 2-4 The basic automotive air-conditioning system.

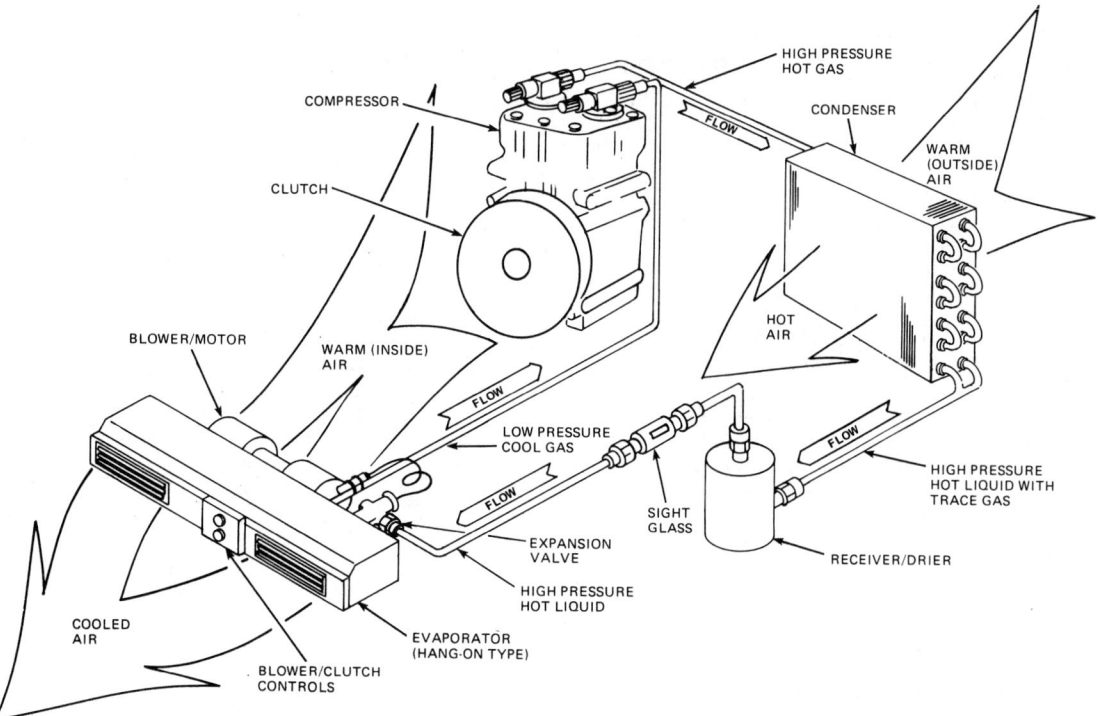

Fig. 2-5 Typical aftermarket (hang-on) automotive A/C.

which, in turn, allows the liquid to pick up heat and change to a vapor before entering the compressor. The compressor increases the pressure of the vapor, which turns it into liquid before returning to the metering device.

To provide for sufficient area for heat exchange to take place, the tubing of the inside coil (evaporator) and outside coil (condenser) have been bent in a serpentine manner. Fins have also been added to these coils to increase their heat transfer characteristics. The basic automotive air-conditioning system is shown in figure 2-4.

There are many variations of the basic system. Those most commonly found in modern automobiles are outlined in chapter four. Figure 2-5 shows a typical aftermarket automotive air-conditioning system.

Compressors

At the present time, over thirty different models of compressors are available for automotive air-conditioning application. Other models are on the drawing boards of compressor manufacturers, some of which will be developed and available for use in the near future.

The prime consideration and need for new compressor design is to reduce weight. Although weight is an important factor, compressors must also be designed to be efficient and durable. The York Vane Rotary compressor was the first rotary compressor developed for automotive air-conditioning use.

FUNCTION

The compressor in the automotive air-conditioning system serves two important functions at the same time. One function is to create a low-pressure condition at the compressor inlet provisions to remove heat-laden refrigerant vapor from the evaporator. This low-pressure condition is essential to allow the refrigerant metering device (thermostatic expansion valve or fixed orifice tube) to admit the proper amount of liquid refrigerant into the evaporator.

The second function of the compressor is to compress the low-pressure refrigerant vapor into a high-pressure vapor. This increased pressure raises the heat content of the refrigerant. A high pressure with high heat content is essential if the refrigerant is to give up its heat in the condenser.

Failure of either function will result in a loss or reduction of circulation of the refrigerant within a system. Without proper refrigerant circulation in the system, the air conditioner will not function properly or may not function at all.

DESIGN

Many types of compressors are used in automotive air-conditioning systems. Regardless of the type, compressors are basically of the same design: reciprocating piston. *Reciprocating* means that the piston moves up and down, to and fro, or back and

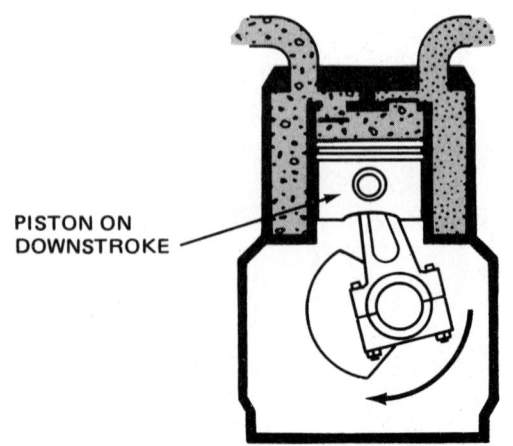
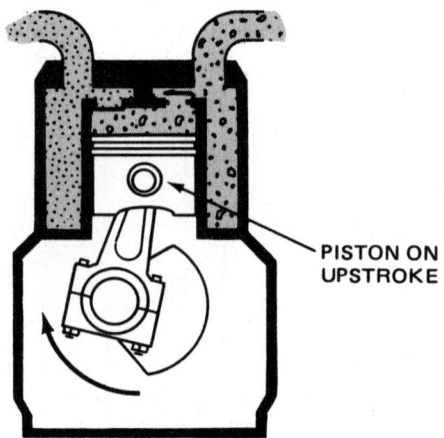

Fig. 2-6 Engine-driven clutch pulley drives crankshaft which, in turn, drives piston in compressor.

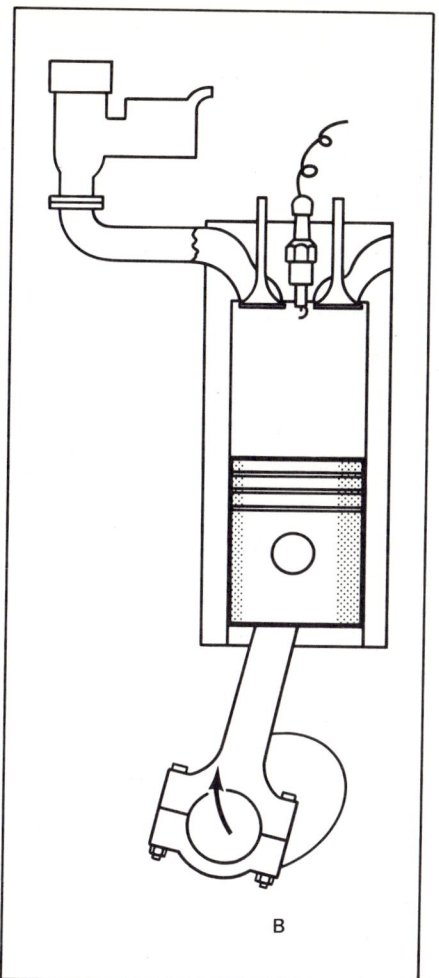

Fig. 2-7 The burning of air/fuel mixture (A) drives the piston which, in turn, rotates the crankshaft (B) in an engine.

forth. Two basic methods of driving the piston are by *crankshaft* or *axial plate*. The axial plate is often called a *swash plate* or *wobble plate*.

Crankshaft

Driving the piston by crankshaft, figure 2-6, is an operation which is very similar to an automobile engine. The main difference is that a compressor crankshaft drives the piston, whereas in an engine the piston drives the crankshaft, figure 2-7. The compressor crankshaft is driven, directly or indirectly, off the engine crankshaft by means of pulleys and belts.

Axial Plate

The other method of driving the piston is by axial plate, figure 2-8. The axial plate, pressed on

Fig. 2-8 Details of compressor axial plate, also referred to as swash plate.

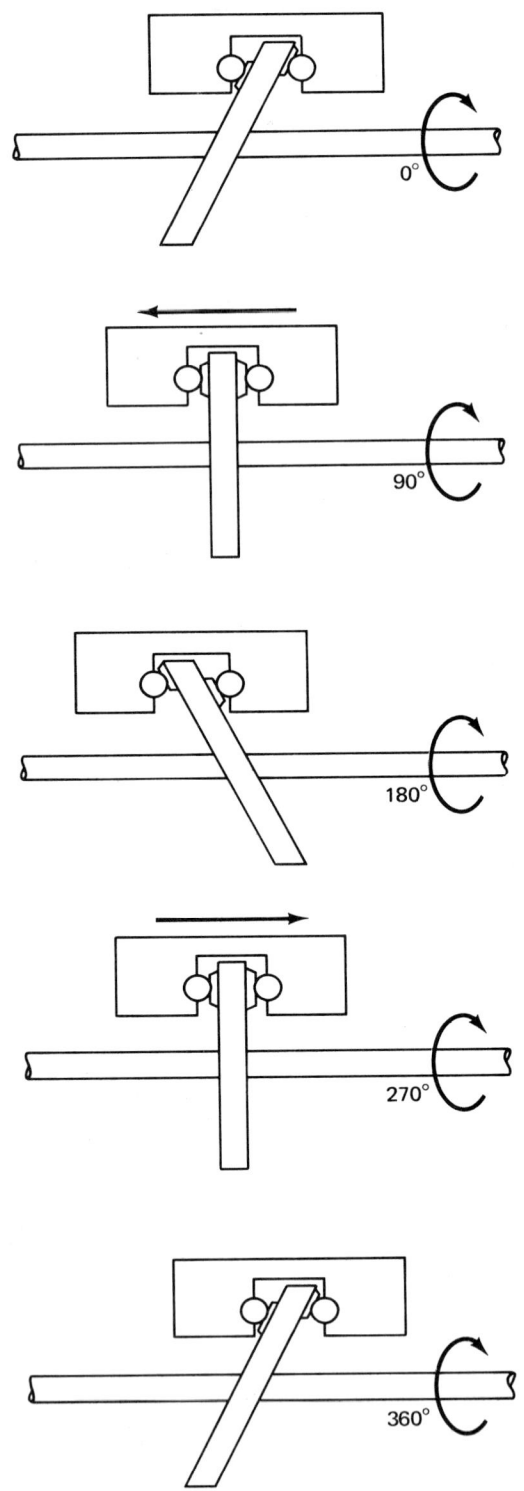

Fig. 2-9 One complete revolution of the crankshaft drives the piston from one end of its travel to the other by action of the axial plate which rotates with the crankshaft.

Fig. 2-10 Clutch mounted on compressor.

the main shaft, provides a reciprocation of the piston motion, figure 2-9. The axial plate is driven by the main shaft off the engine crankshaft, directly or indirectly, by means of pulleys and belts.

DRIVES

All automotive air-conditioning compressors have an electromagnetic clutch attached to their crankshaft or main shaft, figure 2-10. This clutch provides a means of starting and stopping the compressor. Some compressors are driven by one or two belts off the engine crankshaft and have an idler pulley which is used to adjust belt tension. Some use an accessory device, such as an alternator or power-steering pump (pulley), as the belt adjustment provisions.

Other compressors are driven off the water-pump pulley which, in turn, is driven by the engine crankshaft pulley. In this application, the belt is tensioned by adjusting the compressor.

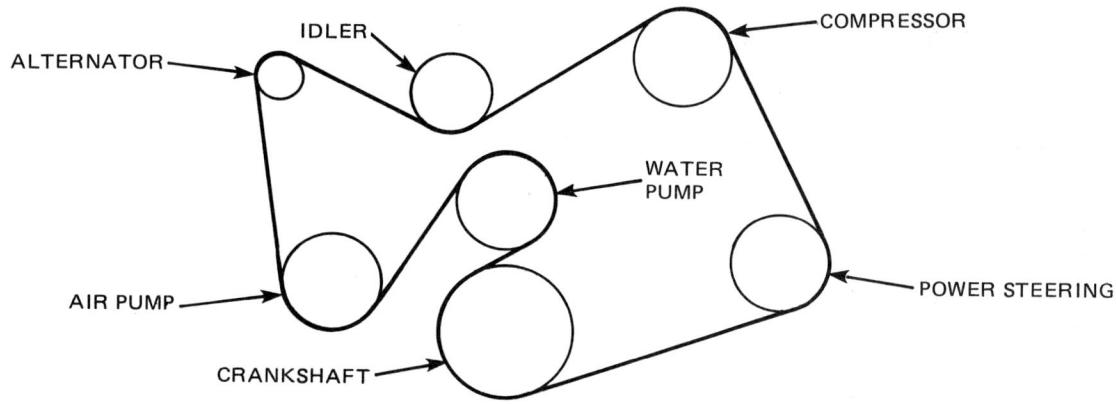

Fig. 2-11 Serpentine belt drive system.

Compressors are also driven off the crankshaft by a single-belt drive, along with such other accessories as the power steering pump, air pump, alternator, and water pump. This system is known as a *serpentine drive*, figure 2-11. The belt, called V-rib or serpentine, is tensioned by a spring-loaded idler pulley which rides on the back (flat) side of the belt.

RECIPROCATING- OR PISTON-TYPE COMPRESSORS

Automotive air-conditioning compressors, depending on design, have one, two, four, five, six, or ten pistons (cylinders). At least one domestic manufacturer, Tecumseh, provides a single-cylinder compressor, figure 2-12. The two-cylinder, V-type compressor, figure 2-13, was manufactured by Chrysler Air-Temp until recent years. Two-cylinder, in-line compressors are currently manufactured by Nippondenso, figure 2-14, Tecumseh, figure 2-15, and York, figure 2-16.

Two four-cylinder, radial-design compressors are available: the R-4, figure 2-17, manufactured by Delco Air (Frigidaire), and the HR-980, figure 2-18, manufactured by Tecumseh.

Sankyo and Delco Air manufacture a five-cylinder compressor. The Sankyo compressor, figure 2-19, is a positive displacement compressor, the Delco Air V-5 compressor, figure 2-20, is of variable displacement design.

Fig. 2-12 Tecumseh single-cylinder compressor.

Fig. 2-13 Chrysler Air-Temp two-cylinder compressor.

Chapter Two, Operation

Fig. 2-14 Nippondenso two-cylinder compressor.

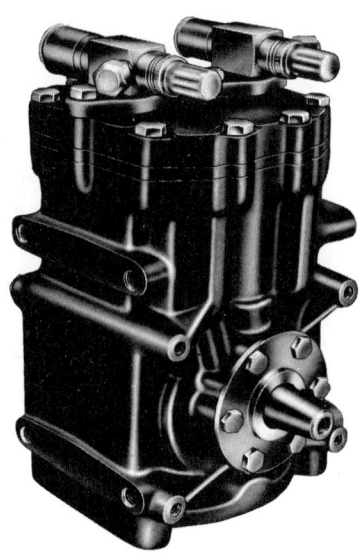

Fig. 2-15 Two-cylinder Tecumesh compressor.

Three six-cylinder compressors are available: the Delco Air A-6, figure 2-21, the Delco Air DA-6, figure 2-22, and the Nippondenso, figure 2-23. These compressors are of the axial design.

A ten-cylinder compressor was introduced by Nippondenso in 1986. Known as model 10P-15, this compressor has the same general appearance as the six-cylinder compressor illustrated in figure 2-23.

Applications

Tecumseh's single-cylinder compressor is used on many aftermarket compact car applications, both domestic and import. Nippondenso's two-cylinder compressor is used on some import car lines. The Tecumseh and York two-cylinder compressors are often found on intermediate and full-size aftermarket applications, as well as on some

Fig. 2-16 Two-cylinder York compressor.

Fig. 2-17 Delco Air 4-cylinder compressor with clutch assembly.

Compressors 17

Fig. 2-18 Tecumseh HR-980 compressor.

Fig. 2-21 Delco Air 6-cylinder compressor with clutch assembly.

Fig. 2-19 Sankyo 5-cylinder compressor with clutch assembly.

Fig. 2-22 Delco Air DA-6 compressor.

Fig. 2-20 Delco Air V-5 compressor.

Fig. 2-23 Nippondenso 6-cylinder compressor.

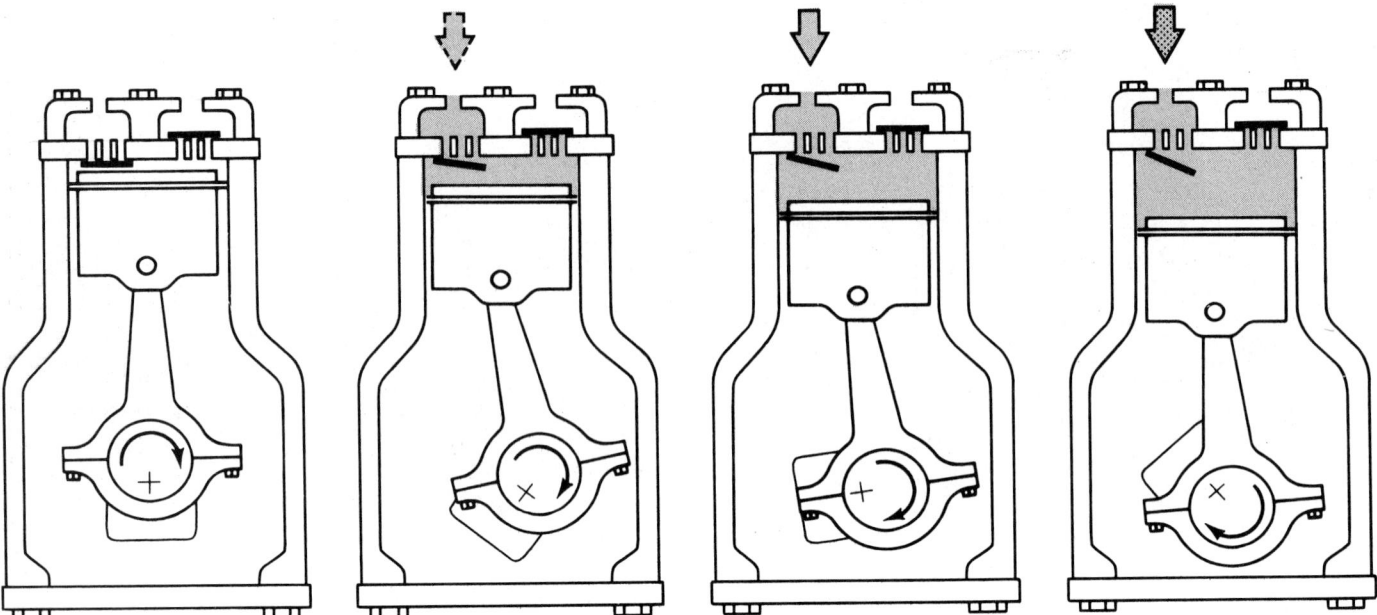

Fig. 2-24 Piston travel, top to bottom. Note position of suction and discharge valves.

American Motors and Ford factory systems.

The Air-Temp two-cylinder, V-type compressor is found only on some Chrysler car lines. The manufacture of this compressor was discontinued by Air-Temp in early 1981. Although it is a very efficient and durable compressor, it is also heavy.

The four-cylinder compressor by Delco Air is standard equipment on some General Motors car lines, and also may be found on some American Motors, Checker, Mercedes-Benz, and Saab car lines. The Sankyo compressor may be found on American Motors, Dodge, Plymouth, BMW, Nissan/Datsun, Fiat, Honda, Jeep, Mazda, Porsche, Subaru, Toyota, and Volkswagen car lines.

Delco Air 6-cylinder compressors may be found on General Motors, Checker, Ford, Lincoln, Mercury, Audi, Avanti, Jaguar, Mercedes-Benz, Peugeot, Rolls-Royce, and Volvo car lines.

The Nippondenso compressor is found on some Chrysler, Dodge, Ford, Lincoln, Mercury, and Plymouth car lines. At the present time, however, the Nippondenso 10-cylinder compressor is found only on some Ford and Mercury car lines.

Also, at the present time, the Delco Air vari-

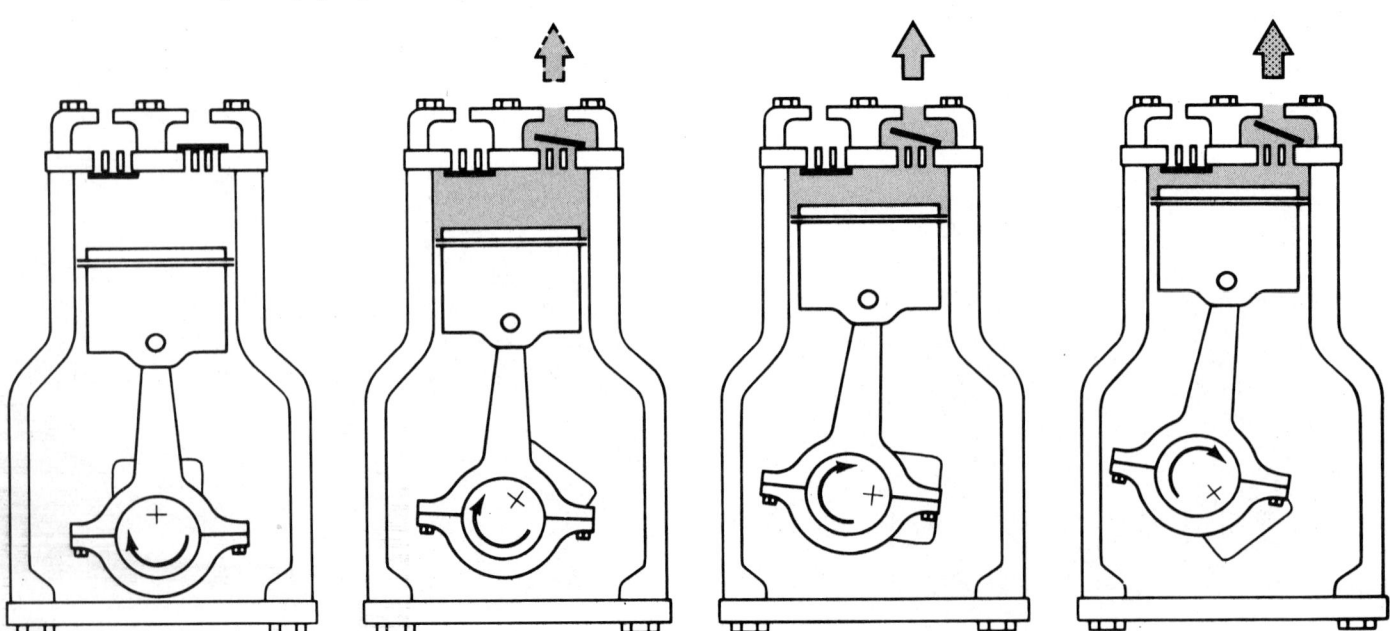

Fig. 2-25 Piston travel, bottom to top. Note position of suction and discharge valves.

Compressors 19

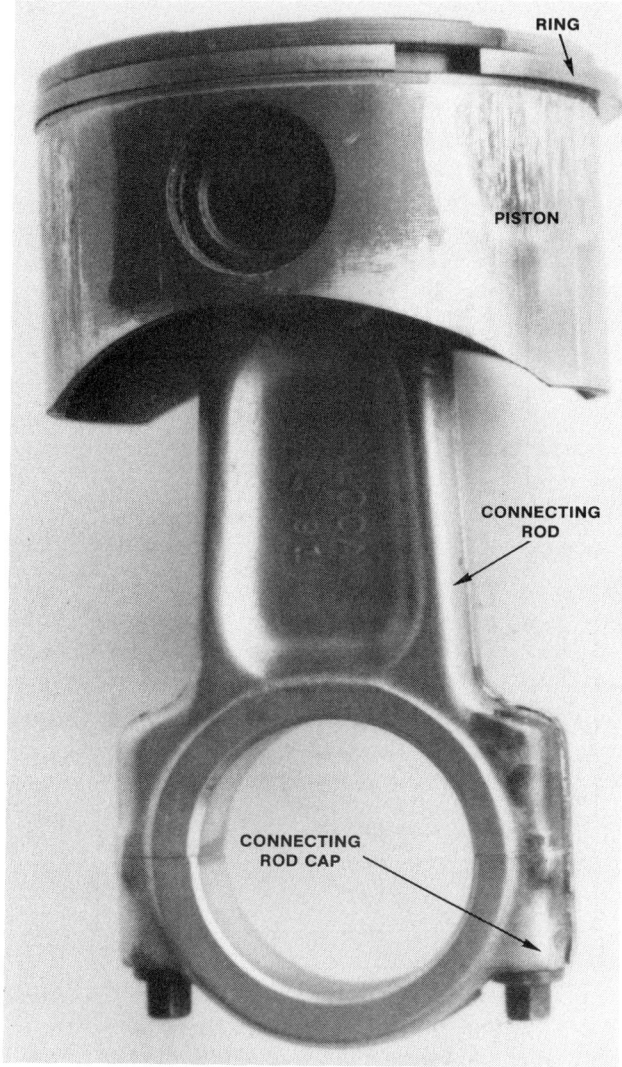

Fig. 2-26 Typical piston fitted with ring.

able displacement compressor, known as the V-5, is found only on some General Motors car lines.

Action (Reciprocating or Piston Type)

Low-pressure refrigerant vapor is compressed to high-pressure refrigerant vapor by action of the pistons and valve plates. For each piston, there is one intake (suction) valve and one outlet (discharge) valve mounted on a valve plate. For simplicity of understanding, a single-cylinder (piston) compressor will be discussed in this section.

By action of the crankshaft, figure 2-24, the piston travels from the top of its stroke to the bottom of its stroke during the first half-revolution of the crankshaft. On the second half-revolution, the piston travels from the bottom of its stroke to the top of its stroke, figure 2-25. The first action, top to bottom, is called the *intake* or *suction* stroke; the second action, bottom to top, is called the *compression* or *discharge* stroke.

The piston is fitted with a piston ring, figure 2-26, to provide a seal between the piston and the cylinder wall. This seal helps provide a negative (low) pressure on the down or intake stroke, and a positive (high) pressure on the up or exhaust stroke.

During the intake stroke, figure 2-27, a low-pressure area is created atop the piston and below the intake and exhaust valves. The higher pressure atop the intake valve, from the evaporator, allows the intake valve to open to admit heat-laden refrigerant vapor into the cylinder chamber. The discharge valve is held closed during this time period. The much higher pressure atop this valve as opposed to the low pressure below it prevents it from opening during the intake stroke.

During the compression stroke, figure 2-28, a high-pressure area is created atop the piston and below the intake and exhaust valves. This pressure becomes much greater than that above the intake valve and closes that valve. At the same time, the pressure is somewhat greater than that above the exhaust valve. The pressure difference is great enough to cause the exhaust valve to open. This allows the compressed refrigerant vapor to be discharged from the compressor.

Piston action is repeated rapidly — once for each revolution of the crankshaft. At road speed, this action may be repeated 1,500 or more times each minute for each cylinder of the compressor.

YORK VANE ROTARY COMPRESSOR

York's vane rotary compressor, figure 2-29, provides the greatest cooling capacity per pound of compressor weight. It has no pistons and only one valve: a discharge valve. The discharge valve actually serves as a check valve to prevent high-pressure refrigerant vapor from entering the compressor through the discharge provisions during the off cycle, or when the compressor is not operating. The function of the rotary vane compressor (or vane rotary compressor, as it is called by York) is the same as that of the piston- or reciprocating-type compressor. Its operation, however, is entirely different.

The concept of rotary-type compressors for refrigeration service is not new. Two basic types of rotary vane compressors have been available for nonautomotive refrigeration use for many years. One type has vanes that rotate with the shaft; the

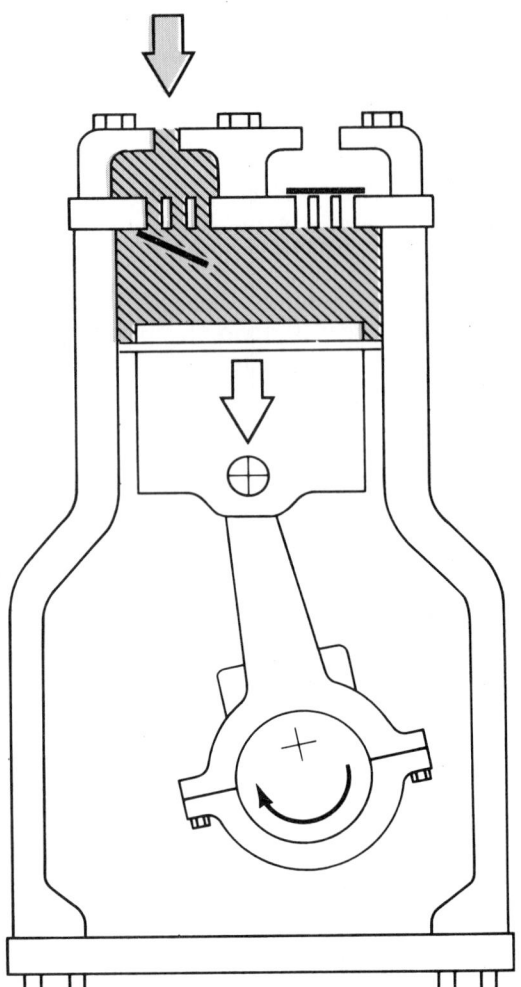

Fig. 2-27 Piston on downstroke (intake) pulls low-pressure refrigerant vapor into cylinder cavity. Note that intake (suction) valve is open and discharge valve is closed.

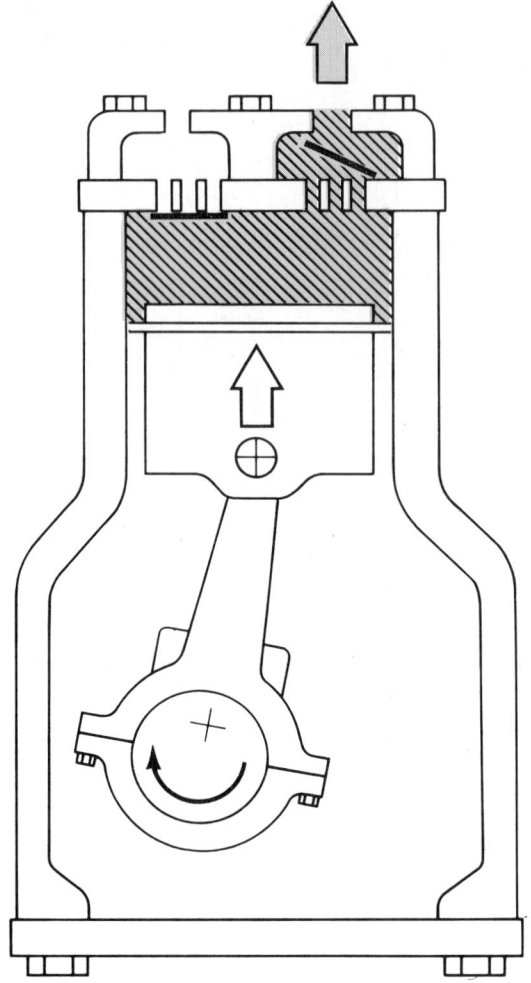

Fig. 2-28 Piston on upstroke (discharge) compresses refrigerant vapor and forces it out through the discharge valve. Note that the intake (suction) valve is closed and the discharge valve is open.

other type has stationary vanes. York's vane rotary compressor, for automotive air-conditioning service, is of the type with vanes that rotate with the shaft.

VARIABLE DISPLACEMENT COMPRESSORS

In 1985, Delco Air introduced a variable displacement compressor which was used that year on some models of all General Motors car lines. Designated as model V-5, this compressor can match any automotive air-conditioning load demand under all conditions. This is accomplished by varying the displacement of the compressor by changing the stroke of the pistons.

The five axially oriented pistons are driven by a variable-angle wobble plate. The angle of the

Fig. 2-29 York vane rotary compressor with clutch assembly.

wobble plate is changed by a bellows-activated control valve located in the rear head of the compressor. This control valve senses suction pressure, and controls the wobble plate angle based on crankcase-suction pressure differential.

When the air-conditioning demand is high, suction pressure will be above the control point, and the control valve will maintain a bleed from the compressor crankcase to the suction side. In this case, there is no crankcase-suction pressure differential, and the compressor will have maximum displacement. The wobble plate is at maximum angle providing greatest stroke (piston travel).

Conversely, when the air-conditioning demand is low and the suction pressure reaches the control point, the control valve will bleed discharge gas into the crankcase, and, in turn, close off a passage from the crankcase to the suction plenum.

The angle of the wobble plate is actually controlled by a force balance on the five pistons. Only a slight increase of the crankcase-suction pressure differential is required to create a force on the pistons sufficient to result in a movement of the wobble plate.

Temperature, then, is maintained by varying the capacity of the compressor, not by cycling the clutch ON and OFF. This action provides a more uniform method of temperature control and, at the same time, eliminates some of the noise problems associated with a cycling clutch system.

ELECTROMAGNETIC CLUTCH

Automotive air-conditioner manufacturers use an electromagnetic clutch as a means of disengaging the compressor when it is not needed. For example, the compressor is disengaged when a defrost cycle is indicated in the evaporator or when the air conditioner is not being used.

Basically, all clutches operate on the principle of magnetic attraction. There are two general types of clutches: those with a stationary field and those with a rotating field.

The Stationary Field Clutch

The stationary field clutch is more desirable than the rotating field clutch for use since it has fewer parts to wear out.

The field is mounted to the compressor by mechanical means, depending upon the type of field and the compressor supplied. The rotor is held on the armature by means of a bearing and snap rings. The armature is mounted on the compressor crankshaft.

When there is no current to the field, a magnetic force is not applied to the clutch. The rotor is free to turn on the armature which remains stationary on the crankshaft.

When the thermostat or switch is closed, current is applied to the field. A magnetic force is established between the field and the armature. As a result, the armature is pulled into the rotor. When the armature becomes engaged with the rotor, the complete unit turns while the field remains stationary. The compressor crankshaft then begins to turn and the refrigeration cycle starts.

When the switch or thermostat is opened, the current to the field is cut off. The armature disengages from the rotor and stops while the rotor continues to turn. The pumping action of the compressor is stopped until current is again applied to the field.

The Rotating Field Clutch

The rotating field clutch operates in the same manner as the stationary field clutch, with the exception of the field placement. In this case, the field is a part of the rotor and turns with the rotor. Current is applied to the field by means of brushes which are mounted on the compressor.

Current applied to the field through the brushes sets up a magnetic field which pulls the armature into contact with the rotor. The complete unit, consisting of the armature, rotor, and field, turns and causes the compressor to turn.

In both types of clutches, slots are machined in the armature and rotor to aid in concentrating the magnetic field and increasing the attraction between them.

Since the clutch engages and disengages at high speeds, as required for the proper temperature control, it is understandable that considerable scoring occurs on the armature and rotor surfaces. Such scoring is allowable and should not be a cause for concern.

The spacing between the coil and the pulley is important. The pulley should be as close to the coil as possible to achieve better magnetic flux travel. However, the pulley should not be so close that the rotor drags on the coil housing.

The spacing between the rotor and the armature is also important. If this spacing is too close, the armature drags on the rotor when the unit is turned off. If the rotor and armature are too far apart, there will be a poor contact between the armature and rotor when the unit is turned on. Either of these situations results in serious clutch malfunctions.

The Receiver/Dehydrator and Accumulator

The receiver/dehydrator (drier) is a very important part of an air-conditioning system. The load on the evaporator varies with temperature increases, increased humidity, or refrigerant losses due to small leaks. Thus, a storage area is necessary to hold extra refrigerant until it is needed by the evaporator. The receiver portion of the receiver/dehydrator unit serves as this storage area. Because of its function in storing liquid refrigerant, the use of a receiver means that it is not necessary to measure precisely the charge of refrigerant into the system. Several ounces (mL) over or under the recommended charge make little difference in system operation. In early air-conditioner units, a separate tank was often used as a receiver. In systems having a receiver tank, a separate dehydrator or drier is used. The drier is usually an in-line type and contains a filter and desiccant or drying material. A sight glass added at the outlet of the drier gives the service technician a means of observing the refrigerant flow in the system.

RECEIVER/DRIER COMPONENTS

The Desiccant

A desiccant is a solid substance which can remove moisture from a gas, liquid, or solid. The desiccant commonly used in the drier is silica gel, molecular sieve, or Mobil-Gel®. The desiccant may be placed between two screens (which also act as strainers) within the receiver, figure 2-30, or it may be placed in a metal mesh bag and suspended from a metal spring. In some cases, the bag of desiccant is simply placed in the tank and is not held in place. It is not uncommon to shake a drier tank and hear the desiccant move. This sound does not mean that the receiver/drier is damaged (depending upon the type of receiver/drier).

The capacity of the desiccant for absorbing moisture depends upon the volume and type of desiccant used. For example, five cubic inches (81.94 cm^3) of silica gel can absorb and hold about 100 drops of water at 150°F (65.56°C).

The Filter

Most driers contain filters through which the refrigerant must pass before it leaves the tank. The filtering material prevents desiccant dust and other solids from being carried with the refrigerant into the air-conditioning system. Some driers have two filters, one on each side of the desiccant.

The Pickup Tube

The pickup tube is a device provided to insure that 100% liquid refrigerant is fed to the thermostatic expansion valve. Since the refrigerant entering the tank can be a mixture of gas and liquid, the tank also acts as a separator. The liquid refrigerant drops to the bottom of the tank and the gaseous part of the refrigerant remains at the top. The pickup tube extends to the bottom of the tank,

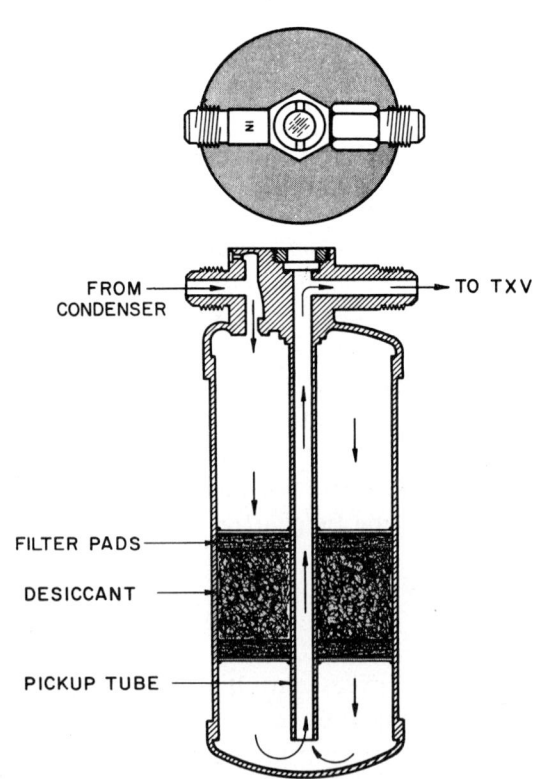

Fig. 2-30 Receiver/drier (cutaway).

thus insuring that a constant supply of gas-free liquid is delivered to the thermostatic expansion valve.

The Strainer

The strainer is made of fine wire mesh and is placed in the tank to aid in removing impurities (in particle form) as refrigerant passes through the receiver/drier. Some tanks have two strainers, one on each side of the desiccant.

The Sight Glass

The sight glass is used to visually observe the flow of refrigerant in the system and to determine if the system is undercharged. The sight glass may be located in the liquid or outlet side of the receiver/drier or it may be found at any point in the liquid line. From these locations, the service technician can readily observe the state of the refrigerant within the system. When the system is operating properly, a steady stream of liquid, free of bubbles, can be observed in the glass. The presence of bubbles or foam often indicates a system malfunction or a loss of refrigerant.

Using the sight glass to determine refrigerant charge is only valid if the ambient temperature is above 70°F (21.1°C). It is normal for continuous bubbles to appear in the sight glass on a cool day. If the sight glass is generally clear and the air conditioner is operating satisfactorily, occasional bubbles do not indicate a shortage of refrigerant. This condition may occur when the heat load changes and/or the compressor cycles OFF and ON.

It should be noted, however, that some systems do not have a sight glass. In such cases, system conditions must be determined with the manifold and gauge set.

ACCUMULATOR

Some air-conditioning installations contain a device that resembles a receiver/drier. This device

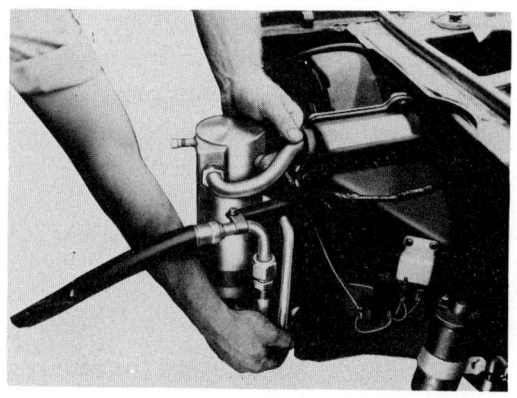

Fig. 2-31 Accumulator located at the outlet of the evaporator.

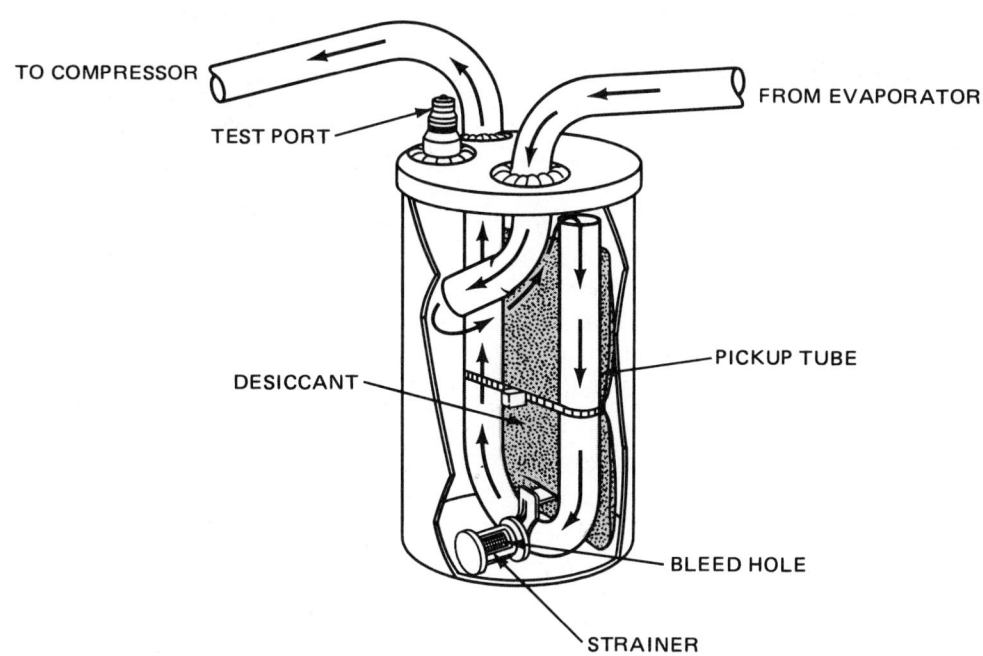

Fig. 2-32 Cutaway view of the accumulator. Note oil bleed hole to prevent oil from being trapped in accumulator.

is known as an *accumulator*, figure 2-31. The accumulator is provided to prevent liquid refrigerant from entering the compressor. The accumulator also serves as a tank to store excess liquid refrigerant and contains a desiccant.

Another name for the accumulator is the *suction accumulator* since it is located in the suction line of the system, figure 2-32. This device is used in systems that, under certain conditions, may have a flooded evaporator. The accumulator separates the liquid refrigerant from the vapor. In other words, it *accumulates* the liquid.

Refrigerant enters the top of the accumulator and liquid refrigerant falls to the bottom of the tank. Gaseous refrigerant remains at the top of the tank and is moved to the compressor through the pickup tube. At the bottom of the tank, the pickup tube contains a small hole or orifice. This orifice allows a very small amount of trapped oil or liquid refrigerant to return to the compressor.

A compressor can be damaged by an excess of liquid since it is a *positive displacement pump* and is not designed to compress liquids. Since only a controlled amount of liquid is allowed to return to the compressor through the pickup tube orifice, the compressor is not damaged.

The characteristics and composition of the desiccant in the accumulator are the same as those for the receiver/drier.

The Thermostatic Expansion Valve and Orifice Tube

The control of the proper amount of refrigerant entering the evaporator core, under varying heat load conditions, is the job of the metering device. This device is known as a *thermostatic expansion valve* (TXV or TEV), H-valve (also called block valve), or fixed orifice tube (also called expansion tube). The TXV or H-valve is usually found outside the evaporator case at the inlet provisions of the evaporator core. The fixed orifice tube (FOT) may be an intregal part of the inlet provisions of the evaporator, or it may be found inside the liquid line anywhere between the condenser outlet and the evaporator inlet. The TXV on some systems is found inside a device known as a valves-in-receiver (VIR) and, on other systems, it is part of a device called a combination valve or combo valve. These various metering devices are covered in this chapter.

Two types of thermostatic expansion valves are in common use: the internally equalized valve and the externally equalized valve. Many factory-installed air conditioners use an externally equalized valve and aftermarket manufacturers commonly use an internally equalized valve. Figure 2-33 illustrates the typical location of the thermostatic expansion valve in the air-conditioning system.

OPERATION OF THE THERMOSTATIC EXPANSION VALVE

The diagram in figure 2-34 illustrates the construction of an expansion valve. The valve has an orifice with a needle-type valve and seat to provide

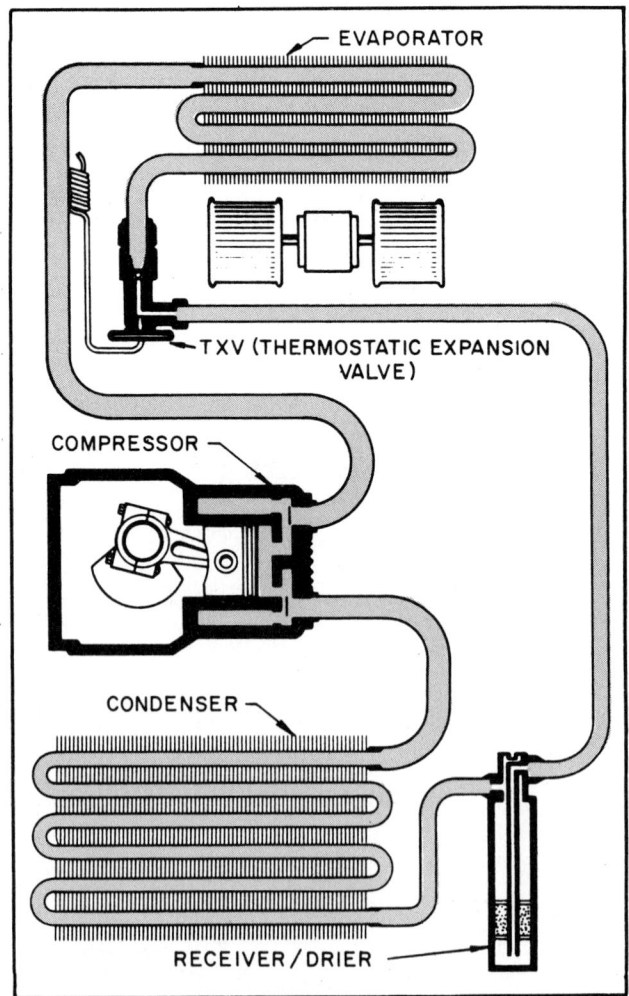

Fig. 2-33 Relation of the thermostatic expansion valve to the air-conditioning system.

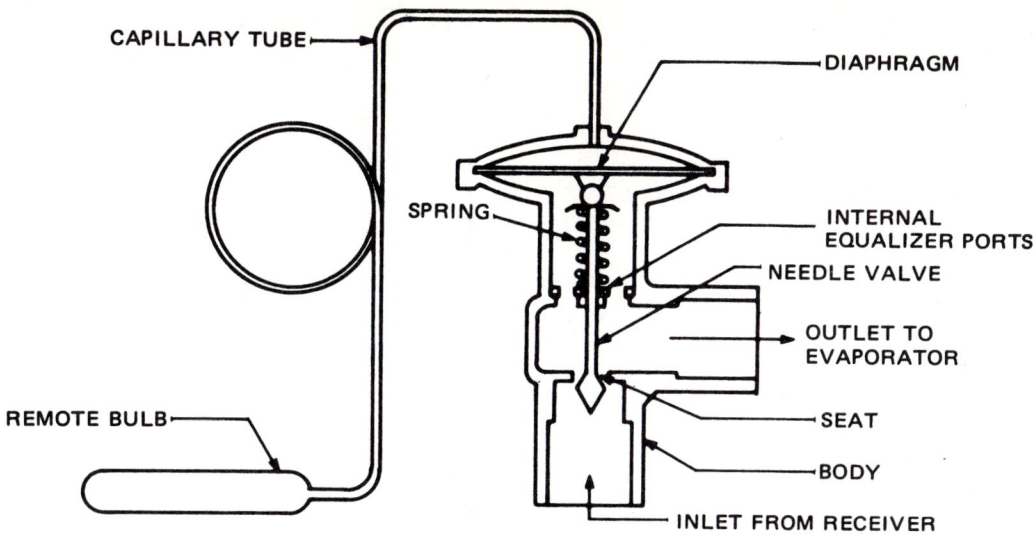

Fig. 2-34 Thermostatic expansion valve (cutaway).

variable metering. The needle is actuated by a diaphragm which is controlled by three forces:

- the evaporator pressure exerted on the bottom of the diaphragm which tends to keep the valve closed.
- the superheat spring pressure against the bottom of the needle valve which tends to keep the valve closed.
- the pressure of the inert liquid in the remote bulb or capillary tube against the top of the diaphragm which tends to open the valve.

Remote Bulb

Several types of inert liquid can be used in the remote bulb. However, for the moment, it is assumed that the fluid in the bulb is the same as that used in the system (Refrigerant 12). Because the same fluid or refrigerant is used, each exerts the same pressure, assuming that the temperature of each fluid is the same.

Under normal design considerations, the liquid refrigerant entering the evaporator boils by picking up heat and is in vapor (gas) form by the time it exits the evaporator coil. In fact, the refrigerant should be all vapor before reaching the end of the evaporator coil, and the vapor should become somewhat superheated. Although the superheated vapor is warmer than the temperature at which evaporation takes place, the pressure of the vapor is not changed. The remote bulb of the expansion valve is clamped onto the suction line. In this location, the bulb senses the warmer temperature of the evaporator outlet. The temperature of the inert fluid within the remote bulb increases, and its corresponding pressure is exerted on the diaphragm.

The increased pressure of the inert fluid exerted on the top of the diaphragm is greater than the combination of the evaporator pressure and the superheat spring pressure. As a result, the needle is moved away from the seat in the orifice. The needle valve opens until the superheat spring pressure and the evaporator pressure are great enough to balance the remote bulb pressure.

For example, when the needle valve is closed, it does not allow enough refrigerant to enter the evaporator. Thus, the evaporator pressure is low and the suction vapor is warm. This condition causes a positive pressure on top of the diaphragm and the needle valve opens.

When the needle valve is open, too much refrigerant is allowed to enter the evaporator. As a result, the evaporator pressure is high and the suction vapor is cool. This condition creates a positive pressure under the diaphragm which closes the needle valve. When the three pressures of the thermostatic expansion valve balance in the manner just described, the evaporator remains fully operational under all load conditions.

The TXV has three main functions: it throttles, modulates, and controls.

Throttling Action

The expansion valve separates the high side of the air-conditioning system from the low side. Since

26   Chapter Two, Operation

there is a pressure drop across the valve, the flow of refrigerant is restricted, or throttled. The state of the refrigerant entering the valve is a high-pressure liquid. The refrigerant leaving the valve is a low-pressure liquid. A drop in refrigerant pressure is accomplished without changing the state of the refrigerant.

Modulating Action

The TXV is designed to meter the proper amount of liquid refrigerant into the evaporator as required for the proper cooling action. The amount of refrigerant required varies with different heat loads. The TXV modulates from the wide-open position, to the closed position. The valve seeks a point between these two positions to insure the proper metering of the refrigerant.

Controlling Action

The expansion valve is designed to change the amount of liquid refrigerant metered into the evaporator in response to load or heat changes. As the load increases, more refrigerant is required by the evaporator. As the load is decreased, the valve closes and less refrigerant is metered into the evaporator core. This controlling action of the thermostatic expansion valve maintains proper refrigerant metering into the evaporator under varying heat-load conditions.

Superheat

The liquid refrigerant delivered to the evaporator coil usually completely vaporizes, or evaporates, before it reaches the coil outlet. Since it is known that the liquid refrigerant boils (vaporizes) at a low temperature (approximately −21.6°F or −29.8°C, at sea-level pressure), it can be seen that the vapor remains cold, even after all of the liquid is evaporated.

The cold vapor flowing through the remainder of the coil continues to absorb heat and becomes superheated. In other words, the temperature of the refrigerant is increased above the point at which it evaporates or vaporizes.

For example, an evaporator operating at a suction pressure of 28.5 psig (196.5 kPa) has a saturated liquid temperature of 30°F (−1.1°C), according to the temperature-pressure chart in figure 2-35. As the refrigerant vaporizes (due to the absorption of heat from the evaporator), the temperature of the vapor rises until the temperature at the coil

TEMPERATURE-PRESSURE CHART

(Evaporator temperature range)

TEMPERATURE		PRESSURE	
°F	°C	psig	kPa
20	−6.6	21	144.7
22	−5.5	22.4	154.4
24	−4.4	23.8	164.1
26	−3.3	25.3	174.4
28	−2.2	26.8	184.7
30	−1.1	28.5	196.5
32	0	30	206.8
34	+1.1	31.7	218.5
36	+2.2	33.4	230.2
38	+3.3	35.1	242
40	+4.4	36.9	254.4

Fig. 2-35 Temperature-pressure chart, TXV range.

outlet, or tailpipe, reaches 35°F (1.67°C). Thus, the difference between the inlet and the outlet temperatures is 5°F (2.7°C).

This difference in temperature is known as *superheat*. All expansion valves are adjusted at the factory to operate under the superheat conditions present in the particular type of unit for which they are designed. When an expansion valve is being replaced, it is important to use a valve having the proper superheat range and the proper size. Although many thermostatic expansion valves look the same, they differ greatly in their applications.

THE THERMOSTATIC EXPANSION VALVE AS A CONTROL DEVICE

The thermostatic expansion valve consists of seven major parts, as shown in figure 2-36:

- valve body
- valve seat
- valve diaphragm
- push rod(s)
- valve stem and needle
- superheat spring with adjuster
- capillary tube with remote bulb

As indicated previously, the remote bulb is fastened to the outlet, or tailpipe, of the evaporator.

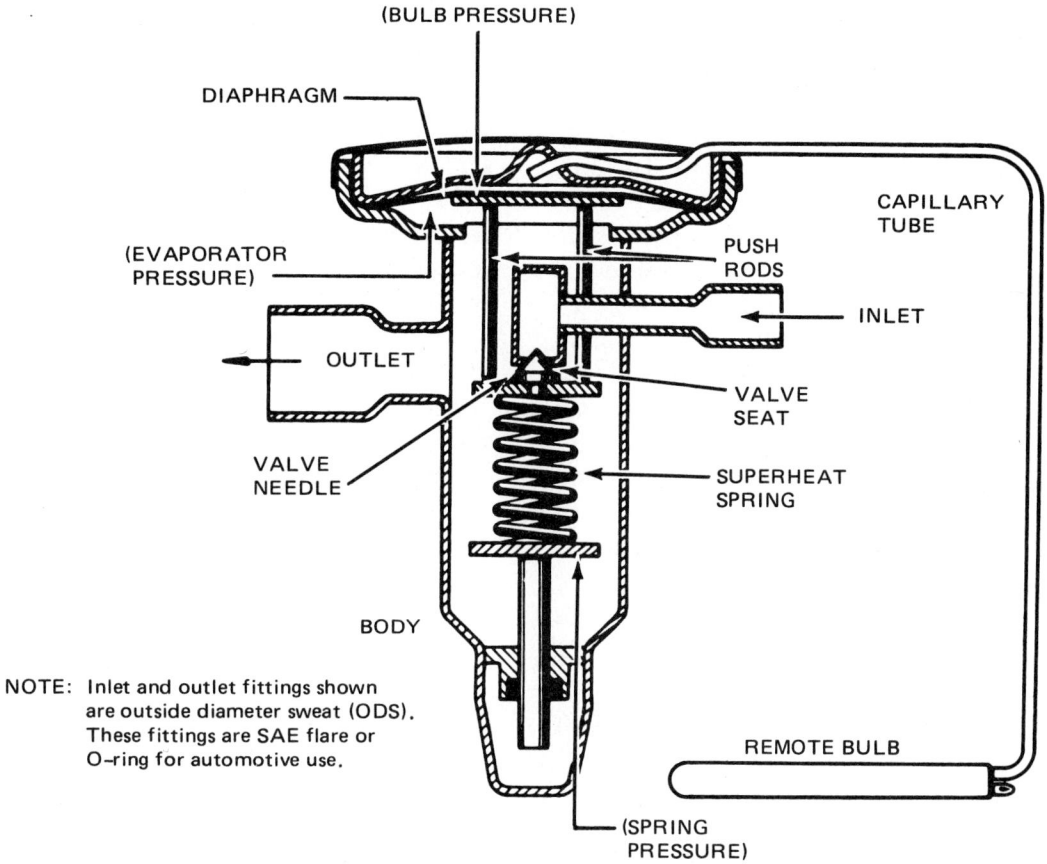

Fig. 2-36 Typical thermostatic expansion valve (cutaway).

The bulb senses tailpipe temperatures and activates the diaphragm in the valve through the capillary tube. In this manner, the proper amount of refrigerant is metered into the evaporator core.

For example, a high evaporator tailpipe temperature means that the evaporator is *starved* for refrigerant. This condition is indicated by an increase in the superheated vapor leaving the evaporator. As a result, the low-side pressure gauge indicates lower-than-normal readings.

The increased heat at the tailpipe causes an increase in the pressure exerted on the diaphragm by the expanding gases in the remote bulb through the capillary tube. The diaphragm, in turn, forces the push rods down against the valve stem and the needle valve, which is then pushed off its seat. In this way, more refrigerant is metered into the evaporator.

When the tailpipe temperature is low, there is less pressure on the remote bulb, capillary tube, and diaphragm, with the result that the needle valve is seated. In this case, the flow of refrigerant into the evaporator is restricted.

EQUALIZERS

It was stated previously that thermostatic expansion valves are either internally or externally equalized. The term *equalized* refers to provisions made for exerting evaporator pressure under the diaphragm. In an internally equalized valve there is a drilled passage from the evaporator side of the needle valve to the underside of the diaphragm. An externally equalized valve functions in the same manner, but can pick up the evaporator pressure at the outlet of the evaporator.

To overcome the effect of a pressure drop in larger evaporators, the externally equalized TXV is used. The external equalizer tube is connected to the tailpipe of the evaporator and runs to the underside of the diaphragm in the expansion valve. This arrangement balances the pressure of the tailpipe through the expansion valve remote bulb. The use of an external equalizer eliminates the effect of the pressure drop across the evaporator coil. Thus, the superheat settings depend only on the adjustment of the spring tension.

FIXED ORIFICE TUBE

A number of terms are used to identify the fixed orifice tube (FOT), such as expansion tube (ET), cycling clutch orifice tube (CCOT), and cycling clutch fixed orifice tube (CCFOT). By any name, this device replaces the thermostatic expansion valve to meter refrigerant into the evaporator in many factory-installed systems. It is found on some car lines in the inlet provisions of the evaporator. On other car lines, the FOT is found in the liquid line between the condenser outlet and the evaporator inlet. The old and new style expansion tubes, figure 2-37, are not interchangeable. The refrigerant entering the evaporator is controlled by the fixed orifice tube in a manner which is based on a pressure difference and the subcooling characteristics of the refrigerant.

Unlike the thermostatic expansion valve, the fixed orifice tube has no moving parts. The tube is not adjustable and its failure is usually a result of becoming clogged. Attempting to clean a clogged fixed orifice tube usually proves to be most difficult, if not impossible. It is best to replace the tube and accumulator.

An air-conditioning system equipped with an expansion tube does not have a receiver/drier. The drying agent for the system is found in an *accumulator*. The accumulator is located at the outlet of the evaporator.

Screen

The thermostatic expansion valve is equipped with a screen in the inlet side of the valve. This screen can be cleaned if it becomes clogged. If the screen requires cleaning, the receiver/dehydrator should be replaced. If the screen is too obstructed for cleaning, a new screen (and receiver/dehydrator) should be installed. The screen *must not be omitted* from the system.

The inlet of early series fixed orifice tubes (FOT) does not contain a screen. A screen was included in later series beginning in 1976. In either case, if the screen or tube becomes clogged, replacement is suggested. In addition, the accumulator should also be replaced to prevent a recurrence of the clogged FOT.

VALVES-IN-RECEIVER (VIR)

On some car lines a capsulized thermostatic expansion valve (TXV) is found in a device known as a *valves-in-receiver* (VIR) or, a later version, *evaporator equalizer valves-in-receiver* (EEVIR), figure 2-38. The VIR or EEVIR also contain the receiver with desiccant and a capsulized suction pressure regulator known as a *positive operated suction throttling valve* (POASTV) or, more simply, a POA valve.

The TXV is capsulized and is placed inside the VIR assembly with the POA valve. Its function and purpose is similar to that of the standard

A OLD STYLE

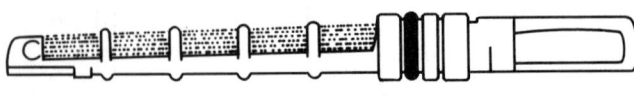

B NEW STYLE

Fig. 2-37 Old- and new-style expansion tube. The two styles are not interchangeable.

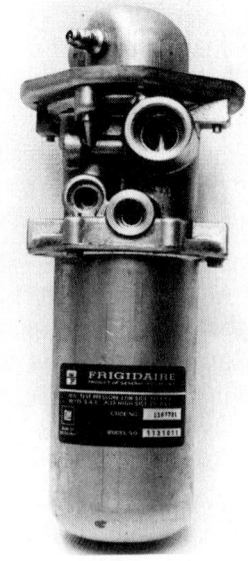

Fig. 2-38 Typical evaporator equalizer valves-in-receiver (EEVIR or VIR).

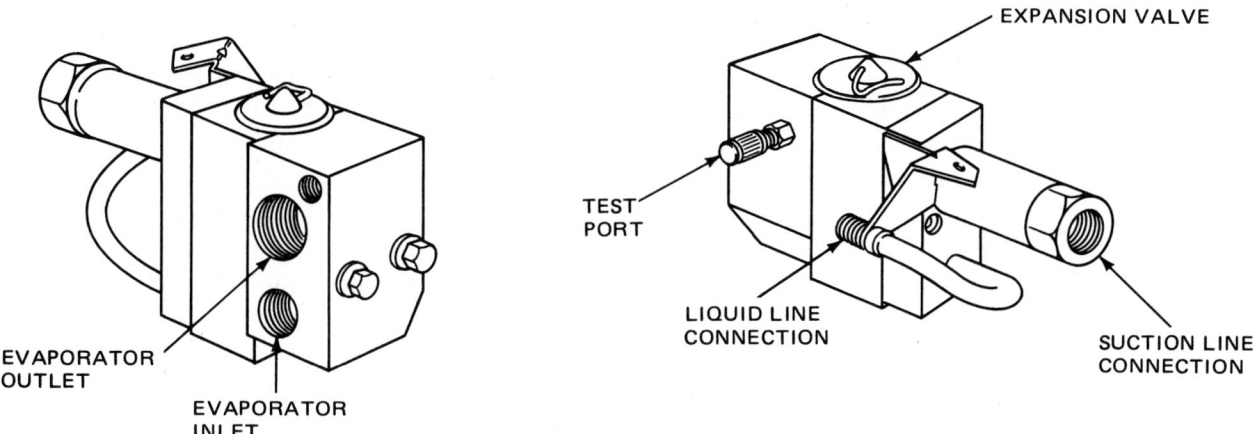

Fig. 2-39 Ford's suction throttling valve and expansion valve assembly (combination valve).

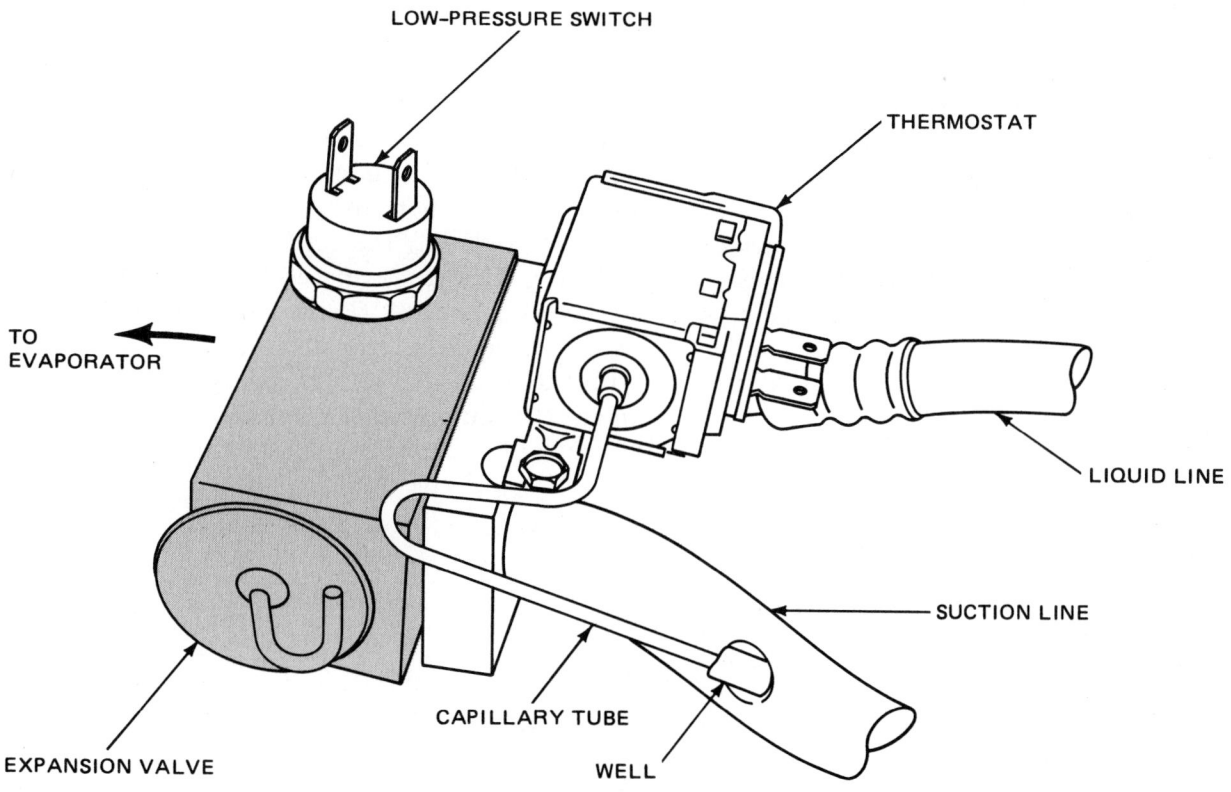

Fig. 2-40 Chrysler's H-valve assembly.

TXV: to meter the proper amount of refrigerant into the evaporator under varying heat load conditions.

COMBINATION VALVE

The *combination valve,* also called *combo valve,* is found on some Ford car lines. The combo valve is similar in operation to the VIR in that it contains a thermostatic expansion valve (TXV) and a suction pressure regulator, known as a *suction throttling valve* (STV). The combo valve, figure 2-39, however, does not include a receiver or desiccant as does the VIR.

The TXV and STV assemblies of the combo valve may be serviced separately. The STV manifold housing separates from the TXV to gain access to the STV capsule. The TXV, which includes the low-side access service fitting, is serviced as a separate assembly.

It should be noted that the TXV of the combination valve has a much shorter capillary tube than does a standard TXV. Only one inch (25.4 mm) or so in length, there is no remote bulb to be secured to the evaporator outlet.

OTHER VALVE TYPES

In certain Chrysler car lines, the thermostatic expansion valve is called an *H-valve*, figure 2-40. Some Ford car lines use a similar valve, called a *block valve*. Like the combination valve, the H-valve and the block valve do not have a capillary tube. Unlike the combination valve, however, the H-valve and the block valve do not have a suction pressure regulator as a part of their assembly. The suction pressure regulator in Chrysler air-conditioning systems equipped with the V-type compressor is found under the low-side compressor service valve assembly.

The H-valve includes a low-pressure cutoff switch which may be serviced separately. The low-pressure cutoff switch, a part of the electrical circuit, interrupts current flow to the compressor clutch if high-side system pressure falls below a predetermined safe level. Testing and service procedures for the H-valve and block valve are similar to those given for other types of thermostatic expansion valves.

EVAPORATOR

The evaporator, figure 2-41, is the part of the refrigeration system where the refrigerant vaporizes as it picks up heat. Heat-laden air is forced through and past the fins and tubes of the evaporator. Heat from the air is picked up by the boiling refrigerant and is carried in the system to the condenser.

Factors which are important in the design of an evaporator include the size and length of the tubing, the number of fins, and the amount of air passing through and past the fins. The heat load is also an important consideration. *Heat load* refers to the amount of heat, in Btu, to be removed.

The evaporator may have two, three, or more rows of tubing as determined by the design to fit a specific housing and still be able to achieve the rated capacity in Btu. The refrigerant as it leaves the evaporator on its way to the compressor is low-pressure gas.

If too much refrigerant is metered into the evaporator, the unit floods. As a result, the unit does not cool because the pressure of the refrigerant is higher and it does not boil away as quickly. In addition, when the evaporator is filled with liquid refrigerant, the refrigerant cannot vaporize properly. This step is necessary if the refrigerant is to take on heat. A flooded evaporator allows an excess of liquid refrigerant to leave the evaporator, with the result that serious damage may be done to the next component, the compressor.

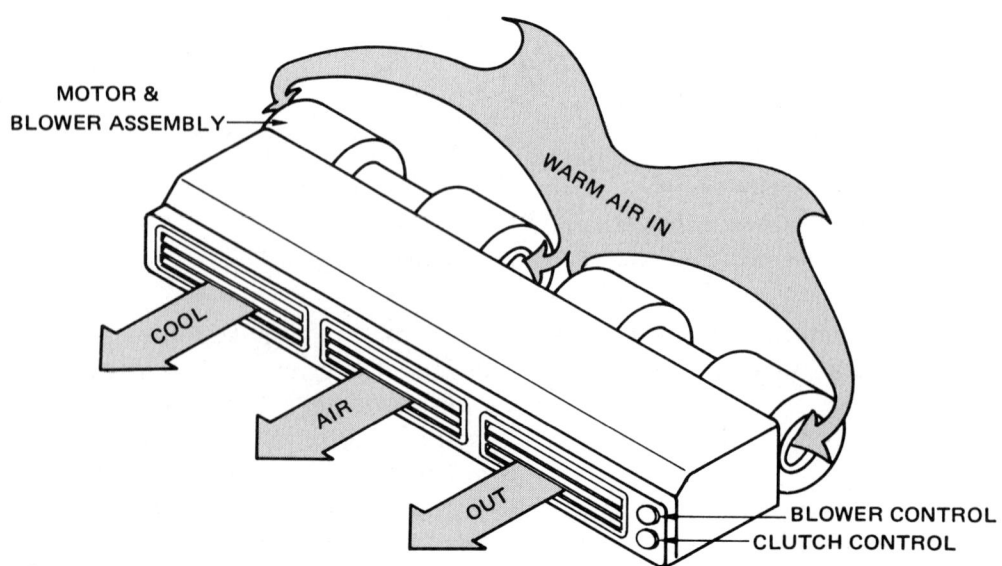

Fig. 2-41 The evaporator (heat is picked up from the air inside the evaporator).

If too little refrigerant is metered into the evaporator, the system is said to be *starved*. Again, the unit does not cool because the refrigerant vaporizes or boils off too rapidly, long before it passes through the evaporator.

BLOWER MOTOR

Many styles and types of blower motors are available, depending upon their application, figure 2-42. Blower motors may have a single shaft or a double shaft. They may be flange mounted or they may have provisions for internal cooling. Regardless of the style or type, the blower motor drives one or two squirrel-cage blowers to move air across the evaporator and/or heater core.

If motor speed control is provided by resistors, the motor will have only one winding. Motor speed control may also be provided by multiwound motors, as well. Resistance for speed control is provided by the motor windings and no external resistors are required.

Automotive blower motors generally are not repairable. If found to be defective they must be replaced. Common causes of failure include worn bushings or brushes, or defective internal wiring. Before replacing a motor thought to be defective, however, always check to insure that the ground wire is secure, since most blower housings are constructed of nonconductive materials.

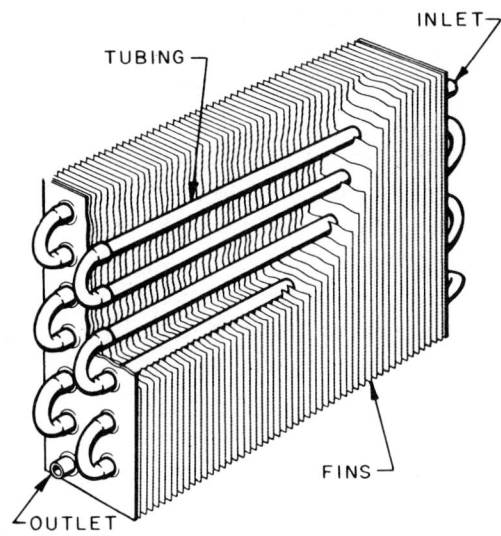

Fig. 2-43 Condenser (cutaway to show tubing and fin detail).

It must be noted that some replacement motors are reversible (REV) whereas many are not. It is important to note whether the defective motor turns clockwise (cw) or counterclockwise (ccw) facing the shaft end of the motor. The replacement motor selected should turn in the same direction.

CONDENSER

The purpose of the condenser is the opposite of that of the evaporator. Refrigerant in the gaseous state liquefies or condenses in the condenser. To do so, the refrigerant must give up its heat in Btu. *Ram air,* or the air passing over the condenser, carries the heat away from the condenser and the gas condenses. The heat removed from the refrigerant (so that it can change to a liquid) is the same heat that was absorbed in the evaporator to change the refrigerant from a liquid to a gas.

The refrigerant is almost 100% gas when it enters the condenser. A very small amount of gas may liquefy in the hot-gas discharge line, but the amount is so small that it does not affect the operation of the system.

The refrigerant is not always 100% liquid when it leaves the condenser. Since only a certain amount of heat can be handled by the condenser at a given time, a small percentage of the refrigerant may leave the condenser in a gaseous state. Again, this condition does not affect the system operation since the next component is the receiver/drier.

As indicated previously, the inlet of the condenser must be at the top of the unit, figure 2-43.

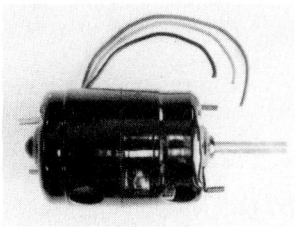 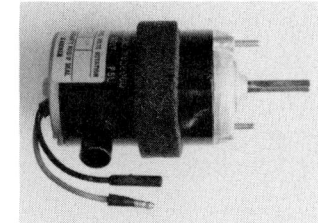
 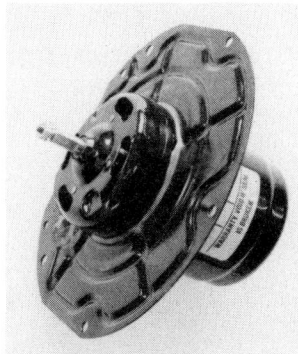

Fig. 2-42 Styles and types of blower motors depend upon their application. Generally, they are not interchangeable from one year/model car to another.

With the inlet in this position, the condensing refrigerant can flow to the bottom of the condenser where it is forced, under pressure, to the receiver/drier through the liquid line.

The refrigerant in the condenser is a combination of liquid and gas under high pressure. Extreme care must be exercised when servicing this component of the system.

From the condenser, the refrigerant continues to the receiver/drier through the liquid line. At this point, the cycle starts over again. The liquid line from the condenser can be either a rubber or a metal line in a variety of sizes.

HOSES

Refrigerant fluid and vapor hoses may be made of copper, steel, or aluminum. They are usually made of a synthetic rubber covered with a nylon braid for strength. The inner core is usually of Buna 'N', a synthetic rubber which is not affected by Refrigerant 12.

CHAPTER 3:
Controls

Within the range of 20 psig (137.9 kPa) and 80 psig (551.6 kPa), the temperature of Refrigerant 12 has a close relationship to its pressure.

Liquid refrigerant is metered into the evaporator by the thermostatic expansion valve (TXV). The amount of refrigerant required is regulated by the heat load on the evaporator. As the heat load decreases, there is a corresponding decrease in the amount of refrigerant that is metered into the evaporator by the expansion valve. In this discussion of pressure controls, the student should recall that water droplets which accumulate on the evaporator freeze when the temperature drops below 32°F (0°C).

SUCTION PRESSURE REGULATORS

The suction pressure regulator controls the pressure of the refrigerant in the evaporator by preventing the pressure from falling below a predetermined range, usually 22 psig (151.6 kPa) to 30 psig (206.8 kPa) (depending on system design). If a setting of 30 psig (206.8 kPa) is assumed, the suction pressure regulator allows evaporator pressures of about 30 psi (206.8 kPa) to be released to the compressor. The control holds all pressures up to 30 psi (206.8 kPa). In this manner, the evaporator can maintain a constant pressure of 30 psig (206.8 kPa).

The operation of the evaporator in this manner is based on the assumption that the thermostatic expansion valve, suction regulator, and compressor are operating properly, figure 3-1. If, for example, the TXV is flooding the evaporator, the pressure in the evaporator rises above 30 psig (206.8 kPa), figure 3-2. This condition can be corrected by replacing the TXV, or by correcting any other problem that may be causing the flooding condition.

Flow through any type of suction pressure regulator is never completely stopped. A bypass is included so that a small amount of refrigerant and refrigeration oil can circulate through the system. This provision helps to eliminate the danger of compressor damage when a malfunction in the suction regulator causes it to close.

EVAPORATOR PRESSURE REGULATOR

The evaporator pressure regulator (EPR) valve is a fully automatic suction pressure control device that is used in certain Chrysler Corporation automotive air-conditioning systems. The EPR valve is located inside the compressor under the suction side service valve, figure 3-3.

The EPR valve, figure 3-4, maintains the evaporator pressure, and thus its temperature, at a point just above freezing. As a result, any evaporator condensate cannot freeze during the normal operation of the evaporator. The pressure in the evaporator is maintained between 22 psig (151.6 kPa) and 26 psig (179.2 kPa) by the action of the EPR valve. If the EPR valve is operating properly, the compressor inlet pressure should be about 15 psig (103.4 kPa). However, this pressure can be higher or lower, depending on the evaporator heat load.

An EPR valve balance is maintained between the control spring pressure and the evaporator refrigerant pressure. A diaphragm seals the chamber and prevents refrigerant leaks. An increase of evaporator pressure against the diaphragm overcomes the control spring tension and moves the valve away from the seated position. As a result, there is an increase in the refrigerant flow from the evaporator to the compressor.

A decrease in evaporator pressure allows the control spring to move the valve toward the seat. The refrigerant flowing from the evaporator is restricted and the evaporator pressure increases until

34 Chapter Three, Controls

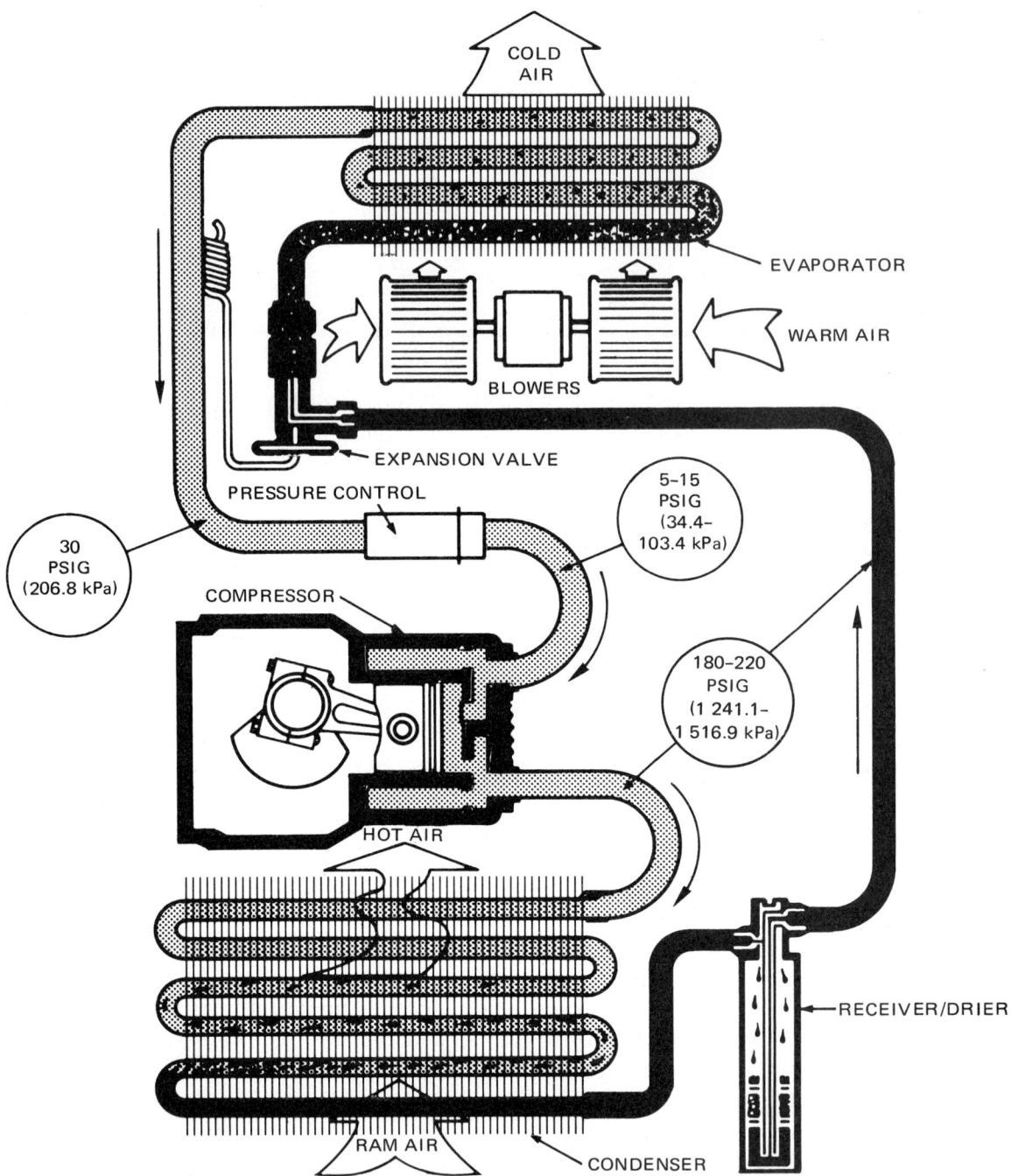

Fig. 3-1 Controlling action of the pressure control with the proper expansion valve metering.

it reaches a value sufficient to reopen the EPR valve.

The opening and closing of the EPR valve continues until a balance is reached between the evaporator pressure and the spring tension. The valve then remains in a constant position until the evaporator heat load or the compressor speed changes and a new balance of pressures is required.

Although the EPR valve is located within the compressor on the suction side, it is not necessary to disassemble the compressor if the valve must be replaced. The EPR valve can be changed without removing the compressor from the engine compartment. Since the valve cannot be adjusted, any malfunction requires unit replacement.

An oil passage which runs inside the compressor between the suction line and the compressor crankcase also runs through the EPR valve. Since oil is carried out of the compressor in the refrigerant, the oil passage permits the oil to be returned to the crankcase, regardless of the condition of the

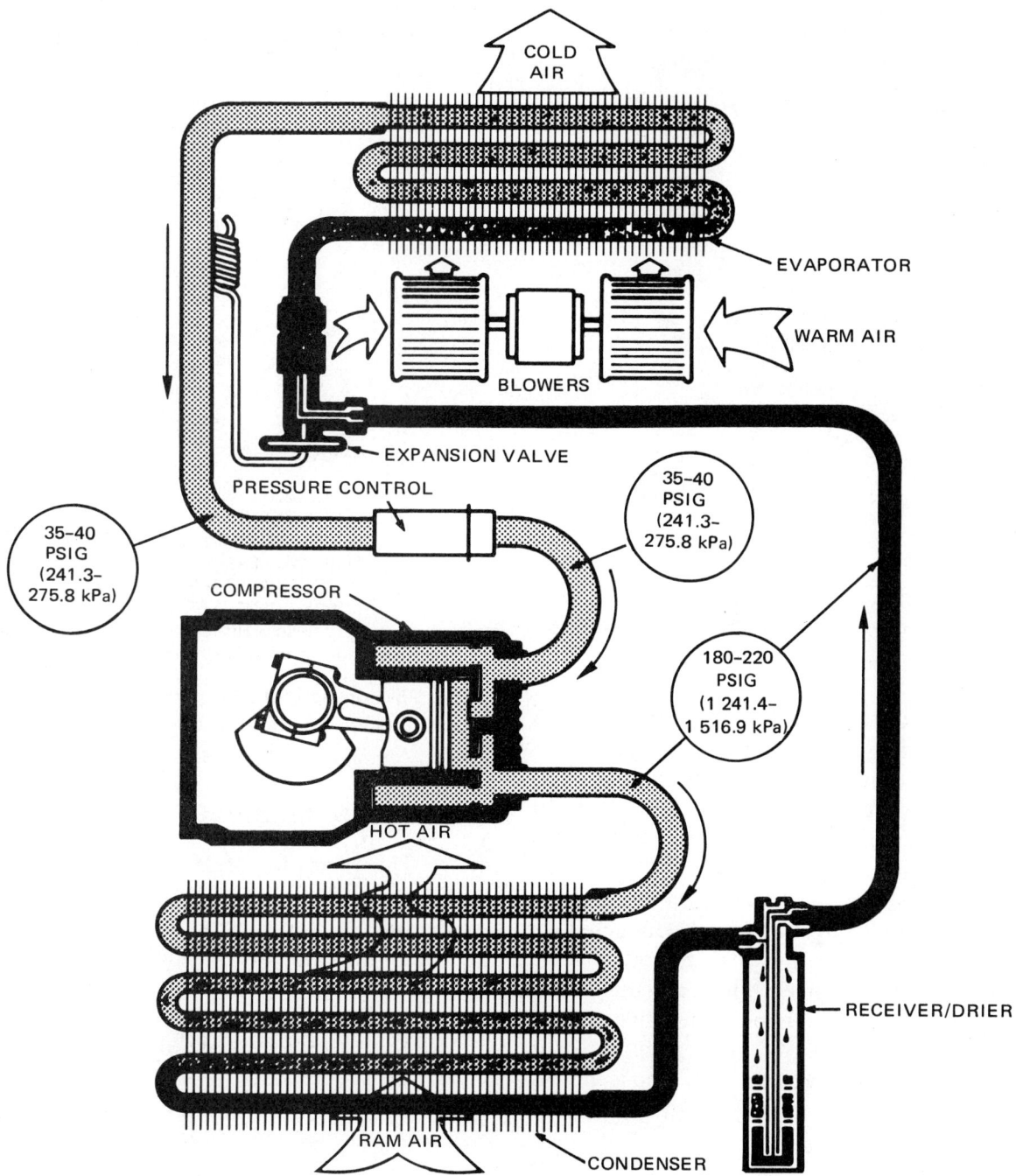

Fig. 3-2 Loss of controlling action of pressure control due to improper expansion valve metering (flooding evaporator).

EPR valve. In addition, the oil passage pressurizes the crankcase and prevents the crankcase pressure from dropping below the normal atmospheric pressure. If this pressure does drop into the vacuum range, atmospheric pressure can enter the system through the crankshaft seal assembly. The moisture content of the incoming air can contaminate the system. Another condition that can result from the addition of air at atmospheric pressure is higher-than-normal head pressures.

SUCTION THROTTLING VALVE

The suction throttling valve (STV) is a flow control device found at the evaporator outlet of some automotive air-conditioning systems, figure 3-5.

Its purpose is to maintain evaporator pressure at a predetermined level. This type of valve provides control with a much greater accuracy than is obtainable with many other types of controls. The

36 Chapter Three, Controls

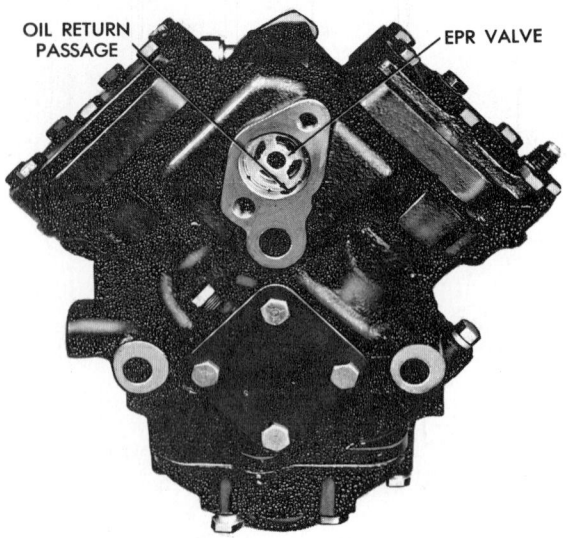

Fig. 3-3 EPR valve and oil return passage.

STV maintains the evaporator pressure to within ±0.5 psig (±3.4 kPa). This means that there is, at most, a variation of one psig (6.895 kPa) between the low pressure and the high pressure in the evaporator.

The valve contains a *pilot valve* that enables it to achieve as close to absolute zero pressure as possible. The absolute pilot serves as the opposing force to the evaporator pressure. The STV does not rely on spring pressures or atmospheric pressure for its operation.

The inlet end of the valve has a test port to which the low-side manifold gauge is connected for testing, figure 3-6. Two other fittings on the valve accommodate the oil bleed line and the external equalizer line of the expansion valve. If the pilot-operated valve is not adjusted properly or is defective, the entire valve assembly must be replaced since it is a sealed unit and cannot be serviced.

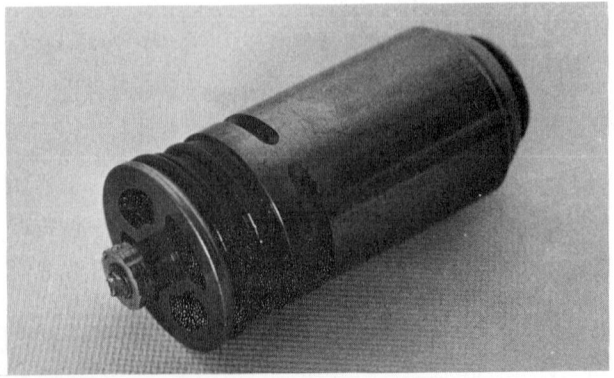

Fig. 3-4 EPR valve located under the low-side (suction) service valve.

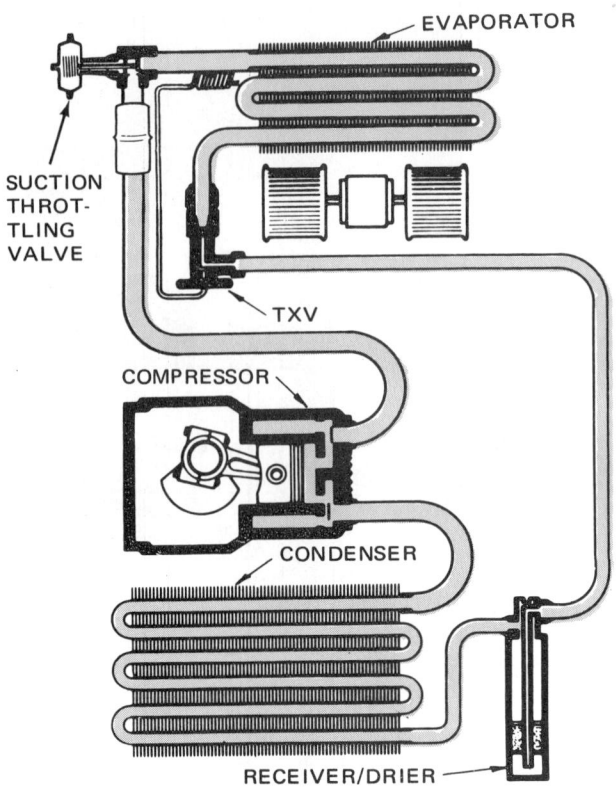

Fig. 3-5 Location of the pilot-operated absolute suction throttling valve in the air-conditioning system.

VALVES-IN-RECEIVER

The valves in receiver (VIR) assembly, figures 3-7 and 3-8, is a combination of three different components: the thermostatic expansion valve, the suction throttling valve, and the receiver/dehydrator (including a sight glass).

Early series are called simply valves-in-receiver (VIR) and later series are called evaporator equalizer valves-in-receiver (EEVIR). Both are essentially the same device; they operate and are serviced in the same manner. Replacement parts or repair

Fig. 3-6 Test port for manifold gauge on STV.

Controls 37

kits are available for field repair.

The VIR assembly is mounted near the evaporator. Both the inlet and the outlet fittings of the evaporator connect to the VIR, as well as to the liquid line and suction line. The VIR is designed to

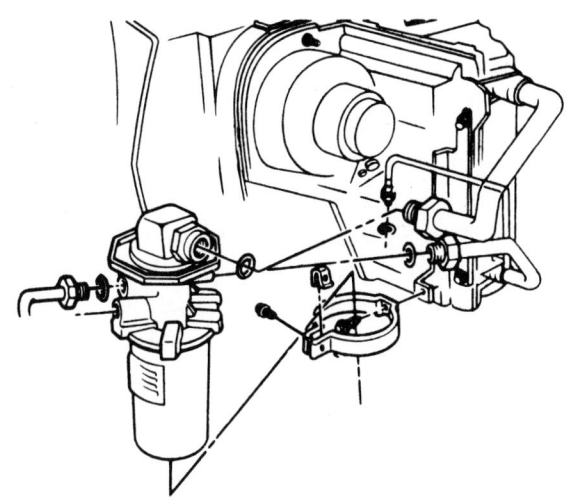

Fig. 3-7 Typical VIR installation.

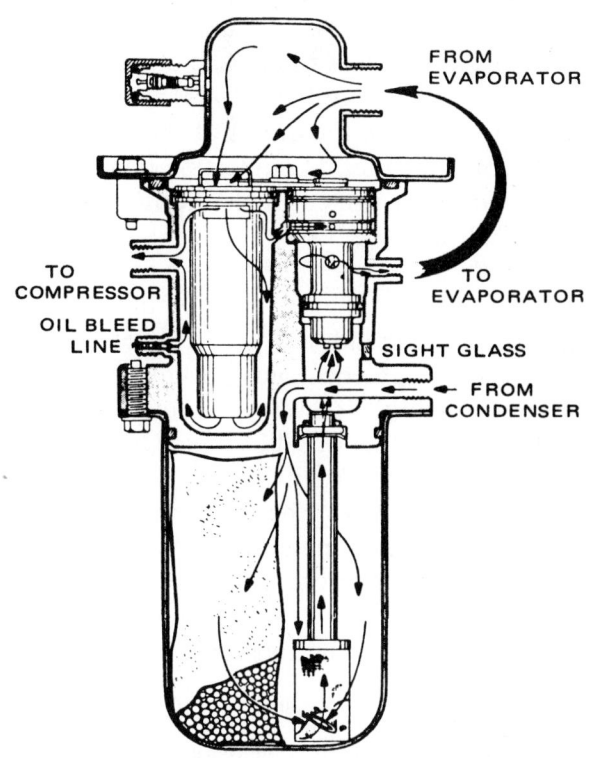

Fig. 3-8 Cutaway section of valves-in-receiver (VIR) showing detail of components and direction of refrigerant flow.

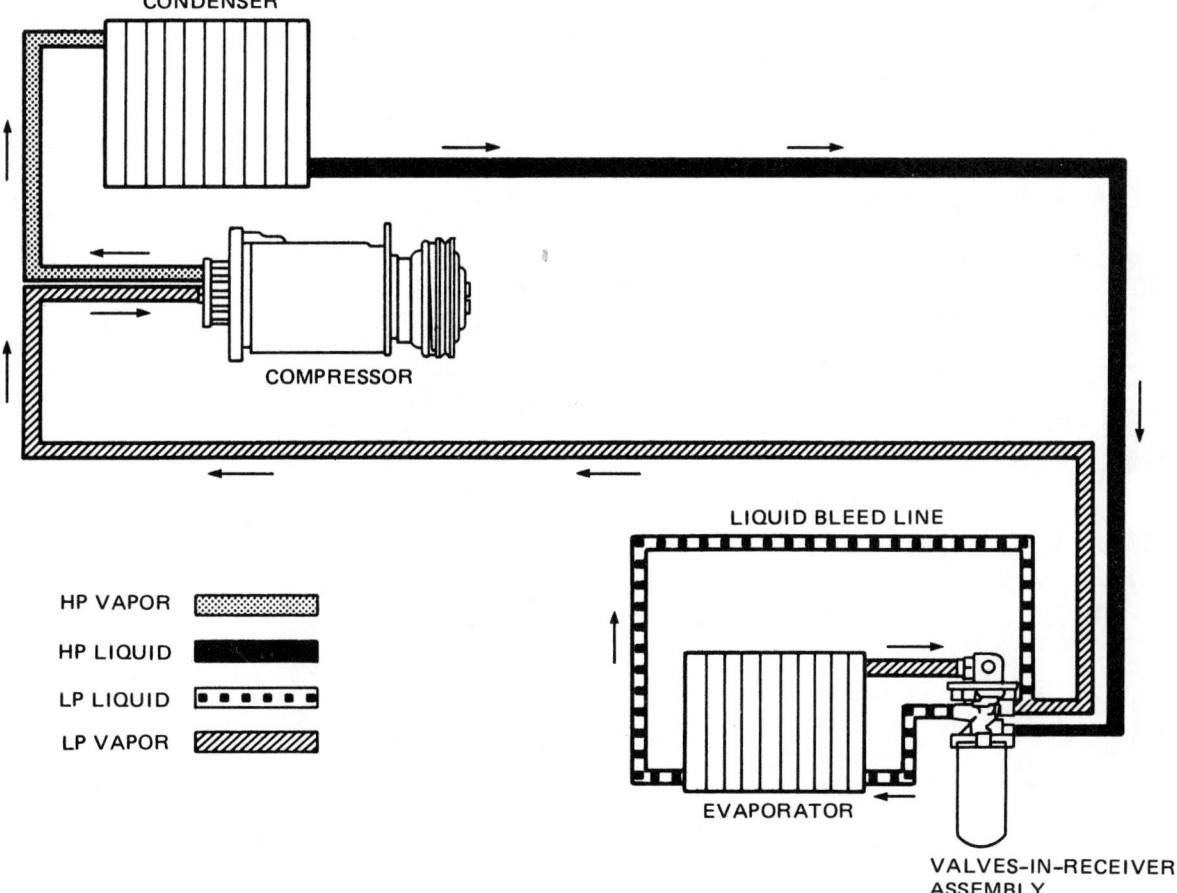

Fig. 3-9 System schematic with valves-in-receiver.

eliminate the need for the equalizer external capillary and the TXV remote bulb. The diaphragm end of the TXV is exposed directly to refrigerant vapor entering the VIR from the outlet of the evaporator. The provision for external equalizing consists of a small hole (orifice) drilled in the housing wall between the STV and the TXV.

The desiccant is contained in the receiver shell and is replaceable. A liquid pickup tube containing a filter screen extends to the bottom of the shell. The filter traps impurities and prevents them from circulating through the system. A replaceable sight glass is located in the VIR housing at the inlet of the TXV.

The components of the VIR function in the same manner as similar separate system components. Because the VIR components are mounted in a common housing, their appearance is somewhat different from that of the individual units covered previously.

Figure 3-9 is a system schematic showing the valves-in-receiver assembly. Figures 3-10 and 3-11 describe the TXV and STV respectively as found in the VIR assembly.

COMBINATION VALVE

The *combination valve,* also called *combo valve,* used on some Ford car lines, is mounted at or near the inlet and outlet provisions of the evaporator. It is similar in function and operation to the valves-in-receiver (VIR). Unlike the VIR, however, the combo valve does not include the receiver and desiccant. The receiver (with desiccant) in a Ford system is usually found in the liquid line near the condenser outlet.

The combo valve, figure 3-12, separates into two sections for each service: the thermostatic expansion valve (TXV) and the suction throttling valve (STV). The STV operates in a manner similar to the evaporator pressure regulator (EPR). Its purpose is to regulate evaporator pressure at a predetermined level, thereby controlling its temperature.

The primary cause of failure is that the STV becomes stuck in the open position. This condition would be noted by a lower-than-normal evaporator

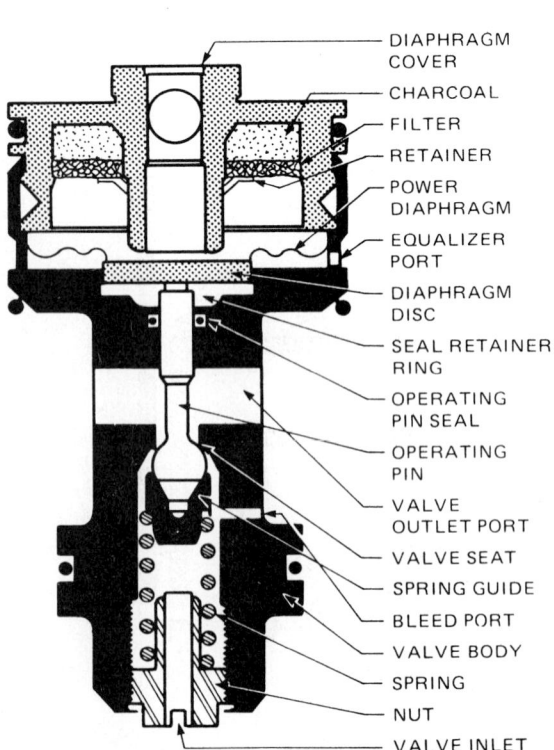

Fig. 3-10 TXV as found in the valves-in-receiver (VIR) assembly.

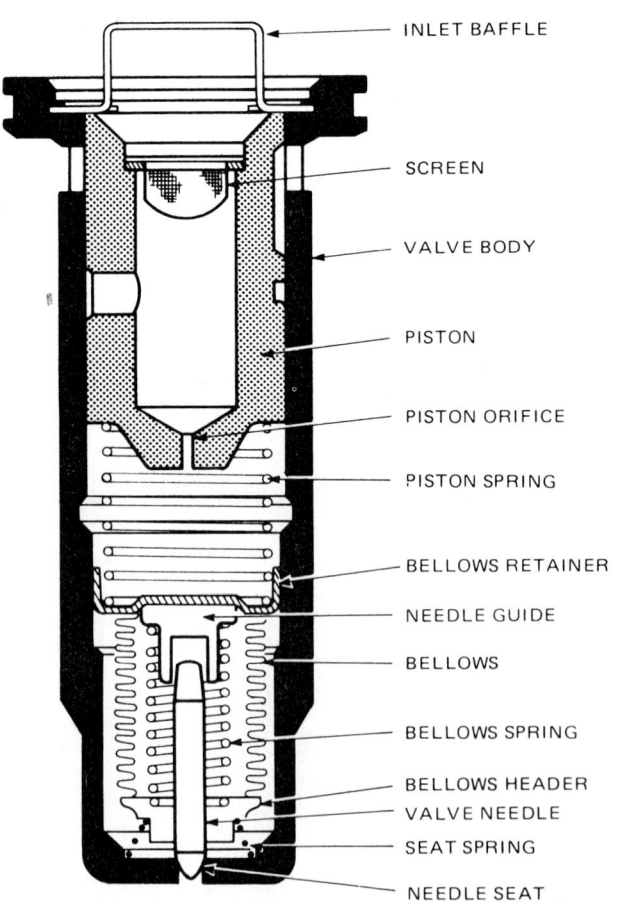

Fig. 3-11 STV as found in the valves-in-receiver (VIR) assembly.

Controls 39

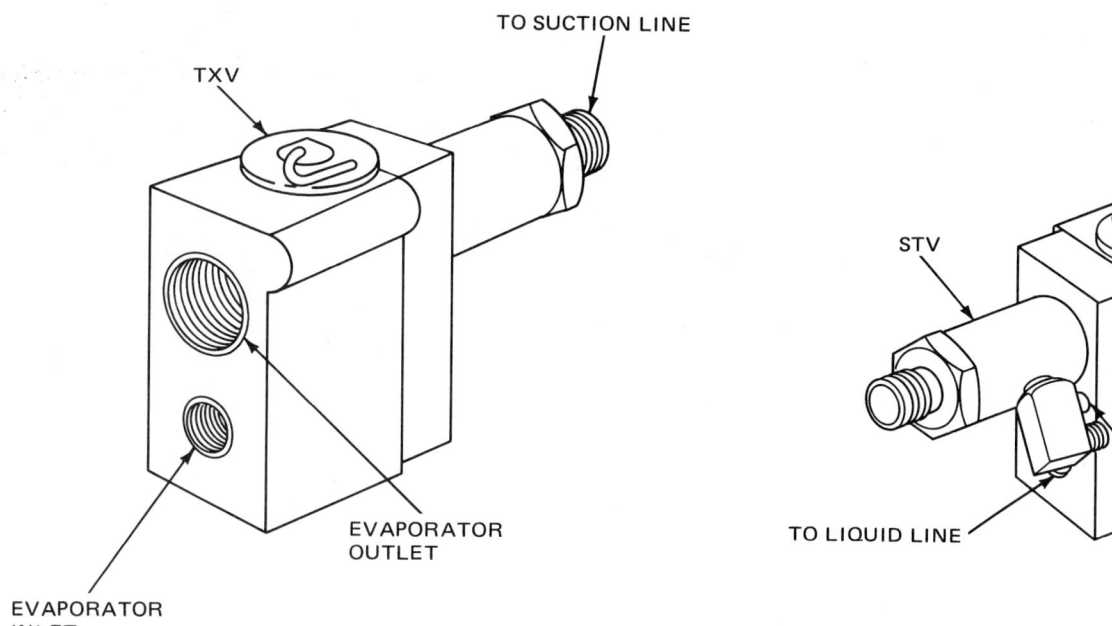

Fig. 3-12 Combination (combo) valve details.

(low-side) pressure as measured at the access port of the TXV. In this case, the pressure taken at the compressor suction port service valve would be the same or nearly the same as that taken at the TXV. If the system is operating properly, a slight to considerable pressure drop between these two ports will be noted, depending upon evaporator load conditions.

MASTER CONTROL

The master control generally includes the blower speed control provisions. The variable (infinite) speed control, also known as a *rheostat*, shown in figure 3-13, is popular with aftermarket systems. Also used are two-, three-, four-, and five-position blower speed controls. Figure 3-14 shows a set of duct-mounted dropping resistors used in multiposition speed controls.

Motor speed resistors are usually made of nichrome wire and are placed in the air conditioning and/or heater air-stream for cooling.

Fig. 3-13 Rheostat, a variable resistor used to provide infinite fan/blower-speed control.

Fig. 3-14 Remote duct-mounted blower motor speed dropping resistors (nichrome wire).

THERMOSTAT

An electromagnetic clutch is used on the compressors of most aftermarket units and on some factory-installed air conditioners to provide a means of temperature control. A device known as a *thermostat*, figure 3-15, controls the clutch. Located in the evaporator, the thermostat is initially set by the driver to a predetermined temperature setting. The clutch cycles at this setting to control the average in-car temperature.

The thermostat is an electrical switch which is actuated by a change in temperature. It senses either evaporator core air temperature or the temperature of the refrigerant as it enters or leaves the evaporator (depending upon design). A temperature above that preselected closes a thermostatic switch and an electrical signal is sent to the clutch. The clutch is energized and the air conditioner will operate. Similarly, a temperature at or below that preselected will open the thermostatic switch to interrupt the electrical signal to the clutch. The clutch becomes deenergized, and the air conditioner will not operate.

Most thermostats have a positive OFF position so that the clutch can be turned off regardless of the temperature. In this way, the air-conditioner fans or blower can be used without a refrigerating effect.

Two types of thermostats are available for the control of the clutch: the bellows type and the bimetallic type. Both types of thermostats are temperature actuated. Although the principle of operation is different for each type of thermostat, they serve the same purpose in that they both control the evaporator temperature by cycling the compressor on and off through the clutch.

PRESSURE CUTOFF SWITCH

Many systems have a low- or high-pressure cutoff switch in the clutch circuit. These switches are sensitive to system pressure and open in the event of abnormal pressure. This interrupts current to the clutch coil to stop compressor action.

The low-pressure cutoff switch is found in the system anywhere between the evaporator inlet and the compressor inlet. In the event of an abnormally low pressure of, say, 5 psi (34.4 kPa) the switch will open to stop the compressor. This prevents further reduction of system pressure and protects the system from the possible entrance of air and/or

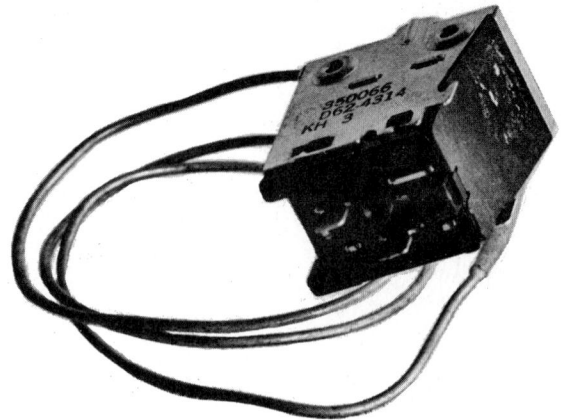

REMOTE SENSING THERMOSTAT
(BELLOWS TYPE)

BIMETALLIC THERMOSTAT

Fig. 3-15 Thermostats.

moisture, as would be the case with a low-side leak.

The high-pressure cutoff switch is found in the system anywhere between the compressor outlet and the evaporator inlet. In the event of an abnormally high pressure of, say, 300 psi (2 068.5 kPa), this switch will open to stop compressor action. This prevents system damage and/or rupture that may be caused by further increase in pressure.

COMPRESSOR DISCHARGE PRESSURE SWITCH

Many factory systems use a compressor discharge pressure switch to disengage the compressor clutch electrical circuit. The action of this switch stops the compressor if the refrigerant charge is not adequate, say, due to a leak, to provide sufficient circulation within the system. The compressor discharge pressure switch is also called a no-charge switch and ambient low-temperature switch, or a low-pressure cutoff switch. The switch is designed to open electrically to shut off the compressor when high-side system pressure drops below 37 psig (255 kPa). This switch also performs the secondary function of an outside ambient air temperature sensor. When outside ambient air temperature falls below 25°F (−3.9°C), the reduced corresponding refrigerant pressure keeps the switch open.

The compressor discharge pressure switch, located in the high-pressure discharge line from the compressor or receiver/drier, cannot be repaired. If it fails in service it must be replaced with a new unit. Its function is to protect the compressor, and it should not be bypassed with a jumper wire.

TIME-DELAY RELAY

The time-delay control unit is designed to prevent the heat cycle from coming on in the automatic unit until the engine coolant has reached a temperature of 110°F (43.34°C). The unit consists of two resistors, capacitors, and transistors. Figure 3-16 shows the time-delay circuit of the wiring diagram.

ELECTROVACUUM RELAY

The *electrovacuum relay* (EVR) contains a normally closed (NC) vacuum solenoid valve and a normally closed (NC) electrical relay. The purpose of the EVR is to prevent blower operation when the system is in the "heat" mode until engine coolant temperature reaches 115–120°F (46.1–48.8°C). When the coolant temperature is below this value, electrical contacts in the *engine temperature (sending) switch* (ETS) are closed. This grounds and completes the EVR circuit to open the ETR relay contacts. The ETR relay contacts, in series with the blower motor, interrupt current to the motor to open this circuit.

AMBIENT SWITCH

The *ambient switch* is an electrical switch actuated by changing ambient temperature. The ambient switch is used in many custom and automatic systems. (The student should not confuse the ambient switch with the ambient sensor.)

The ambient switch is located outside the engine area where it can sense the ambient temperature only. The actual switch location depends on its design. The switch is never mounted where it is possible to sense the engine heat.

If the master switch is pressed, the ambient switch will turn the air-conditioning compressor ON at 35°F (1.67°C). The switch turns the compressor OFF if the ambient temperature falls to 25°F (−3.89°C).

Whenever the ambient temperature is in the range 64°F (17.78°C) and 55°F (12.78°C), the ambient switch bypasses the master control and the time-delay relay and allows the blowers to run regardless of the engine coolant temperature.

When the air-conditioning compressor or blower is operated at low ambient temperatures, the humidity of the incoming air is reduced by condensing the moisture from it. In this way, window fogging is prevented when an automobile is being operated during rainy, damp, or cool weather conditions.

THERMOSTATIC VACUUM VALVE

The thermostatic vacuum valve (TVV) is a vacuum-control valve which is sensitive to temperature. The TVV is used only on late model automatic systems and is mounted where it can sense coolant temperature, such as on the side of the heater core. The TVV consists of a power element cylinder with a piston, vacuum parts, and spring. The power element is filled with a temperature-sensitive compound so that when the engine is cold

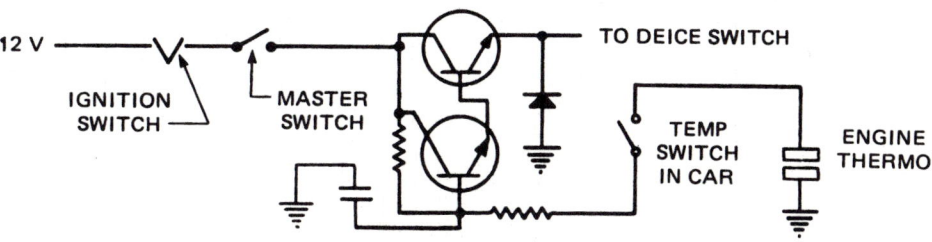

Fig. 3-16 Time-delay relay schematic.

and the coolant is not warm, the inlet part of the TVV is blocked and the outlet part is vented. When the coolant temperature reaches a specified range, usually 100°F to 125°F (37.78°C to 51.67°C), the compound in the cylinder expands and moves the piston until vacuum flow starts.

In the automatic temperature control system, the vacuum flow proceeds from the selector vacuum disc switch to the program vacuum disc switch, the master switch, the vacuum diaphragm, and the outside-recirculate air-cooled diaphragm. On cold days, the TVV serves only as a time delay.

SUPERHEAT SWITCH

The superheat switch is located in the rear head of some six-cylinder compressors. This device is a temperature/pressure-sensitive electrical switch which is normally in the open position, figure 3-17. The switch remains open during system high-temperature and high-pressure conditions or low-temperature and low-pressure conditions. The switch closes when the system experiences high-temperature and low-pressure conditions.

The high-temperature and low-pressure condition of the system is usually caused by a loss of refrigerant. This loss may result in compressor or system damage if the air-conditioning system remains in operation.

The superheat switch offers a failsafe method of stopping the compressor until the problem is corrected. When the superheat switch closes, a circuit is completed through a heater of the thermal fuse. The fuse blows, opens the clutch circuit, and stops the compressor.

The superheat switch was replaced in 1978 with a switch which is pressure-actuated only. The difference in appearance is that the late-model switch does not have the thermal sensing tube. It is important to note that the two switches are not interchangeable. Using the wrong switch can result in reduced voltage to the clutch, causing erratic clutch and compressor operation. This condition can lead to a loss of compressor oil and result in a seized (ruined) compressor.

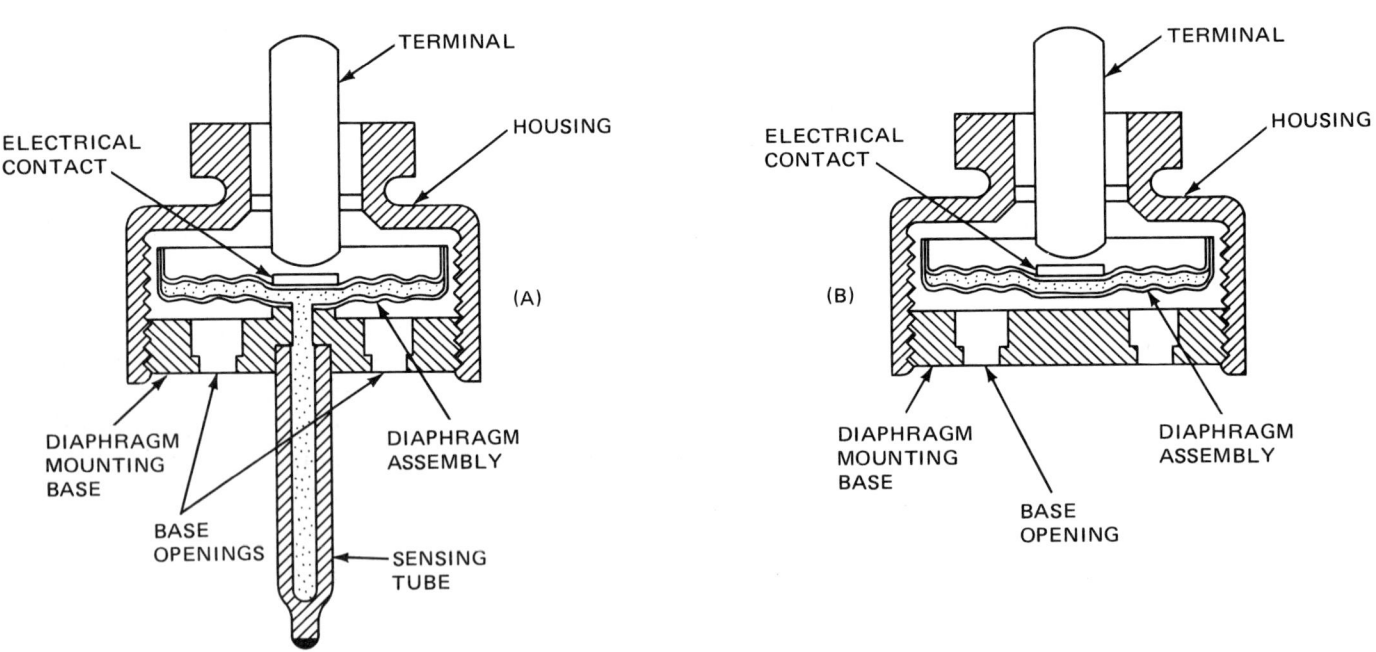

Fig. 3-17 Cutaway view of details of early model (A) and late model (B) superheat switch.

CHAPTER 4:

Basic Systems

Types of Systems

There have been many different types of automotive air-conditioning systems since the first "window shaker" was modified for automotive application in the early 1940s. Temperature control was achieved with a Hot Gas By-Pass Valve which was later replaced by an evaporator pressure regulator. The following are brief descriptions of air-conditioning systems found on both late-model and older cars.

CYCLING CLUTCH SYSTEM

The most simple system found in today's automobile is the cycling clutch system, figure 4-1. This system consists of five major components: compressor, condenser, receiver/drier, thermostatic expansion valve, and evaporator. Temperature control is accomplished by an electromagnetic clutch which cycles the compressor ON and OFF based on evaporator temperature as sensed by the thermostat.

The accumulator system, figure 4-2, is the most popular today. It is called Ford Fixed Orifice Tube (FFOT) or Fixed Orifice Tube (FOT) by Ford and Cycling Clutch Orifice Tube (CCOT) by General Motors.

In the accumulator system, the Thermostatic Expansion Valve (TXV) is replaced by a Fixed Orifice Tube (FOT), and the receiver/drier is replaced by the accumulator. It should be noted that the accumulator is found in the suction line, figure 4-2, while the receiver is found in the liquid line, figure 4-1. The accumulator, like the receiver, contains desiccant and filters which remove moisture and impurities from the system. Also, the accumulator is located where it can prevent liquid refrigerant from entering the compressor. As its name implies, it *accumulates* excess liquid.

Temperature control is maintained by cycling the clutch in one of two ways: some systems use a thermostat to sense evaporator temperature, and others use a high- and/or low-pressure cut-out switch. Measuring pressure is a more accurate method of temperature control.

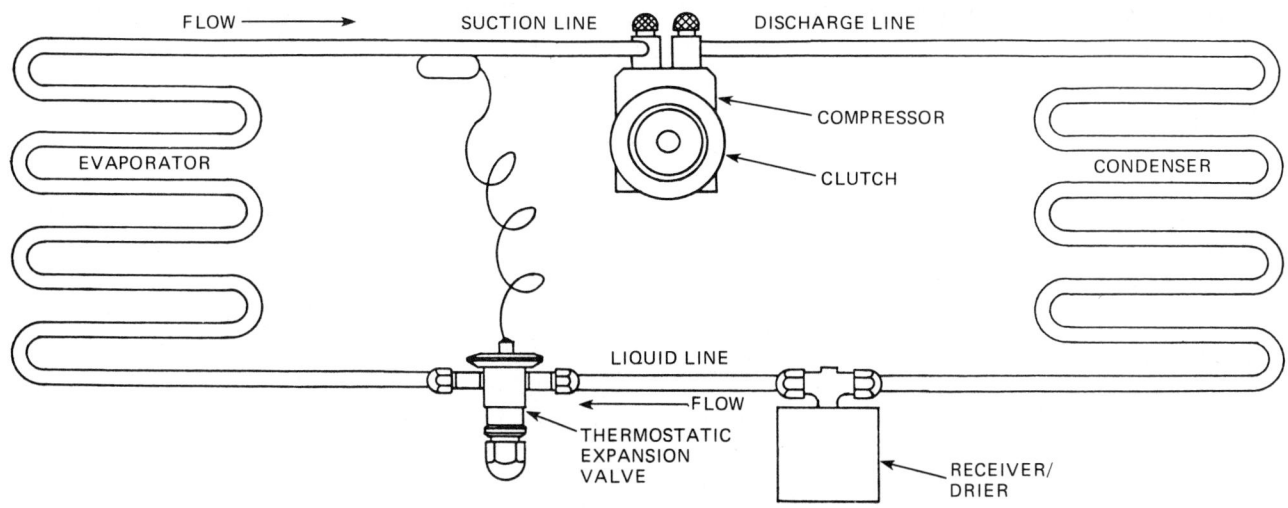

Fig. 4-1 Typical cycling clutch system with thermostatic expansion valve.

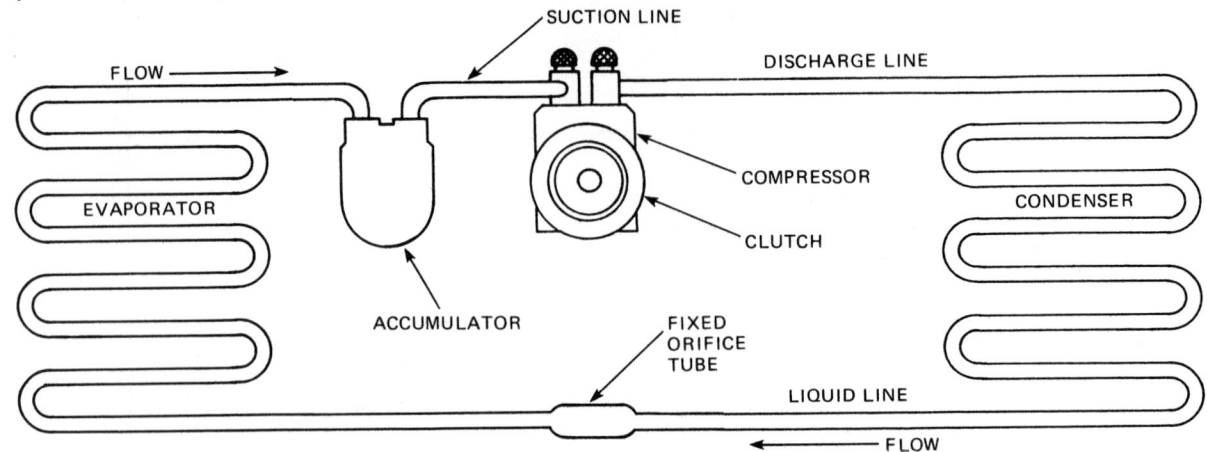

Fig. 4-2 Typical cycling clutch system with fixed orifice tube (FOT).

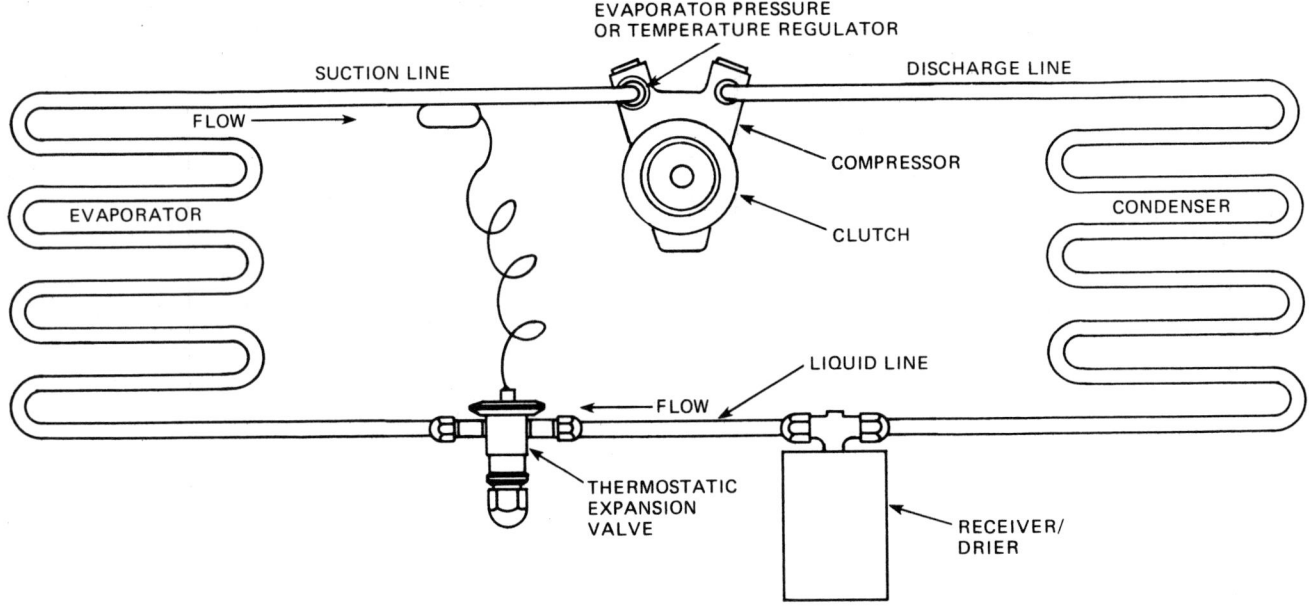

Fig. 4-3 The Evaporator Pressure Regulator is found under the suction service valve of the compressor on Chrysler systems.

EVAPORATOR PRESSURE REGULATOR

The Evaporator Pressure Regulator (EPR) will be found on some Chrysler applications through model year '79 and some Dodge truck applications through '81. Some systems were equipped with an electrically controlled device called an Evaporator Temperature Regulator (ETR) which was not successful and, as they failed, were replaced with the EPR. This system consists of six major parts: compressor, condenser, receiver/drier, thermostatic expansion valve, evaporator, and ETR/EPR.

The magnetic clutch is used to turn the system on and off. It has no role in temperature control. Temperature control is accomplished by maintaining evaporator pressure. The EPR valve is found under the suction fitting of the compressor, figure 4-3.

SUCTION THROTTLING VALVE

Temperature control by controlling evaporator pressure was also used by Volvo, Audi, and most Ford and General Motors car lines. This device is known as a Suction Throttling Valve (STV), figure 4-4. By 1983, however, this method of temperature control had been discontinued. This device was also known as a POA valve, or Positive Operated Absolute Suction Throttling Valve (POASTV).

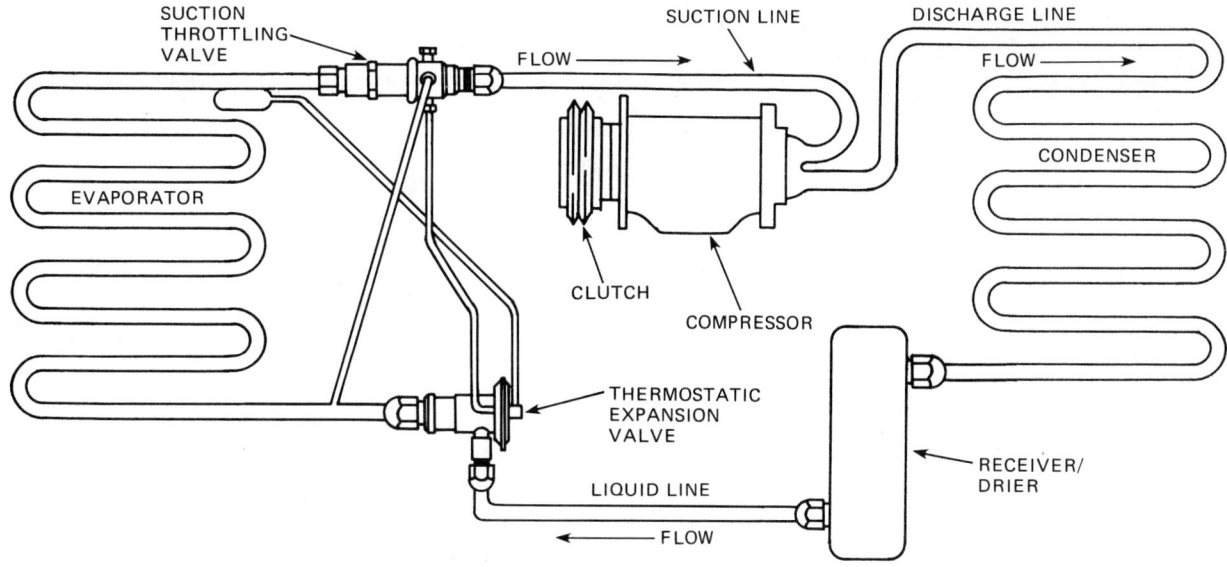

Fig. 4-4 Typical suction throttling valve system.

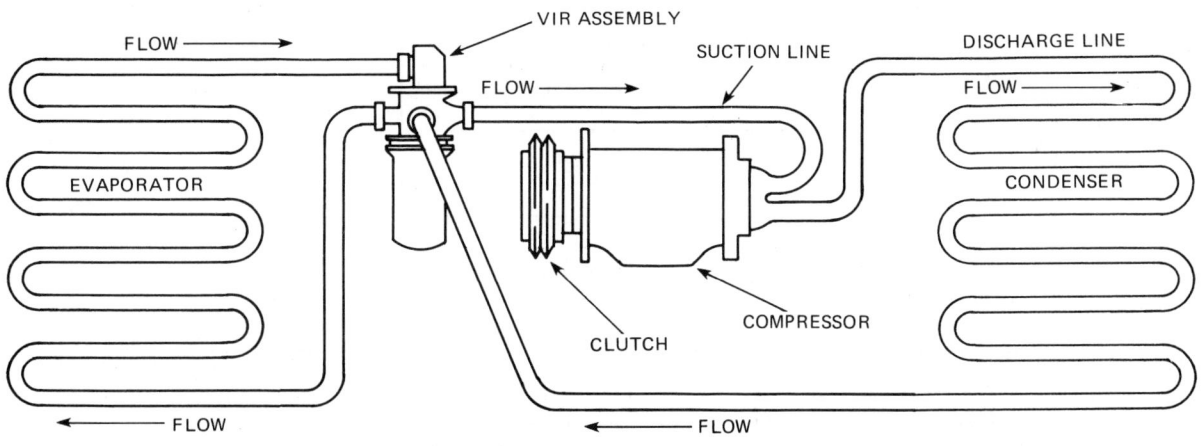

Fig. 4-5 Typical valves-in-receiver system.

VALVES-IN-RECEIVER

The Valves-In-Receiver (VIR) system was used for several years by General Motors through 1978 and by Audi through 1983. The VIR system, figure 4-5, operates on the same basic principal as any suction pressure control system. Both the thermostatic expansion valve (TXV) and suction throttling valve (STV) are found in the VIR. The receiver/dehydrator is also a part of the VIR. Like the EPR system, the magnetic clutch is used only as a means of turning the system on and off.

SUMMARY

Over the years there have been many methods used to control the temperature of the evaporator in automotive applications. All of them, of course, accomplish the task; some, however, are more costly to operate than others. The ultimate goal is to produce the greatest number of British thermal units (Btu) for the least cost. In the trades, this correlation is known as Energy Efficiency Ratio (EER).

CHAPTER 5:
Automatic Temperature Controls

Many different types of semiautomatic and automatic temperature control systems are found in use today; so many, it is not possible to cover each system individually in this text. Systems are modified or changed from year to year and from car model to car model.

Since diagnostic testing procedures differ, typical testing procedures are not recommended. For example, test point *12* of one car line may be test point *10* or *14* of another car line. The *shorting* of the wrong test point could destroy an expensive component.

Some components are so sensitive that the 1.5-volt battery used in an analog ohmmeter may destroy it. A digital ohmmeter, then, must be used whenever a manufacturer's specifications suggest that component resistance measurements be taken. Some components and circuits are so sensitive to

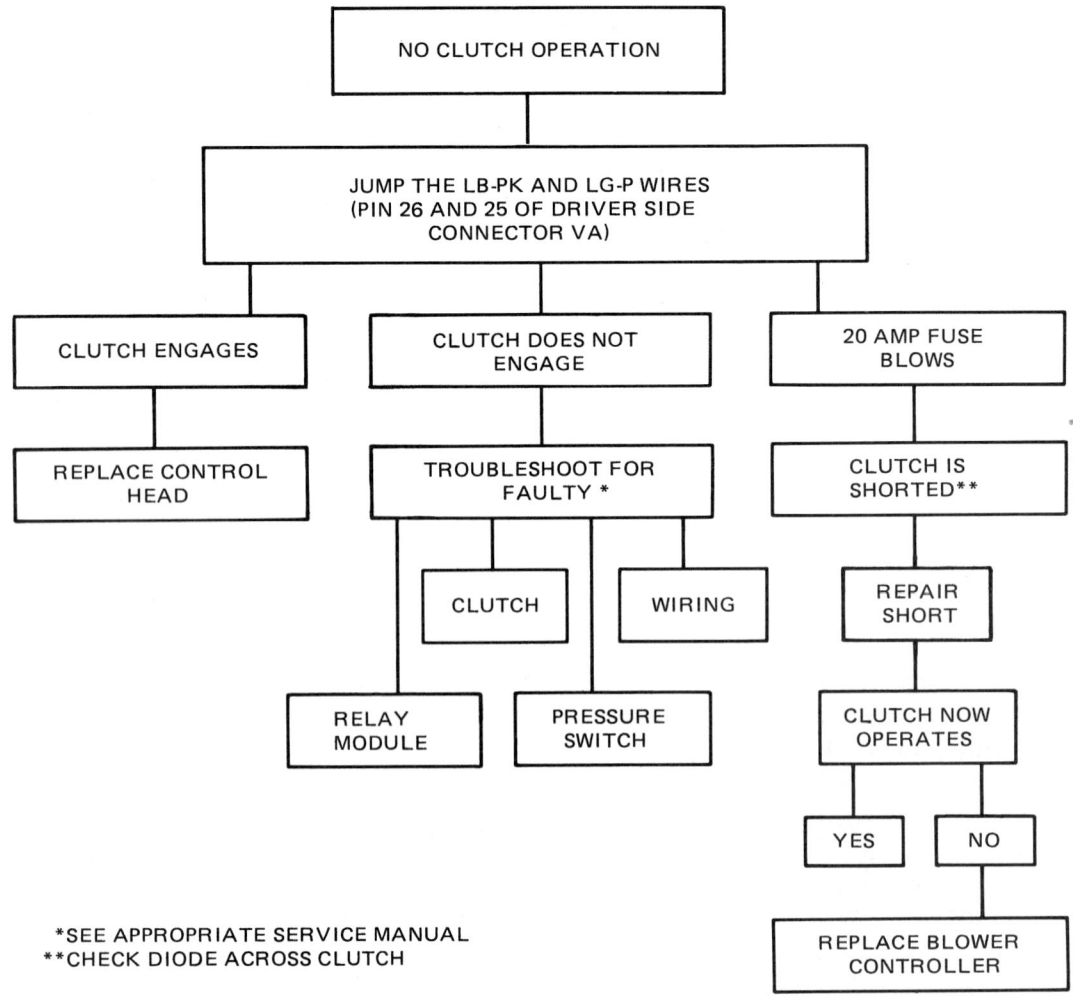

Fig. 5-1 Typical flow chart for no clutch operation.

outside influence, however, that some schematics are labeled "do not measure resistance." Heed this caution, when it is noted, to avoid unnecessary damage to delicate electronic components.

Though the systems differ in many respects, all are designed to provide in-car temperature and humidity conditions at a preset level (within system limitations), regardless of the temperature conditions outside the car.

The temperature control also functions to hold the relative humidity within the car to a healthful level and to prevent window fogging.

For example, if the desired temperature is 75°F (23.89°C), the automatic control system will maintain an in-car environment of 75°F (23.89°C) at 45 to 55 percent humidity, regardless of the outside weather conditions.

In even the hottest weather, a properly operating system can rapidly cool the automobile interior to the predetermined temperature (75°F or 23.89°C). The degree of cooling then cycles to maintain the desired temperature level. In mild weather conditions, the passenger compartment can be held to this same predetermined temperature (75°F or 23.89°C) without resetting or changing the control.

During cold weather, the system rapidly heats the passenger compartment to the predetermined 75°F (23.89°C) level, and then automatically maintains this temperature level.

The intent of this chapter is to give an overall understanding of the components of the various systems, not to cover any particular system in detail. These components include, but are not limited to, *coolant temperature sensor, in-car temperature sensor, outside temperature sensor, high-side temperature switch, low-side temperature switch, low-pressure switch, vehicle speed sensor, throttle position sensor, sunload sensor,* and *power steering cutout switch.*

Many automotive electronic temperature control systems have self-diagnostic test provisions whereby an on-board microprocessor-controlled subsystem will display a code. This code (number, letter, or alphanumeric) is displayed to tell the technician the cause of the malfunction. Some systems also display a code to indicate which computer detected the malfunction. Manufacturers' specifications must be followed to identify the malfunction display codes since they differ from car to car. For example, in some General Motors car lines ".7.0" will be displayed to indicate no malfunction if "no trouble" codes are stored in the

Fig. 5-2 Typical thermistor.

computer. On some Ford car lines the "no trouble" code is "888."

It is also possible for the air-conditioning system to malfunction even though self-check testing indicates there are no problems. It is then necessary to follow a manufacturer's step-by-step procedures to troubleshoot and check the system. Again, typical diagnostic procedures are not practical because of the many different types of systems now found in service. For example, figure 5-1 illustrates diagnostic procedures for "no

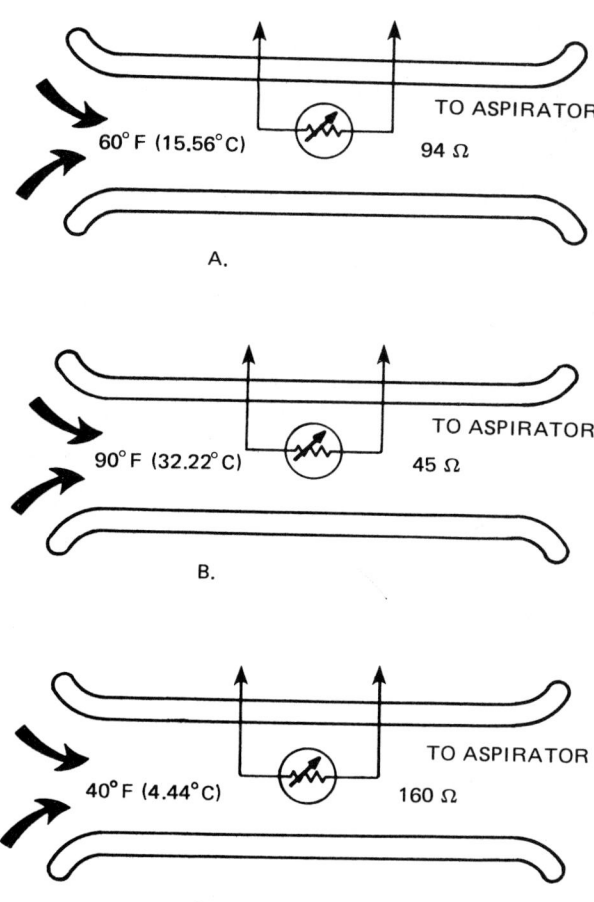

Fig. 5-3 The resistance of a thermistor changes as temperature changes.

clutch operation" for a particular year/model car. This procedure may not be applicable for that same car in another model year or for other similar cars in that same model year.

SENSORS

Although they may vary in physical appearance, sensors all have the same general operating characteristics. That is, they are extremely sensitive to slight changes in temperature. The change in resistance value of each sensor is inversely proportional to a temperature change. For example, when the temperature decreases, the resistance of the sensor increases; and, when the temperature increases, the sensor resistance decreases.

The sensor is actually a resistor whose resistance value is determined by its temperature. This type of resistor is called a *thermistor*, figure 5-2. While the theory of thermistor operation is not covered in this text, the student should be able to gain a good understanding of thermistor operation from the following description and figure 5-3, A through C.

In figure 5-3A, one thermistor is installed in a duct. With air at a temperature of 60°F (15.56°C) passing through the duct, the resistance of the thermistor is 94 ohms. If the temperature in the duct is 90°F (32.22°C), figure 5-3B, then the resistance of the thermistor decreases to about 45 ohms. If, however, the temperature is decreased to 40°F (4.44°C), the thermistor resistance is increased to 160 ohms, figure 5-3C.

ELECTRONIC TEMPERATURE CONTROL SYSTEMS

Many types of electronic temperature control systems are in use. The flow charts of figures 5-4 and 5-5 illustrate two typical systems. The following information relates to many of the components found in an electronic temperature control system. Not all components, however, are found in all systems.

CONTROL PANEL

The control panel is found in the instrument panel at a convenient location for both driver and front-seat passenger access. Any of three types of control panel may be found: manual, figure 5-6; push button, figure 5-7; or touch pad, figure 5-8. All serve the same purpose: to provide operator control of the air-conditioning and heating system. Some control panels have features that other panels do not have, such as provisions to display in-car and outside air temperature in English or metric units.

Provisions are made on the control panel for operator selection of an in-car temperature be-

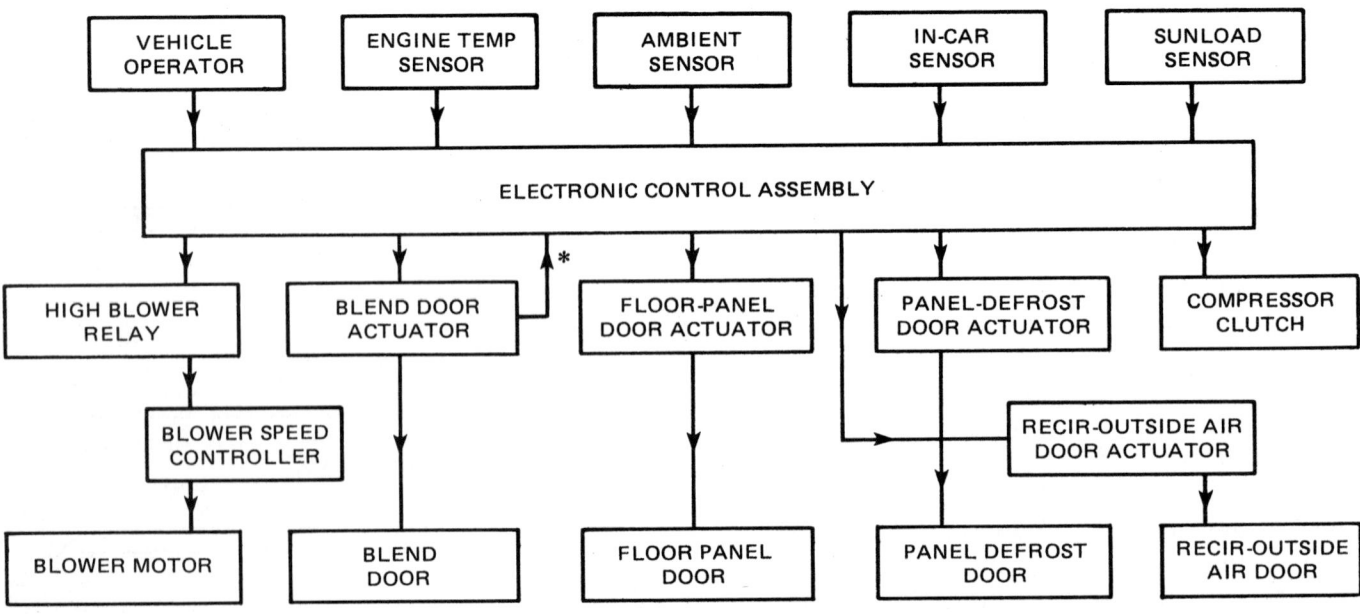

Fig. 5-4 Typical flow chart for electronic temperature control system with five inputs.

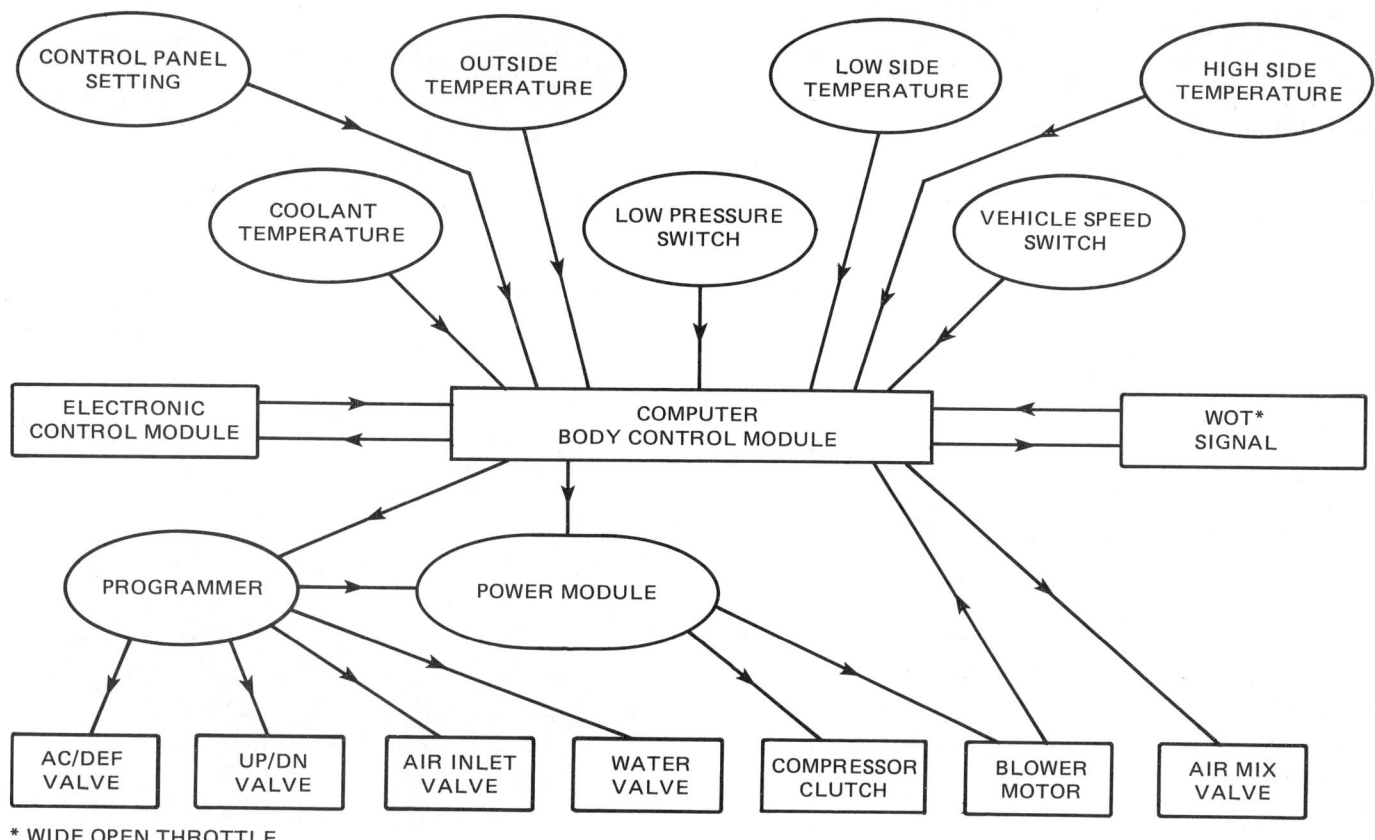

Fig. 5-5 Typical flow chart for electronic temperature control system with nine inputs.

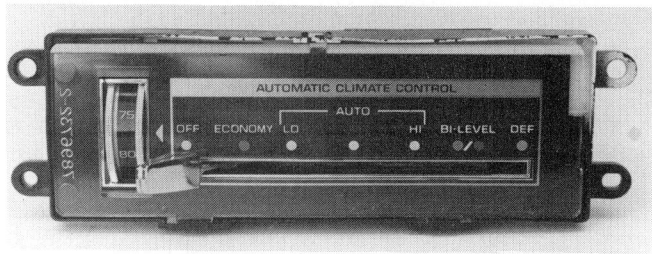

Fig. 5-6 Manual control panel.

Fig. 5-7 Push-button control panel.

tween 65°F (47.2°C) and 85°F (56.6°C) in one-degree increments. Some have an override feature that provides for a setting of either 60°F (42.2°C) or 90°F (72.2°C). Either of these two settings will override all in-car temperature control circuits to provide maximum cooling or heating conditions.

Usually, a microprocessor is located in the control head to input data to the programmer, based on operator-selected conditions. When the ignition switch is turned off, a memory circuit will remember the previous setting. These conditions will be restored the next time the ignition switch is turned on. If the battery is disconnected, however, the memory circuit is cleared and must be reprogrammed.

PROGRAMMER

The programmer, figure 5-9, receives electrical input signals from sensors and the main control panel. Based on all inputs, the programmer provides output signals to turn ON/OFF the compressor clutch, OPEN/CLOSE the heater water valve, determine blower speed, and position all MIX/BLEND mode doors.

BLOWER AND CLUTCH CONTROL

The blower and clutch control, figure 5-10, functions to convert low-current signals from the control panel to high-current feed to the blower motor. Blower speeds with this control are infinitely variable. The speed is controlled through a resistor strip on the temperature door actuator. The resistor strip, then, functions the same as a rheostat to input data to the control panel. The control panel, in turn, inputs the blower-speed signal to the blower control.

A power transistor circuit is included in the blower control which functions to engage the compressor clutch circuit. The metal strip on which the transistor is mounted serves as a heat sink. This assembly is located in the blower airstream to aid in heat dissipation.

POWER MODULE

The power module, figure 5-11, controls the operation of the blower motor. The power module amplifies the blower-drive signal from the programmer; its output signal is proportional to its input signal. This provides variable blower speeds as determined by in-car conditions. If the in-car temperature is considerably higher than the selected air-conditioner temperature, the blower will start at high speed and decrease to low speed as the in-car temperature is lowered.

Conversely, if the in-car temperature is considerably lower than the selected heater temperature, the blower will start at high speed and decrease to low speed as the in-car temperature rises.

CLUTCH DIODE

The clutch coil is an electromagnet, which generates a strong magnetic field when current is applied. This magnetic field is constant as long as power is applied. When power is removed, the magnetic field collapses and creates high-voltage *spikes*. These spikes are harmful to the computer and must be prevented.

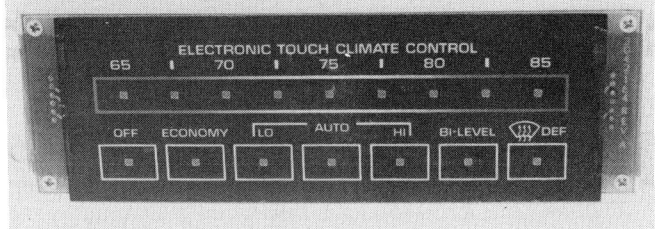

Fig. 5-8 Touch pad control panel.

Fig. 5-9 A typical programmer.

Fig. 5-10 A typical blower and clutch control.

A diode placed across the clutch coil, figure 5-12, provides a "short" for these harmful spikes, holding the spikes to a safe level. This diode is usually found inside the clutch coil connector, across the 12-volt lead and ground lead.

HIGH-SIDE TEMPERATURE SWITCH

The high-side temperature switch is located in the air-conditioning system liquid line between the condenser outlet and the orifice tube inlet, figure 5-13. Though it is a temperature-sensing device, it provides air-conditioner system pressure data to the processor. System temperature is determined by system pressure based on the temperature/pressure relationship of Refrigerant 12.

Fig. 5-11 A typical power module.

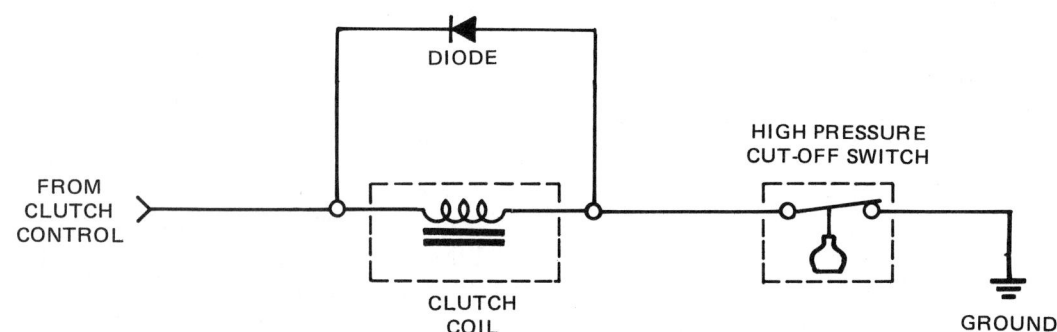

Fig. 5-12 A diode is placed across the clutch coil to reduce *spikes* as the clutch is cycled ON and OFF.

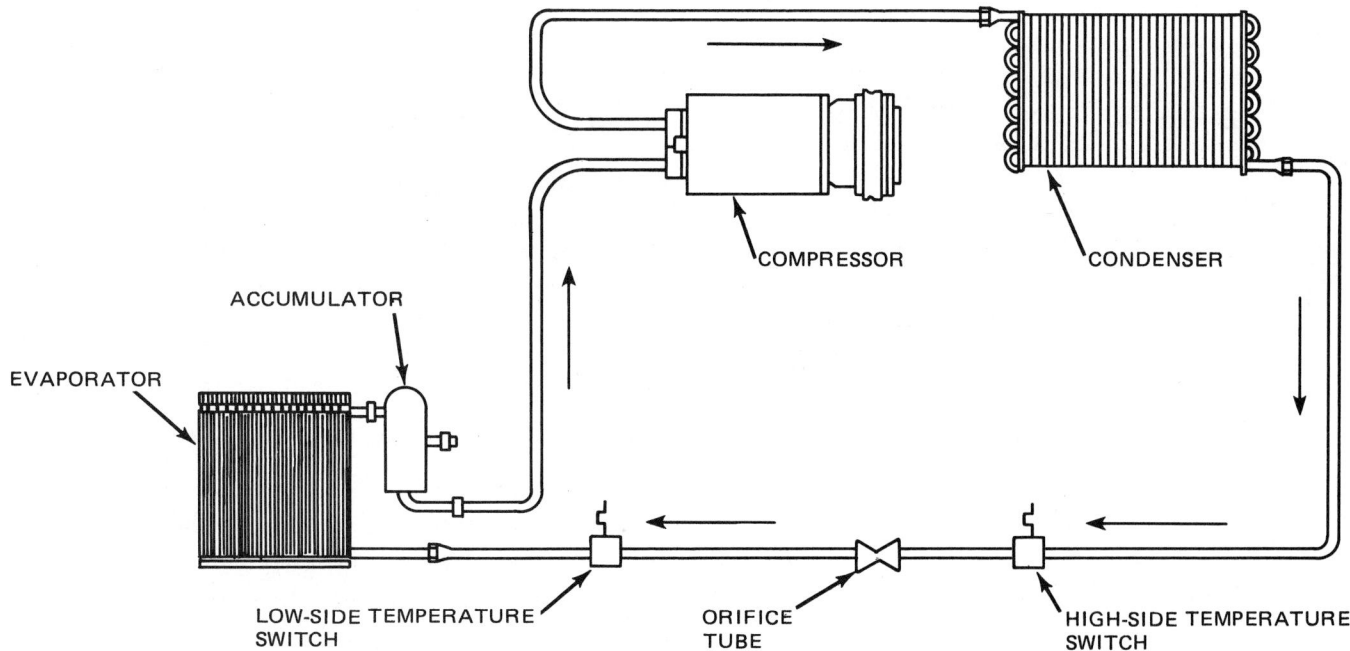

Fig. 5-13 Note the location of the high- and low-side temperature switch in the system.

LOW-SIDE TEMPERATURE SWITCH

The low-side temperature switch is located in the air-conditioning system line between the orifice tube outlet and the evaporator inlet. Refer again to figure 5-13. Its purpose is to sense low-side refrigerant pressure and to provide this information to the processor.

HIGH-PRESSURE SWITCH

The high-pressure switch is normally closed (NC) and opens if air-conditioning system pressure exceeds 425-435 psig (2 930-2 953 kPa). It recloses when the system pressure drops to below 200 psig (1 379 kPa). This switch provides for system safety if, for any reason, pressures exceed safe limits. Unlike the low-pressure switch, the high-pressure switch does not provide data to the processor. This switch is usually in-line with the compressor clutch circuit.

LOW-PRESSURE SWITCH

The low-pressure switch is located in the low side of the air-conditioning system, usually on the accumulator, figure 5-14. This normally closed (NC) switch opens when system low-side pressure drops below 2-8 psig (13.8-55.2 kPa). An open

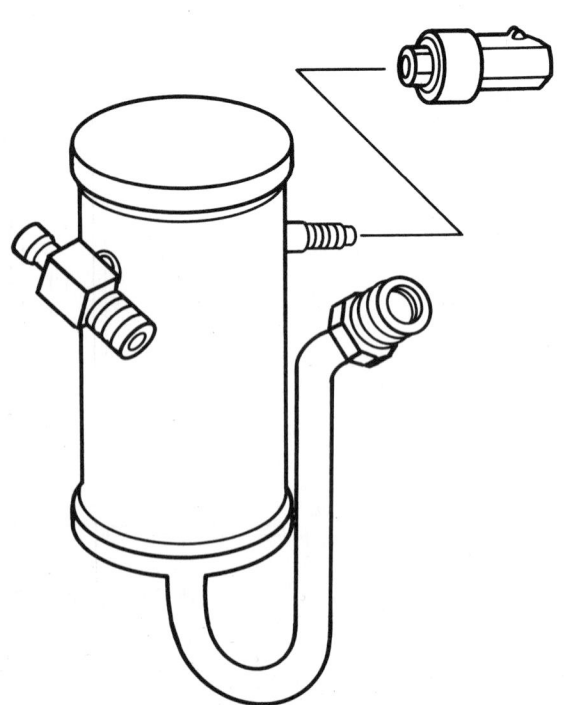

Fig. 5-14 The low-pressure switch is usually located on the accumulator.

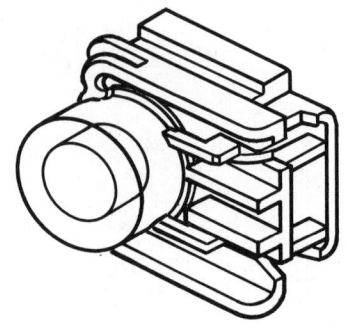

Fig. 5-15 A typical sunload sensor.

low-pressure switch signals the processor to disengage the compressor clutch circuit to prevent compressor operation during low-pressure conditions. Low-pressure conditions may result due to a loss of refrigerant or a clogged orifice tube.

PRESSURE CYCLING SWITCH

The pressure cycling switch is found on some systems. It is used as a means of temperature control by opening and closing the electrical circuit to the compressor clutch coil. On cycling clutch systems, this switch usually opens at a low pressure of 25-26 psig (172.4-179.3 kPa) and closes at a high pressure of 46-48 psig (317.2-331 kPa). On some systems, this switch may be in-line with the compressor clutch coil. On other systems, it may send data to the processor to turn the compressor on and/or off.

SUNLOAD SENSOR

The sunload sensor, figure 5-15, is usually found atop the dashboard, adjacent to one of the radio speaker grilles. The sunload sensor is a photovoltaic diode that sends an appropriate signal to the processor to aid in regulating the in-car temperature.

OUTSIDE TEMPERATURE SENSOR

The outside temperature sensor is usually located just behind the radiator grille and in front of the condenser. Its purpose is to sense outside temperature conditions to provide data to the processor.

This sensor circuit has several programmed memory features to prevent false ambient temperature data input during periods of low-speed driving or when stopped, such as when waiting for a traffic signal.

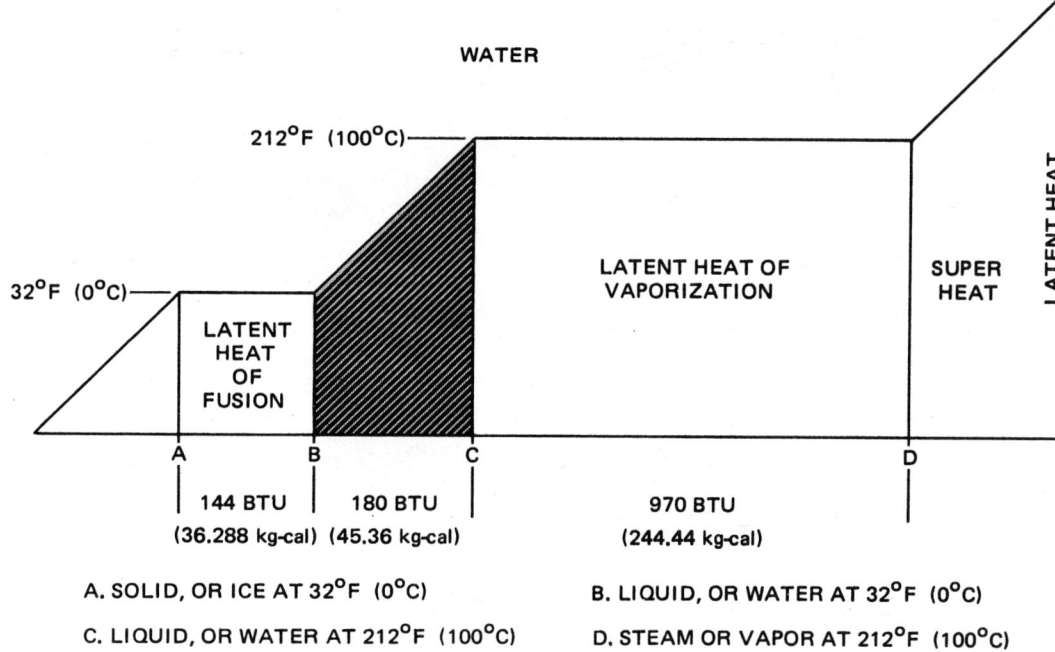

Fig. 1-3 Latent and sensible heat values for water.

exceptions to this statement are ammonia (NH_3) with a specific heat of 1.100, and hydrogen (H) with a specific heat of 3.410.

COLD — THE ABSENCE OF HEAT

What is meant by the word cold? *Cold* is the absence of heat. If cold is to be understood, then the student must first understand what heat is. *Heat* is energy and it is present in all things. Heat cannot be contained. The molecular structure of all things is changed into one of three forms by heat.

Heat is molecular movement. For example, water is liquid between 32°F (0°C) and 212°F (100°C). If heat is added to water at 212°F (100°C), its molecular movement is increased. As a result, water vaporizes and turns to steam. When heat is removed from water at 32°F (0°C), its molecular movement is decreased. The water then solidifies and turns to ice.

All matter generates heat which is called specific heat. The body generates heat that must be overcome if one is to feel cool. The food stored in the refrigerator generates heat that must be overcome if the food is to be kept at a safe temperature as required for short-term or long-term storage. Any matter that is to be cooled must first have its specific heat removed or overcome.

If it is now asked, "What is cold?", it appears that the answer is that cold is the absence of heat. If this is true, at what point is all the heat removed from matter? Ice, at 32°F (0°C), is said to be cold.

Absolute cold, then, is the absence of all heat. Complete absence of heat does not occur until the temperature of −459.67°F (−273.16°C) is reached. All temperature above this value contains heat. For example, −459°F still contains 0.67°F of heat; −273°C still contains 0.16°C of heat.

Absolute cold, like other absolutes, has not yet been achieved by scientists. A Dutch physicist, Wander de Haas, working at the University of Leiden (Holland), achieved a temperature of 0.004 4°C above absolute zero. In 1957, Dr. Arthur Spohr, working at the U.S. Naval Research Laboratory, achieved a temperature of less than one-millionth of a degree kelvin (K) above absolute zero (0.000 001°K). The Kelvin scale, used in physics, uses 0°K for absolute cold, 273°K as the freezing point for water, and 373°K as its boiling point.

In summary then, cold is the absence of heat energy. According to current scientific theory, absolute zero is the point at which all molecular movement stops. Since molecular movement causes heat energy, it follows that if there is no movement there is no heat.

Body Comfort

The normal temperature of the adult human body is 98.6°F (37°C). This temperature is sometimes called subsurface or deep-tissue temperature as opposed to surface or skin temperature. An understanding of the process by which the body maintains its temperature is helpful to the student because it explains how air conditioning helps keep the body comfortable.

As calories are taken into the body, they are converted into energy and stored for future use. The conversion process generates heat. All body movements use up the stored energy and, in doing so, add to the heat generated by the conversion process.

The body consistently produces more heat than it requires. Therefore, for body comfort, all of the excess heat produced must be given off by the body.

THE BODY REJECTS HEAT

The constant removal of body heat takes place through three natural processes which all occur at the same time. As shown in figure 1-4, these processes are:

- convection
- radiation
- evaporation

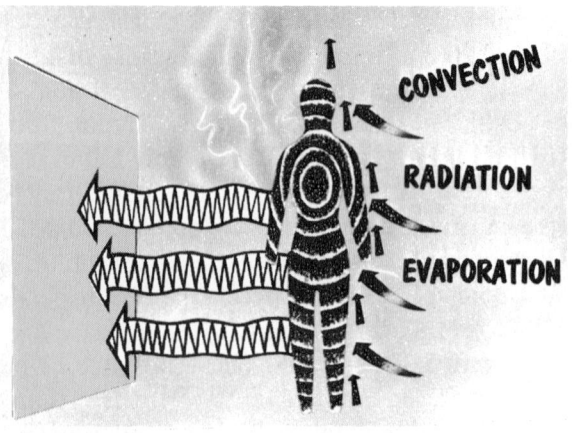

Fig. 1-4 Processes by which heat is removed from the body.

Convection

The *convection* process of removing heat is based on two phenomena:

- Heat flows from a hot surface to a surface containing less heat. For example, heat flows from the body to the air surrounding the body when the air temperature is less than the skin temperature.
- Heat rises. This is evident by watching the smoke from a burning cigarette, or the steam from boiling water.

When these two phenomena are applied to the body process of removing heat, the following occurs:

- The body gives off heat to the surrounding air (which has a lower temperature).
- The surrounding air becomes warmer and moves upward.
- As the warmer air moves upward, air containing less heat takes its place. The convection cycle is then completed.

Radiation

Radiation is the process which moves heat from a heat source to an object by means of heat rays. This principle is based on the phenomenon that heat moves from a hot surface to a surface containing less heat. Radiation takes place independently of convection. The process of radiation does not require air movement to complete the heat transfer. This process is not affected by air temperature, although it is affected by the temperature of the surrounding surfaces.

The body quickly experiences the effects of sun radiation when it moves from a shady to a sunny area.

Evaporation

Evaporation is the process by which moisture becomes a vapor. As moisture vaporizes from a warm surface, it removes heat and thus cools the surface. This process takes place constantly on the surface of the body. Moisture is given off through the pores of the skin. As the moisture evaporates, it removes heat from the body.

IN-CAR TEMPERATURE SENSOR

The in-car temperature sensor, also called an in-vehicle sensor, figure 5-16, is located in a tubular device, called an *aspirator*. A small amount of in-car air is drawn through the aspirator across the in-car sensor to provide average in-car temperature data to the processor.

ASPIRATOR

The aspirator is a small duct system which is so designed that it causes a small amount of in-car air to pass through it, figure 5-17. The main airstream causes a low pressure (suction) at the inlet end of the aspirator. This causes in-car air to be drawn into the in-car sensor plenum. The in-car sensor, located in the plenum, is continuously exposed to average in-car air to monitor the in-car air temperature.

COOLANT TEMPERATURE SENSOR

The coolant temperature sensor is a thermistor that provides engine coolant temperature information to the processor. This sensor also provides input information to other on-board

Fig. 5-16 A typical in-car temperature sensor.

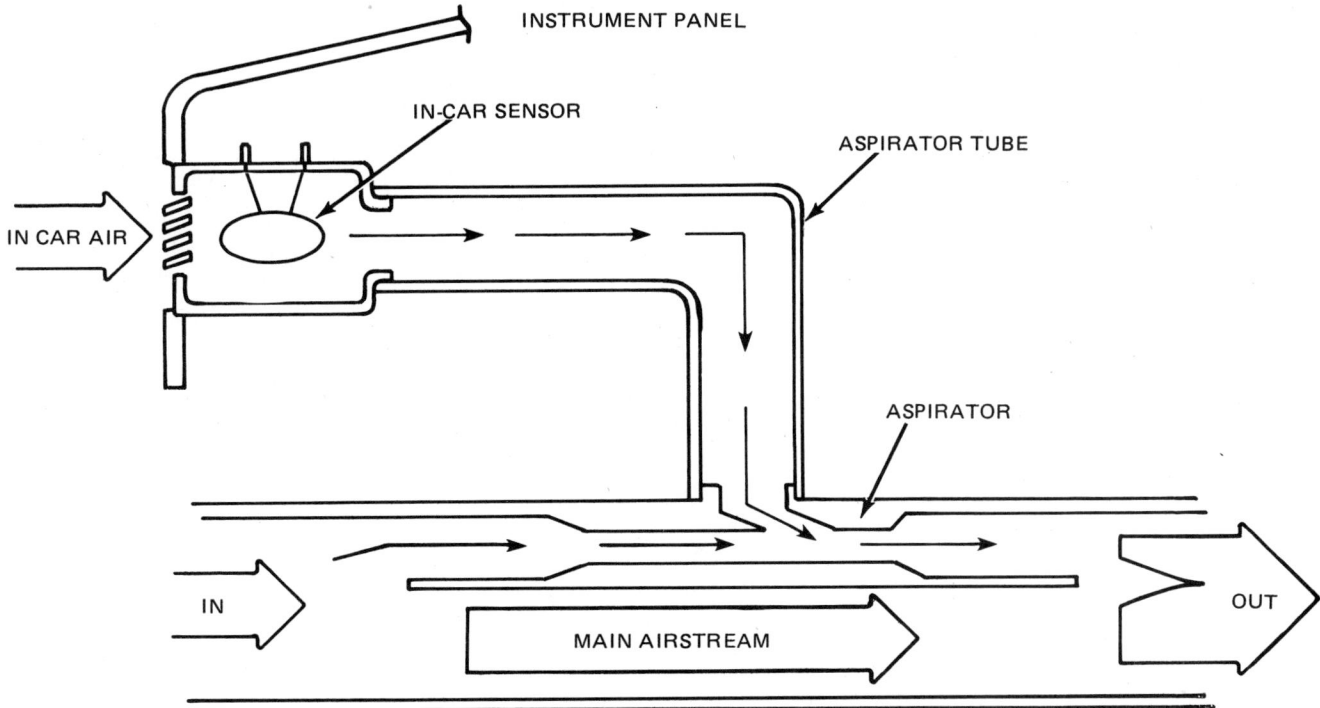

Fig. 5-17 A typical aspirator. Note the location of the in-car temperature sensor.

computers to provide data for fuel enrichment, ignition timing, exhaust gas recirculate operation, canister purge control, idle speed control, and closed-loop fuel control.

A defective coolant temperature sensor will cause poor engine performance, which will probably be evident before poor air-conditioning performance is noticed.

VEHICLE SPEED SENSOR

The vehicle speed sensor is a pulse generator located at the transmission output shaft. It provides actual vehicle speed data to the processor as well as other subsystems, such as the electronic control module.

THROTTLE POSITION SENSOR

The throttle position sensor is actually a potentiometer with a voltage input from the processor. The processor, then, determines throttle position based on the return voltage signal. At the wide-open throttle (WOT) position the compressor clutch is disengaged to provide maximum power for acceleration. This device is often called the WOT sensor and is most often found on diesel engine-equipped vehicles.

HEATER DELAY SWITCH

The heater turn-on switch is usually a bimetallic snap-action switch found in the coolant stream of the engine. Its purpose is to prevent blower operation when engine coolant temperature is below 120–122°F (48.9–50°C), if heat is selected.

If cooling is selected, the programmer will override this switch to provide immediate blower operation, regardless of engine coolant temperature.

BRAKE BOOSTER VACUUM SWITCH

The brake booster vacuum switch is found on some cars. It is used to disengage the air-conditioning compressor when braking requires maximum effort. This switch is usually in-line with the compressor clutch electrical circuit and does not provide data to the processor.

POWER STEERING CUTOFF SWITCH

The power steering cutoff switch, found on some cars, is used to disengage the air-conditioning compressor when the power steering system requires maximum effort. This switch may be in-line with the compressor control relay and may not provide data to the programmer. On other applications, this switch is in the electronic control module which provides feedback data to the processor.

MODE ACTUATOR

Two types of mode actuators are used to position the mode doors: vacuum and electric. Vacuum-operated actuators are often called "pots" or "motors."

Electric mode actuators have both drive and feedback circuitry. This provides the means for them to be stopped at any specified position through 360° of travel. Mode actuators are not reversible and travel in one direction only. The feedback circuit provides constant data to the control panel relative to the position in which it is stopped. If the feedback circuit is interrupted through faulty or broken wiring or dirty connections, the actuator will continue to run. However, if the correct feedback signal is not received by the control panel within twenty seconds, power to the actuator will be turned off. If this occurs, on many systems an LED will flash on the control panel to warn the operator that there is a problem with the system.

Figure 5-18 shows how a vacuum motor is used to operate the mode doors. In figure 5-18A, the device is shown in the relaxed position. In figure 5-18B, it is in the applied position.

In the relaxed position, the spring keeps the arm extended. In the applied position, the vacuum overcomes the spring pressure and the arm is pulled to the IN position. The normal, or OFF, position of the vacuum motor is the relaxed position.

WATER VALVE ACTUATOR

Two types of water valve actuators are available: vacuum and electric.

The electric water valve actuator, figure 5-19, operates in a manner similar to the mode actuator. It differs only in that it is reversible and only

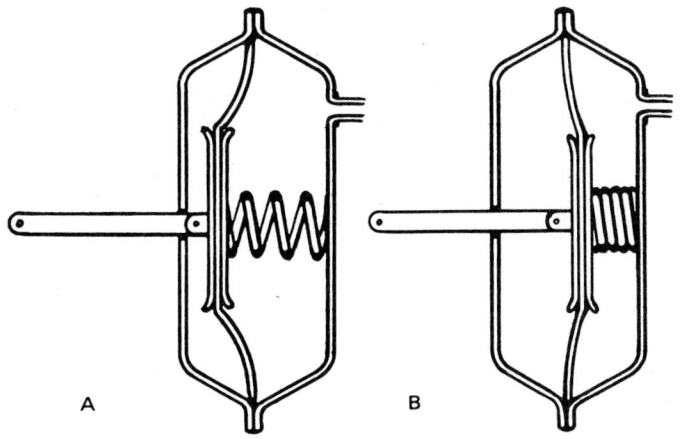

Fig. 5-18 Vacuum motor or pot (cutaway).

Fig. 5-19 A typical electric water valve actuator.

Fig. 5-20 Water valve.

travels 90°. Its purpose is to turn on and off the water valve. The water valve provides water to the heater core which is located in the air-conditioning/heating duct system.

The heater control valve may be located on the engine, on the fender well, near the heater core, or inside the heater case. In some systems, the control is actuated by a cable. However, for the automatic temperature system, the control is vacuum actuated. The operation of the control is governed by varying vacuum levels. A typical vacuum-operated hot water heater control valve is shown in figure 5-20.

SUMMARY

Many of the components of an automatic temperature control system are covered in this chapter. Others are covered throughout this text. Because of the complexity of the automatic system and its number of variations, it is essential that manufacturers' specifications, manuals, and schematics be consulted for any specific year/model to be serviced.

CHAPTER 6:

Troubleshooting and Diagnosis

A comprehensive glossary of terms, acronyms, and abbreviations used in the automotive air-conditioning trade is found in the back of this book.

An accurate diagnosis and determination of automotive air-conditioning system function and, more importantly, malfunction, depend largely upon the ability of the technician to interpret gauge pressure readings. The importance of a refrigeration technician's manifold and gauge set is often compared to that of a physician's stethoscope.

An improper gauge reading will relate to a specific problem. More than one problem may be associated with a particular gauge reading, however. A system operating normally will have a low-side gauge pressure reading that corresponds with the temperature of the liquid refrigerant as it becomes a vapor while removing heat in the evaporator. The high-side gauge readings should correspond with the temperature of the refrigerant vapor as it becomes a liquid while giving up its heat in the condenser. The use of a third gauge, in some systems, is to monitor the pressure of the refrigerant vapor as it enters the compressor. This compound gauge relates to the pressure drop in the system after the refrigerant has passed through the suction pressure control device.

Any deviation from normal gauge readings, other than slight, indicates a malfunction. This malfunction, if within the system, may be caused by a faulty control device, a restriction, or a defective component. It should be noted that improper mounting or location of components in a newly installed system may affect system performance. An overheated engine cooling system or an improperly tuned engine may also affect system performance, and will be noted as abnormal gauge readings.

Diagnosis of system malfunction is made easier with the knowledge that the low-side temperature (°F) and pressure (psig) are closely related. This is true of Refrigerant 12, and is easily determined in the English system of measure between 20 psig and 60 psig. The English temperature-pressure chart, figure 6-1, shows that there is only a slight variation between the temperature and pressure in this range.

It may, therefore, be correct to assume that for every pound (psig) pressure change in the low side that the temperature will correspondingly change by one degree (°F). For example, a pressure of 33.1 psig indicates (on the chart) an evaporating temperature of 36°F. A pressure increase of two pounds (2 psig) to 35.1 psig will result in a temperature increase of 2°F to 38°F.

SERVICE PROCEDURE 1:

TROUBLESHOOTING THE AIR-CONDITIONING SYSTEM

This procedure is given as a quick reference to enable the service technician to isolate many of the conditions that can cause improper air-conditioning system operation or noise.

ENGLISH TEMPERATURE-PRESSURE CHART					
Low-Side Pressure psi		Temperature °F	High-Side Pressure psi		Temperature °F
Absolute	Gauge		Absolute	Gauge	
25.9	11.2	4	120	105	60
27	12.3	6	124	109	62
28.1	13.4	8	128	113	64
29.3	14.6	10	132	117	66
30.5	15.8	12	137	122	68
31.8	17.1	14	141	126	70
33	18.3	16	147	132	72
34.4	19.7	18	152	137	74
35.7	21	20	159	144	76
37.1	22.4	22	167	152	78
38.5	23.8	24	175	160	80
40	25.3	26	180	165	82
41.5	26.8	28	185	170	84
43.1	28.4	30	190	175	86
44.7	30	32	195	180	88
46.4	31.7	34	200	185	90
47.8	33.1	36	204	189	92
49.8	35.1	38	208	193	94
51.6	36.9	40	215	200	96
53.5	38.8	42	225	210	98
55.4	40.7	44	235	220	100
57.3	42.6	46	243	228	102
59.3	44.6	48	251	236	104

Fig. 6-1 English temperature-pressure chart.

- Part I *noisy system*. Suggests causes of noise and how to correct the problem.
- Part II *intermittent cooling*. Used as an aid to troubleshoot the customer complaint, "Sometimes it works; sometimes it does not." Suggested causes and corrections are given.
- Part III *insufficient cooling*. "It just is not cool enough," is a common customer complaint. Causes of insufficient cooling and suggested remedies are given.
- Part IV *no cooling*. "It does not cool at all," is the easiest complaint to diagnose. Possible causes and corrections are given.

PROCEDURE, PART I

NOISY SYSTEM

Possible Cause

Loose electrical connection causing "clutch chatter."
Defective clutch coil.
Defective clutch.
Defective clutch bearing(s).
Loose belt(s).

Possible Correction

Tighten or repair the connection, as necessary.
Replace the clutch coil.
Replace the clutch.
Replace the clutch bearing(s).
Tighten the belt(s). Do not overtighten.

58 Chapter Six, Troubleshooting and Diagnosis

Broken belt (if two-belt drive). — Replace both belts as a pair.
Worn or frayed belt(s). — Replace belt(s).
Loose compressor mount. — Tighten the compressor mount.
Loose compressor brace(s). — Tighten the compressor brace(s).
Broken compressor mount. — Repair or replace the compressor mount.
Broken compressor brace(s). — Repair or replace the compressor brace(s).
Blower fan rubbing against case. — Adjust or reposition the blower fan.
Defective blower motor. — Replace the blower motor.
Idler pulley bearing(s) defective. — Replace the idler pulley assembly or bearing(s), as applicable.

NOISY COMPRESSOR

Overcharge of refrigerant. — Purge the system until the charge is correct or recharge the system.
Undercharge of refrigerant. — Locate and repair the leak. Recharge the system.
Overcharge of oil. — Remove excess oil or replace the oil.
Undercharge of oil. — Locate and repair the leak. Replace the oil to the proper level.
Moisture in the system. — Purge the system, replace the drier, and evacuate and recharge the system.
Defective compressor. — Repair or replace the compressor.

PROCEDURE, PART II

SYSTEM COOLS INTERMITTENTLY

Possible Cause — **Possible Correction**

Defective circuit breaker. — Replace the circuit breaker.
Circuit breaker trips on overload. — Correct the problem: short circuit or excessive current draw.
Loose wiring. — Repair or replace the wiring.
Defective blower speed control. — Replace the control (switch).
Defective blower speed resistors. — Replace the resistor block.
Defective blower motor. — Replace the blower motor.
Defective clutch coil. — Replace the clutch coil.
Loose belt(s). — Tighten the belt(s). Do not overtighten.
Defective clutch brush set. — Replace the brush set.
Loose ground connection at blower. — Tighten or repair the ground connection.
Loose ground connection at clutch coil. — Tighten or repair the ground connection.
Loose ground connection at clutch brush set. — Tighten or repair the ground connection.
Clutch slipping; low voltage. — Determine the cause and correct it.
Clutch slipping; excessive wear. — Replace worn clutch part(s).
Thermostat improperly adjusted. — Adjust the thermostat.
Defective thermostat. — Replace the thermostat.
Defective low-pressure control. — Replace the low-pressure control.
Defective high-pressure control. — Replace the high-pressure control.
Defective suction pressure regulator. — Replace the suction pressure regulator.

| Moisture in the system. | Purge the system, replace the drier, and evacuate and recharge the system. |

PROCEDURE, PART III

INSUFFICIENT COOLING

Possible Cause

Blower motor "sluggish" (runs slow).

Clutch slipping; low voltage.
Clutch slipping; excessive wear.
Clutch cycles too often.

Defective thermostat.
Defective low-pressure control.
Defective suction pressure regulator.
Insufficient airflow from evaporator.

Insufficient airflow over condenser.

Partially clogged screen in receiver-drier.
Partially clogged screen in expansion valve.
Partially clogged screen in fixed orifice tube.

Partially clogged screen in inlet of compressor.

Thermostatic expansion valve remote bulb loose.
No insulation on TXV remote bulb.
Moisture in system.

Air in system.

Excess refrigerant in system.

Excess oil in system.

Partially clogged accumulator.
Partially clogged receiver-drier.
Defective thermostatic expansion valve.
Undercharge of refrigerant.

Possible Correction

Check for loose connections. If none, replace the motor.
Determine the cause and correct it.
Replace worn clutch part(s).
Adjust or replace the thermostat. Replace the low-pressure control.
Replace the thermostat.
Replace the low-pressure control.
Replace the suction pressure regulator.
Clean the evaporator and/or repair sticking or binding "blend" doors.
Clean the condenser and/or correct the cooling system problem(s).
Replace the receiver-drier.
Clean the screen and replace the drier.
Clean the screen and replace the accumulator.
Clean the screen, determine the cause, and correct as necessary.
Clean the contact area and tighten the remote bulb. Wrap with cork tape.
Insulate the remote bulb with cork tape.
Purge the system, replace the drier, and evacuate and recharge the system.
Purge the system. Evacuate and recharge the system.
Purge the system until correct or purge and recharge the system.
Drain oil to the proper level or change the oil.
Replace the accumulator.
Replace the receiver-drier.
Replace the thermostatic expansion valve.
Repair the leak, and evacuate and charge the system.

PROCEDURE, PART IV

NO COOLING

Possible Cause

Blown fuse.

Defective circuit breaker

Possible Correction

Correct the problem, if any, and replace the fuse.
Correct the problem, if any, and replace the circuit breaker.

Broken electrical wire.	Repair or replace the wire.
Disconnected electrical wire.	Reconnect the wire.
Corroded electrical wire (high-resistance connection).	Clean and reconnect or replace the connector.
Defective clutch coil.	Replace the clutch coil.
Defective or worn clutch brush set.	Replace the brush set.
Defective blower motor.	Replace the blower motor.
Defective thermostat.	Replace the thermostat.
Defective low-pressure control.	Replace the low-pressure control.
Loose compressor drive belt(s).	Tighten the belt(s). Do not overtighten.
Broken drive belt(s).	Replace the belt(s).
Defective compressor suction valve plate(s).	Replace the suction valve plate(s) and gasket(s).
Defective compressor discharge valve plate(s).	Replace the discharge valve plate(s) and gasket(s).
Blown compressor head or valve plate gasket(s).	Replace head and valve plate gasket(s).
Defective compressor.	Rebuild the compressor or replace with a new or rebuilt compressor.
Undercharge or no charge of R-12:	Locate and repair the leak.
a. Compressor shaft seal leaking.	Replace the shaft seal and gasket set.
b. Defective hose (leaking R-12).	Replace the defective hose.
c. Fusible plug leaking R-12.	Replace the fusible plug (do not repair).
d. Refrigerant leak in system.	Locate and correct the leak, as required.
Plugged (clogged) line or hose.	Clean or replace the line or hose.
Clogged inlet screen in expansion valve.	Clean the screen and replace the drier.
Defective thermostatic expansion valve.	Replace expansion valve.
Clogged expansion tube.	Clean or replace the expansion tube. Replace the accumulator.
Clogged screen in receiver-drier.	Replace the receiver-drier.
Excessive moisture in system.	Replace the drier, and evacuate and charge the system.
Clogged screen in accumulator.	Replace the accumulator.
Defective suction pressure control.	Repair or replace the control.

SYSTEM DIAGNOSIS 1:

THE COMPRESSOR—CYCLING CLUTCH TXV OR FOT SYSTEM

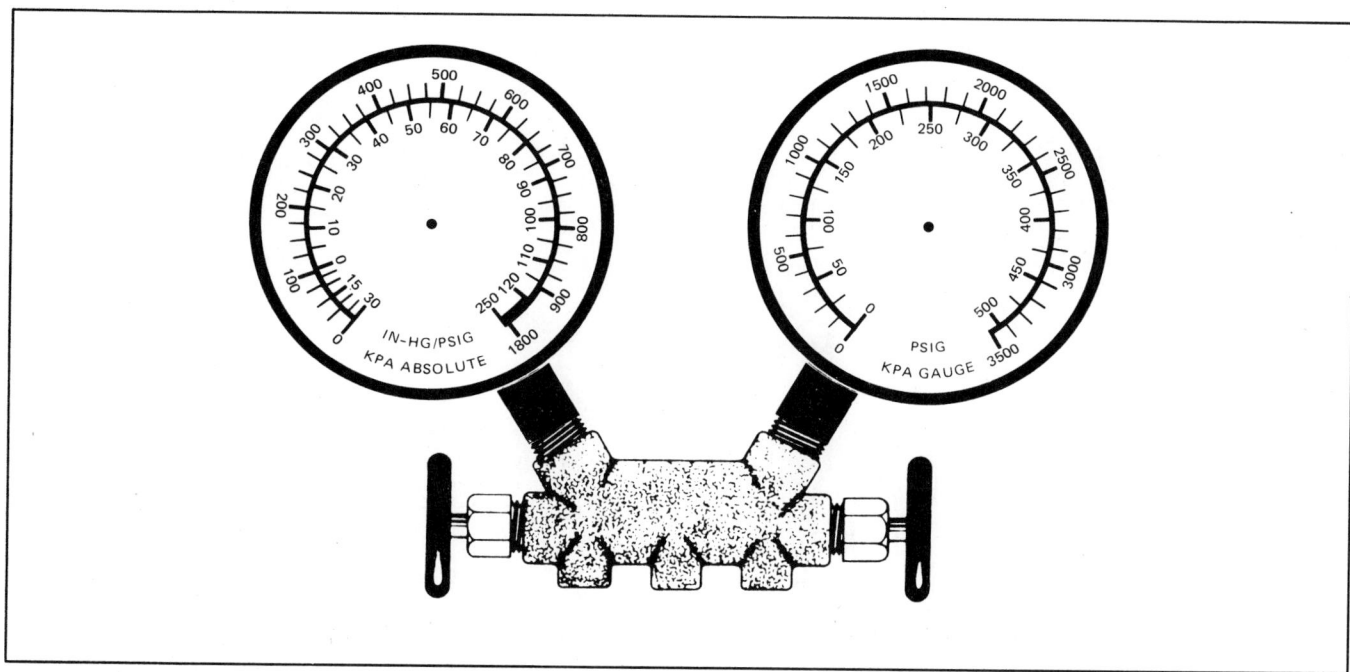

CONDITIONS

Ambient temperature: 90°F (32.2°C)
Low-side gauge: 50 psig (446 kPa absolute)
High-side gauge: 120 psi (827 kPa)

DIAGNOSIS

1. Show the high- and low-side readings on the gauges in the diagram.

2. What should the normal high-side reading be? _____ psi
   _____ kPa

3. What is the evaporator temperature in this problem? _____ °F
   _____ °C

4. A low-side reading of 50 psig (446 kPa absolute) is (high, low). _____

5. A high-side reading of 120 psi (827 kPa) is (high, low). _____

6. This condition results in (good, poor, no) cooling from the evaporator. _____

7. An internal _____ of the compressor is indicated by these conditions. _____

8. To correct this condition, a new _____ and/or _____ must be installed. _____
   _____

9. This condition is generally caused by excessive _____. _____

SYSTEM DIAGNOSIS 2:

THE CONDENSER—CYCLING CLUTCH TXV OR FOT SYSTEM

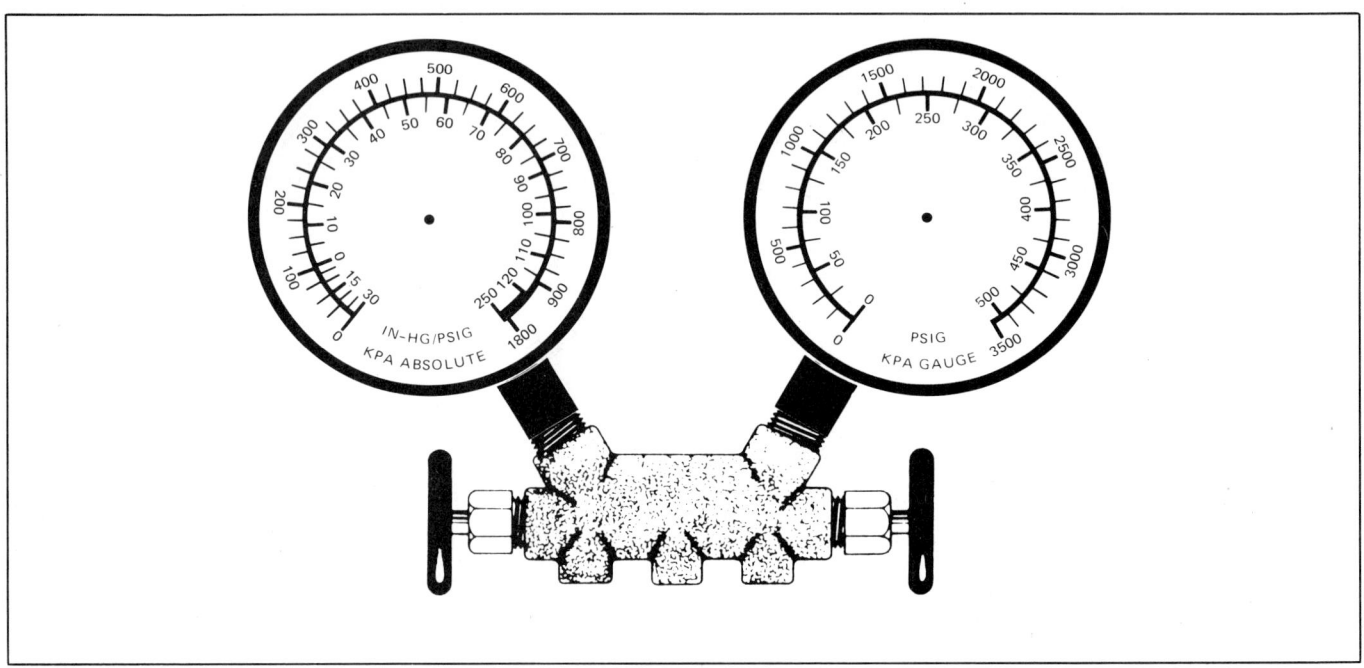

CONDITIONS
Ambient Temperature: 95°F (35°C)
Low-side gauge: 55 psig (499 kPa absolute)
High-side gauge: 300 psi (2 069 kPa)

DIAGNOSIS
1. Show the high- and low-side gauge readings on the gauges in the diagram.
2. What should the normal high-side gauge reading be? _____ psi
   _____ kPa
3. What is the evaporator temperature in this problem? _____ °F
   _____ °C
4. A low-side reading of 55 psig (499 kPa absolute) is (high, low). _____
5. A high-side pressure reading of 300 psi (2 069 kPa) is (high, low). _____
6. This condition results in (good, poor, no) cooling from the evaporator. _____
7. Give two conditions outside the air-conditioning system that can cause this pressure.
   _____
   _____
8. Give two conditions inside the air-conditioning system that can cause this pressure.
   _____
   _____
9. Give one type of damage that can occur by operating the air conditioner with this head pressure. _____

SYSTEM DIAGNOSIS 3:

THE DEHYDRATOR—CYCLING CLUTCH TXV SYSTEM

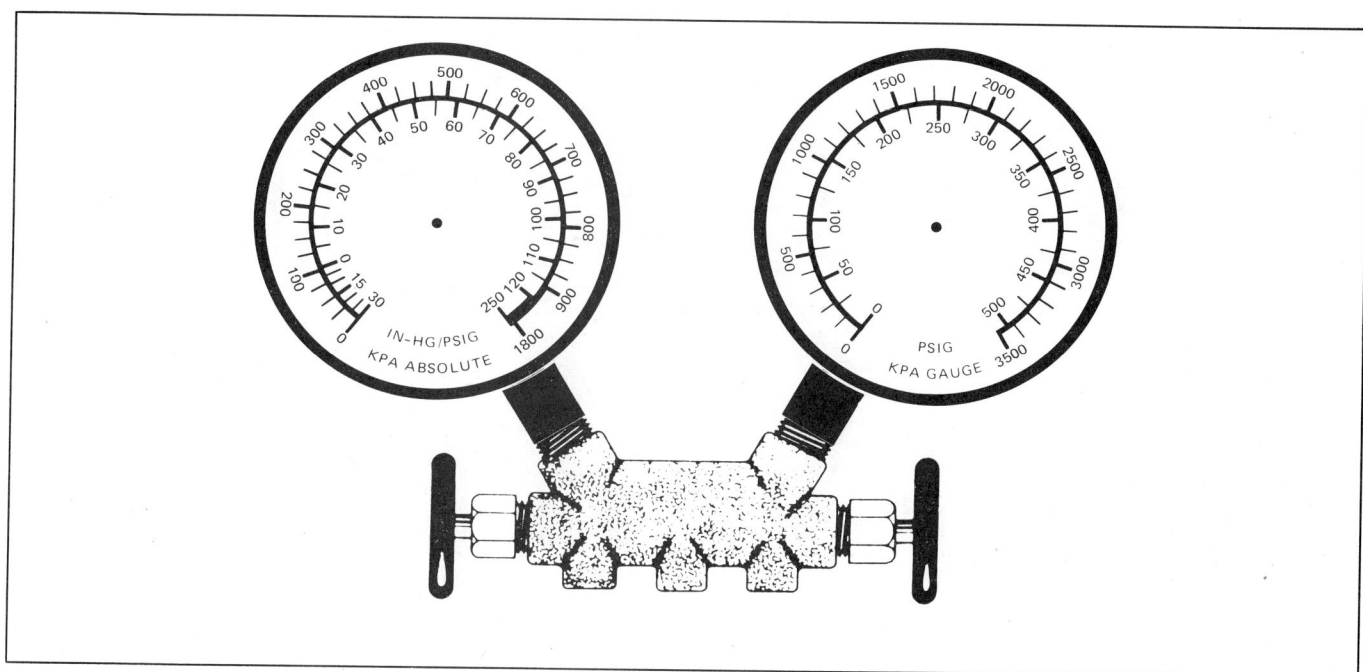

CONDITIONS

Ambient temperature: 100°F (37.8°C)
Low-side gauge: 5 psig (136 kPa absolute)
High-side gauge: 305 psi (2 103 kPa)

DIAGNOSIS

1. Show the high- and low-side gauge readings on the gauges in the diagram.

2. What should the normal high-side reading be? _____ psi
   _____ kPa

3. What is the evaporator temperature in this problem? Explain. _____ °F
   _____ °C
   _____

4. A low-side reading of 5 psig (136 kPa absolute) is (high, low). _____

5. A high-side reading of 305 psi (2 103 kPa) is (high, low). _____

6. This condition results in (good, poor, no) cooling from the evaporator. _____

7. A restriction at the _____ is indicated by these readings. _____

8. Frosting is likely to occur at the point of _____. _____

9. How can this system be repaired? _____
   _____
   _____

SYSTEM DIAGNOSIS 4:

THE ACCUMULATOR—CYCLING CLUTCH FOT SYSTEM

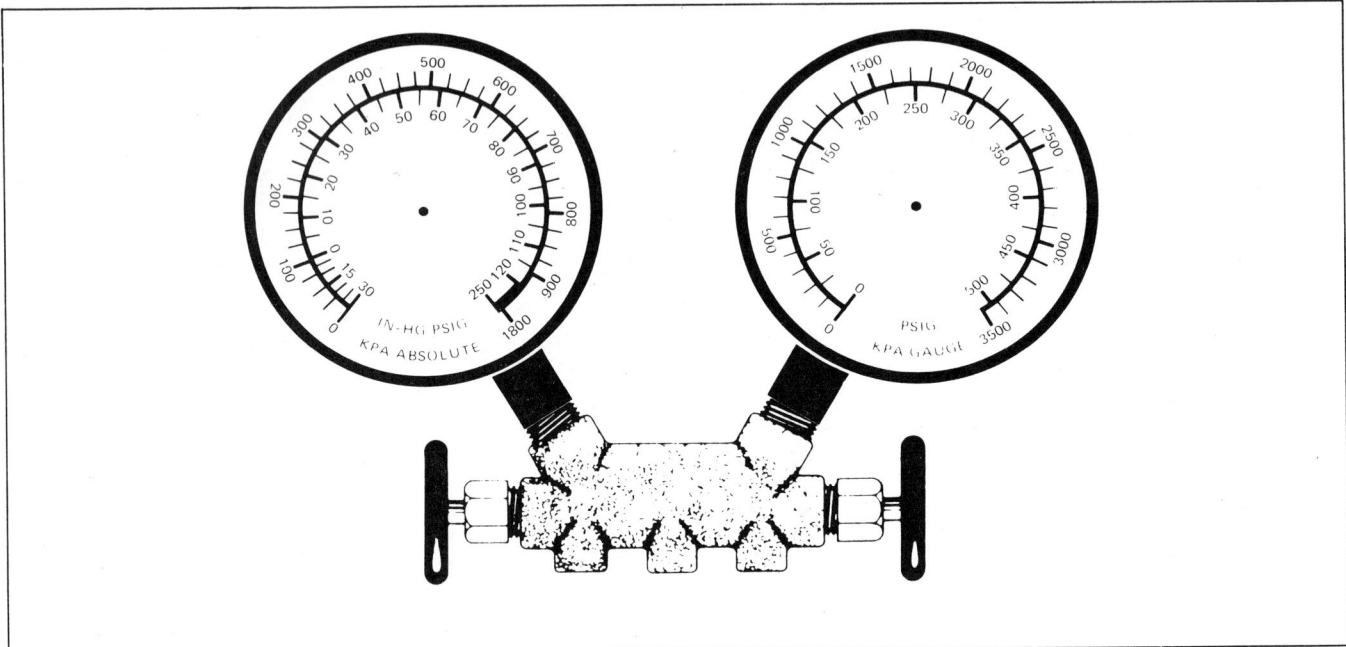

CONDITIONS
Low-side service valve located on accumulator
Ambient temperature: 95°F (35°C)
Low-side gauge: 45 psig (412 kPa absolute)
High-side gauge: 165 psig (1 138 kpa)

DIAGNOSIS

1. Show the high- and low-side gauge readings on the gauges in the diagram.

2. What should the normal high-side reading be? _____ psig
   _____ kPa

3. What is the evaporator temperature in this problem? _____ °F
   Explain. _____ °C

   _____

4. A low-side reading of 45 psig (412 kPa absolute) is (high, normal, low). _____

5. A high-side reading of 165 psig (1 138 kPa) is (high, normal, low). _____

6. This condition results in (good, poor, no) cooling from the evaporator. _____

7. A restriction in the _____ is indicated by these readings. _____

8. Frosting is likely to occur at the point of _____ . _____

9. How can this system be repaired? _____

SYSTEM DIAGNOSIS 5:

THE ACCUMULATOR—CYCLING CLUTCH FOT SYSTEM

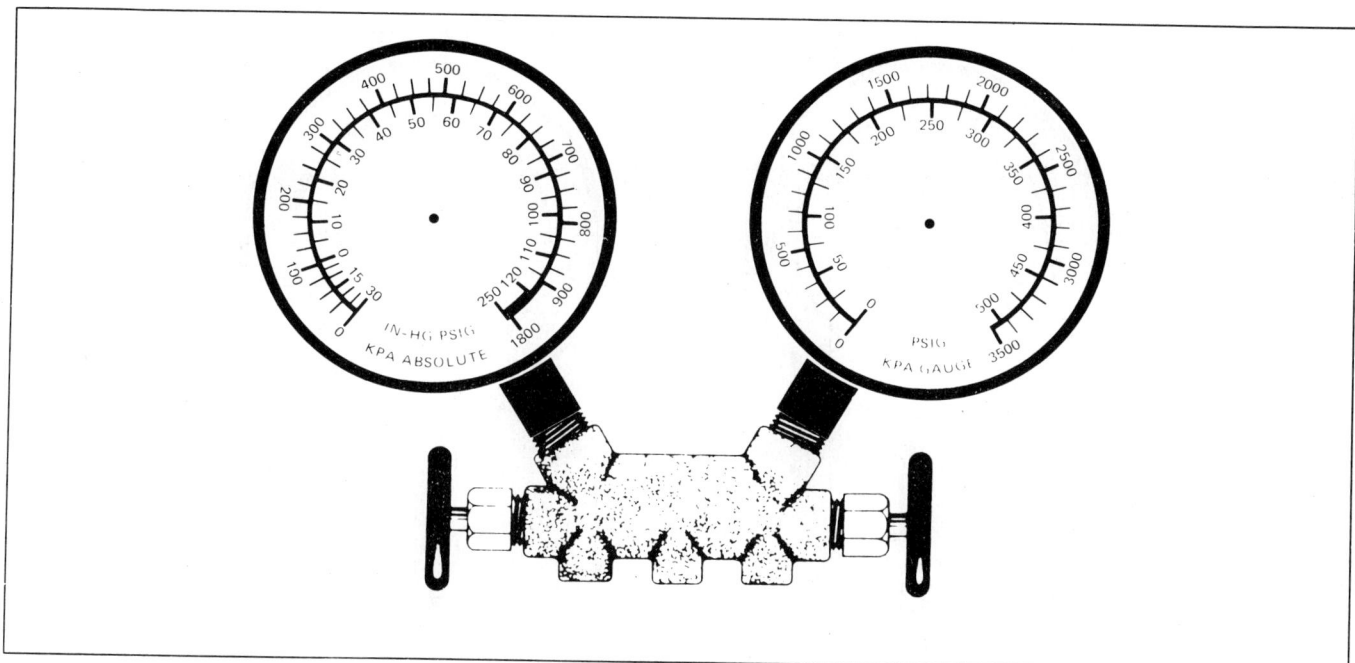

CONDITIONS

Low-side service valve located downstream of the accumulator
Ambient temperature: 95°F (35°C)
Low-side gauge: 5 psig (136 kPa absolute)
High-side gauge: 165 psig (1 138 kPa)

DIAGNOSIS

1. Show the high- and low-side gauge readings.
2. What should the normal high-side reading be? _____ psig
   _____ kPa
3. What is the evaporator temperature in this problem? Explain. _____ °F
   _____ °C
   _____
4. A low-side reading of 5 psig (136 kPa absolute) is (high, normal, low). _____
5. A high-side reading of 165 psig (1 138 kPa) is (high, normal, low). _____
6. This condition results in (good, poor, no) cooling. _____
7. A restriction in the _____ is indicated by these readings. _____
8. Frosting is likely to occur at the point of _____ . _____
9. How can this system be repaired? _____

SYSTEM DIAGNOSIS 6:

THERMOSTATIC EXPANSION VALVE—CYCLING CLUTCH TXV SYSTEM

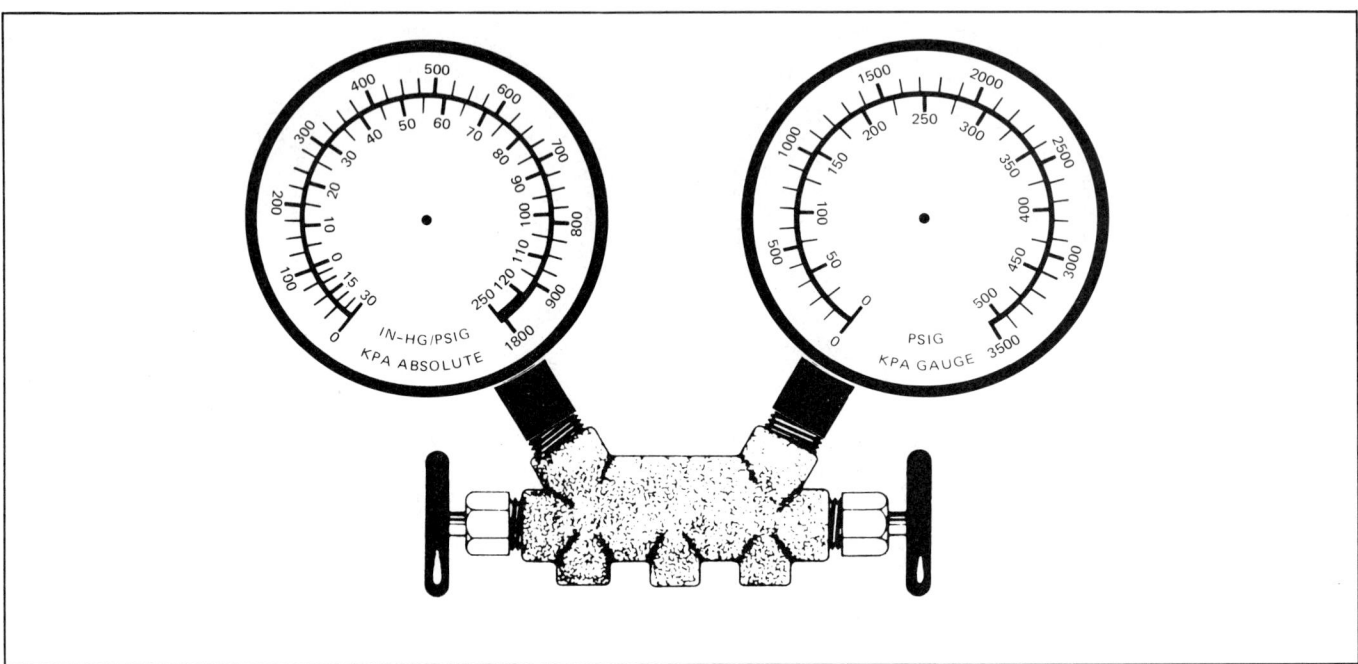

CONDITIONS
Ambient temperature: 95°F (35°C)
Low-side gauge: 2 psig (115 kPa absolute)
High-side gauge: 170 psi (1 172 kPa)

DIAGNOSIS

1. Show the high- and low-side manifold readings on the gauges in the diagram.
2. What should the normal high-side reading be? _____ psi
   _____ kPa
3. What is the evaporator temperature in this problem? Explain. _____ °F
   _____ °C
4. A low-side reading of 2 psig (115 kPa absolute) is (high, normal, low). _____
5. A high-side reading of 170 psi (1 172 kPa) is (high, normal, low). _____
6. This condition results in (good, poor, no) cooling from the evaporator. _____
7. This condition indicates a (starved, flooded) evaporator due to a defective _____. _____
8. This condition is usually accompanied by frosting at the valve _____. _____
9. How can this condition be corrected? _____

SYSTEM DIAGNOSIS 7:

THERMOSTATIC EXPANSION VALVE—CYCLING CLUTCH TXV SYSTEM

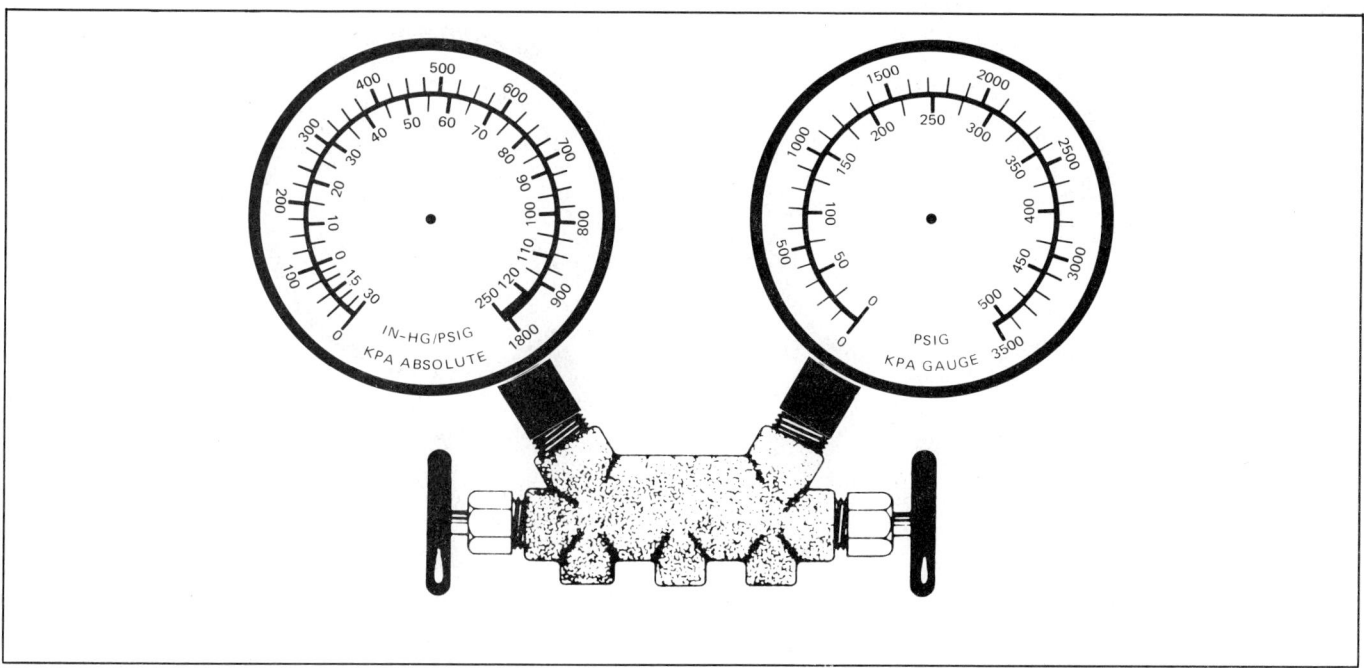

CONDITIONS
Ambient temperature: 95°F (35°C)
Low-side gauge: 55 psig (481 kPa absolute)
High-side gauge: 160 psi (1 103 kPa)

DIAGNOSIS
1. Show the high- and low-side manifold readings on the gauges in the diagram.
2. What should the normal high-side reading be? _____ psi
   _____ kPa
3. What is the evaporator temperature in this problem? _____ °F
   _____ °C
4. A low-side reading of 55 psig (481 kPa absolute) is (high, normal, low). _____
5. A high-side reading of 160 psi (1 103 kPa) is (high, normal, low). _____
6. This condition results in (good, poor, no) cooling from the evaporator. _____
7. This condition indicates a (starved, flooded) evaporator due to a malfunctioning _____. _____
8. List two possible causes for this malfunctioning. _____
9. Can moisture in the system cause this system malfunction? Explain. _____

SYSTEM DIAGNOSIS 8:

THE ORIFICE TUBE—CYCLING CLUTCH FOT SYSTEM

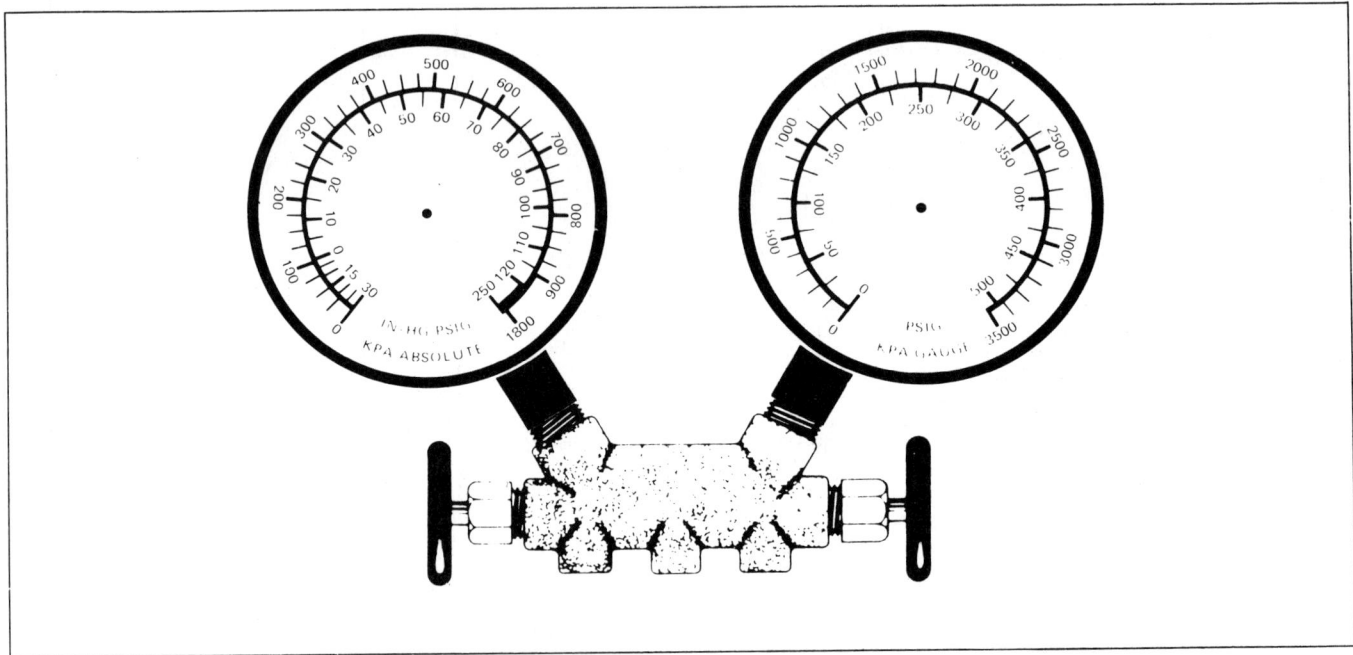

CONDITIONS
Ambient temperature: 95°F (35°C)
Low-side gauge: 3 psig (122 kPa absolute)
High-side gauge: 172 psig (1 186 kPa)

DIAGNOSIS

1. Show the high- and low-side gauge readings.
2. What should the normal high-side reading be? _____ psig
   _____ kPa
3. What is the evaporator temperature? _____ °F
   Explain. _____ °C
   _____
4. A low-side reading of 3 psig (122 kPa absolute) is (high, _____
   normal, low).
5. A high-side reading of 172 psi (1 186 kPa) is (high, _____
   normal, low).
6. This condition results in (good, poor, no) cooling. _____
7. This condition indicates a (starved, flooded) evaporator. _____
8. This condition indicates a clogged _____. _____
9. This condition is usually accompanied by frosting at
   the _____. _____
10. How can this condition be corrected? _____
    _____

68

SYSTEM DIAGNOSIS 9:

THE THERMOSTAT—CYCLING CLUTCH TXV OR FOT SYSTEM

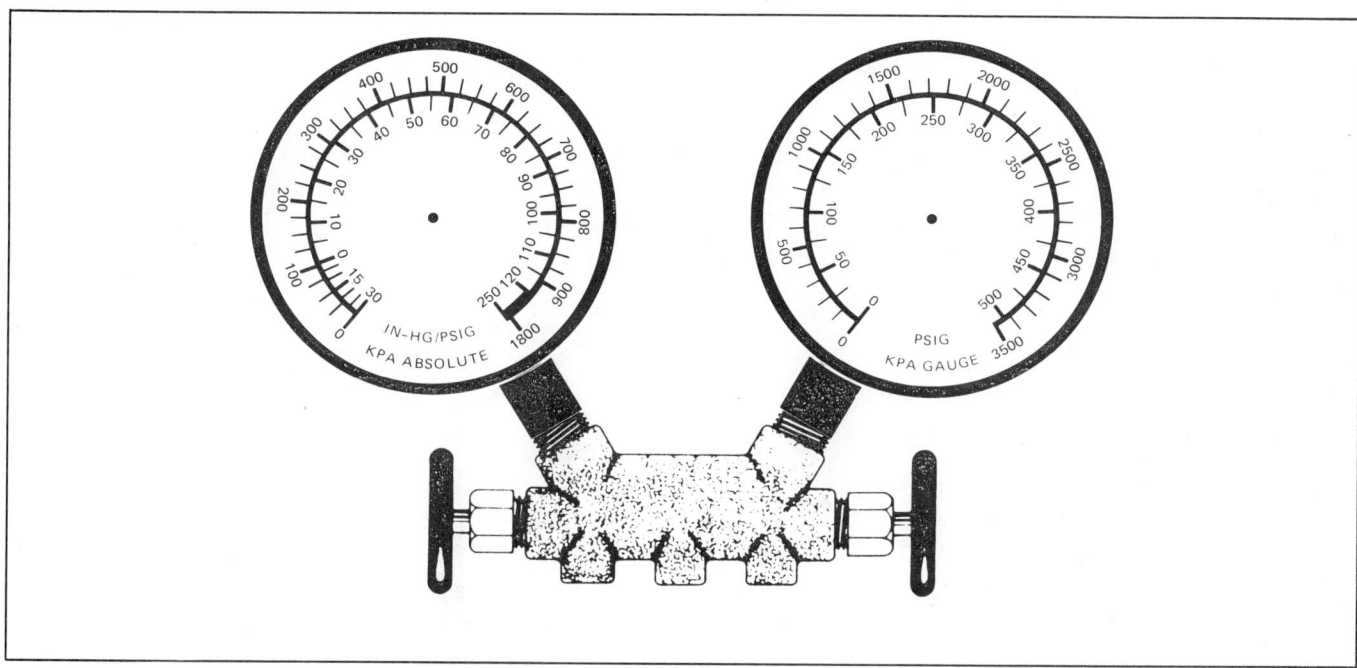

CONDITIONS
Ambient temperature: 97°F (36°C)
Low-side gauge: 10 psig (170 kPa absolute)
High-side gauge: 205 psi (1 413 kPa)

DIAGNOSIS

1. Show the high- and low-side gauge readings on the gauges in the diagram.
2. A high-side pressure of 205 psi (1 413 kPa) in this problem is (high, normal, low). _____
3. A low-side pressure of 10 psig (170 kPa absolute) in this problem is (high, normal, low). _____
4. What is the evaporator temperature in this problem? _____ °F
   _____ °C
5. This condition results in (good, poor, no) cooling from the evaporator. _____
6. This condition can be accompanied by frosting of the _____, which blocks off airflow and results in poor _____.
7. List two possible causes of a malfunctioning thermostat that can result in this problem.
   _____
   _____
8. How can the customer unintentionally cause this problem? _____
   _____
9. List two types of thermostats. _____
   _____
10. Are all thermostats adjustable? _____

SYSTEM DIAGNOSIS 10:

THE THERMOSTAT—CYCLING CLUTCH TXV OR FOT SYSTEM

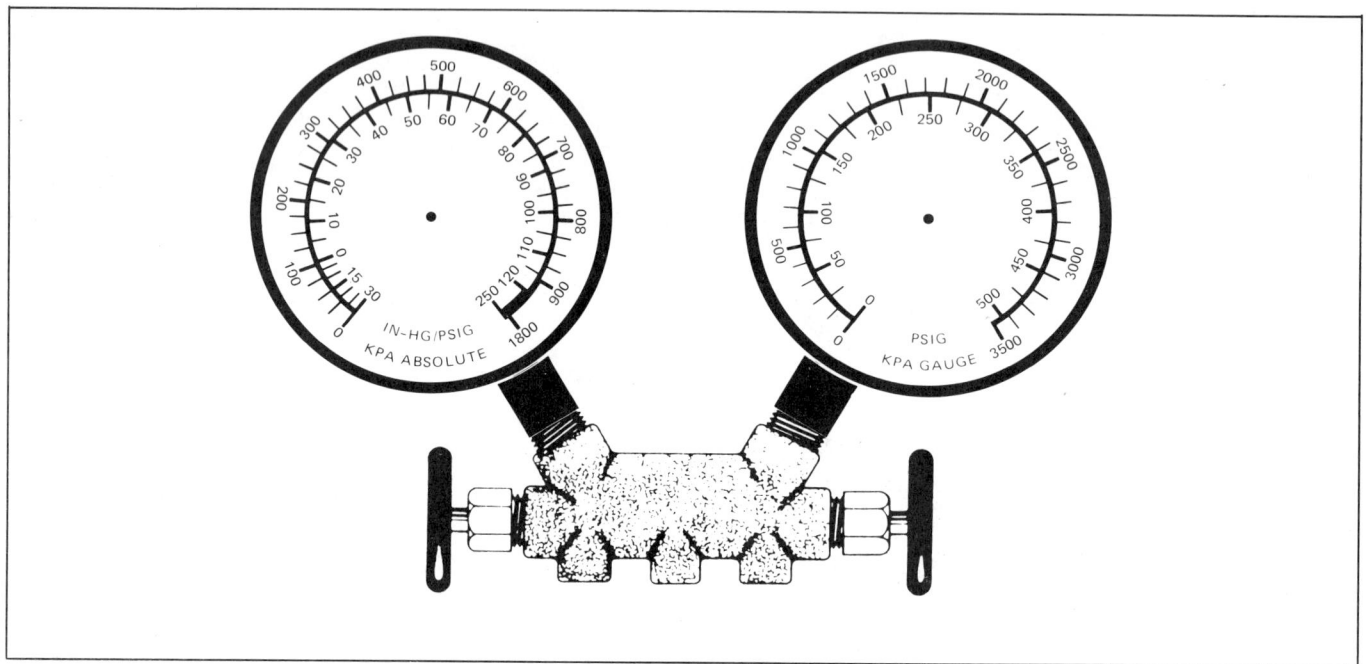

CONDITIONS

Ambient temperature: 98°F (36.7°C)
Low-side gauge: 60 psig (515 kPa absolute)
High-side gauge: 210 psi (1 448 kPa)

DIAGNOSIS

1. Show the high- and low-side gauge readings on the gauges in the diagram.
2. A high-side pressure of 210 psi (1 448 kPa) in this problem is (high, normal, low). _____
3. A low-side pressure of 60 psig (515 kPa absolute) in this problem is (high, normal, low). _____
4. What is the evaporator temperature? _____ °F
   _____ °C
5. This condition results in (good, poor, no) cooling from the evaporator. _____
6. Give two possible causes for this malfunction. _____
   _____
   _____
7. How can the customer unintentionally cause this problem? _____
   _____
   _____
8. Can all thermostats be adjusted? Explain. _____

SYSTEM DIAGNOSIS 11:

THE SYSTEM—CYCLING CLUTCH TXV OR FOT SYSTEM

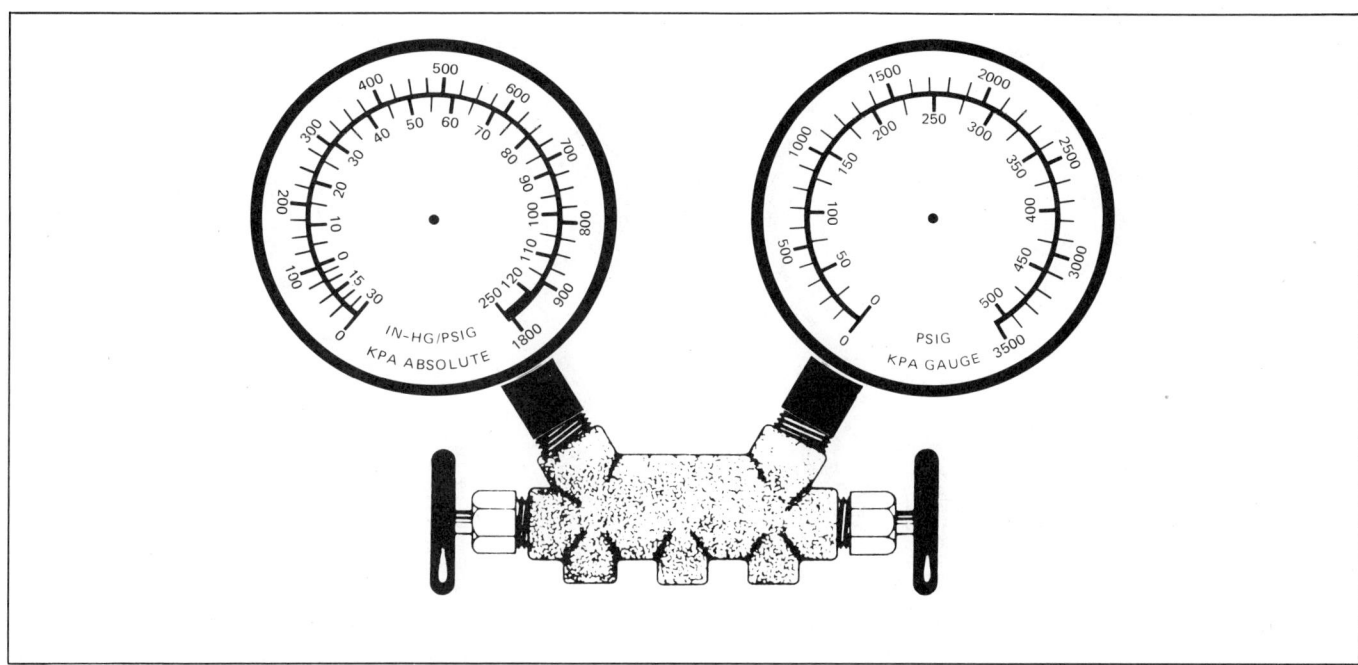

CONDITIONS

Ambient temperature: 90°F (32°C)
Low-side gauge: 80 psig (653 kPa absolute)
High-side gauge: 80 psi (552 kPa)

DIAGNOSIS

1. Show the high- and low-side gauge readings on the gauges in the diagram.

2. What should the normal high-side reading be? _____ psi
   _____ kPa

3. The high side is (high, normal, low). _____

4. The low side is (high, normal, low). _____

5. List three possible problems with this system.
   a. _____
   b. _____
   c. _____

SYSTEM DIAGNOSIS 12:

THE SYSTEM—CYCLING CLUTCH TXV OR FOT SYSTEM

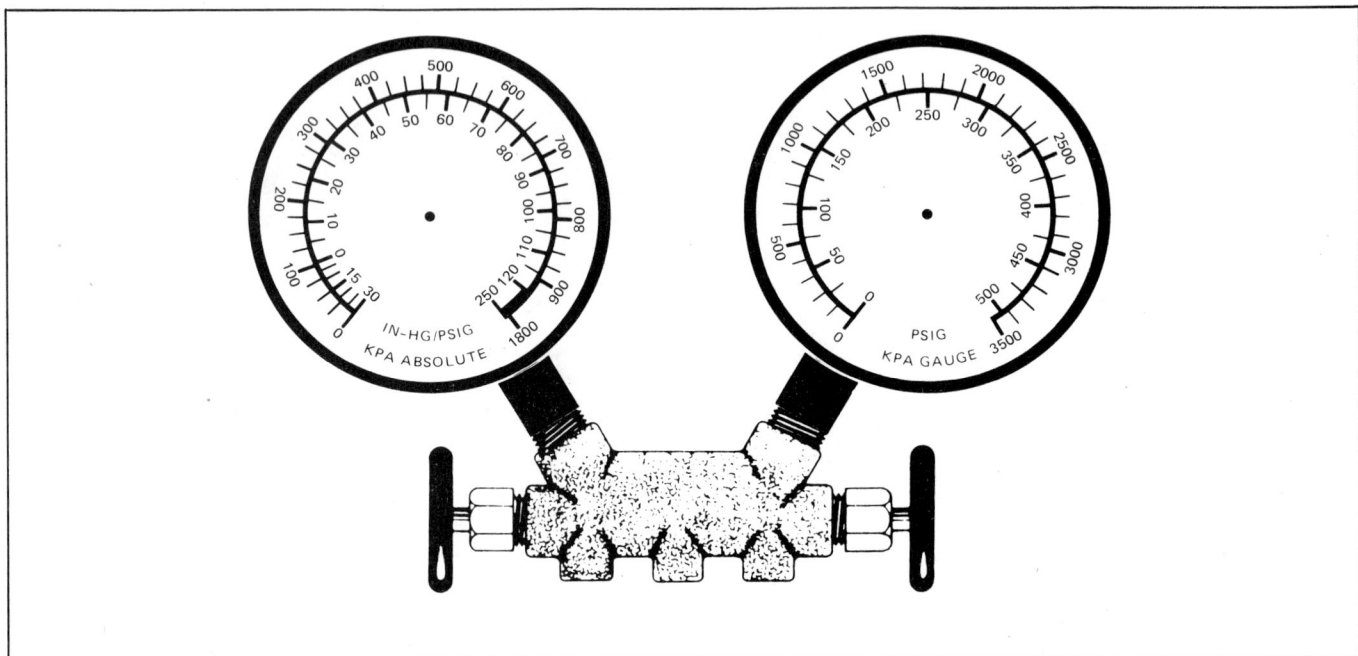

CONDITIONS

Ambient temperature: 80°F (27°C)
Low-side gauge: 20 psig (339 kPa absolute)
High-side gauge: 155 psi (1 069 kPa)

DIAGNOSIS

1. Show the high- and low-side gauge readings on the gauge set in the diagram.

2. The low-side gauge is (low, normal, high). _____

3. List four possible problems with this system.
   a. _____
   b. _____
   c. _____
   d. _____

SYSTEM DIAGNOSIS 13:

THE SYSTEM—CYCLING CLUTCH TXV OR FOT SYSTEM

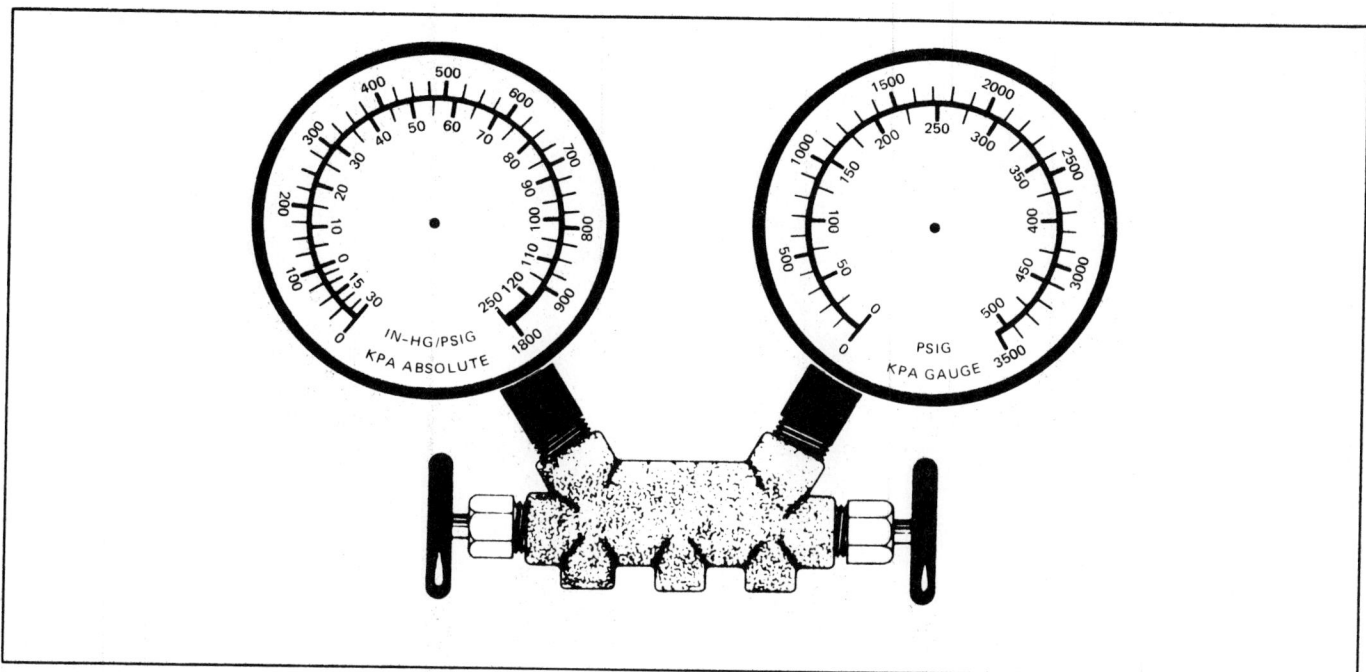

CONDITIONS

Ambient temperature: 83°F (28°C)
Low-side gauge: 37 psig (356 kPa absolute)
High-side gauge: 160 psi (1 103 kPa)

DIAGNOSIS

1. Show the gauge readings on the gauge set in the diagram.
2. What is the evaporator temperature in this problem? This temperature is (low, normal, high). _____ °F   _____ °C
3. List four possible causes for this malfunction.
   a. _____
   b. _____
   c. _____
   d. _____

SYSTEM DIAGNOSIS 14:

THE SYSTEM—CYCLING CLUTCH TXV OR FOT SYSTEM

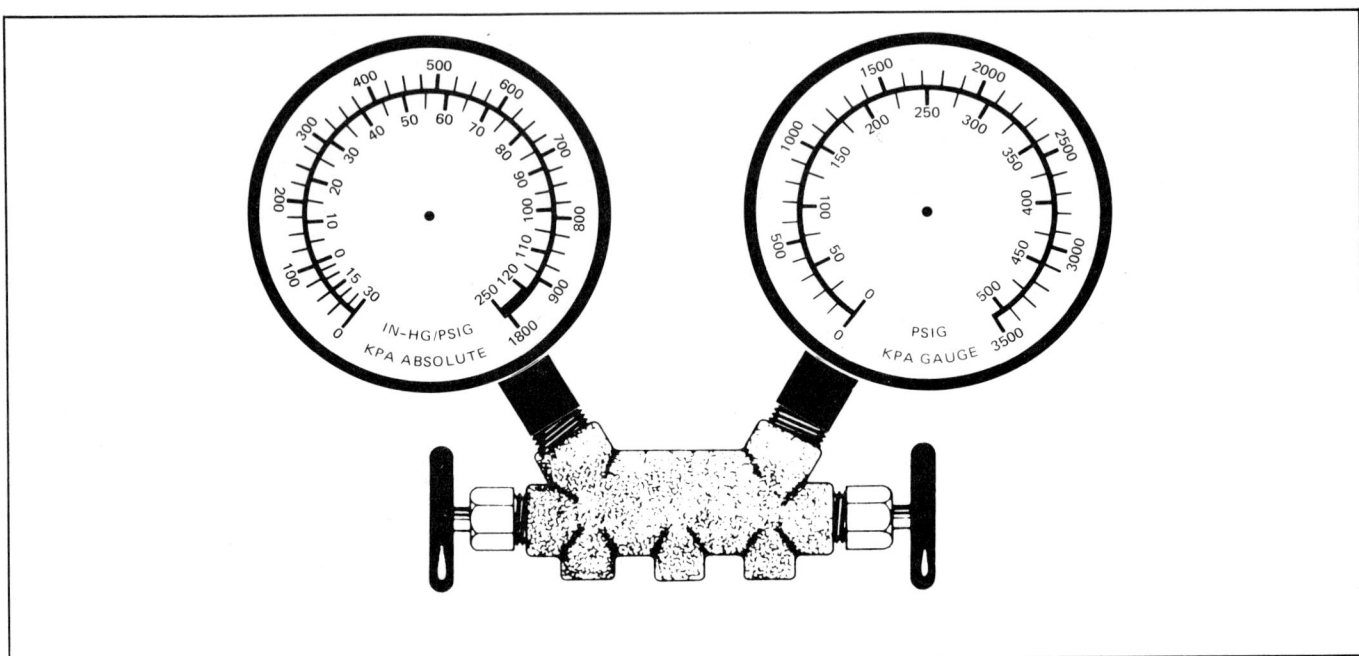

CONDITIONS

Ambient temperature: 90°F (32°C)
Low-side gauge: 50 psig (346 kPa absolute)
High-side gauge: 170 psi (1 172 kPa)

DIAGNOSIS

1. Show the gauge readings on the gauge set in the diagram.
2. The high-side pressure is (high, normal, low). _____
3. List four possible causes for this malfunction.
   a. _____
   b. _____
   c. _____
   d. _____

SYSTEM DIAGNOSIS 15:

THE SYSTEM—CYCLING CLUTCH TXV OR FOT SYSTEM

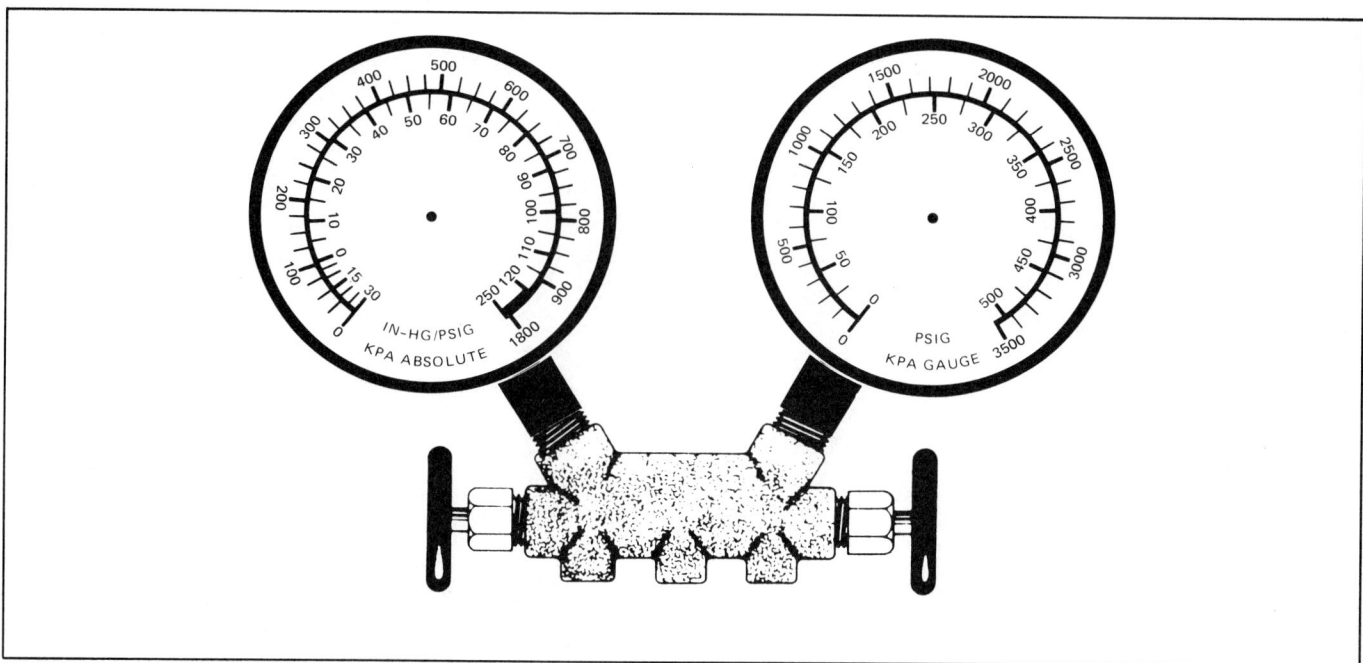

CONDITIONS

Ambient temperature: 95°F (35°C)
Low-side gauge: 37 psig (356 kPa absolute)
High-side gauge: 250 psi (1 724 kPa)

DIAGNOSIS

1. Show the gauge readings on the gauge set in the diagram.
2. The low-side gauge is (high, normal, low). _____
3. The high-side gauge is (high, normal, low). _____
4. List two possible causes for this malfunction.
   a. _____
   b. _____
5. An (undercharge, overcharge) of refrigerant can cause _____ this problem.

SYSTEM DIAGNOSIS 16:

THE SYSTEM—CYCLING CLUTCH TXV OR FOT SYSTEM

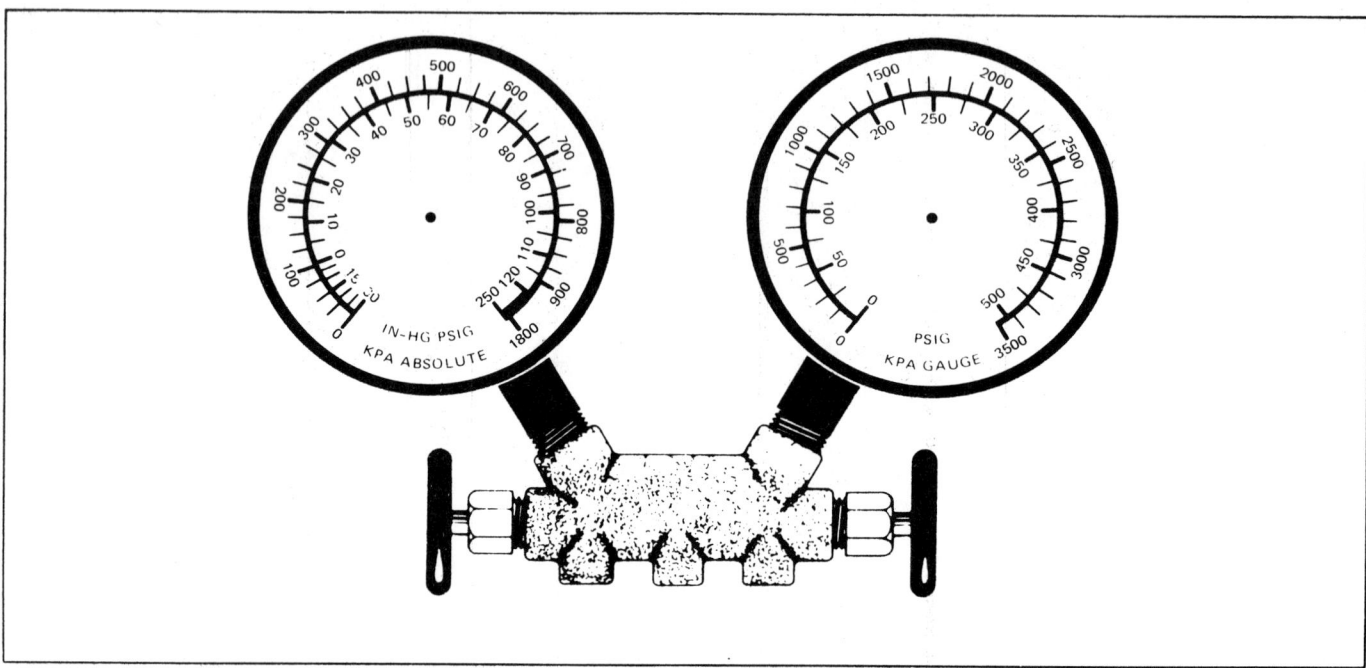

CONDITIONS

Ambient temperature: 96°F (36°C)
Low-side gauge: 39 psig (370 kPa absolute)
High-side gauge: 325 psi (2 241 kPa)

DIAGNOSIS

1. Show the gauge readings on the gauge set in the diagram.
2. List six possible causes of excessive head pressure.
    a. _____
    b. _____
    c. _____
    d. _____
    e. _____
    f. _____
3. High head pressure is (always, not always) accompanied _____
   by high suction pressure.

CHAPTER 7:

Servicing

Safety

It must be recognized that the skills and procedures of individuals performing the service work vary greatly. It is not possible to anticipate all conceivable ways or conditions under which service work may be performed. Therefore, it is impossible to provide precautions for every possible hazard that may result.

The following precautions are basic, and apply to any type of automotive service.

1. Wear safety glasses or goggles for eye protection when working under the hood of a car.
2. Set the parking brake. Place the gear selector in PARK if equipped with an automatic transmission, or in NEUTRAL if a manual transmission.
3. Unless required otherwise for the procedure, be sure that the ignition switch is in the OFF position.
4. Operate the engine, if required for the procedure, in a well-ventilated and lighted area.
5. Avoid loose clothing. Tie long hair securely behind the head. Remove rings, watches, and loose-hanging jewelry.
6. Keep clear of all moving parts when the engine is running.
7. Keep hands, clothing, tools, and test leads away from the cooling fan. Electric cooling fans may start without warning even when the ignition switch is in the OFF position.
8. Avoid contact with hot parts such as the radiator, exhaust manifold, and high-side refrigerant lines.
9. If in doubt, ASK; do not take chances.

SAFETY CAUTION: The technician must exercise extreme caution and pay heed to every established safety practice when performing these or any automotive air-conditioning service procedures.

Manifold and Gauge Set

A basic tool for the air-conditioning service technician is the manifold and gauge set. Since system pressures accurately indicate total system performance, a means must be provided to make these measurements on any air-conditioning unit. The

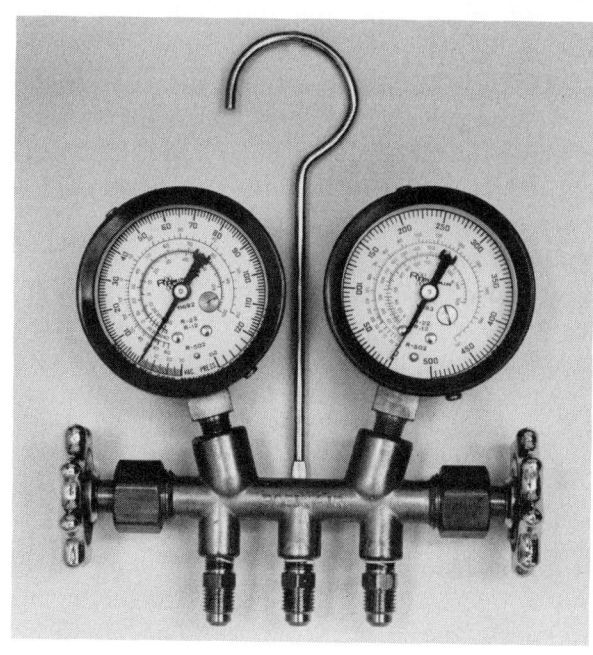

Fig. 7-1 Manifold and gauge set, side wheel.

Fig. 7-2 Manifold and three-gauge set, front wheel.

manifold and gauge set is essential in making these measurements. The servicing of most automotive air conditioners requires the use of a two-gauge manifold set, figure 7-1. Some systems, however, require a three-gauge set, figure 7-2.

For a two-gauge set, one gauge is used on the low (suction) side of the system. The other gauge is used on the high (discharge) side of the system. Systems requiring the use of a third gauge have a second low-side fitting which requires a low-pressure gauge.

MANIFOLD

The gauges are connected into the air-conditioning system through a manifold and high-pressure hoses. The manifold contains provisions for fittings to which gauges and hoses can be connected. In addition, two hand wheels are provided on the manifold for controlling the flow of refrigerant through the manifold.

The low-side hose fitting is directly below the low-side gauge and the high-side hose fitting is below the high-side gauge. The center hose fitting of the manifold is used for charging, evacuation, or any other service that is required.

Both the low and high sides of the manifold are provided with hand shutoff valves. When the hand valve is turned all the way to the right, in a clockwise (cw) direction, the manifold is closed. However, the gauge indicates the system pressure in the hose. Figure 7-3 shows both manifold hand valves in the closed position. For this condition, pressures can still be recorded on each gauge.

The hand valve is opened by turning it to the left or counterclockwise (ccw). When the hand valve is open, the system is opened to the center hose port of the manifold set. This condition is desirable only when refrigerant must be allowed to enter or leave the system.

If the low-side manifold hand valve is opened, figure 7-4, the passage is complete between the low-side port and the center port only. The low-side gauge indicates only the low-side pressure. The high side remains closed and the high-side gauge indicates only the high-side pressure.

Similarly, when only the high-side hand valve is opened, figure 7-5, the passage is complete between the high-side port and the center port. Again, the low-side and high-side gauges indicate only the pressure in their respective sides.

If both hand valves are opened, figure 7-6, both the low-side and high-side ports are open to the center port. However, the pressures indicated on the gauges are not accurate when both hand valves are opened. Some of the high-side pressure feeds through the manifold to the low-side gauge, with the result that the high-side pressure indication is decreased and the low-side pressure indication is increased.

The manifold is used to perform nearly all of the air-conditioning system tests and diagnostic procedures. Manifolds are available in a front valve type, a side valve type, and an offset valve type.

LOW-SIDE GAUGE (ENGLISH)

The English scaled gauge used on the low side of the system is called a *compound gauge*. It is designed to give both vacuum and pressure indications. This gauge is connected through the manifold and the high-pressure hose to the low side of the air-conditioning system.

The vacuum scale of a compound gauge generally is calibrated to show pressures from thirty

Manifold and Gauge Set

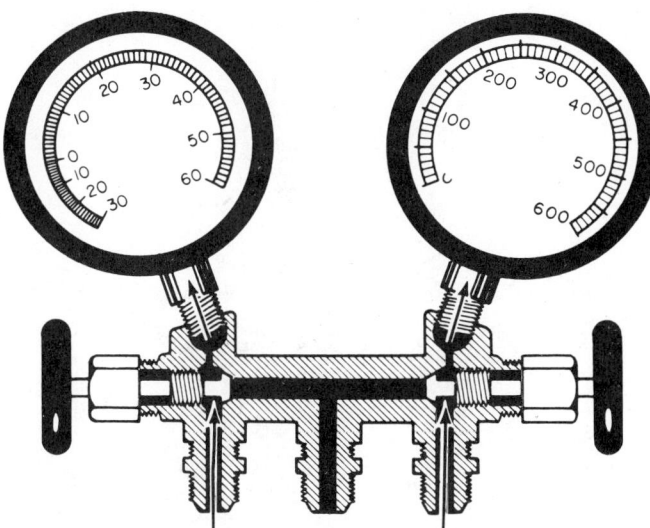

Fig. 7-3

inches of mercury (30 inHg) to zero inches of mercury (0 inHg). The pressure scale is calibrated to indicate pressures from zero pounds per square inch gauge (0 psig) to one hundred twenty pounds per square inch gauge (120 psig). The compound gauge is constructed so as to prevent any damage to the gauge if the pressure should reach a value as high as 250 psig. The gauge described in this paragraph is designated in the following manner:

30"-0-120 psi, with retard to 250 psi.

Pressures above 80 psig are rarely experienced in the low side of the system. However, such pressures may result if the manifold hoses are crossed so that the manifold gauges are connected backwards to the air-conditioning system. (Even experienced service technicians can make this type of error.)

HIGH-SIDE GAUGE (ENGLISH)

The high-side gauge indicates the pressure in the high side of the system. Pressures in this area under normal conditions seldom exceed 250 psig. However, as a safety factor, it is recommended that the minimum scale indication of the gauge be 300 psig. A popular scale for the high-side gauge is 0-500 psig.

The high-side gauge is not calibrated as a compound gauge. Therefore, it cannot be damaged whenever the system is pulled into a vacuum.

GAUGE CALIBRATION AND SCALES

Many gauges are provided with calibration adjustment screws. A good gauge is reasonably accu-

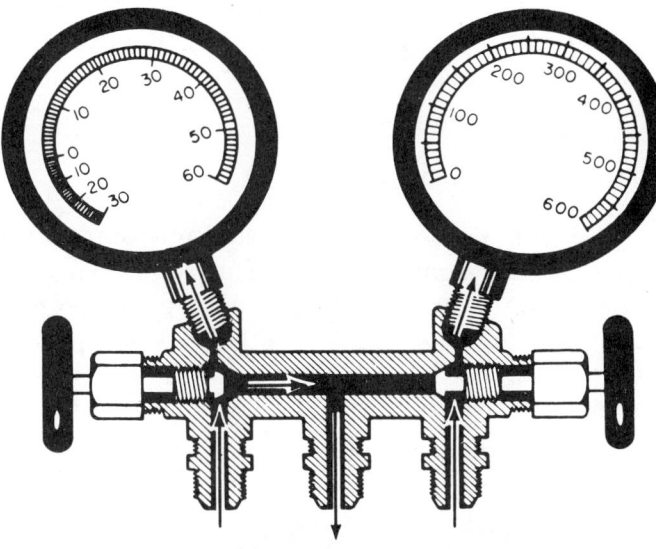

Fig. 7-4

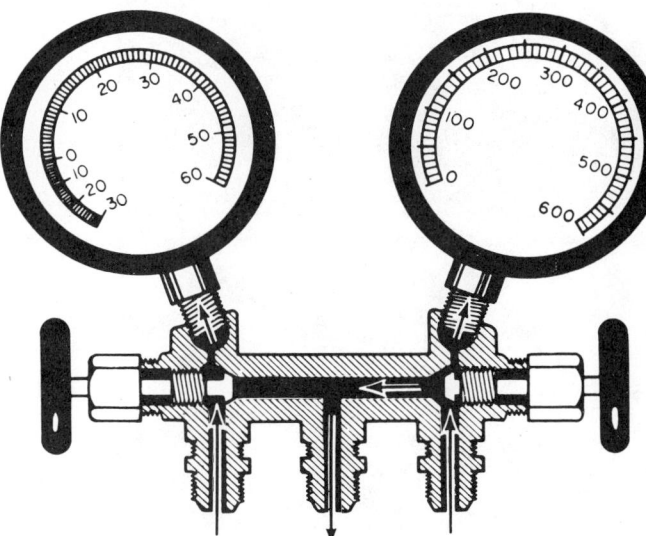

Fig. 7-5

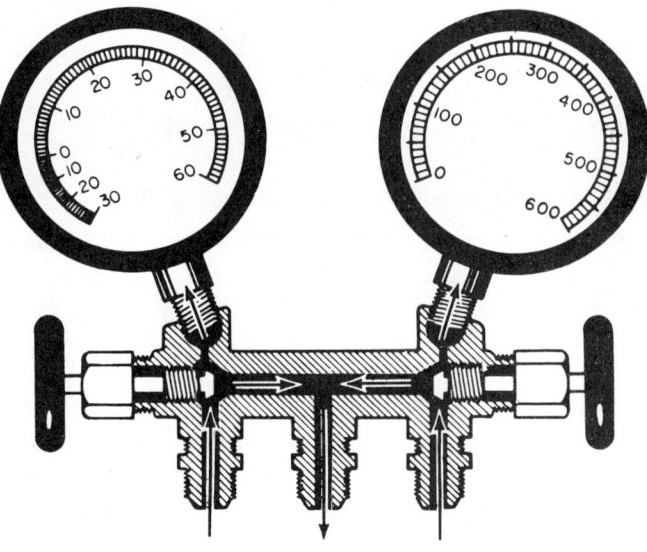

Fig. 7-6

rate to about two percent of the total scale reading when it is calibrated so that the needle rests on zero when there is no applied pressure.

To calibrate a gauge, it is necessary to remove the glass or plastic cover and the retaining ring (bezel). A small screwdriver can then be used to turn the adjusting screw in either direction until the pointer is lined up with the zero mark, figure 7-7. The adjusting screw must not be forced—to do so can damage the gauge.

Many gauges have inner scales which indicate the temperature-pressure relationship of three popular types of refrigerant: R-12, R-22, and R-502. Refrigerants R-22 and R-502 are not used in automotive air conditioners primarily because of their higher operating pressures. R-22 is used in packaged and split air-conditioning and heat pump systems. R-502 is used in lower-temperature applications, such as commercial ice makers.

HOSES

A charging hose is constructed to withstand working pressures in excess of 500 psi (344 8 kPa). Charging hoses may have a burst-pressure rating of up to 2 000 psi (13 790 kPa).

Hoses are available in several colors: white, yellow, red, and blue. Thus, a standard color code can be used when connecting the hoses. Blue is used on the low side, red is used on the high side, and white or yellow is used for the center port. The

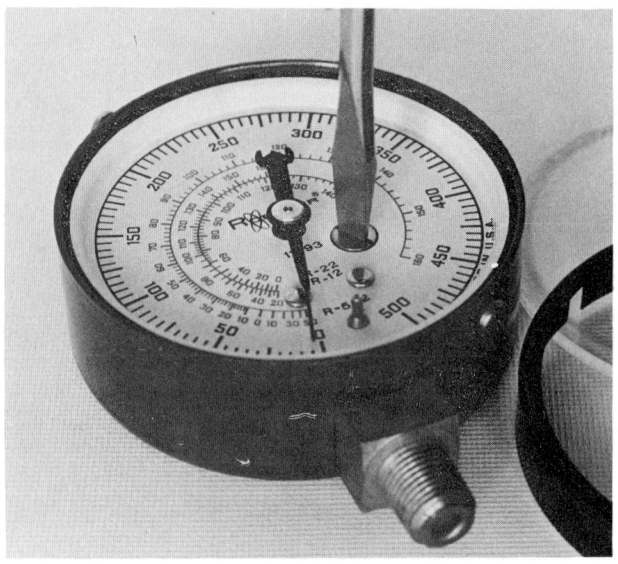

Fig. 7-7 Screwdriver used to recalibrate gauge to zero.

color-coded hoses lessen the chance of accidentally reversing the manifold connections to the air-conditioning system.

THE THIRD GAUGE

Some air conditioners require a third gauge for testing system pressures. This additional gauge is used on systems having some type of pressure control for the evaporator. The two low-side gauges are used to determine the pressure drop across the control device. Figure 7-8 shows the use of a three-gauge manifold.

Fig. 7-8 Three-gauge manifold set used to check system pressures.

Leak Detectors

The methods of detecting leaks in an air-conditioning system range from using a soap solution to the use of an expensive self-contained electronic instrument.

The most popular detection instrument is the halide gas torch. Its popularity is due to its initial low cost, ease of handling, and simplicity of construction and operation.

HALIDE LEAK DETECTOR

The halide leak detector, figure 7-9, can detect a leak as slight as one pound (0.453 6 kg) in ten years. However, a great deal of practice and experience are required to be able to recognize such a slight leak.

Air is drawn through the search hose into the burner and the area of the copper reactor plate. When the gas and air mixture is ignited, the flow of gas is regulated until the flame burns about one-quarter inch (6.35 mm) above the opening in the reactor plate. This plate is heated by the flame to a red-hot temperature.

When the search hose comes into contact with leaking refrigerant, the refrigerant is drawn into the search tube and is brought to the reactor plate. As a result, the flame turns violet. In some cases, if the leak is severe enough, the flame is extinguished.

SAFETY CAUTION: A halide leak detector must be used in well-ventilated spaces only. It must never be used in a place where explosives, such as gases, dust, or vapors, are present. The vapors or fumes from the halide leak detector must not be inhaled; they may be poisonous.

LEAK DETECTION USING A SOAP SOLUTION

A soap solution may be a more efficient method of locating small leaks. Since leaks often occur in areas of limited access, a halide or electronic leak detector cannot be used to locate such leaks.

To perform the soap solution leak test, mix one-half cup of soap powder with water to form a thick solution which is just light enough to make

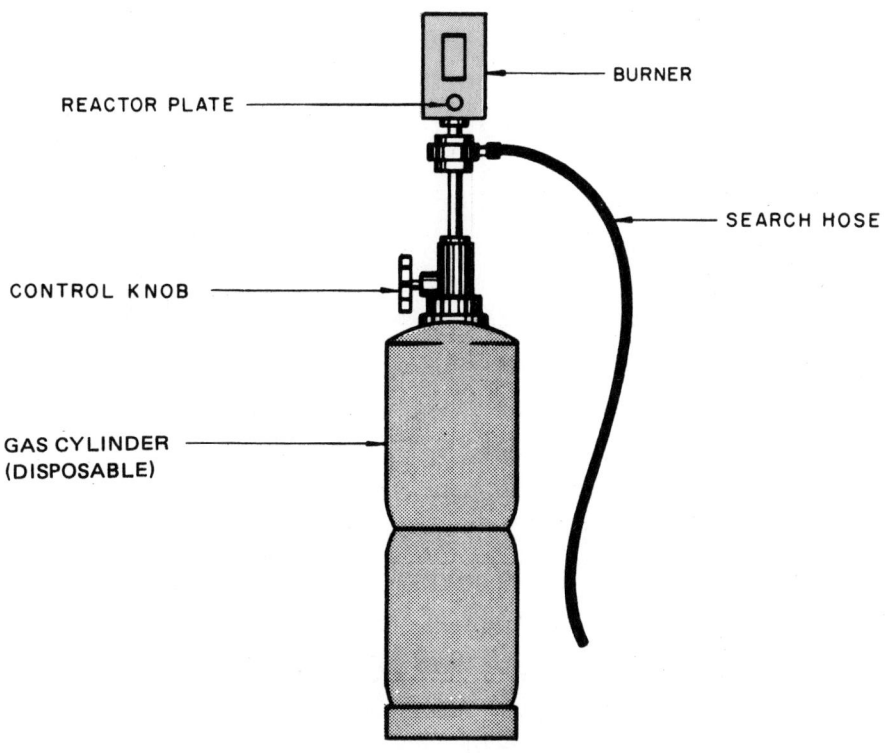

Fig. 7-9 Halide leak detector.

Fig. 7-10 Using soap solution as leak detector. Leak is revealed by bubbles.

suds with a small paintbrush. When this solution is applied to the area of a suspected leak, soap bubbles reveal the leak, figure 7-10.

In many instances, the leak in an air-conditioning system can be either a cold leak or a pressure leak. A cold leak occurs only when the unit is not at its operating temperature, such as in a car that is parked overnight. A pressure leak occurs at periods of high pressure within the system, such as when the automobile is slowly moving in heavy traffic on a very warm day.

LEAK DETECTION USING DYE

To locate either a cold leak or a pressure leak, it may be desirable to introduce a dye solution into the system. This dye is available in either yellow or red forms. The dye is safe for air-conditioning system use and does not affect the operation of the system.

When a leak cannot be detected in the shop, a dye solution is then added. After the automobile is driven a few days, the leak can be detected by the dye trace.

Once a dye is introduced into the system, it will remain there unless the complete system is cleaned out, the oil changed, and the drier replaced.

ELECTRONIC LEAK DETECTORS

Electronic leak detectors are the most sensitive of all leak detection devices. The initial purchase price of an electronic leak detector is higher than that of a halide leak detector. In addition, this more sophisticated device requires more frequent maintenance than the halide leak detector.

Electronic leak detectors are also known as halogen leak detectors. Such a device can detect a Refrigerant 12 rate of loss as slow as one-half ounce (14.1 g) per year. This value corresponds to one hundred parts of refrigerant to one million parts of air (100 ppm).

Fig. 7-11 Computerized electronic portable leak detector.

An example of a portable halogen leak detector is the model 5500 TIF manufactured by Thermal Industries, figure 7-11. This instrument is powered by two ordinary "C" cell flashlight batteries. This instrument is capable of calibrating itself automatically while in use.

Service Valves

The service technician almost always must enter the air-conditioning system to perform diagnostic, testing, and service procedures. This is necessary to record the pressures within the system as an aid in determining a problem, if any.

Most air-conditioning systems have two service valves: one on the low side of the system and one on the high side of the system. Some General Motors, Chrysler, and Ford systems have three valves. The third valve is on the low side of the system.

Basically, there are two types of service valve: the Schrader (automatic) valve, and the hand shutoff (manual) valve. Though different in appearance and operation, they both serve the same purpose.

SCHRADER VALVE

The Schrader-type valve is, by far, the most popular service valve today. The Schrader-type service valve is very similar to a tire valve in appearance and operation. This valve, figure 7-12, has only two positions: *cracked* (open) and *back seated* (closed). The normal operating position of this valve is back seated. This valve is cracked or opened by a pin or a bar in the end of the manifold hose or in a special hose adapter. Whenever the hose or adapter is screwed onto the Schrader valve, system pressures are impressed on corresponding gauges.

Several types of adapters are shown in figure 7-13. Another fitting, often found in the high side of the system, is the quick connect/disconnect type, figure 7-14. This fitting also requires a special adapter to connect the high-side hose into the system.

The different size or type of fitting on the high-pressure side of the system helps to prevent reversing the hoses of the manifold and gauge set.

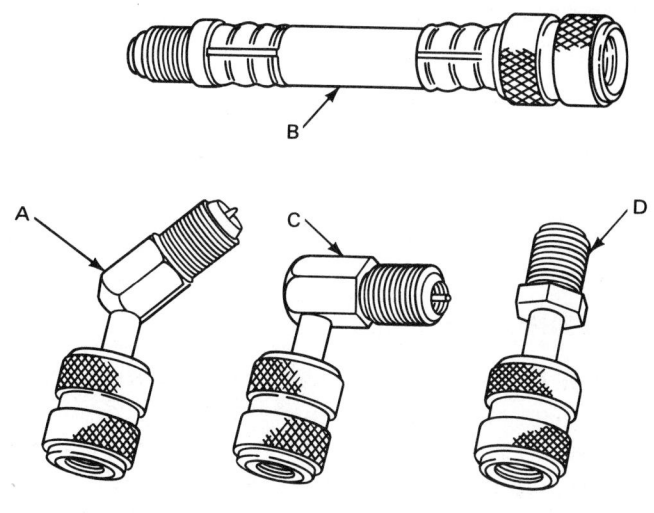

A – 45° adapter
B – flexible adapter
C – 90° adapter
D – straight adapter

Fig. 7-13 Adapters used to connect high-side gauge hose into the system.

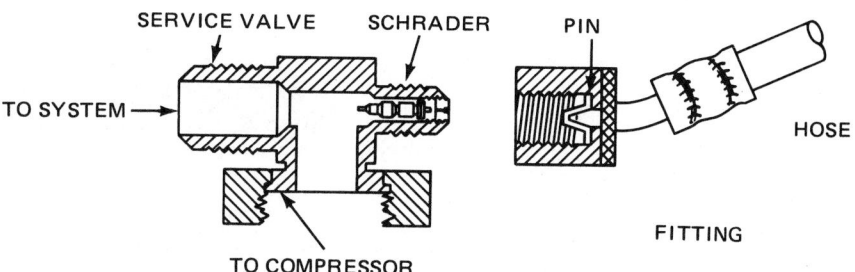

Fig. 7-12 Pin in fitting of service hose cracks (opens) the Schrader valve when hose is attached to service valve.

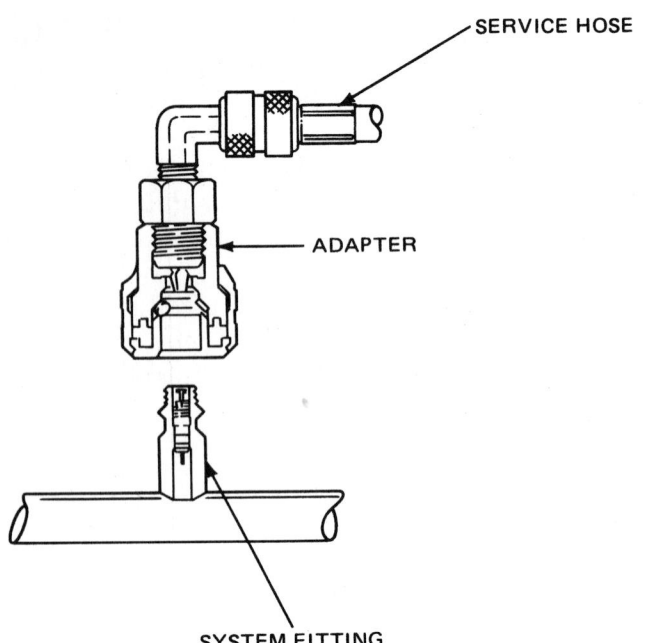

Fig. 7-14 Quick connect/disconnect fitting and adapter.

valve shows that the gauge port connects to the compressor only. If the compressor is operated with the service valve in the front-seated position, and the gauge port is capped, the compressor will surely be damaged. This is because there is no area into which to pump the compressed refrigerant.

Normal Refrigerant Operation — Gauge Port Out of the System

As shown in figure 7-15B, a service valve in this position is said to be back seated. In this case, the compressor and hose outlet are connected and refrigerant is free to flow if the compressor is started. The gauge port is closed off and pressure readings cannot be taken when the service valve is back seated. All service valves should be in this position when the system is operating normally.

HAND SHUTOFF VALVE

The hand shutoff service valve is often referred to as a manual valve. Although it is not as common as in past years, it is still found on some systems. The hand shutoff valve has a 1/4-inch (square end) stem that is used for opening and closing the valve. For these operations, some technicians use pliers or vise grips, but it is recommended that a service-valve wrench be used to position this type of valve.

The service valve is back seated when the stem is turned fully counterclockwise (ccw). It is cracked when the stem is turned one or two turns clockwise (cw) off the back-seated position. The valve is front seated when the stem is turned fully clockwise (cw).

The hand shutoff valve is a three-position device that can be used for the three functions shown in figure 7-15.

No Refrigerant Flow — Gauge Port Out of the System

In the position shown in figure 7-15A, the service valve is said to be front seated. For this case, the refrigerant is trapped in the hose end of the service valve. The gauge port fitting is toward the atmosphere. Tracing the path through the

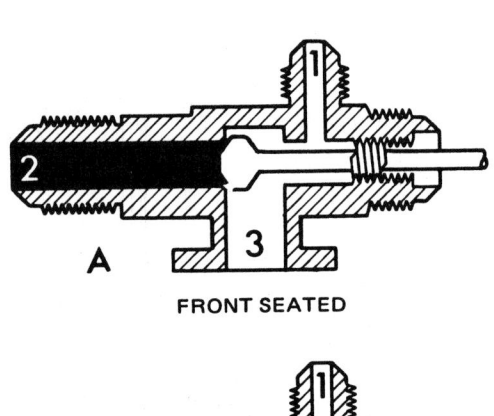
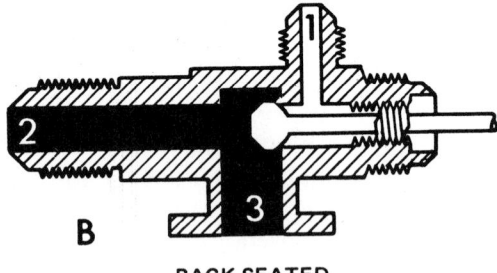

Fig. 7-15 Service valves, hand shutoff type.

Normal Refrigerant Operation — Gauge Port in the System

When the service valve is in the position shown in figure 7-15C, it is said to be in the cracked or midposition. In this case, the system can be operated while pressures are recorded through the gauge port openings.

Actually, in the cracked position the service valve is not really midpositioned. The service valve is cracked when the valve stem is turned from one-half to one full turn clockwise (cw) off the back-seated position.

MOISTURE REMOVAL

Many problems can arise due to excessive moisture in a refrigeration system. After any repair work, the system must be pumped down (evacuated) to remove any moisure present in the system. This section shows how a refrigeration system is pumped down and explains how a vacuum is used to remove moisture. Recall that a pressure below zero pounds gauge pressure (0 psig or 0 kPa gauge) is referred to in terms of inches of mercury (inHg) English or kilopascals absolute (kPa absolute) metric.

The removal of moisture from a system can cause serious problems for the service technician who is not equipped with the proper tools. A vacuum pump is a must for air-conditioning service. Although other methods can be used, the vacuum pump is still the most efficient means of moisture removal.

Moisture is removed in the air-conditioning system by creating a vacuum. In a vacuum, the moisture in the system boils. The pumping action of the vacuum pump then pulls the moisture in the form of a vapor from the system. When the pressure is increased on the discharge side of the pump, the vapor again liquefies. This process usually occurs inside the pump.

At higher altitudes, the atmospheric pressure has a lower value than at sea level. A vacuum pump can simulate conditions at a higher altitude by mechanical means. A good vacuum pump is capable of evacuating a system to a pressure of 29.76 inHg (0.81 kPa absolute) or better. At this pressure, water boils at 40°F (4.44°C). In other words, if the ambient temperature is 40°F (4.44°C) or higher, the water boils out of the system.

At 0 inHg (101.3 kPa absolute) at sea level, water boils at 212°F (100°C). To find the boiling point of water in a vacuum (absolute pressure), use the table in figure 7-16. Note that the boiling point

System Vacuum Inches Mercury	Temperature °F Boiling Point
24.04	140
25.39	130
26.45	120
27.32	110
27.99	100
28.50	90
28.89	80
29.18	70
29.40	60
29.66	50
29.71	40
29.76	30
29.82	20
29.86	10
29.87	5
29.88	0
29.90	-10
29.91	-20

Fig. 7-16 Boiling point of water in a vacuum (English).

of water is lowered only 112°F (62.2°C) to 100°F (37.7°C) as the pressure is decreased from 0 inHg (101.3 kPa absolute) at sea level to 28 inHg (0.98 kPa absolute). However, the boiling point drops by 120°F (66.6°C) as the pressure decreases from 28 inHg (0.98 kPa absolute) to 29.91 inHg (0.30 kPa absolute).

The degree of vacuum achieved and the amount of time the system is subjected to a vacuum determine the amount of moisture removed from the system.

Moisture (water) boils at a lower temperature at higher altitudes. However, it must be pointed out that vacuum pump efficiency is reduced at higher altitudes.

For example, the altitude of Denver, Colorado is 5,280 feet (1,609 m) above sea level. Water boils at 206.2°F (96.78°C) at this altitude, but the maximum efficiency of a vacuum pump is reduced. A vacuum pump that can pump 29.92 inHg (0.27 kPa absolute) at sea level can only pump 25.44 inHg (15.44 kPa absolute) at this altitude.

The English formula for determining vacuum pump efficiency at a given atmospheric pressure is:

$$\frac{\text{Atmospheric Pressure in Your Location}}{\text{Atmospheric Pressure at Sea Level}} \times \text{Pump Rated Efficiency} = \text{Actual Efficiency}$$

Assume that a vacuum pump has a rated efficiency of 29.92 inHg at sea level (0.27 kPa absolute) and that the atmospheric pressure at Denver is 12.5 psia (86.18 kPa absolute). To determine the actual efficiency at this location, the formula is:

$$\frac{12.5}{14.7} \times 29.92 = 25.44 \text{ inHg}$$

Another method of moisture removal is the *sweep* or *triple evacuation* method. Although this method cannot remove all of the moisture, it should be sufficient to reduce the moisture to a safe level if the system is otherwise sound and a new drier is installed.

TRIPLE EVACUATION METHOD

The basic steps in the triple evacuation method are given here.

Procedure

1. Connect a manifold and gauge set to the system. Insure that all hoses and connections are tight and secure.
2. Pump a vacuum to the highest efficiency for 15-20 minutes.
3. Break the vacuum by adding Refrigerant 12. Increase the pressure to 1-2 psig, (6.8-13.7 kPa).
4. Pump a vacuum to the highest efficiency for 15-20 minutes (second time).
5. Break the vacuum by adding Refrigerant 12. Increase the pressure to 1-2 psig (6.8-13.7 kPa).
6. Pump a vacuum to the highest efficiency for 25-30 minutes (third time).
7. The system is now ready for charging.

SERVICE PROCEDURE 1:

CONNECTING THE MANIFOLD AND GAUGE SET INTO THE SYSTEM

This procedure can be used when it becomes necessary to install the manifold and gauge set on the air-conditioning system to perform any one of the many operational tests. This Service Procedure is given in two parts. Part I is used when installing a manifold and gauge set into a system equipped with three-way (hand shutoff) compressor service valves. Part II is used when installing a manifold and gauge set into a system equipped with Schrader-type service valves.

> *SAFETY WARNING:* Safety glasses should be worn while working with a refrigerant. Remember, liquid refrigerant splashed in the eyes can cause blindness.

PROCEDURE, PART I

Prepare the System

1. Place a fender cover on the car to avoid damage to the finish of the car.
2. Use a wrench of the correct size to remove the protective caps from the service valve stems. Some caps are made of light metal and can be removed by hand.
3. Using the correct wrench, remove the protective acorn caps from the service ports.

> *SAFETY WARNING:* Remove the caps slowly to insure that no refrigerant leaks past the service valve.

Connect the Manifold Gauge Service Hoses to the Compressor

1. Connect the low-side manifold hose to the suction side of the compressor.
2. Connect the high-side manifold hose to the discharge side of the compressor. Both of the connections (1 and 2) are to be fingertight.
3. Make sure the hand shutoff valves are closed on the manifold set before the next step.

Purge the Service Hoses

1. Use a service valve wrench and rotate the suction-side service valve stem two or three turns clockwise.
2. Repeat the procedure in step 1 with the discharge service valve stem.
3. Purge the air from the low-side hose by cracking the low-side hand valve for a few seconds; then close the valve.
4. Repeat the procedure in step 3 with the high-side hand valve to purge the air from the high-side hose.

PROCEDURE, PART II

Prepare the System

1. Place a fender cover on the car to avoid damage to the finish of the car.
2. Using a wrench of the correct size to avoid damage, remove the protective acorn caps from the high- and low-side service ports.

SAFETY WARNING: Remove the caps slowly to insure that no refrigerant is leaking past a defective Schrader valve.

Connect the Manifold Gauge Service Hoses

1. Service hoses must be equipped with a Schrader valve depressing pin. If the hoses are not so equipped, a suitable adapter must be used.
2. Make sure that the manifold hand shutoff valves are closed before the next step.
3. Connect the low-side manifold hose to the suction side of the system fingertight.
4. Connect the high-side manifold hose to the discharge side of the system fingertight.

   NOTE: A special adapter must be connected to the manifold hose (before it is connected to the system) if the high-side fitting is 3/16 inch.

Purge the Service Hoses

1. Purge the air from the low-side hose by cracking the low-side service valve on the manifold for a few seconds; then close the valve.
2. Repeat step 1 with the high-side manifold valve to purge the air from the high-side hose.

SERVICE PROCEDURE 2:

LEAK TESTING THE SYSTEM

Three popular methods of leak detection are soap bubbles, halide gas, and halogen electronic testing. This procedure is given in three parts: Part I for soap bubble testing, Part II for halide gas testing, and Part III for halogen electronic testing.

The soap solution method of leak detection is often required when it is impossible or impractical to pinpoint the exact location of a leak using halide or halogen leak detectors. A commercially available solution, such as that shown in figure 7-17, is more effective than a household solution.

The halide leak detector is essentially a propane torch. This device, figure 7-18, is the most popular form of leak detector for the service technician because of its low initial cost and low upkeep.

SAFETY WARNING: A halide leak detector must only be used in a well-ventilated area. It must never be used in spaces where explosive gases are present. When refrigerant comes into contact with an open flame, toxic gases are formed. Never inhale the vapors or fumes from the halide leak detector—they can be poisonous.

The halogen electronic leak detector is the most sensitive of all types of leak detectors, figure 7-19. Some of these electronic detectors can sense a refrigerant leak as small as one-half ounce per year. The initial cost and upkeep are the controlling economic factors to be considered in purchasing electronic leak detectors.

SAFETY WARNING: A halogen electronic leak detector must be used in a well-ventilated area only. It must never be used in spaces where explosive gases are present.

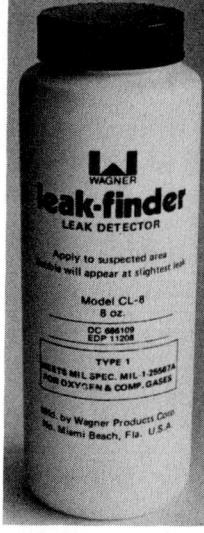

Fig. 7-17 Typical liquid leak detector.

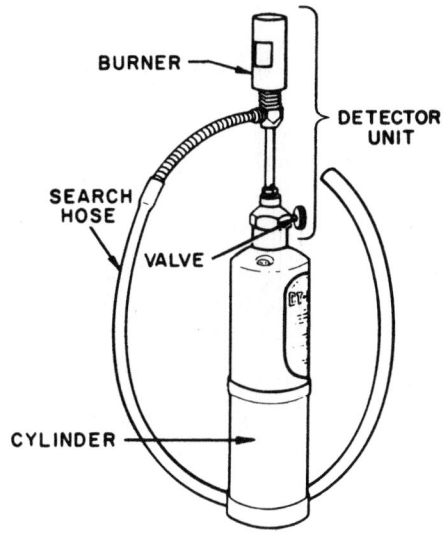

Fig. 7-18 Leak detector (torch).

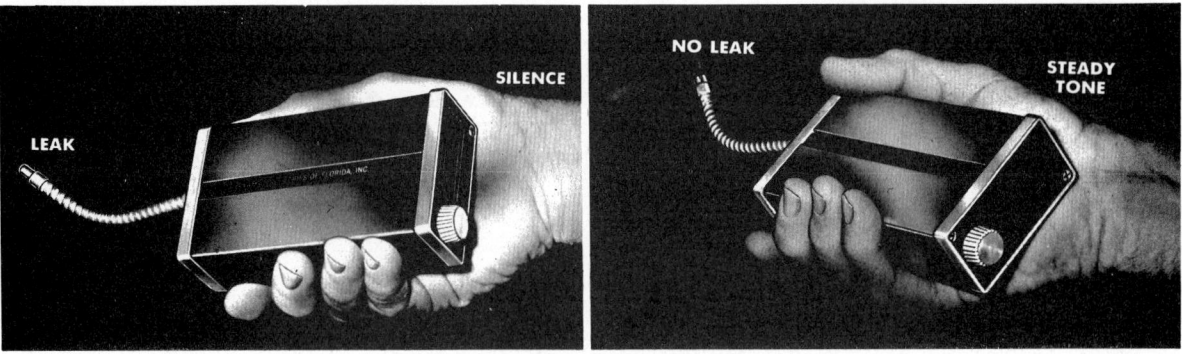

Fig. 7-19 Leak detector (electronic).

PREPARE THE SYSTEM (ALL METHODS)

1. Connect the manifold and gauge set to the system.
2. Place the high- and low-side compressor service valves in the cracked position.
3. Place the high- and low-side manifold hand valves in the closed position.
4. Determine the presence of refrigerant in the system. A minimum value of 50 psig (348 kPa) is needed for leak detection.
5. If there is an insufficient charge of refrigerant in the system, continue with the next step, *Add Refrigerant for Leak Test Pressure (all methods)*. If the charge is sufficient, omit the next step and go to PROCEDURE, PART I, II, or III.

ADD REFRIGERANT FOR LEAK TEST PRESSURE (ALL METHODS)

1. Open the high- and low-side hand valves to purge the hoses of air. Then close the valves.
2. Attach the center manifold hose to the refrigerant container.
3. Open the refrigerant container service valve.
4. Open the high-side manifold hand valve until a pressure of 50 psig (348 kPa) is reached on the low-side gauge. Then close the high-side hand valve.
5. Close the refrigerant container service valve and remove the hose.

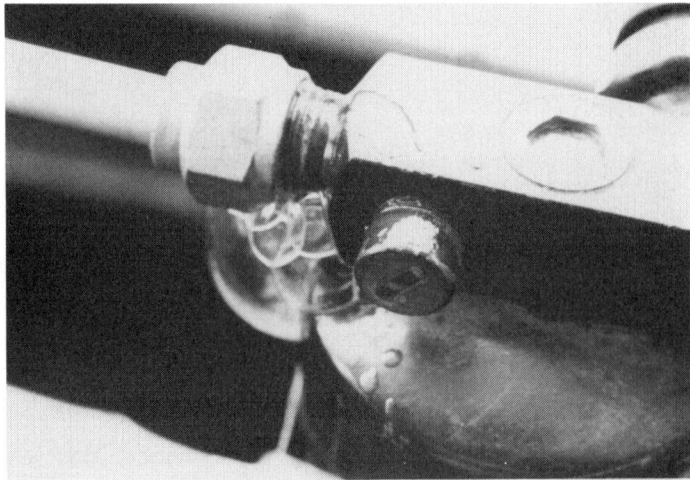

Fig. 7-20 Bubbles reveal point of leak when using soap solution.

PROCEDURE, PART I
SOAP SOLUTION METHOD

Prepare the Leak Detector

1. Apply solution to all joints and/or suspected areas by:
   a. using dauber supplied with commercial solution.
   b. using small brush with household solution.

2. Leaks are exposed when a bubble forms, as shown in figure 7-20.

3. Repair leak as outlined in "Repair System (All Methods)."

PROCEDURE, PART II
HALIDE GAS METHOD

Prepare the Leak Detector

1. Open the valve and light the gas. Adjust for a low flame; that is, one which burns about 1/2 inch above the reactor plate.

2. Allow the flame to burn until the copper reactor plate becomes cherry red in color.

3. Lower the flame until it is about 1/4 inch above or just even with the reactor plate.

Check for Leaks in the Air-conditioning System

1. Move the search hose under all of the joints and connections in the system. Check all seals and control devices.

2. Disconnect any vacuum hoses connected to the system. Check the vacuum hose ports for refrigerant vapors.

3. Repair leak as outlined in "Repair Service (All Methods)."

PROCEDURE, PART III
HALOGEN ELECTRONIC METHOD

Prepare the Leak Detector

NOTE: Follow the procedure as outlined in the manufacturer's instructions provided with the leak detector. Although the procedures may vary considerably for different leak detectors, the following steps can be used as a guide.

1. Turn the controls and the sensitivity knobs to off or zero.

2. Plug the leak detector into an approved voltage source and turn the switch on. Allow a warmup period of about five minutes (unless battery powered).

3. After the warmup period, place the probe at the reference leak and adjust the controls and sensitivity knob until the detector reacts. Remove the probe — the reaction should stop. If the reaction continues, the sensitivity adjustment is too high. If the reaction stops, the adjustment is adequate.

Check the System for Leaks

1. Move the search hose under all of the joints and connections. Check all seals and control devices.

2. Disconnect any vacuum hoses connected to the system. Check the vacuum hose ports for refrigerant vapor (indicating a control leak).
3. When a leak is located, the detector reacts as it does when placed by the reference leak.

REPAIR SYSTEM (ALL METHODS)

1. After the leak is located, purge the system of refrigerant.
2. Repair the leak as indicated. Check the compressor oil.
3. Add oil and refrigerant. Recheck for leaks.
4. If no leaks are found, purge the system, evacuate, and charge the system.
5. Perform other service procedures as necessary.

SERVICE PROCEDURE 3:

EVACUATING THE SYSTEM

The air-conditioning system must be evacuated whenever the system is serviced to the extent that it is purged of refrigerant. Evacuation rids the system of air and moisture that was allowed to enter the unit. The table in figure 7-21 illustrates the effectiveness of moisture removal for a given vacuum.

System Vacuum, inHg	Temperature, °F
27.99	100
28.89	80
29.40	60
29.71	40
29.82	20
29.88	0

Fig. 7-21 Boiling point of water in a vacuum (English).

PROCEDURE

Prepare the System

1. Connect the manifold and gauge set to the system.
2. Place the high- and low-side compressor service valves in the cracked position.
3. Place the high- and low-side manifold hand valves in the closed position.
4. Connect the center manifold hose to the inlet of the vacuum pump.

Evacuate the System

1. Start the vacuum pump.
2. Open the low-side manifold hand valve and observe the compound gauge needle. The needle should be pulled down to indicate a slight vacuum.
3. After about five minutes, the compound gauge should indicate below 20 inHg (33.8 kPa absolute) and the high-side gauge needle should be slightly below the zero index of the gauge.
4. Operate the pump for 15 minutes and observe the gauges. The system should be at a vacuum of 24–26 inHg (20.3-13.5 kPa absolute) minimum if there is no leak.
5. If the system is not down to 24-26 inHg (20.3-13.5 kPa absolute), close the low-side hand valve and observe the compound gauge. If the compound gauge needle rises, indicating a loss of vacuum, there is a leak which must be repaired before the evacuation is continued. Leak check the system as outlined.
6. If no leak is evident, continue with the pumpdown.

Complete the Evacuation

1. Pump for a minimum of 30 minutes, longer if time permits.
2. After pumpdown, close the high- and low-side manifold hand valves. (The high-side valve can be opened after the system is checked for blockage.)
3. Shut off the vacuum pump, disconnect the manifold hose, and replace its protective caps.

SERVICE PROCEDURE 4:

ADDING DYE OR TRACE SOLUTION TO THE AIR-CONDITIONING SYSTEM

A dye or trace solution can be introduced into an air-conditioning system to aid in pinpointing a small leak. The dye shows the exact location of a leak by depositing a colored film around the leak. Depending on the dye used, the film may be orange-red or yellow. Once the dye is introduced into the air-conditioning system, it remains until the system is cleaned. The trace solution or dye is formulated for use in air-conditioning systems and does not affect system operation in any way.

NOTE: Some refrigerant manufacturers produce refrigerants which include a red dye solution, figure 7-22. This product is introduced into the system following the standard charging procedures. This procedure is for adding dye solution which is not previously mixed with refrigerant, figure 7-23.

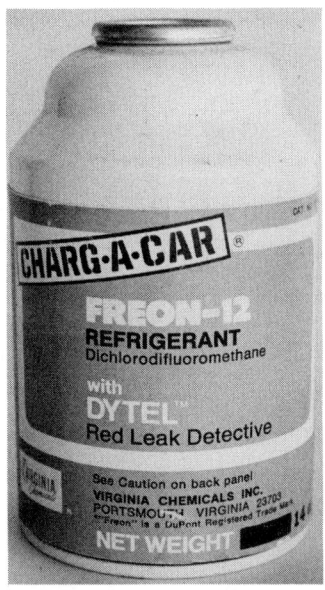

Fig. 7-22 Typical "pound" can of Refrigerant 12 with a red dye additive. "Freon" and "Dytel" are trademarks of E.I. DuPont.

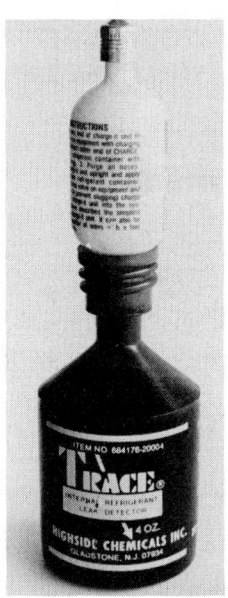

Fig. 7-23 Typical dye solution which is compatible with Refrigerant 12.

PROCEDURE

Prepare the System

1. Connect the manifold and gauge set to the system. If the system is charged with refrigerant, purge it from the system.
2. Construct a charging line using a six-inch (152-mm) piece of copper tubing and two flare nuts.
3. Remove the center hose from the manifold and connect the copper tubing (from step 2) to the center manifold connection.
4. Connect the dye solution to the copper tubing. Reconnect the center manifold hose to the dye solution.
5. Secure the other end of the center manifold hose (charging line) to a source of Refrigerant 12.

Add Dye to the System

1. Start the engine and operate it at idle speeds. Set the controls for maximum cooling.
2. Open the low-side manifold hand valve slowly and allow the trace dye to enter the system.
3. Charge the system to at least half capacity. Allow to operate for 15 minutes.
4. Shut off the air conditioner and the car engine.

Observe the System

1. Observe the hoses and fittings for signs of the dye solution. If no signs of a leak are evident, arrange to have the car available the following day for diagnosis and repair.
2. If one or more leaks is detected, make repairs as required. The dye solution can remain in the system without causing harm to the system.

Return the System to Normal Operation

1. Remove the manifold and gauge set.
2. Replace the protective caps.

SERVICE PROCEDURE 5:

PURGING THE AIR-CONDITIONING SYSTEM

To *purge* an air-conditioning system is to remove all of the refrigerant, moisture, and air from the system. This is usually necessary when a system component is to be serviced or replaced. This procedure outlines the steps to purge the refrigerant to the atmosphere, a common practice in most automotive shops. The Environmental Protection Agency (EPA) in recent years has criticized this practice, claiming that damaging contamination of the ionosophere is partly due to refrigerant "dumping." Some larger repair shops have installed refrigerant recovery systems which enable them to dry, clean, and reuse refrigerants purged from systems.

SAFETY WARNING: Adequate ventilation must be maintained during this operation. Do not discharge Refrigerant 12 near an open flame—toxic gas is formed.

PROCEDURE

Prepare the System

1. Connect the manifold and gauge set into the system, figure 7-24. Set all controls to the maximum cold position.
2. Set the engine speed to 1 000-1 200 r/min and operate for 10-15 minutes.
3. This procedure should be followed whenever possible to stabilize the system. However, certain system malfunctions may make this procedure impossible.

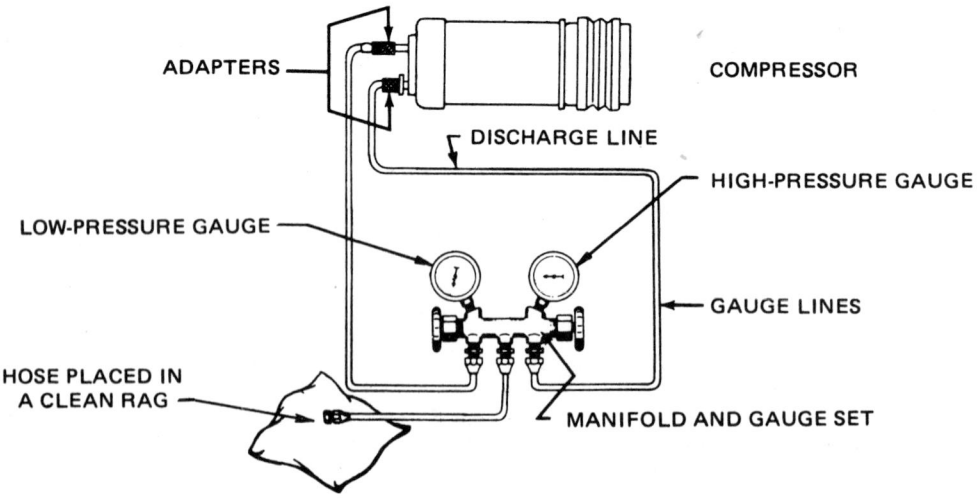

Fig. 7-24 Manifold hookup to purge system.

Purge Refrigerant from the System

1. Return the engine speed to normal to prevent dieseling. Shut off the engine.
2. Open the low- and high-side manifold valves slowly to allow refrigerant to bleed off through the center hose.
3. Open the hand valves only enough to bleed off the refrigerant. Rapid purging draws excessive oil from the system.
4. The center hose can be placed on a clean rag. If any refrigeration oil is pulled out of the system, it shows on the rag.

    NOTE: If it is apparent that a measurable amount of oil is being drawn from the system, place the center hose into a graduated container. The amount of oil drawn from the system must be replaced with clean, fresh oil.

System Purged of Refrigerant

1. Both manifold gauges read zero when the system is purged.
2. Close the hand manifold valves when the refrigerant ceases to bleed off.
3. The system is now purged of refrigerant and can be opened for service as required.
4. Cap all openings and hoses to avoid the possibility of dirt or foreign matter entering the system.

SERVICE PROCEDURE 6:

CHARGING THE SYSTEM

Two methods of charging an automotive air-conditioning system are given in this procedure: using pound cans with the system off (Part I), and using pound cans with the system operating (Part II).

Containers of refrigerant are commonly called *pound cans,* but actually hold 14 ounces (396.9 g) of refrigerant. Pound cans are popular and are used in many shops, including those with a large volume of business and those operating on a smaller scale.

SAFETY WARNING: Above 130°F (54.4°C), liquid refrigerant completely fills a container and hydrostatic pressure builds up rapidly with each degree of temperature added.

- *Never heat a refrigerant container above 125°F (51.7°C). (It should never be necessary to heat a refrigerant container at all.)*
- *Never apply a direct flame to a refrigerant container or place an electric heater close to the container.*
- *Do not abuse a refrigerant container.*
- *Use only approved wrenches to open and close the valves.*
- *Store the container in an upright position.*
- *Do not handle refrigerant without suitable eye protection and do not discharge refrigerant into an enclosed area having an open flame.*

With the refrigerant can or tank inverted, vapor rises to the top of the container and liquid refrigerant is forced into the charging hoses. Do not invert the refrigerant container with low-side pressures in excess of 40 psig (377 kPa absolute). Regulating the valve on the container or the manifold hand valve insures a pressure of 40 psig (377 kPa absolute) or below. Liquid refrigerant entering the compressor low side can cause serious damage to internal parts such as pistons, reed valves, head, and head gaskets.

If the ambient temperature is lower than 80°F (26.7°C), do not invert the refrigerant container. The car engine and air-conditioning system should be at operating temperature.

PREPARE THE SYSTEM (BOTH METHODS)

1. With both manifold hand valves in the closed position, connect the manifold and gauge set into the system, figure 7-25 or 7-26.
2. Place the high- and low-side compressor service valves in the cracked position, if the unit is so equipped.
3. Place the system under a vacuum after an adequate pumpdown.

INSTALL THE CAN TAP VALVE ON THE CONTAINER OF REFRIGERANT (BOTH METHODS)

1. The valve stem should be in the out, or counterclockwise, position.
2. Attach the valve to the can. Secure the locking nut, if the valve is so equipped.

3. Connect the center manifold hose to the can tap port.
4. Pierce the can by closing the can tap shutoff valve. Turn the valve stem all the way in the clockwise direction.

PURGE THE LINE OF AIR (BOTH METHODS)

1. Once the can is pierced, back the can tap valve out as far as possible (turn in a counterclockwise direction).
2. The center hose is now charged with refrigerant. *Do not crack* the high- or low-side hand valves.
3. Loosen the center hose connection at the manifold set until a hiss can be heard. Allow gases to escape for a few seconds, then retighten the connection.
4. The system is now purged and under a vacuum.

CHECK THE SYSTEM FOR BLOCKAGE (BOTH METHODS)

1. Open the high-side gauge manifold hand valve. Observe the low-side gauge pressure. Close the high-side hand valve.
2. If the low-side gauge does not move from the vacuum range into the pressure range, system blockage is indicated.
3. Correct the blockage, if indicated. Then evacuate and continue with the next operation.

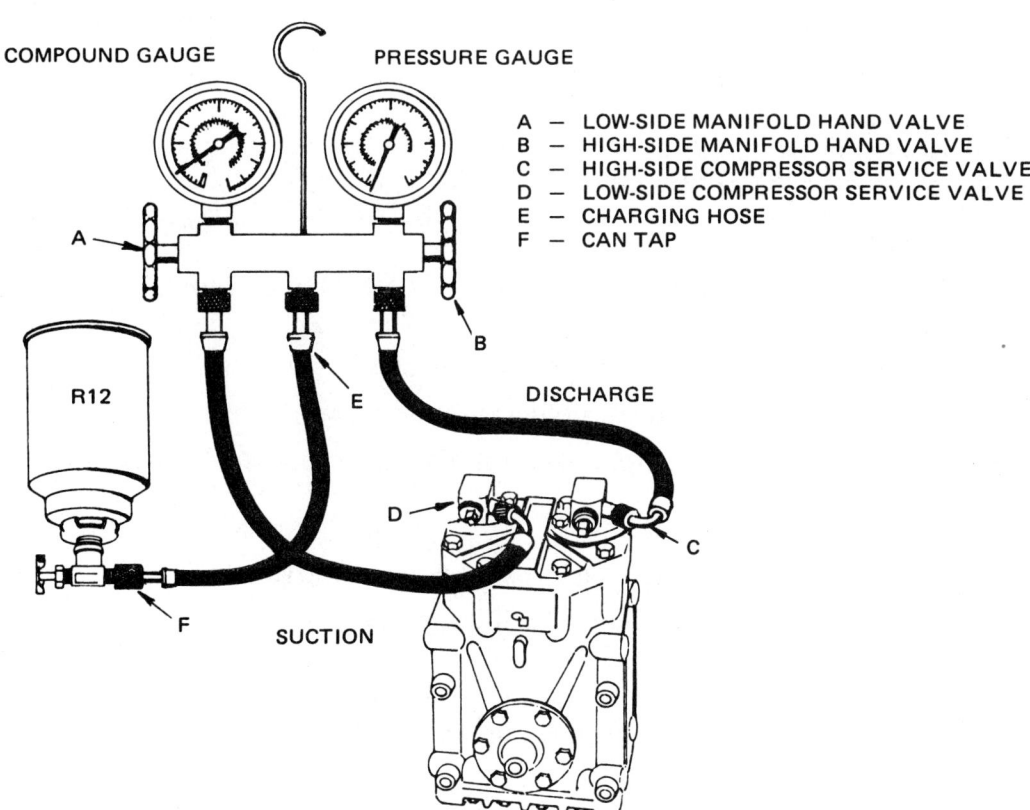

Fig. 7-25 Charging the system with liquid (can upside down).

PROCEDURE, PART I
USING POUND CANS (SYSTEM OFF)

Charge the System

1. Open the high-side gauge manifold hand valve.
2. Observe the low-side gauge pressure. If the gauge indication does not move from the vacuum range into the pressure range, system blockage is indicated.
3. If the system is blocked, correct the condition, evacuate, and continue with the procedure.
4. Invert the container and allow the liquid refrigerant to enter the system.
5. Tap the refrigerant container on the bottom. The can is empty if it gives a hollow ring.
6. Repeat this procedure with additional cans of refrigerant as required to charge the air conditioner completely. Refer to the manufacturer's specifications regarding the system capacity.

Complete the System Charge

1. Close the high-side manifold hand valve.
2. Remove the can tap from the center hose.
3. Rotate the compressor clutch by hand through two or three revolutions to insure that liquid refrigerant has not entered the low side of the compressor.
4. Start the engine and set it to fast idle.
5. Engage the clutch to start the compressor. Set all controls to maximum cooling.
6. Conduct a performance test, if indicated.
7. Back seat the compressor service valves. Remove the manifold gauge set from the system.
8. Replace all protective caps and covers.

PROCEDURE, PART II
USING POUND CANS (SYSTEM OPERATIONAL)

Charge the System

1. Start the engine and adjust the speed to about 1 250 r/min by turning the idle screw or the setting on the high cam.
2. Insure that both of the manifold hand valves are closed.
3. Adjust the controls for maximum cooling with the blower on high speed.
4. Open the low-side gauge manifold hand valve to allow gaseous refrigerant to enter the system.
5. After the pressure on the low side drops below 40 psig (377 kPa absolute), the can should be inverted to allow more rapid removal of the refrigerant.
6. Tap the can on the bottom to determine if it is empty. An empty can will give a hollow ring.
7. Repeat this procedure with additional cans of refrigerant as required to charge the system completely. Refer to the manufacturer's specifications regarding the capacity of the system.

    NOTE: If the system capacity is not known, charge the unit until the sight glass is clear, then add another 1/4 pound (113.4 g) of refrigerant.

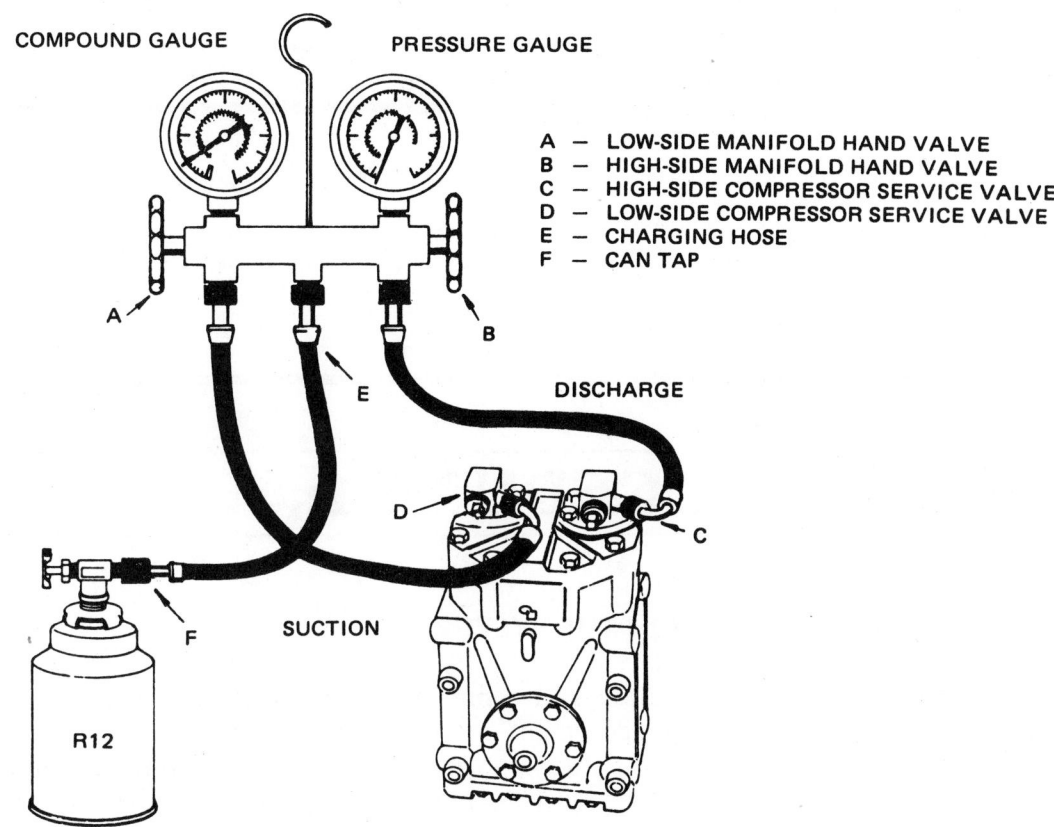

Fig. 7-26 Charging the system with gas (can upright).

Complete the System Charge

1. Close the low-side manifold hand valve.
2. Remove the can tap from the center hose.
3. Conduct the performance test if indicated.
4. Back seat the compressor service valves and remove the manifold and gauge set.
5. Replace all protective caps and covers.

CHAPTER 8:

Repair

SERVICE PROCEDURE 1:

ISOLATING THE COMPRESSOR FROM THE SYSTEM

When a system has both high- and low-side compressor service valves, the compressor can be isolated from the system. The refrigerant can be retained in the system while the compressor is serviced. If a system uses a Schrader-type service port, the compressor cannot be isolated. In this situation, the system must be purged of refrigerant to perform any service procedures.

PROCEDURE

Prepare the System

1. With the manifold and gauge set connected into the system, set both hand valves in the closed position.
2. Set both compressor service valves in the cracked position.
3. Stabilize the system by running the car engine at about 1 200 r/min with the air-conditioner controls turned on maximum cooling for about 10 minutes.

Isolate the Compressor

1. Return the car engine to idle speed, about 500 r/min.
2. Close the low-side service valve until the low-side gauge reads 10 inHg (68 kPa absolute).
3. Turn off the car motor. Completely close (front seat) the low-side service valve.
4. Close the high-side service valve.
5. Open the low-side manifold hand valve and allow trapped refrigerant to escape.
6. Repeat step 5 with the high-side hand valve. Close both valves when the gauges read zero.
7. The compressor is now isolated and can be removed from the car if necessary. Service valves must be removed from the compressor. Do not attempt to remove the hoses.

SERVICE PROCEDURE 2:

PERFORMING A VOLUMETRIC TEST OF THE AIR-CONDITIONING COMPRESSOR

The volumetric or compressor capacity test is performed to determine the condition of the discharge reed valves and the piston rings.

PROCEDURE

Prepare the System for Volumetric Test

1. Attach the gauge and manifold set to the compressor.
2. Start the engine and adjust the speed to 1 000–1 200 r/min.
3. Adjust the controls for maximum cooling. Operate the system for about 10–15 minutes.
4. After 10–15 minutes, shut off all of the air-conditioning controls.
5. Return the engine speed to idle to prevent dieseling. Shut off the engine.
6. If the compressor is equipped with high- and low-side service valves, the compressor can be isolated, the valves removed, and another set of valves substituted for this test. If service valves are provided, follow the procedure outlined in "Isolating the Compressor from the System," Service Procedure 1.
7. If the compressor is equipped with Schrader-type service valves, the system must be purged of refrigerant. Follow the procedure outlined in Chapter 7.
8. When the system is purged of refrigerant, disconnect the high-side hose from the compressor outlet. Cap the hose end to prevent dirt and moisture from entering while the compressor check is being made. Repeat the procedure with the low-side hose.
9. If the compressor is isolated, remove the high- and low-side service valves and substitute other valves for this test.

SAFETY WARNING: Do not remove the high- and low-side compressor hoses if the compressor is isolated.

10. Seal the compressor inlet fitting with the correct size of flare cap.
11. Connect the high-side gauge hose to the high-side compressor service valve. Open the high-side manifold hand valve.
12. Disconnect the low-side gauge hose from the compressor and the manifold.
13. Remove the center hose on the manifold and install a 1/4-inch test cap on the manifold fitting. The test cap is made by drilling a 1/4-inch acorn cap with a #71 drill to give an orifice of 0.026 inch.
14. If a Schrader-type valve is used, install an adapter to open the low side of the compressor to the atmosphere. If service valves are used, *both sides must be cracked or front seated.* The acorn nut must be removed from the low-side valve.

Perform the Volumetric or Capacity Test

1. Start the engine and allow it to idle at exactly 500 r/min.
2. Engage the clutch and operate the compressor as an air pump.

    NOTE: Never operate the air-conditioning compressor as an air pump for more than

15 seconds at a time. To do so can seriously damage the compressor because of improper lubrication. The manufacturer's warranty is void if compressor failure is due to a lack of lubrication.

Air is drawn in at the compressor inlet and is pressurized to the center of the gauge manifold and the high-side gauge.

3. As soon as the maximum pressure is reached, turn off the compressor.
4. Read the high-side manifold gauge. The high-side gauge should read 180–200 psi (1 241–1 379 kPa).
5. If the reading is low, a faulty reed valve or a faulty valve plate gasket is indicated.
6. Make repairs as required.

Recheck the System

1. If necessary repairs are made, the compressor should be rechecked. Follow the procedure outlined.

Return the Compressor to Service

1. Remove all caps and plugs. Reconnect all lines and service valves.
2. If the system was purged, evacuate the system and recharge it.
3. If the compressor was isolated, purge the compressor of air as follows:
    a. Open the high-side manifold hand valve.
    b. Crack the compressor low-side service valve from the front-seated position.
    c. After a few seconds of purging, close the high-side manifold hand valve.
    d. Midposition the low- and high-side compressor service valves.

SERVICE PROCEDURE 3:

PERFORMANCE TESTING THE AIR CONDITIONER

Humidity is an important factor in the temperature of the air delivered to the interior of the car. The service technician must understand the effect that humidity has on the performance of the system. When the humidity is high, the evaporator has a double function to perform. The evaporator must lower the air temperature as well as the temperature of the moisture carried in the air. The process of condensing the moisture in the air transfers a great deal of heat energy into the evaporator. As a result, the amount of heat that the evaporator can absorb from the air is reduced.

The evaporator capacity used to reduce the amount of moisture in the air is not wasted, however. Lowering the moisture content of the air entering the vehicle adds to the comfort of the passengers.

This procedure serves as a guide to the service procedures related to performance testing of the automobile air conditioner. The technician should refer to the manufacturer's service manuals for specific data.

PROCEDURE

Prepare the System

1. With the manifold and gauge set connected into the system, set both hand valves in the closed position.
2. Set the compressor high- and low-side service valves in the cracked position.
3. Run the engine at the high cam setting or adjust the idle screw to about 1 500–1 700 r/min.
4. Place the fan in front of the radiator to assist the ram airflow.
5. Turn on the air conditioner. Set all controls to maximum cooling.
6. Insert a thermometer in the air-conditioning duct as close as possible to the evaporator core. Set the blower on medium or low speed.

Visual Check of the Air Conditioner

1. The low-pressure gauge should be indicating within the range 20–30 psig (239–310 kPa absolute).
2. The high-side gauge should be within the specified range of 160–220 psig (1 103–1 517 kPa).
3. The discharge air temperature should be within the specified range of 40°F–50°F (4.4°C–10°C).

Inspect the High Side and Low Side of the System for Even Temperatures

1. Feel the hoses and components in the high side of the system to determine if the components are evenly heated.

SAFETY WARNING: Certain system malfunctions cause the high-side components to become superheated to the point that a serious burn can result if care is not taken when handling these components.

2. Note the inlet and outlet temperatures of the drier assembly. Any change in the temperature indicates a clogged or defective drier.
3. All lines and components on the high side should be warm to the touch.
4. All lines and components on the low side of the system should be cool to the touch.
5. Note the condition of the thermostatic expansion valve. If the valve is frosted or cold on the inlet side, the valve may be defective.

Test the Thermostats and Control Devices

1. Refer to the service manual for the performance testing of the particular type of control device used.
2. Determine that the thermostat engages and disengages the clutch. There should be about a 12°F (6.7°C) temperature rise between the cutout and cut-in point of the thermostat.
3. Figures 8-1A and 8-1B are guides for determining the proper gauge readings and temperatures.
4. The relative humidity at a particular temperature is a factor in the quality of the air as indicated by figures 8-2A and 8-2B. (These figures should be regarded as guides only.)
5. Complete the performance test as outlined in the manufacturer's service manual.

Ambient Air Temperature, °F	70	80	90	100	110
Average Compressor Head Pressure, psig	150-190	170-220	190-250	220-300	270-370
Average Evaporator Temperature, °F	38-45	39-47	40-50	42-55	45-60

Fig. 8-1A (English).

Ambient Air Temperature, °C	21	27	32	38	43
Average Compressor Head Pressure, kPa	1 034-1 310	1 172-1 517	1 310-1 724	1 517-2 069	1 862-2 551
Average Evaporator Temperature, °C	3.3-7.2	3.9-8.3	4.4-10	5.5-12.8	7.2-15.6

Fig. 8-1B (metric).

Ambient Temperature, °F	70			80			90			100		
Relative Humidity, %	50	60	90	50	60	90	40	50	60	20	40	50
Discharge Air Temperature, °F	40	41	42	42	43	47	41	44	49	43	49	55

Fig. 8-2A (English).

Ambient Temperature, °C	21			27			32			38		
Relative Humidity, %	50	60	90	50	60	90	40	50	60	20	40	50
Discharge Air Temperature, °C	4.4	5	5.5	5.5	6.1	8.3	5	6.6	9.4	6.1	8.3	12.7

Fig. 8-2B (metric).

SERVICE PROCEDURE 4:

SERVICING REFRIGERANT HOSES AND FITTINGS

Many types of connectors are used to join refrigerant hoses to the various components of the air-conditioning system. Cleanliness is important. Be certain to clean all foreign matter from inside and outside hoses and fittings before assembly.

This procedure is given in five parts: Part I for installing an insert (barb) fitting, Part II for repairing a hose using an insert fitting, Part III for repairing a damaged "factory" fitting, Part IV for servicing spring lock fittings, and Part V for O-ring service.

PROCEDURE, PART I

INSERT BARB FITTING

Prepare the Hose

1. a. Measure and mark the required length of replacement hose, or
   b. Determine how much hose must be cut ahead of the damaged fitting.
2. Use a single-edge razor blade and cut the hose.
   NOTE: Single-edge razor blades are available at most cleaning supply houses or hardware stores.
3. Trim the end of the hose to be used to insure that the cut is at right angle (square).

Insert the Fitting

1. Apply clean refrigeration oil to the inside of the hose to be used.
2. Insure that the fitting is free of all nicks and burrs.
3. Coat the fitting liberally with clean refrigeration oil.
4. Slip the insert fitting into the refrigeration hose in one constant, deliberate motion.
5. Install the hose clamp and tighten it to a torque of 30 ft-lb (40.6 N·m).

   NOTE: The hose clamp should be placed at the approximate location of the fitting barb closest to the nut end of the fitting, figure 8-3.

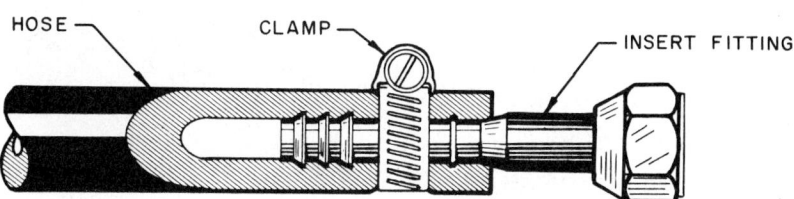

Fig. 8-3 Insert fitting detail (hose cutaway).

PROCEDURE, PART II

HOSE REPAIR USING INSERT FITTING

Prepare the Hose

1. Determine how much of the damaged hose must be cut out and mark hose.
2. Use a single-edge razor blade and cut the hose. Remove the damaged section.
3. Trim the ends of the hose to insure that the cut is at right angle.

Insert the Fitting

1. Apply clean refrigeration oil to the inside of the hoses to be joined.
2. Coat the splice fitting liberally with clean refrigeration oil.
3. Slip the fitting into the hoses in one constant, deliberate motion.
4. Install the hose clamps and tighten to 30 ft-lb (40.6 N·m).

PROCEDURE, PART III

REPAIRING A DAMAGED FACTORY FITTING

Prepare the Hose

1. Remove the hose from the car and place the damaged fitting securely in a vise or other holding device.
2. Use a hacksaw and cut through the ferrule.
3. Use pliers to "peel" off the ferrule.
4. Slice the hose end, figure 8-4, with a single-edge razor blade and remove the hose.
5. Cut off the damaged end of the hose, figure 8-5.

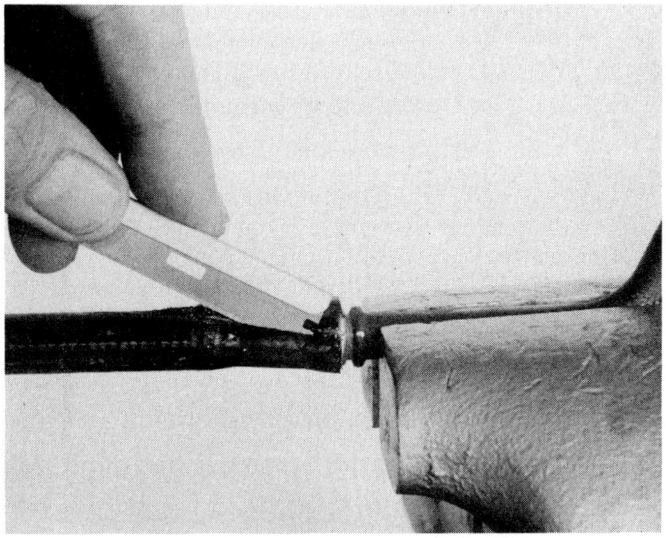

Fig. 8-4 Slice the hose end with a blade and "peel" off the fitting.

Rejoin the Hose

1. Apply clean refrigeration oil to the inside of the hose.
2. Coat the fitting liberally with clean refrigeration oil.
3. Slip the hose onto the fitting with one constant, deliberate motion.
4. Install a hose clamp and tighten to 30 ft-lb (40.6 N·m).

Fig. 8-5 Cut off the damaged end of the hose.

Service Procedure Four 109

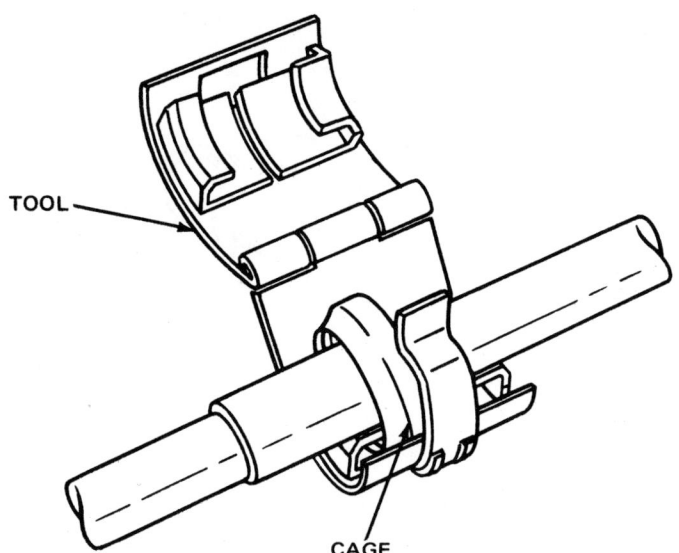

Fig. 8-6 Installing special tool to disconnect spring lock connector.

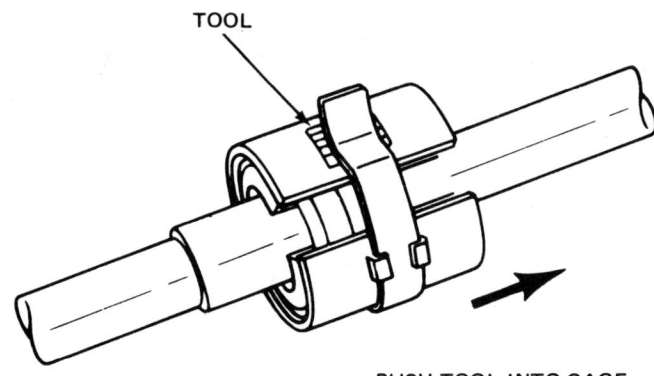

Fig. 8-7 After closing, push tool into the cage to release fitting from garter spring.

PROCEDURE, PART IV

SERVICING SPRING LOCK FITTINGS

Separate Spring Lock Fittings

1. Install the special tool onto the coupling so it can enter the cage to release the garter spring, figure 8-6.
2. Close the tool, figure 8-7, and push it into the cage to release the female fitting from the garter spring.
3. Pull the male and female coupling fittings apart, figure 8-8.
4. Remove the tool from the now disconnected spring lock coupling, figure 8-9.

Join Spring Lock Fittings

1. Lubricate two new O-rings with clean refrigeration oil and install them on the male fitting.
   NOTE: The O-ring material is of a special composition and size. To avoid leaks, use the proper O-rings.
2. Insert the male fitting into the female fitting and push together to join.

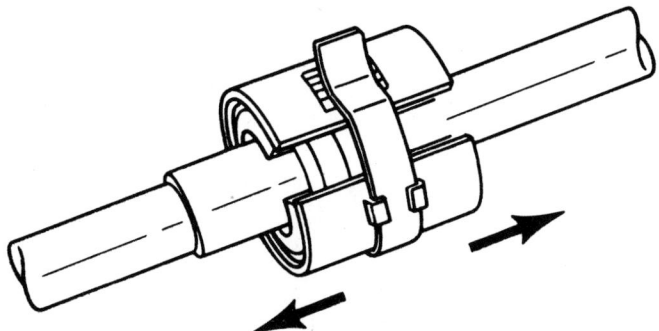

Fig. 8-8 Pull the coupling apart.

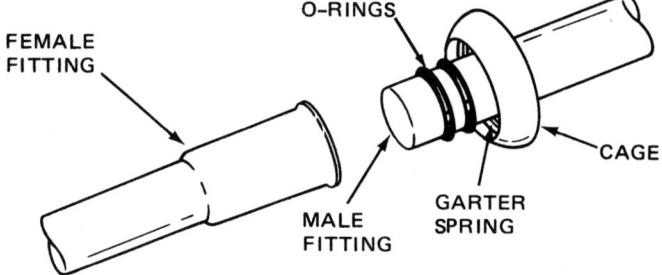

Fig. 8-9 Separated male and female fittings with tool removed.

110 Chapter Eight, Repair

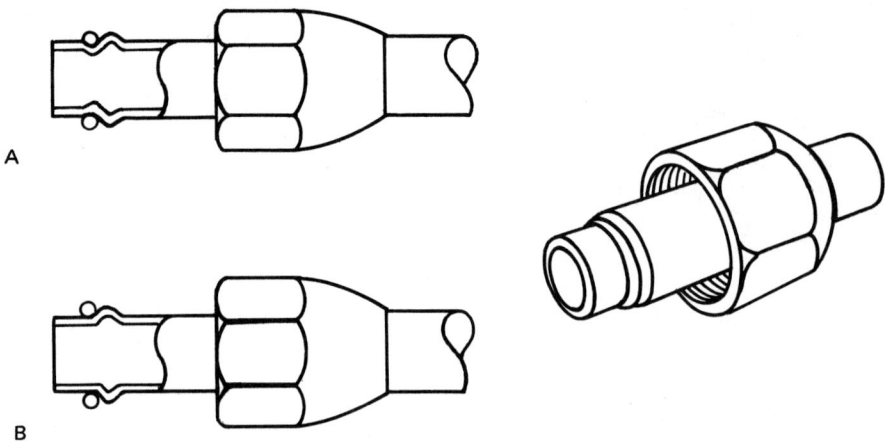

Fig. 8-10 Captive (A) and standard (B) O-ring fittings.

PROCEDURE, PART V

SERVICING O-RINGS

O-rings are replaced whenever a component fitting is removed. They do not usually leak if not disturbed. On occasion, however, an O-ring may be found to be leaking and must be replaced.

If it becomes necessary to replace an O-ring, one should be aware of the two different types of O-ring fittings: captive and standard, figure 8-10. When replacing O-rings it is important to use the proper O-ring for the fitting. The inside diameter (ID) of the two types is slightly different.

SERVICE PROCEDURE 5:

TESTING THE PERFORMANCE OF THE VALVES-IN-RECEIVER (VIR)

The valves-in-receiver (VIR), also known as the evaporator equalizer valves-in-receiver (EEVIR), replaces the thermostatic expansion valve, receiver/drier, and the POA valve by combining these components into one assembly. Each component, however, functions in the same manner as in other systems. This procedure can be used to determine which part, if any, of the VIR or EEVIR is defective.

PROCEDURE

Prepare the System for Test

1. Connect the compound manifold gauge to the service port of the VIR or EEVIR.
2. Connect the high-side manifold gauge to the high-side service port.
3. Start the engine and adjust the engine speed to 2 000 r/min.
4. With the hood open, fully open all of the windows.
5. Set the controls for maximum cooling with the blower on high.

Conduct the Test

1. Note the delivery air temperature by placing the thermometer in the right air duct.
2. Note the evaporator pressure as observed on the compound gauge.
3. If the head pressure is not normal, check for conditions which can cause an abnormal pressure reading.
4. Note the condition of the refrigerant in the sight glass.

   NOTE: Some VIRs have a moisture-indicating sight glass. A *dry* system is indicated by a blue color, a *wet* system by pink, and a *saturated* system by white. If either pink or white, the drier desiccant bag assembly should be replaced.

5. Compare the observations with the chart, figure 8-11.

EVAPORATOR PRESSURE	SIGHT GLASS	AIR DELIVERY	PROBABLE SYSTEM DEFECT	NOTE
28–30 psig (193–207 kPa)	CLEAR	40°–50°F (4.4°–10°C)	NORMAL	
LOW	CLEAR	WARMER	TXV	1 & 2
HIGH	CLEAR	WARMER	POA	
NORMAL-LOW	CLEAR	COLDER	POA	1, 3 & 4
HIGH	CLOUDY	WARMER	POA	1
NORMAL-LOW	CLOUDY	WARMER	LOW CHARGE	1
NORMAL-LOW	CLOUDY	WARMER	DRIER RESTRICTED	1

NOTES:
1. Can cause the superheat to close and blow the thermal fuse link in the compressor clutch circuit.
2. Turn the system off to warm up and equalize the system. Repeat the test. If the system performs properly on the second test, the system probably contains excess moisture. Replace the desiccant.
3. The evaporator can become clogged with ice, thus restricting the airflow.
4. The system can go into a low pressure (or vacuum) when the blower is disconnected.

Fig. 8-11 Valves-in-receiver status chart.

SERVICE PROCEDURE 6:

REBUILDING THE VALVES-IN-RECEIVER (VIR)

The valves-in-receiver (VIR), also known as the evaporator equalizer valves in receiver (EEVIR), should be removed from the car if it is necessary to rebuild the assembly. However, the sight glass, the liquid line valve core, and the evaporator gauge valve core can be easily replaced without removing the assembly from the car.

The following procedure is given in three parts: Part I deals with sight glass replacement, Part II covers the replacement of either (or both) of the valve cores, and Part III covers the rebuilding of the assembly.

PROCEDURE, PART I

SIGHT GLASS

Preparation

1. Purge the system of refrigerant.
2. Remove the sight glass retaining nut using a 7/16 in Allen wrench, figure 8-12.

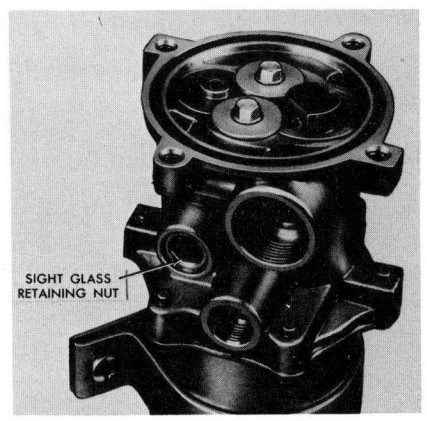

Fig. 8-12 Location of the valves-in-receiver (VIR) sight glass.

Remove the Sight Glass

1. Place a finger over the sight glass to hold it in place.
2. Slightly pressurize the system with refrigerant vapor.
3. Shift the finger pressure on the sight glass from side to side until the sight glass is free of the opening. The system pressure (as applied in step 2) should force the glass from the opening.
4. Discard the sight glass O-ring, thrust washer, and nut. Inspect the sight glass. If it is damaged, discard the sight glass.

Install the Sight Glass

1. Coat the new O-ring, nylon thrust washer, and sight glass retaining nut with refrigeration oil.
2. Install the parts in the cavity in the opposite order from that in which they were removed.
3. Tighten the retaining nut to a torque of 20–25 in-lb (2.3–2.8 N•m).

PROCEDURE, PART II

VALVE CORE(S)

Preparation

1. Purge the system of refrigerant.
2. Determine if one or both of the valve cores must be replaced.

Remove the Valve Core

1. Remove the protective cap from the evaporator gauge valve core and/or the liquid bleed line from the bleed valve fitting of the VIR.
2. Using a numbered tool, remove either (or both) of the valve cores.
3. Discard the core(s) removed.

Install the Valve Core(s)

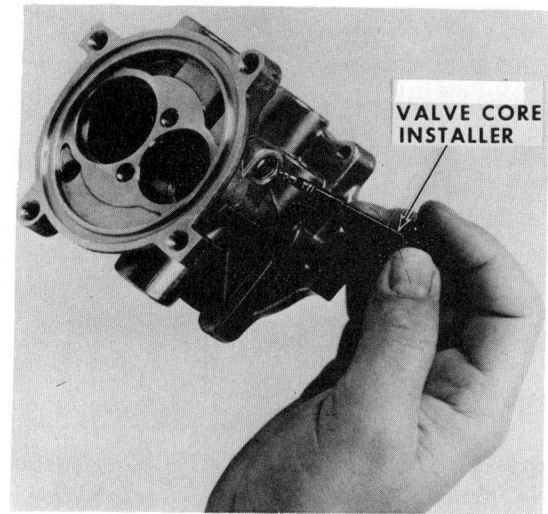

1. Note the different colors of the cores. The evaporator gauge core is blue and the oil bleed line valve core is gold or red.
2. Using the numbered tool, figure 8-13, install the valve core(s).
3. When the core just begins to tighten, note the location of the tool handle and turn it an additional 180° (half turn). This provides a torque of about 24–36 in-oz (0.17–0.25 N·m).
4. Replace the oil bleed line. Tighten the fitting but do not overtighten it.

Fig. 8-13 Location of the valves-in-receiver (VIR) valve core.

PROCEDURE, PART III

REBUILDING THE VIR ASSEMBLY

Preparation

1. Purge the system of refrigerant.
2. While purging, clean the exterior surface of the VIR.
3. Disconnect the oil bleed line.
4. Disconnect the inlet and outlet hoses (from the compressor and the condenser).
5. Disconnect the inlet and outlet lines from the evaporator.
6. Discard all O-rings.
7. Remove the mounting clamp(s) and lift the VIR from the car.

Disassembly of the VIR

1. Note the location of the parts shown in figure 8-14.
2. Loosen the six receiver shell-to-valve housing retaining screws. Turn the screws approximately three turns. *Do not* completely remove the screws until instructed to do so in step 5.
3. Hold the VIR valve housing and push on the lower end of the receiver shell. This should break the seal between the shell and the housing.
4. If step 3 does not break the seal, *carefully* pry between the receiver shell mounting flange and the valve housing. Take care not to mar or scratch the mating surfaces.
5. Remove the six retaining screws (loosened in step 2).
6. Lower the receiver shell to clear the pickup tube and screen. Keep the assembly in an upright position.

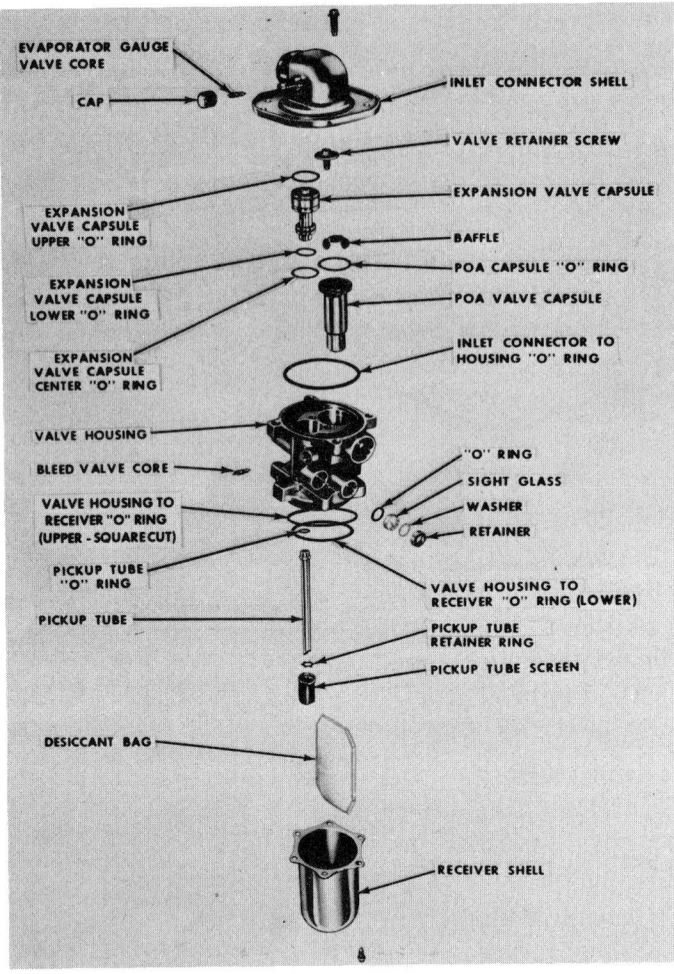

Fig. 8-14 Exploded view of the valves-in-receiver (VIR).

7. Remove and discard the bag of desiccant.
8. Drain, measure, and discard any oil found in the receiver. Note the amount of oil drained.
9. Remove, but do not discard, the pickup tube filter screen.
10. Remove the four inlet connector shell-to-valve housing screws.
11. Carefully slip the inlet connector shell off the valve housing. Do not scratch the mating surfaces.
12. Loosen both valve capsule retaining screws about 3/16 in (4.8 mm). *Do not* remove the screws entirely until instructed to do so in step 17.
13. Attach the valve capsule remover tool to the tapered groove projection on the expansion valve capsule as shown in figure 8-15.
14. Position the tool over one of the screws (step 12) and press down on the handle to loosen the expansion valve capsule.
15. Insert the opposite side of the valve capsule remover tool under the STV baffle. The edge of the tool must clear the edge of the capsule, figure 8-16.
16. Taking care not to damage the valve housing O-ring groove area, press down on the handle to loosen the STV capsule.
17. With both capsules loose, remove both retaining screws (step 12).
18. Remove the expansion valve and the STV capsules from the valve housing.
19. Remove and discard all O-rings and/or gaskets.

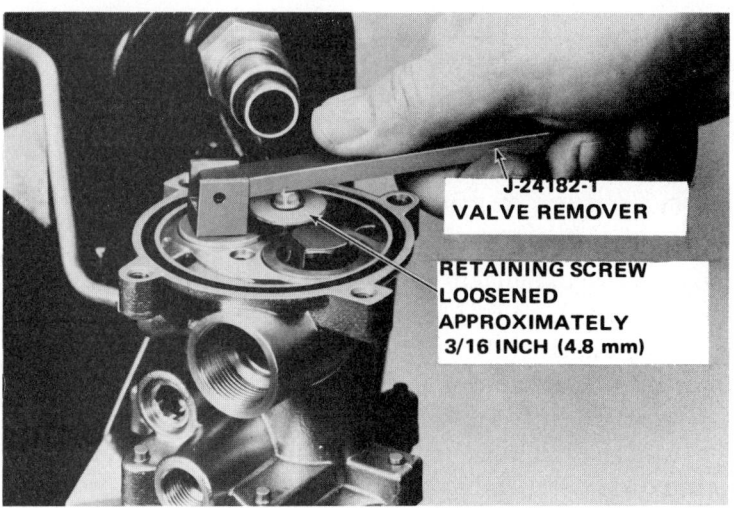

Fig. 8-15 Removing the expansion valve capsule.

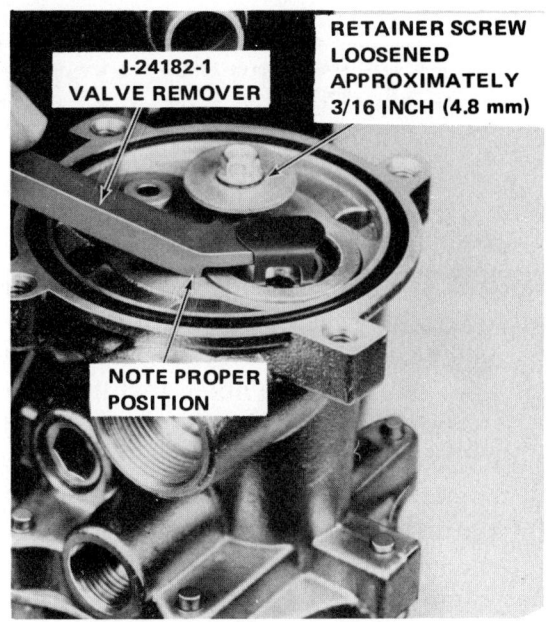

Fig. 8-16 Removing the STV capsule.

Cleaning and Inspection

1. Clean all parts in a good solvent, such as stoddard or kerosene. Trichlorethylene or naphtha, however, are the preferred solvents.
2. Carefully inspect all parts for nicks, scratches, or any other flaws.
3. Place all of the parts to be reassembled (except the desiccant bag) into a container of clean refrigeration oil.
4. Check the pickup tube filter screen to insure that it is clear of any contaminants.

Reassembly of the VIR

1. Reassemble the VIR components in the reverse order of their disassembly.
2. The capsule retaining screws should be tightened to a torque of 5–7 ft-lb (6.8–9.5 N•m).
3. The inlet connector shell screws should be torqued to 10 ft-lb (13.5 N•m).
4. The pickup tube screen must be in place before the receiver shell is replaced. In addition:
   a. place a new bag of desiccant into the shell, and
   b. replace the oil using the quantity noted when the old oil was removed. If less than one ounce (29.57 mL) of oil was removed, replace one ounce (29.57 mL). If more than one ounce (29.57 mL) was removed, replace with the same amount. *Use new, clean refrigeration oil.*
5. The receiver shell screws should be torqued to 10 ft-lb (13.5 N•m).
6. Check the work area. If there are any parts such as O-rings on the bench, they may have been left out of the VIR assembly.

SERVICE PROCEDURE 7:

TESTING AND/OR REPLACING THE FIXED ORIFICE TUBE (FOT)

The fixed orifice tube (FOT) is also known as an expansion tube or, more simply, as an orifice tube. This device is used on systems referred to as CCOT or CCFOT which are the abbreviations for cycling clutch orifice tube or cycling clutch fixed orifice tube.

It must be noted that not all orifice tubes are of the same size. For example, the orifice tube used on 1981 Ford car lines has a slightly smaller diameter than orifice tubes used by Ford in prior years. Though the same service tool may be used to remove and replace either size, the orifice tubes are not interchangeable. When replacing the orifice tube, it is most important that the correct replacement be used.

Some car lines have a nonaccessible orifice tube in the liquid line. Its exact location, anywhere between the condenser outlet and evaporator inlet, is determined by a circular depression or three indented notches in the metal portion of the liquid line. An orifice tube replacement kit is used to replace this type orifice tube and 2 1/2 inches (63.5 mm) of the metal liquid line.

Testing the fixed orifice tube is reasonably simple. There are only two basic problems that one may find: moisture in the system freezing at the orifice tube, or a clogged tube.

This service procedure is given in three parts. Part I covers testing the FOT, Part II covers replacing the accessible FOT, and Part III covers replacing the nonaccessible FOT.

PROCEDURE, PART I

TESTING THE FOT

Prepare the System

1. Attach the manifold and gauge set.
2. Start the engine and adjust the speed to 1 000-1 200 r/min.
3. Adjust all air-conditioning controls to maximum (MAX) cooling.
4. Operate the system for 10-15 minutes.
5. Observe the low-side gauge. An abnormally low low-side gauge reading indicates that the orifice tube is not metering a sufficient amount of refrigerant into the evaporator.

Test the Orifice Tube

NOTE: It may be necessary to bypass the low-pressure switch to prevent clutch cycling on CCOT systems. Bypass the switch only long enough to perform the test. The following steps are to determine if the problem is caused by moisture or by a restriction.

1. Place a warm rag 125°F (52°C) around the fixed orifice tube.
2. Observe the low-side gauge. If the pressure rises to normal, or near normal, moisture in the system is indicated.
3. If moisture is found in the system, the accumulator must be replaced. If moisture is not indicated, the orifice tube is probably clogged. Follow the procedure outlined in Part II of this procedure.

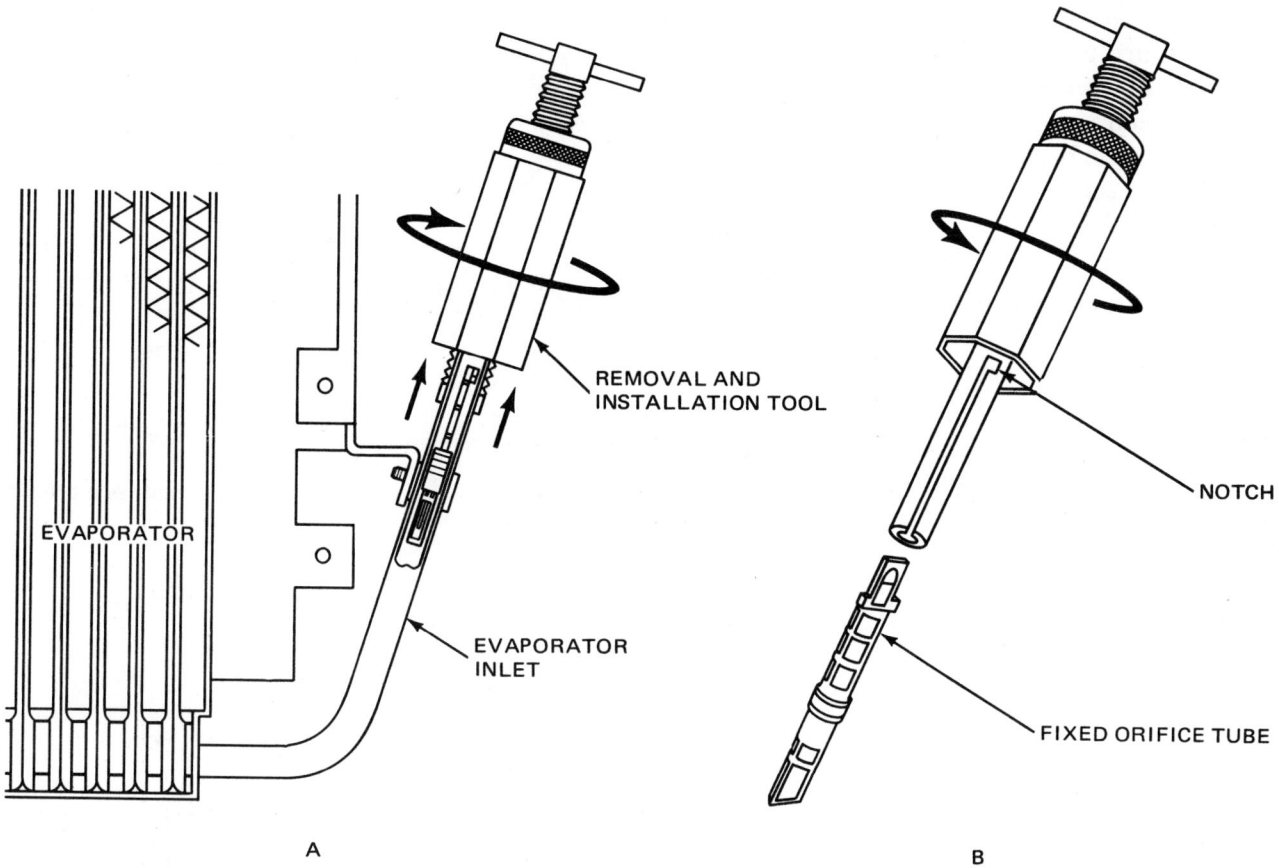

Fig. 8-17 Remove the fixed orifice tube by turning the outer sleeve only. *Do not turn the handle. The handle is turned only enough to engage the notch of the tool onto the fixed orifice tube, detail B.*

PROCEDURE, PART II

SERVICING THE ACCESSIBLE FOT

Remove the Fixed Orifice Tube

1. Purge the system of refrigerant.
2. Using the proper open-end wrenches, remove the liquid line connection at the inlet of the evaporator to expose the FOT.
3. Pour a small quantity of clean refrigeration oil into the FOT well to lubricate the seals.
4. Insert the FOT removal tool, figure 8-17, onto the FOT.
5. Turn the T-handle of the tool *only enough* to engage the tool onto the tabs of the FOT—slightly clockwise (cw).
6. Hold the T-handle and turn the outer sleeve or spool clockwise (cw) to remove the FOT. *Do not turn the T-handle.*

   NOTE: Sometimes the FOT will break during removal. If this happens, proceed with step 7. If not, proceed with "Install the Fixed Orifice Tube." A second tool, known as an *extractor,* is used to remove a broken orifice tube.

118 Chapter Eight, Repair

7. Insert the extractor into the well and turn the T-handle clockwise (cw) until the threaded portion of the tool is securely inserted into the brass portion of the broken FOT, figure 8-18.

8. Pull the tool. The broken FOT should slide out.
NOTE: The brass tube may pull out of the plastic body. If this happens, remove the brass tube from the puller and reinsert the puller into the plastic body. Repeat steps 7 and 8.

Install the Fixed Orifice Tube

1. Coat the new FOT liberally with clean refrigeration oil.
2. Place the FOT into the evaporator well and push it in until it stops against the evaporator tube inlet dimples.
3. Install a new O-ring and replace the liquid line.
4. Replace the accumulator.

Fig. 8-18 Using an extractor tool to remove a broken fixed orifice tube.

PROCEDURE, PART III

SERVICING THE NONACCESSIBLE FOT

Remove the FOT

1. Purge the system.
2. Remove the liquid line from the car. Note how the liquid line was routed so it can be replaced in the same manner.
3. Locate the orifice tube. A circular depression, figure 8-19, or three notches identify the outlet side of the orifice tube.
4. Use a sharp tube cutter to remove a 2 1/2 inch (63.5 mm) section of the liquid line, as shown in figure 8-20. Allow at least 1 inch (25.4 mm) of exposed tube at any bend.
NOTE: Do not use excessive pressure on the feed screw of the tube cutter to avoid distorting the liquid line. A hacksaw should not be used. If a hacksaw must be used; however, flush both pieces of the liquid line to remove all contaminants, such as metal chips.

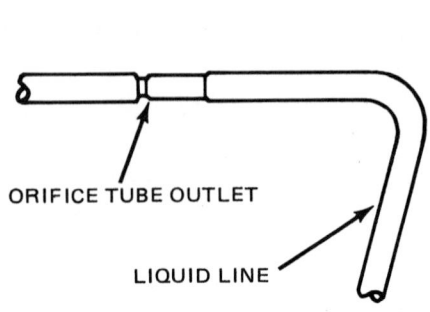

Fig. 8-19 Locating the orifice tube.

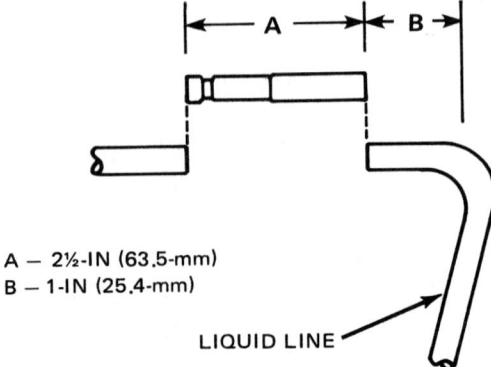

Fig. 8-20 Cut out old orifice tube.

Replace the FOT

1. Slide a compression nut onto each section of the liquid line.
2. Slide a compression ring onto each section of the liquid line with the taper portion toward the compression nut.
3. Lubricate the two O-rings with clean refrigeration oil and slide one onto each section of the liquid line.
4. Attach the orifice tube housing, with the orifice tube inside, to the two sections of the liquid line. Hand tighten both compression nuts. Note the flow direction indicated by the arrows, figure 8-21. The flow should be *toward* the evaporator.
5. Hold the orifice tube housing in a vise to tighten the compression nuts. Insure that the hose bends are in the same configuration as when removed for ease in replacing the liquid line.
6. Tighten each compression nut to 65-70 ft-lb (87-94 N·m) torque.

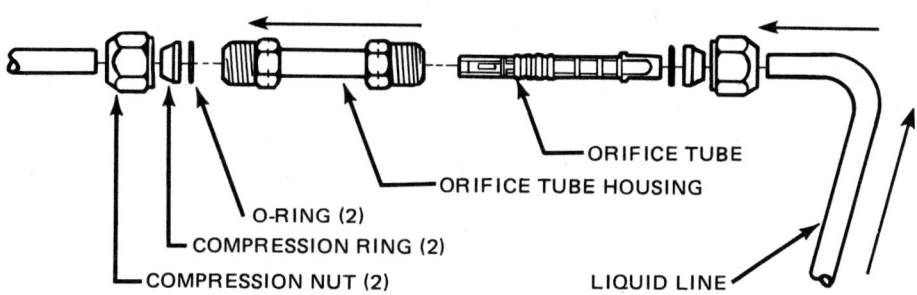

Fig. 8-21 Exploded view of new orifice tube assembly.

SERVICE PROCEDURE 8:

CHECKING THE COMPRESSOR OIL LEVEL (AIR-TEMP, TECUMSEH, YORK COMPRESSORS)

PROCEDURE

Prepare the System

1. The compressor must be isolated from the system. Follow the procedure outlined in this text.

Check the Oil Level

1. Remove the plug from the compressor body to gain access to the compressor crankcase.
2. Use the correct dipstick and measure the oil.
3. Compare the measurements with the chart, figure 8-22, to determine the proper oil level.
4. Add refrigeration oil as necessary to bring the oil level to the proper height.

	York	Tecumseh	Air-Temp
Vertical	1 1/4 in (31.8 mm)	7/8 in (22.2 mm)	
Inclined	2 in (50.8 mm)	1 1/4 in (31.8 mm)	
Horizontal	7/8 in (22.2 mm)	1 1/8 in (28.6 mm)	
R.H. Mount			2 3/4 in (69.9 mm)
L.C. Mount			3 1/8 in (79.4 mm)

Fig. 8-22 Oil level chart.

SERVICE PROCEDURE 9:

CHECKING THE COMPRESSOR OIL LEVEL (SANKYO COMPRESSORS)

The Sankyo compressor is factory charged with seven fluid ounces (201 mL) of Suniso 5GS oil.

PROCEDURE

Prepare the System

1. Start the engine and run the air conditioner so that the compressor operates at idle speed for ten minutes.
2. Turn off the air conditioner and stop the engine.
3. Purge the system of refrigerant slowly to prevent a loss of oil.
4. Position the angle gauge tool across the top flat surfaces of the two mounting ears.
5. Center the bubble and read the inclination angle.
6. Remove the oil filler plug. Rotate the clutch front plate to position the rotor at the top dead center (TDC), figure 8-23.
7. Face the front of the compressor. If the compressor angle is to the right, rotate the clutch front plate counterclockwise (ccw) by 110°. If the compressor angle is to the left, rotate the plate clockwise (cw) by 110°, figure 8-24.

Check the Oil Level

NOTE: A dipstick tool for this procedure is marked in eight increments. Each increment represents one ounce (29.57 milliliters) of oil.

1. Insert the dipstick until it reaches the stop position marked on the dipstick.
2. Remove the dipstick and count the number of increments of oil.
3. Compare the compressor angle and the number of increments with the table in figure 8-25.
4. If necessary, add oil to bring the oil to the proper level. *Do not overfill.* Use only clean refrigeration oil of the proper grade.

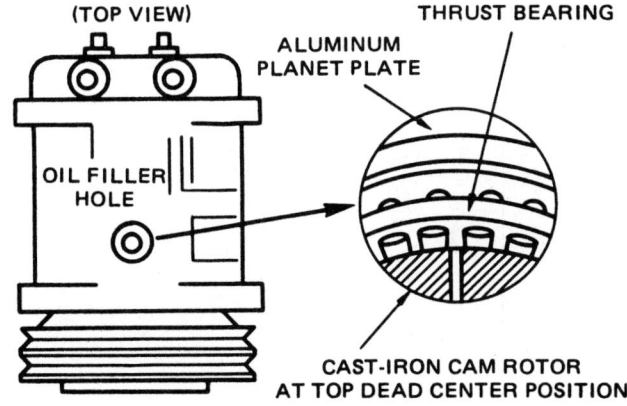

Fig. 8-23 Position the rotor to top dead center (TDC).

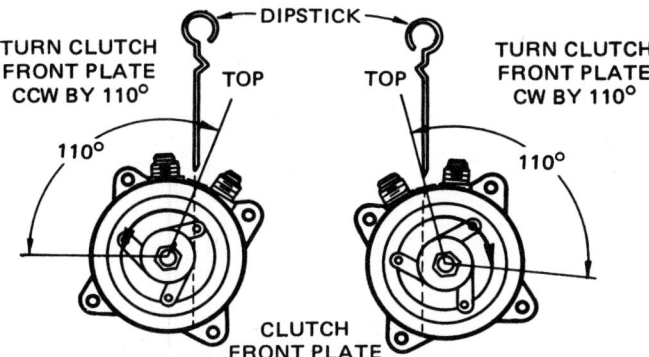

Fig. 8-24 Rotate the clutch front plate.

Inclination Angle In Degrees	Acceptable Oil Level In Increments
0	6-10
10	7-11
20	8-12
30	9-13
40	10-14
50	11-16
60	12-17

Fig. 8-25 Dipstick reading versus inclination angle.

SERVICE PROCEDURE 10:

CHECKING AND ADDING OIL, DELCO AIR FOUR-CYLINDER COMPRESSORS (R-4)

Four-cylinder compressors are factory charged with 5.50 to 6.50 fluid ounces (163 to 192 mL) of 525 viscosity refrigeration oil.

In this procedure, it is assumed that the compressor is isolated or purged of refrigerant and is removed from the car.

PROCEDURE

1. Position the compressor with the shaft end up over a graduated container.
2. Drain the compressor. Allow it to drain for at least ten minutes. Measure and note the amount of oil removed, then discard the old oil.
3. Add new oil in the same amount as the oil drained.

    NOTE: If the replacement compressor is new, drain it as outlined in steps 1 and 2, then add new oil in the amount drained from the old compressor.

SERVICE PROCEDURE 11:

CHECKING AND ADDING OIL, DELCO AIR SIX-CYLINDER COMPRESSORS (A-6 AND DA-6)

Six-cylinder compressors are fully charged at the factory: model A-6 with 11 ounces (325 mL) and model DA-6 with 8 ounces (237 mL) of 525 viscosity refrigeration oil.

To check the compressor oil charge, the compressor must be removed from the car and drained. The oil is then measured. Whenever the oil is checked, the amount of oil drained from the compressor is noted. The old oil is then discarded.

PROCEDURE

Drain the Compressor

1. Remove the oil drain plug located in the compressor oil sump, A-6 only.
2a. Place the compressor in a horizontal position with the drain hole facing downward over a graduated container, A-6 only.
2b. Place the compressor in a vertical position with the suction/discharge ports facing downward over a graduated container, DA-6 only.
3. Drain the compressor. Measure and note the amount of oil removed. Discard the old oil.

Add New Oil (System Stabilized)

NOTE: If the system is not stabilized before the compressor is removed from the car, as in the case of an inoperative compressor, omit this section. Instead, use the following procedure, *"Add New Oil (System Not Stabilized)."*

1. If the quantity of oil drained from the compressor is four ounces (118 mL) or more, add the same amount of new oil to the compressor.
2. If the quantity of oil drained from the compressor is less than four ounces (118 mL), add six ounces (177 mL) of new oil to the compressor.

Add New Oil (System Not Stabilized)

NOTE: If the system is stabilized before the compressor is removed from the car, omit this section. Use the previous procedure, *"Add New Oil (System Stabilized)."*

1. If the quantity of oil removed is less than 4 ounces (118 mL) and the system shows no signs of a greater loss, add six ounces (177 mL) of new oil.
2. If the quantity of oil removed is greater than 4 ounces (118 mL) and the system shows no signs of a greater loss, add the same amount of new oil.
3. If the compressor is replaced with a rebuilt unit, replace the oil in the amount as indicated in steps 1 or 2 and then add one more ounce (29.57 mL).

SERVICE PROCEDURE 12:

CHECKING AND/OR ADDING OIL: NIPPONDENSO COMPRESSOR (INCLUDES FORD FS-6 AND CHRYSLER C-171)

The Nippondenso compressor is factory charged with 13 ounces (384 mL) of 500 SUS (viscosity) refrigeration oil.

To check the oil level, the compressor must be removed from the car. The oil is drained and measured. The amount of oil drained is noted; then the oil is discarded.

PROCEDURE

Drain the Compressor

1. Drain the compressor oil through the suction and discharge service ports into a graduated container.
2. Rotate the crankshaft one revolution to insure that all oil is drained.
3. Note quality and quantity of oil drained and discard.

Refill Compressor

1. Add oil, as follows:
   a. If the amount of oil drained was 3 ounces (89 mL) or more, add an equal amount of clean refrigeration oil.
   b. If the amount of oil drained was less than 3 ounces (89 mL), add 5 to 6 ounces (148 to 177 mL) of clean refrigeration oil.
2. If the compressor is to be replaced, drain all of the oil from the new or rebuilt compressor and replace oil as outlined in step 1 (a or b, as applicable).

   NOTE: Oil is added into the suction and/or discharge port(s). Rotate the compressor crankshaft at least five revolutions by hand after adding oil.

SERVICE PROCEDURE 13:

CHECKING AND ADDING OIL TO THE TECUMSEH HR-980 COMPRESSOR SYSTEM

This compressor is factory-charged with 8 oz (236.6 mL) of 500 viscosity refrigeration oil. In a balanced system, approximately 4 oz (118.3 mL) of oil will be found in the compressor, 3 oz (88.7 mL) in the evaporator, 1 oz (29.6 mL) in the condenser, and 1 oz (29.6 mL) in the accumulator.

PROCEDURE

1. If replacing the compressor: drain the new or rebuilt compressor and replace with 4 oz (118.3 mL) of clean refrigeration oil.

2. If replacing the evaporator: add 3 oz (88.7 mL) of clean refrigeration oil to the new evaporator before installing.

3. If replacing the condenser: add 1 oz (29.6 mL) of clean refrigeration oil to the new condenser before installing.

4. If replacing the accumulator: drain the oil from the old accumulator, through pressure switch fitting, into a graduated container. Add the same amount of clean refrigeration oil to the new accumulator, plus 1 oz (29.6 mL). If no oil was drained from the old accumulator, add 1 oz (29.6 mL) of oil to the new accumulator.

SERVICE PROCEDURE 14:

CHECKING AND ADDING OIL, YORK VANE ROTARY COMPRESSOR

Normal oil charge is six to nine ounces (177 to 266 mL) depending upon system refrigerant capacity, as noted in the chart of figure 8-26. The normal oil charge (level) in the compressor sump is two to four ounces (59 to 118 mL) regardless of the refrigerant charge.

This procedure is given in two parts: Part I for checking the oil charge during system service (on the car), and Part II for bench checking the oil charge (off the car).

System R-12 Charge		Oil Charge	
Pounds	Liters	oz	mL
2	0.946	6	177.4
3	1.419	7	207.0
4	1.892	8	236.6
5	2.365	9	266.2

Fig. 8-26 Oil chart for York vane rotary compressor based on system refrigerant capacity.

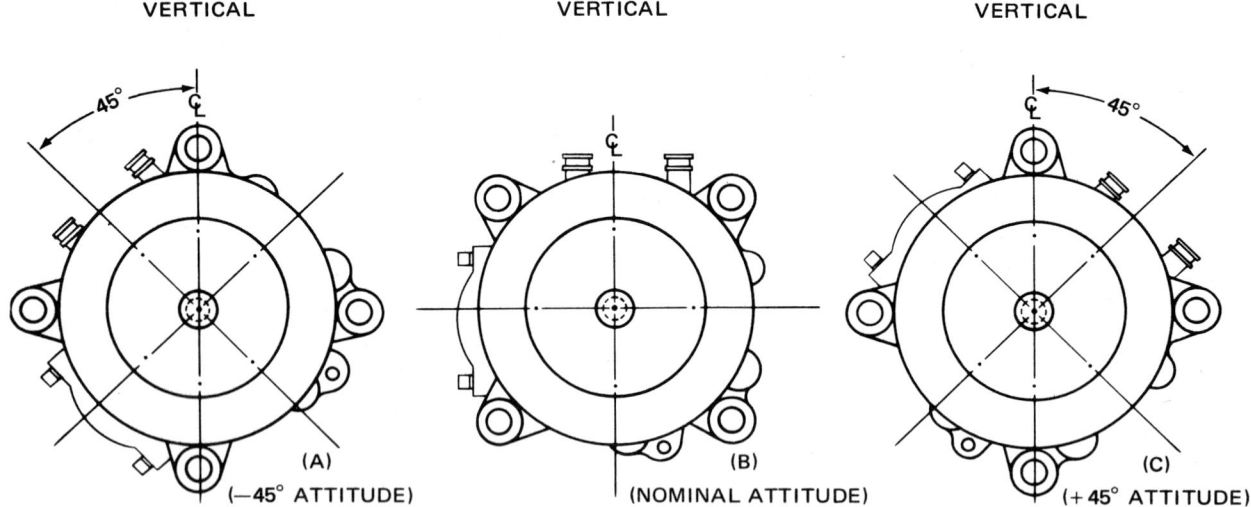

Fig. 8-27 Adjust attitude of compressor so service valves are in vertical position as shown in B.

PROCEDURE, PART I

OIL CHARGE—ON VEHICLE

Prepare the Compressor

1. Start and run the engine at idle speed for 10 minutes with the air-conditioning controls set for maximum cooling and medium fan speed.
2. Stop the engine. Slowly discharge the refrigerant.

3. Loosen the mounting hardware and belt(s) to adjust the attitude of the compressor, figure 8-27, so that the service valves are vertical.
4. Remove the suction and discharge fittings. Discard the O-rings.
5. Rotate the compressor shaft, by hand, counterclockwise (ccw) five to ten turns.

Check Oil Level

1. Use the proper dipstick to measure the oil level.

    NOTE: The oil level should be 2 to 4 ounces (59 to 118 mL).

2. If less than 2 ounces (59 mL), add oil to the correct level; if more than 2 ounces (59 mL), the oil level is considered adequate.

    NOTE: Oil may be added through the discharge port (stamped "D" on the compressor).

PROCEDURE, PART II

OIL CHARGE—BENCH CHECK

1. Remove the oil drain plug and discard the O-ring.
2. Drain the oil into a graduated container. Drain oil from drain hole *and* suction and discharge ports.

    NOTE: If the amount of oil drained is less than 2 ounces (59 mL), replace with 2 ounces (59 mL); if more than 2 ounces (59 mL), replace with same amount as drained.

3. Replace oil (see note above). Oil may be added through the oil drain hole or the discharge port.
4. Replace oil drain plug with new O-ring.

CHAPTER 9:

Compressor Repair

The procedures given in this section are intended as typical. They are to be used as a guide only. Because of the great number of variations in automotive air-conditioning and heating systems, it would be impossible to include all specific and detailed information in this text. When specific or more detailed information is needed, the service technician should consult the appropriate manufacturer's service manual for that particular year-model automobile. Some general service manuals are now available that cover, in greater detail, most service procedures for automobiles of a specific year, make, and model. One such manual, covering the past ten years only, has little theory and is more than four inches (102 mm) thick.

The information in this section, then, is given only as a guide to enable the learning technician to perform many typical service procedures normally required. Proper service and repair procedures are vital to the safe, reliable operation of the system. More importantly, proper service procedures and techniques are essential to provide personal safety to those performing the repair service.

Safety

It must be recognized that the skills and procedures of individuals performing the service work vary greatly. It is not possible to anticipate all conceivable ways or conditions under which service work may be performed. Therefore, it is impossible to provide precautions for every possible hazard that may result.

The following precautions are basic, and apply to any type of automotive service.

1. Wear safety glasses or goggles for eye protection when working under the hood of a car.
2. Set the parking brake. Place the gear selector in PARK if equipped with an automatic transmission, or in NEUTRAL if a manual transmission.
3. Unless required otherwise for the procedure, be sure that the ignition switch is in the OFF position.
4. Operate the engine, if required for the procedure, in a well-ventilated area.
5. Avoid loose clothing. Tie long hair securely behind the head. Remove rings, watches, and loose-hanging jewelry.
6. Keep clear of all moving parts when the engine is running.
7. Keep hands, clothing, tools, and test leads away from the cooling fan. Electric cooling fans may start without warning even when the ignition switch is in the OFF position.
8. Avoid contact with hot parts such as the radiator, exhaust manifold, and high-side refrigerant lines.
9. If in doubt, ASK; do not take chances.

SAFETY CAUTION: The technician must exercise extreme caution, and pay heed to every established safety practice, when performing these or any automotive air-conditioning service procedures.

SERVICE PROCEDURE 1:

SERVICING THE NIPPONDENSO COMPRESSOR (INCLUDES CHRYSLER C-171 AND FORD FS-6)

The Nippondenso compressor is also known as the Chrysler C-171 and the Ford FS-6 compressor. This compressor may be equipped with either a Nippondenso or Warner clutch assembly. Though these two clutches are similar in appearance, their parts are not interchangeable. Complete clutch assemblies are, however, interchangeable on the Nippondenso compressor.

Seal replacement for this compressor is somewhat different from other compressors; the front-head assembly must first be removed.

This service cannot be performed with the compressor on the car; it must first be removed from the engine.

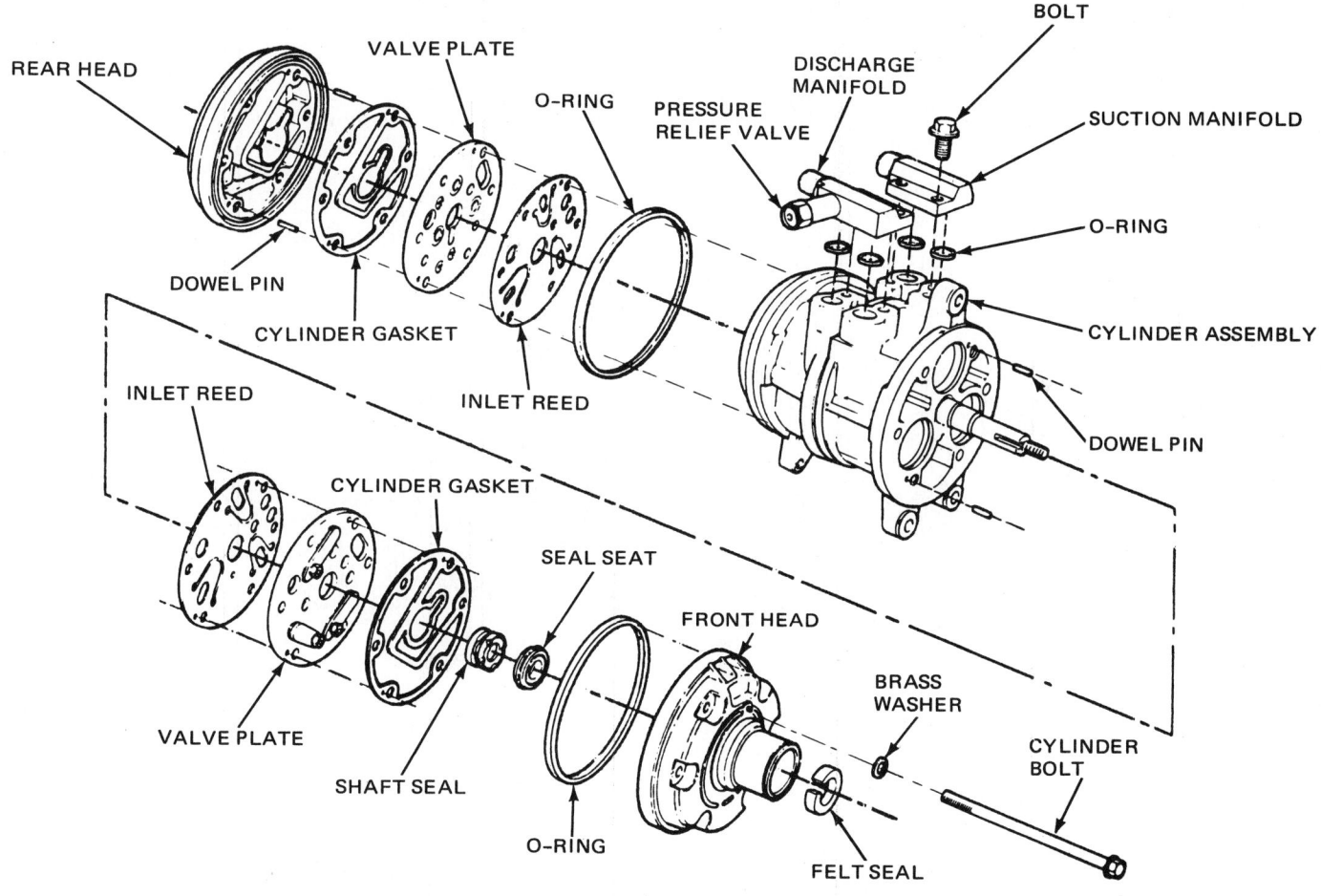

Fig. 9-1 Exploded view of Nippondenso compressor.

Chapter Nine, Compressor Repair

PROCEDURE

Remove the Clutch

1. Remove the hub nut.
2. Use the hub remover and remove the clutch hub, figure 9-2.

    NOTE: The shaft/hub key need not be removed. Take care not to lose the shim washer(s).

3. Use the snap ring plier to remove the pulley retainer snap ring.
4. With the shaft protector in place, figure 9-3, remove the pulley and bearing assembly with the 3-jaw puller.

    NOTE: Make certain that the puller jaws are firmly and securely located behind the pulley to avoid damage.

5. Use the snap ring plier to remove the field coil retaining snap ring, figure 9-4.
6. Note the location of the coil electrical connector and lift the field coil from the compressor.

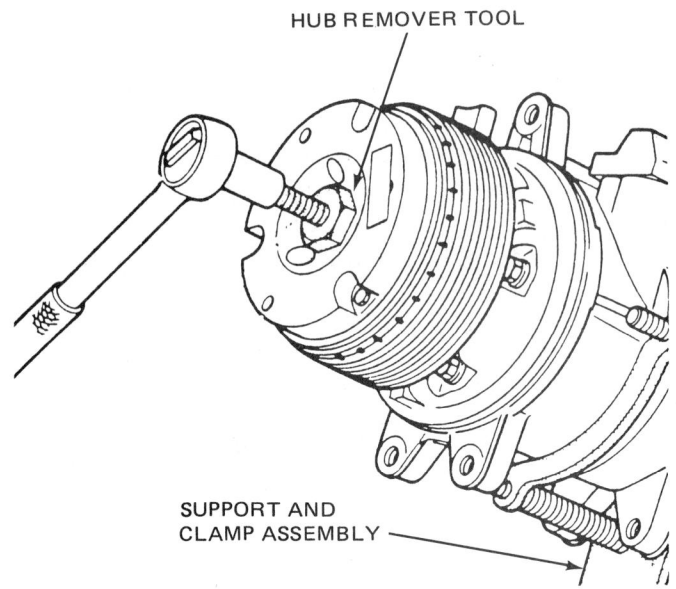

Fig. 9-2 Using the hub remover tool to remove the clutch hub.

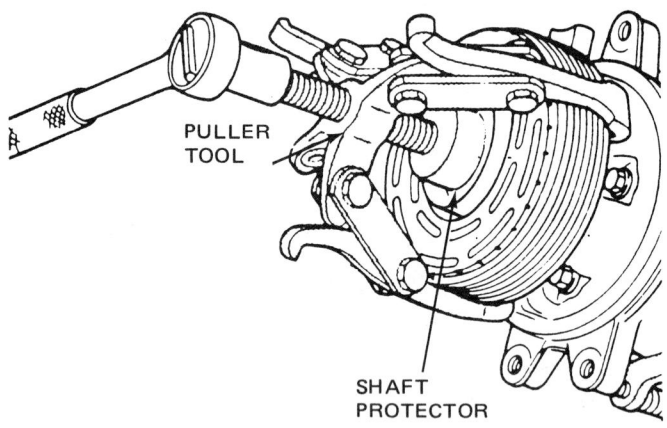

Fig. 9-3 Using a 3-jaw puller with shaft protector to remove pulley and bearing assembly.

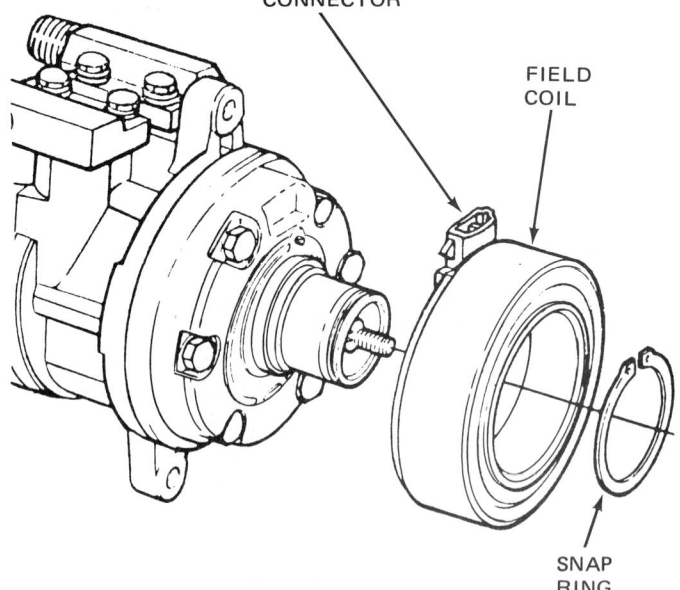

Fig. 9-4 Field coil is held in place with snap ring. Note location of connector and use snap ring plier to remove snap ring — then lift off field coil.

Replace the Pulley Bearing

NOTE: If Nippondenso clutch, use a small screwdriver and remove the bearing retaining snap ring before proceeding.

1. Support the pulley with the proper clutch pulley support, figure 9-5 (see introductory statements).
2. Drive out bearing(s) using hammer and bearing remover.

3. Lift out the dust shield and retainer or leave in place. Make sure the dust shield is in place *before* installing bearing.
4. Install new bearing(s) using the bearing installer and the hammer, figure 9-6. Bearing(s) must be fully seated in the rotor.
5. Replace the wire snap ring if Nippondenso. If Warner, stake the bearing in place using the prick punch and the hammer.

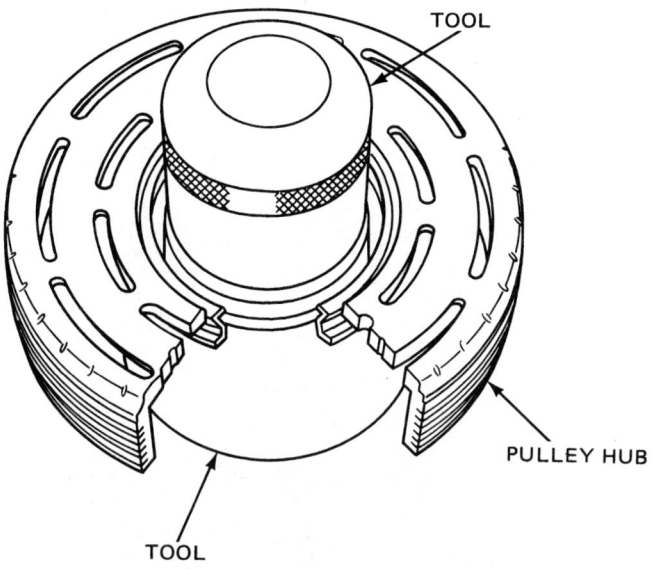

Fig. 9-5 With pulley supported, use tool to drive out pulley bearing.

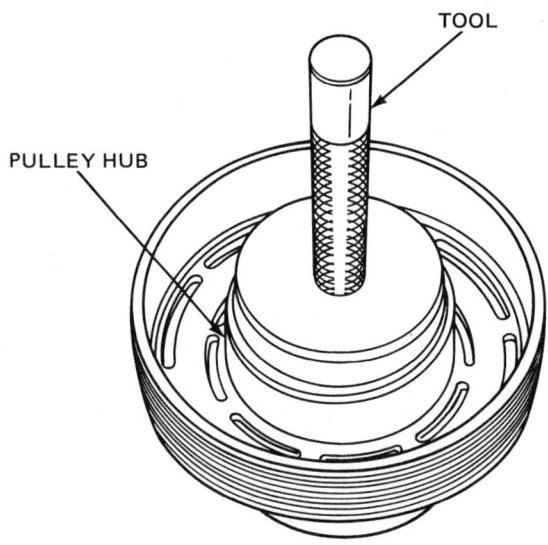

Fig. 9-6 Use bearing installer tool (and hammer) to drive new bearing into pulley hub.

Remove the Seal

1. Using the shaft key remover, remove the shaft key, figure 9-7.
2. Remove the felt oil absorber and retainer from the front head cavity.

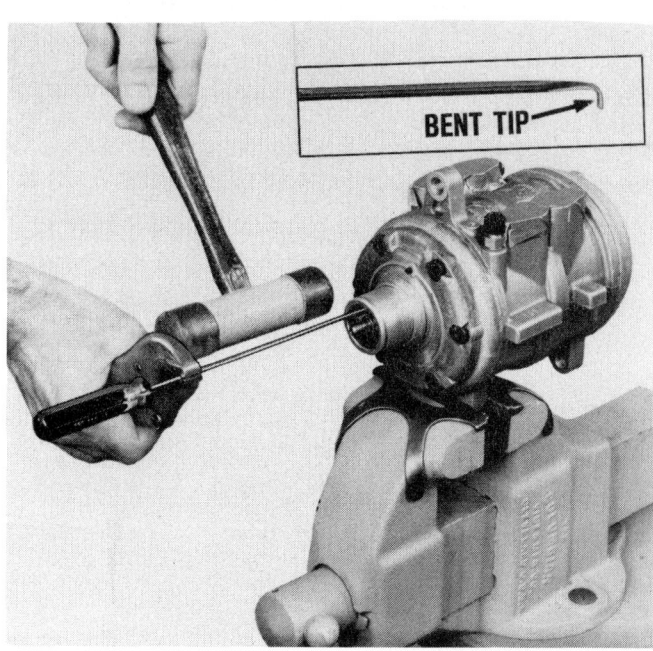

Fig. 9-7 Removing crankshaft key.

132 Chapter Nine, Compressor Repair

3. Drain the compressor oil into a graduated measure.
4. Remove the six through bolts from the front head. Use the proper tool; some require a 10-mm socket and others require a 6-mm Allen wrench.
5. Discard the six brass washers (if equipped) and retain the six bolts.
6. Gently tap the front head with a plastic hammer to free it from the compressor housing.
7. Remove and discard the head-to-housing O-ring and the head-to-valve plate gasket.
8. Place the front head on a piece of soft material, such as cardboard, cavity side up.
9. Use the shaft seal seat remover to remove the seal seat, figure 9-8.
10. Using both hands, remove the shaft seal cartridge, figure 9-9.

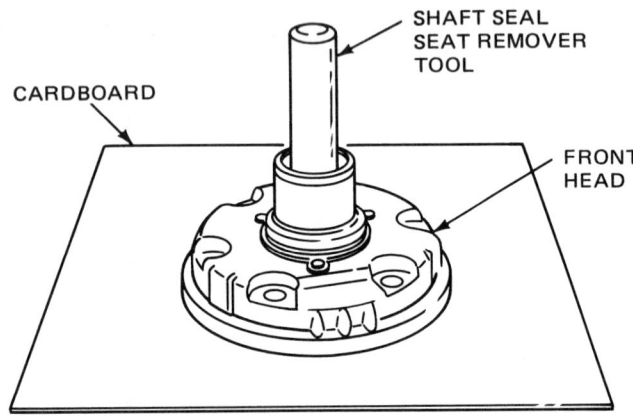

Fig. 9-8 Using the shaft seal seat remover tool to remove the seal seat from the front head.

Fig. 9-9 Removing the shaft seal.

Open the Compressor

1. Tap the rear head with a plastic hammer and remove the head.
2. Discard the head to housing O-ring.
3. Remove the valve plate from the head using the valve plate remover, figure 9-10.
4. Discard head to valve plate gasket.
5. Tap on the compressor body lugs, figure 9-11, to separate the front and rear housings.
   NOTE: Separate no more than one inch (25.4 mm), figure 9-12.

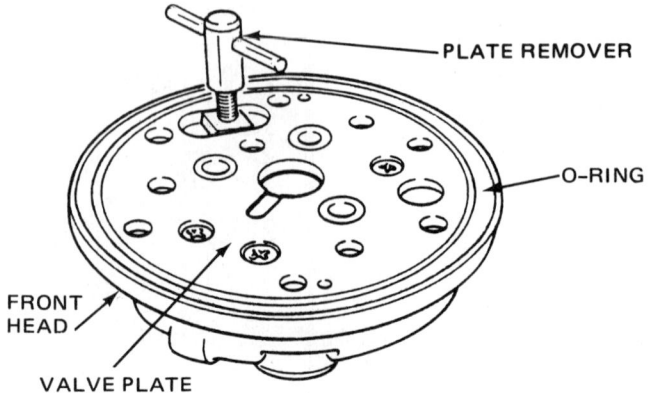

Fig. 9-10 Use special tool to remove valve plate from the head.

Close the Compressor

1. Liberally coat all O-rings and gaskets with clean refrigeration oil.
2. Position the front-to-rear housing O-ring and slide the two housings together.
3. Install the rear head to the valve plate gasket. Install the discharge valve plate and the suction valve plate.
4. Install the rear head O-ring and mount the rear head/valve plate assembly to the compressor housing. The rear head alignment pins must engage in corresponding holes in the compressor housing.
5. Position the compressor on the rear head and install the suction valve plate, the discharge valve plate, and the head to valve plate gasket.
   NOTE: Make sure the valve plates and gasket are aligned with the alignment pins in the compressor housing.

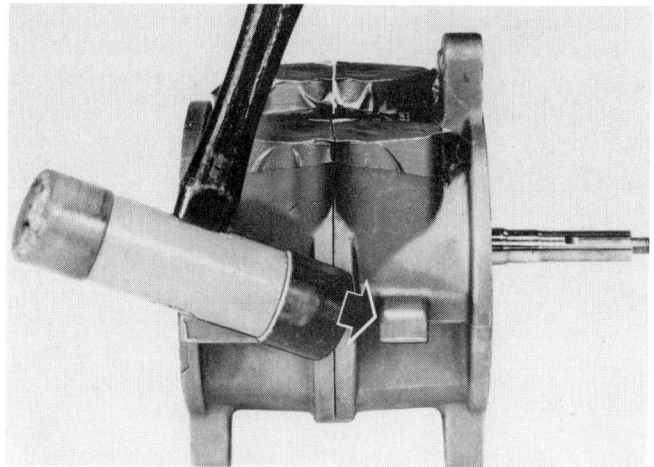

Fig. 9-11 Separating the front and rear housings.

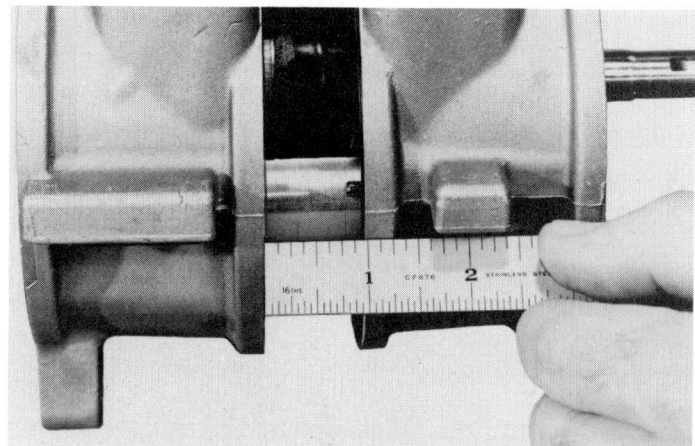

Fig. 9-12 Separate the housings no more than one inch (25.4 mm).

6. Liberally coat all seal parts, compressor shaft, head cavity, and gaskets with clean refrigeration oil.
7. Carefully install the shaft seal cartridge, figure 9-13, making sure to index the shaft seal on the crankshaft slots.
8. Install the seal seat into the front head using the seal seat installer, figure 9-14.
9. Install head-to-valve plate gasket over alignment pins in the compressor housing.
10. Install the head-to-housing O-ring.
11. Carefully slide head onto compressor housing insuring that the alignment pins engage in holes in the head.
12. Using six new brass washers (if required), install the six compressor through bolts.
13. Using a 10-mm socket or 6-mm Allen wrench, as required, tighten the bolts to a 260 lb-in (29.4 N·m) torque.
14. Replace the oil with clean refrigeration oil.

134 Chapter Nine, Compressor Repair

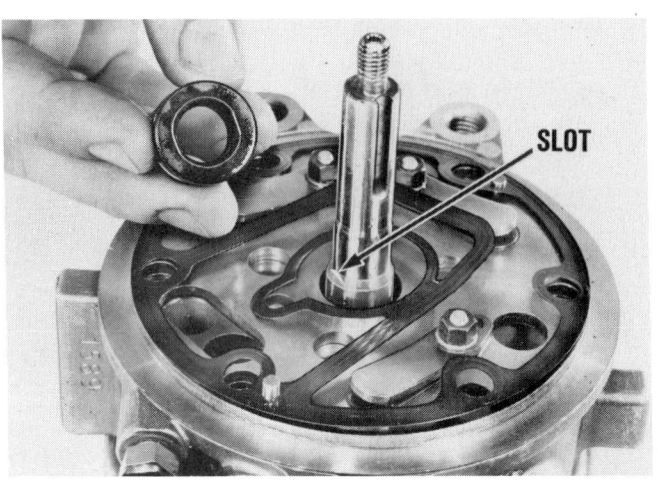

Fig. 9-13 Index flat on shaft seal with slot on crankshaft.

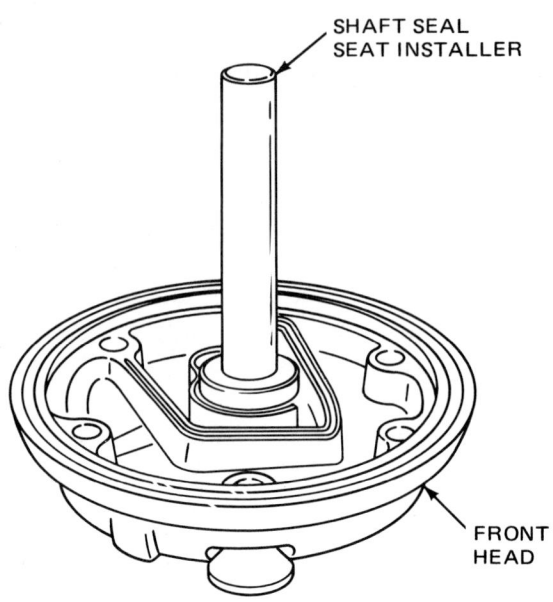

Fig. 9-14 Install the shaft seal seat into the front head using the seal seat installer.

Install the Clutch

1. Install the field coil. Be sure the locator pin on the compressor engages with the hole in the clutch coil.
2. Install the snap ring. Be sure the bevel edge of the snap ring faces out.
3. Slip the rotor/bearing assembly squarely on the head. Using the bearing remover/pulley installer tool, *gently tap* the pulley on the head, figure 9-15.
4. Install the rotor/bearing snap ring. The bevel edge of the snap ring must face out.

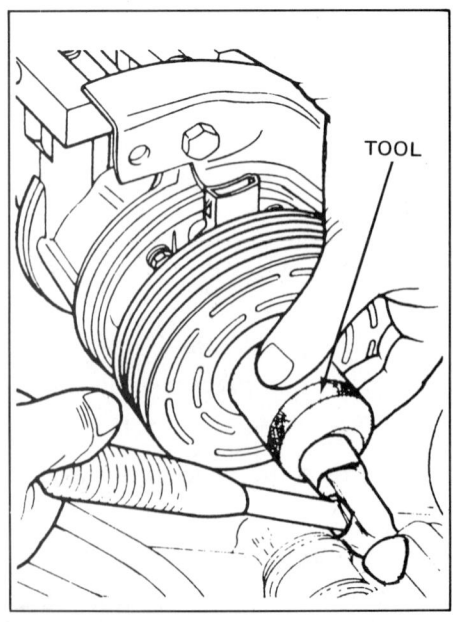

Fig. 9-15 Gently *tap* the pulley onto the compressor head.

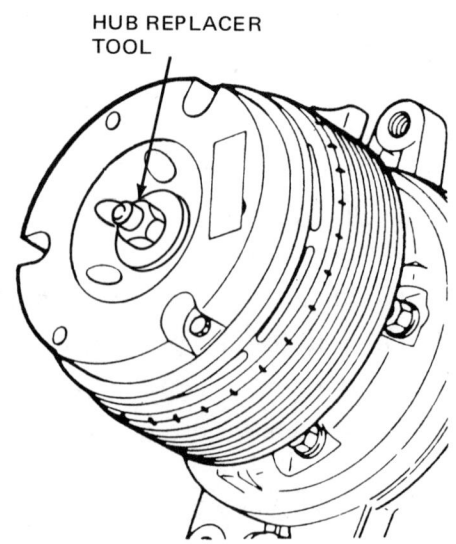

Fig. 9-16 Press the hub onto the compressor shaft using the hub replacer tool only. *Do not drive or hammer hub onto the shaft.*

5. Install shim washers and/or be sure they are in place. Check shaft/hub key to insure proper seating.
6. Align the hub keyway with the key in the shaft. Press the hub onto the compressor shaft using the hub replacer tool, figure 9-16. *Do not drive (hammer) the hub on; to do so will damage the compressor.*
7. Using a nonmagnetic feeler gauge, check the air gap between hub and rotor, figure 9-17.

    NOTE: Air gap should be 0.021–0.036 in (0.53–0.91 mm).
8. Turn the shaft (hub) one-half turn and recheck the air gap. Change the shim(s) as necessary to correct the air gap.
9. Install the locknut and tighten to 10–14 ft-lb (13.6–19.0 N·m).
10. Recheck the air gap. See steps 7 and 8.

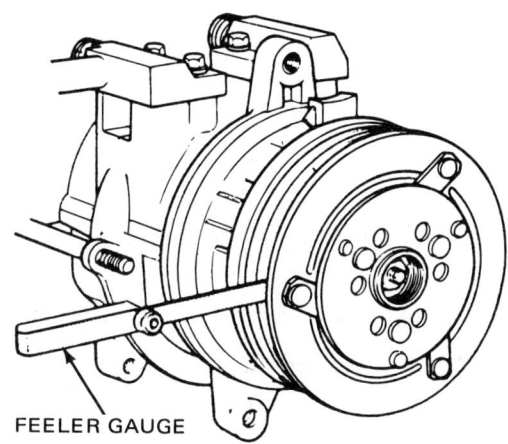

Fig. 9-17 Check air gap between hub and rotor.

SERVICE PROCEDURE 2:

SERVICING THE NIPPONDENSO TEN-CYLINDER COMPRESSOR, MODEL 10P15

The Nippondenso 6- and 10-cylinder compressors are similar in appearance. Unlike the 6-cylinder compressors, the 10-cylinder model shaft seal may be serviced without removing the head.

Service to the 10-cylinder compressor is limited to the clutch and shaft seal. It is not advisable to attempt internal repairs.

Procedures are given in two parts: Part I for clutch service, and Part II for seal service.

PROCEDURE, PART I

CLUTCH SERVICE

Remove Clutch

1. While holding the clutch plate with a strap wrench or clutch plate holding tool, remove the shaft nut with a 12-mm socket and handle.
2. Use the clutch plate remover, figure 9-18, to remove the clutch plate.
3. Remove the clutch plate shim(s) and set them aside for later reassembly.
4. Use the snap ring pliers, figure 9-19, to remove the pulley retaining snap ring.
5. Use the plastic hammer, figure 9-20, to tap the pulley off the compressor. Take care not to damage the pulley.
6. Remove the clutch coil ground wire from the compressor.
7. Use the snap ring pliers to remove the clutch coil retaining snap ring.
8. Lift the coil from the compressor.

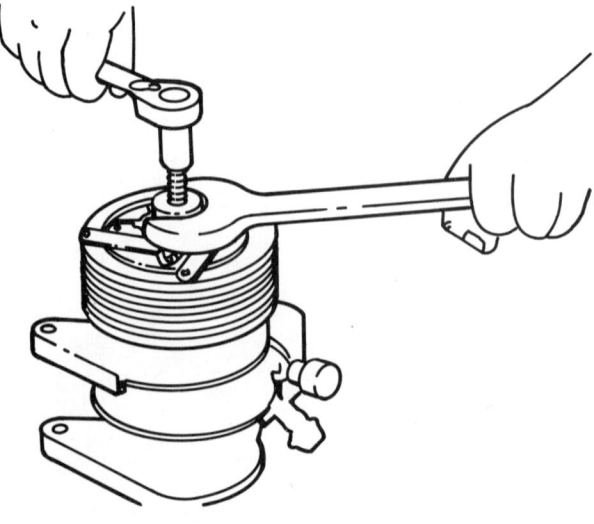

Fig. 9-18 Use clutch plate remover to remove clutch plate.

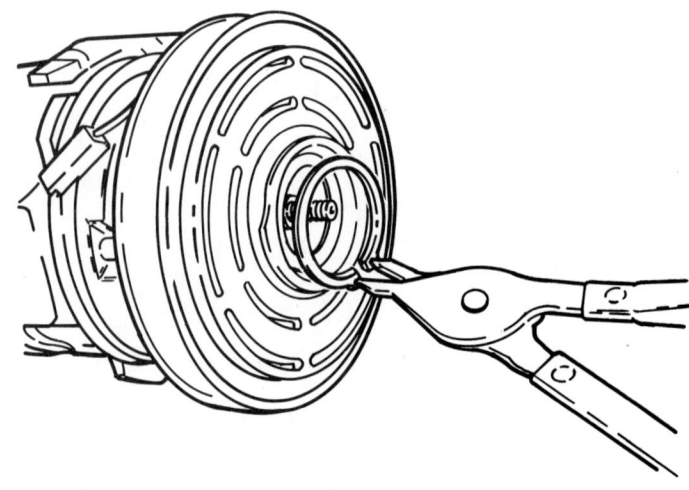

Fig. 9-19 Remove the pulley retaining snap ring.

Replace Bearing

1. Assemble the pulley with the pulley support and bearing remover on a hydraulic press, as shown in figure 9-21. Make sure that the tools and the pulley are *in-line*.

2. Press the bearing from the pulley rotor. Discard the bearing.

3. Assemble the pulley with the pulley support, the bearing replacer tool, and the new bearing, as shown in figure 9-22. Make certain that the tools, the pulley, and the bearing are *in-line*.

4. Carefully press the bearing into the pulley.

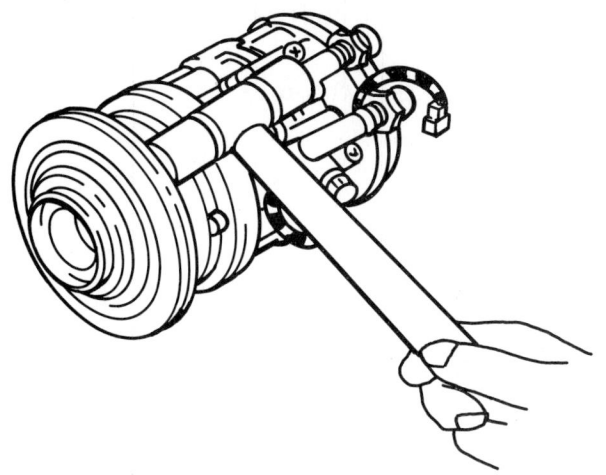

Fig. 9-20 Use plastic hammer to tap pulley off the compressor.

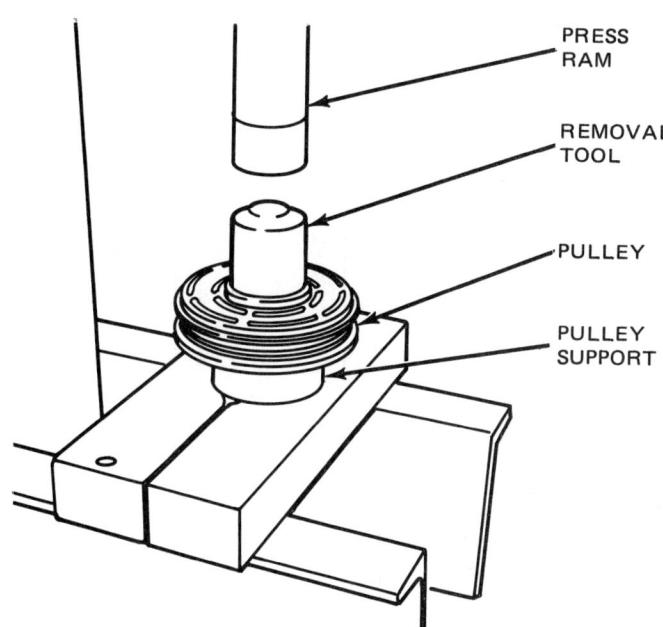

Fig. 9-21 Use a hydraulic press to remove pulley bearing.

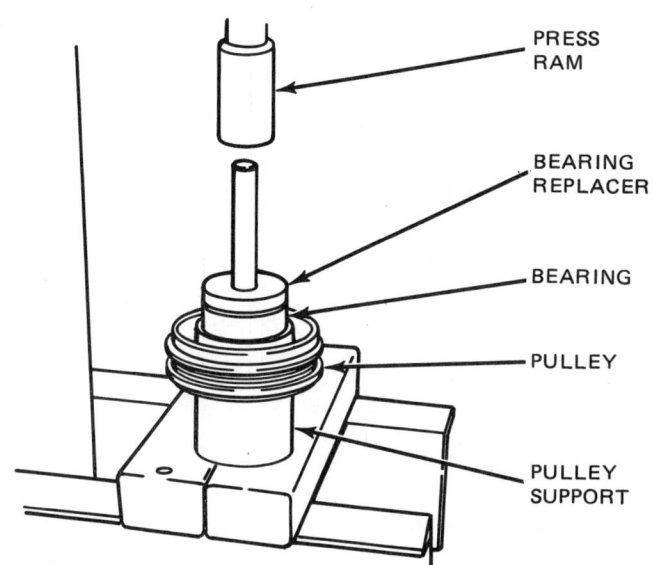

Fig. 9-22 Use a hydraulic press to replace pulley bearing.

Replace Clutch Assembly

1. Place the clutch coil into position and secure it with a snap ring. Be sure that the snap ring is seated.

2. Replace the clutch coil ground wire.

3. Use the plastic hammer to gently tap the pulley onto the compressor. Take care not to damage the pulley.

4. Replace the pulley snap ring. Make sure it is fully seated.

5. Replace the clutch plate shim(s).

6. Replace the clutch plate.

7. Use a nonmetallic feeler gauge and check the clutch plate clearance. Clearance should

138 Chapter Nine, Compressor Repair

be 0.016 inch (4 mm) to 0.028 inch (7 mm). If necessary, add or subtract shim(s) to obtain the proper clearance.

8. Replace the compressor shaft nut and torque to 10-14 ft-lb (13.6-19.0 N·m).
9. Recheck the air gap. Adjust it if necessary. See step 7.

PROCEDURE, PART II

SHAFT SEAL SERVICE

Remove Seal

1. Remove the clutch and coil assembly as outlined in Part I.
2. Remove the felt seal from the seal cavity.
3. Using the O-ring pliers, remove the thrust plate snap ring.
4. Use the shaft key remover, figure 9-23, to remove the shaft key. Set the key aside for reuse.
5. Insert the shaft thrust plate remover/installer into the seal cavity to engage the thrust plate.
6. Hold down on the holder ring and pull out on the T-handle to remove the thrust plate. Discard the thrust plate.
7. Insert the shaft thrust seal remover/installer into the seal cavity and engage the shaft thrust seal. Press against the seal while turning the tool clockwise (cw).
8. Pull the tool out of the seal cavity to remove the seal. Discard the shaft thrust seal.

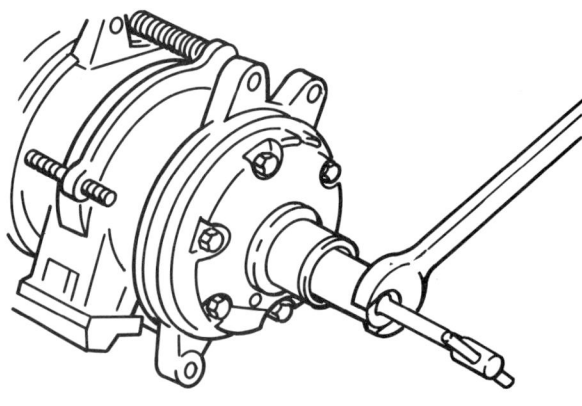

Fig. 9-23 Use the shaft key remover to remove shaft key.

Replace Seal

1. Install the new seal on the thrust seal remover/installer. Engage the seal to the tool by turning the tool or seal clockwise (cw) while applying pressure.
2. Coat the seal and seal cavity liberally with clean refrigeration oil.
3. Insert the seal into the seal cavity until it is fully seated.
4. Rotate the tool counterclockwise (ccw) to release the tool from the seal. Remove the tool from the seal cavity.
5. Use the thrust plate remover/installer to install the new thrust plate.
6. Replace the thrust plate snap ring. Be sure the snap ring is fully seated.
7. Replace the felt seal.
8. Replace the shaft key.
9. Replace the clutch and coil assembly, as outlined in Part I of this procedure.

SERVICE PROCEDURE 3:

SERVICING THE SANKYO COMPRESSOR

Servicing the Sankyo compressor is limited to the shaft oil seal, clutch, and rear head and/or valve plate. This procedure presumes that the compressor has been removed from the vehicle for service.

PROCEDURE

Removing the Clutch

1. Use a 3/4-in. hex socket and spanner wrench to remove the crankshaft hex nut.
2. Remove the clutch front plate, using the clutch front plate puller.
3. Using the snap ring pliers, remove the internal and external snap rings, figures 9-24A and 9-24B.
4. Using the pulley puller, figure 9-25, remove the rotor assembly.
5. If the clutch coil is to be replaced, remove the three retaining screws and the clutch field coil. Omit this step if the coil is not to be replaced.

Fig. 9-24A Removing the internal snap ring

Fig. 9-24B Removing the external snap ring.

Fig. 9-25 Removing the rotor assembly.

140 Chapter Nine, Compressor Repair

Remove the Shaft Seal

1. Remove the shaft key and spacer shims and set aside.
2. Using the snap ring pliers, remove the seal seat retaining snap ring.
3. Remove the seal seat, using the seal seat remover and installer, figure 9-26.
4. Remove the seal, figure 9-27, using the seal remover tool.
5. Remove the shaft seal seat O-ring, figure 9-28, using the O-ring remover.

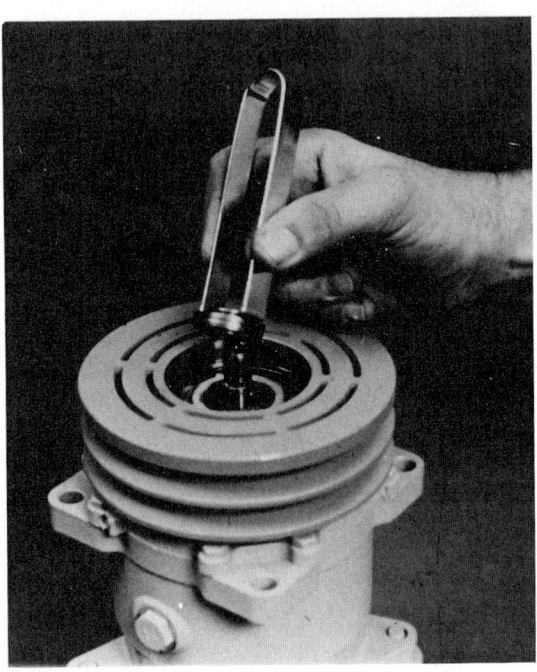

Fig. 9-26 Removing the seal seat.

Fig. 9-27 Removing the seal.

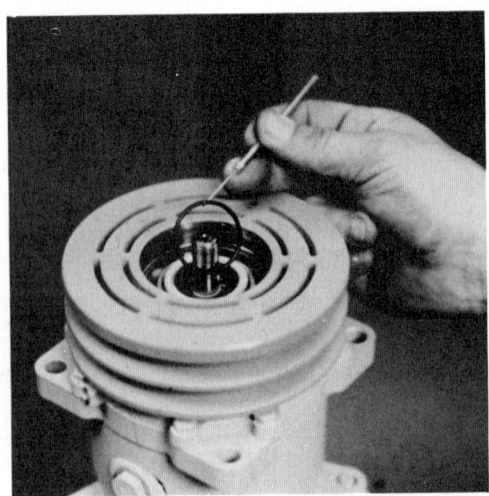

Fig. 9-28 Removing the O-ring.

Install the Shaft Seal

1. Clean the inner bore of the seal cavity by flushing it with clean refrigeration oil.

2. Coat the new seal parts with clean refrigeration oil. *Do not touch* the carbon ring face with the fingers. Normal body acids will etch the seal and cause early failure.

3. Install the new shaft seal seat O-ring. Make sure it is properly seated in the internal groove. Use the remover tool to position the O-ring properly.

4. Install the seal protector on the compressor crankshaft. Lubricate the part liberally with clean refrigeration oil.

5. Place the new shaft seal in the seal installer tool and carefully slide the shaft seal into place in the inner bore. Rotate the shaft seal clockwise (cw) until it seats on the compressor shaft flats.

6. Rotate the tool counterclockwise (ccw) to remove the seal installer tool.

7. Remove the shaft seal protector.

8. Place the shaft seal seat on the remover/installer tool and carefully reinstall it in the compressor seal cavity.

9. Replace the seal seat retainer.

10. Reinstall the spacer shims and shaft key.

Fig. 9-29 Reinstalling the front clutch plate and checking the air gap.

Replace the Clutch

1. Reinstall the field coil (or install a new field coil, if necessary) using the three retaining screws.
2. Align the rotor assembly squarely with the front compressor housing.
3. Using the rotor two-piece installer tools and a soft hammer, carefully drive the rotor into position until it seats on the bottom of the housing.
4. Reinstall the internal and external snap rings using the snap ring pliers.
5. Align the slot in the hub of the front plate squarely with the shaft key.
6. Drive the front plate on the shaft using the installer tool and a soft hammer. *Do not use unnecessary hard blows.*
7. Check the air gap with *go* and *no-go* gauges (see figure 9-29).
8. Replace the shaft nut and tighten it to a torque of 25–30 ft-lb (33.9–40.7 N·m) using the torque wrench.

Remove the Valve Plate Assembly

1. Remove the five screws from the cylinder head using a 13-mm hex socket wrench.
2. Remove the head and valve plate assembly from the cylinder block by tapping lightly with a soft hammer on the gasket scraper which is placed between the valve plate and the cylinder head, figure 9-30.
3. To remove the valve plate, insert the gasket scraper between the valve plate and the cylinder block, figure 9-31. *Do not damage the mating surfaces.*
4. Carefully remove all gasket material, figure 9-32, from the mating surfaces. *Do not nick or scratch the surfaces.*

Install the Valve Plate Assembly

1. Apply a thin coat of clean refrigeration oil to all gaskets and mating surfaces.
2. Install the valve plate gasket on the cylinder block. The alignment pin insures that the gasket is installed properly.
3. Place the valve plate into position. The alignment pin must pass through the pin hole in the valve plate.
4. Install the head gasket on the valve plate. Check for the proper alignment of the gasket.
5. Reinstall the cylinder head and check for the proper alignment.

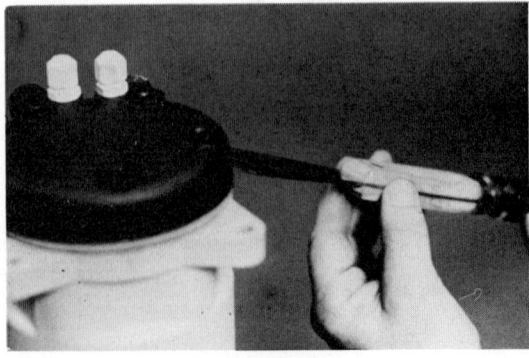

Fig. 9-30 **Removing the rear head.**

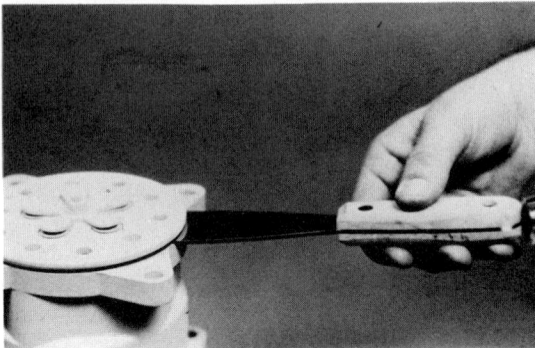

Fig. 9-31 **Removing the valve plate.**

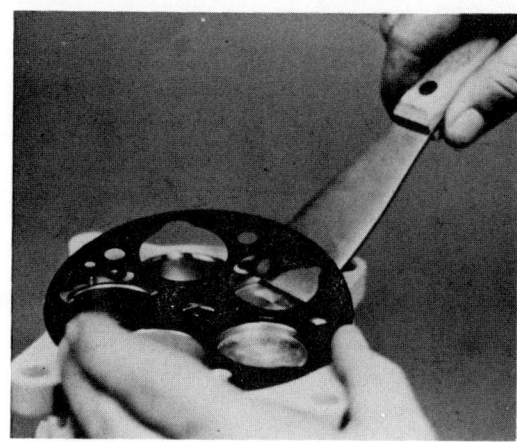

Fig. 9-32 Removing the gasket material.

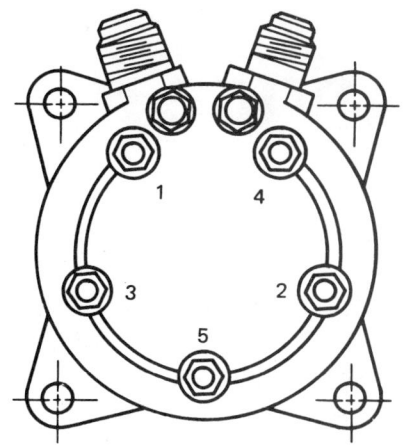

Fig. 9-33 Rear head torque sequence.

6. Install the five hex head screws and tighten them to a snug fit.
7. Tighten the five screws to a torque of 22–25 ft-lb (29.8–33.8 N·m). Tighten the screws in the sequence shown in figure 9-33. *Do not undertighten or overtighten the screws.*
8. Add 1 or 2 ounces (29.5 or 59 mL) of oil to the compressor to compensate for any loss that occurs as a result of this repair.

SERVICE PROCEDURE 4:

SERVICING THE TECUMSEH HR-980 COMPRESSOR

The Tecumseh HR–980 compressor requires special tools for servicing. Since the internal assembly is not accessible, service is limited to shaft seal and clutch repairs.

This service procedure is for servicing the clutch and for replacing the seal.

PROCEDURE

Remove Clutch Assembly

1. Remove retaining nut.
2. Use the hub remover tool and remove the clutch hub from the compressor shaft, figure 9-34. Remove and retain shim(s).
3. Using a spanner wrench, remove the clutch pulley retaining nut.
4. Remove the pulley and bearing assembly from the compressor. If the assembly cannot be removed by hand, use the shaft protector and pulley remover, figure 9-35.
5. Remove the field coil from the compressor.
6. Clean the front of the compressor to remove any dirt and/or corrosion.

Replace Clutch Bearing

1. Place the pulley on the clutch pulley support, as shown in figure 9-36.
2. Use the pulley replacer tool to drive out the bearing.

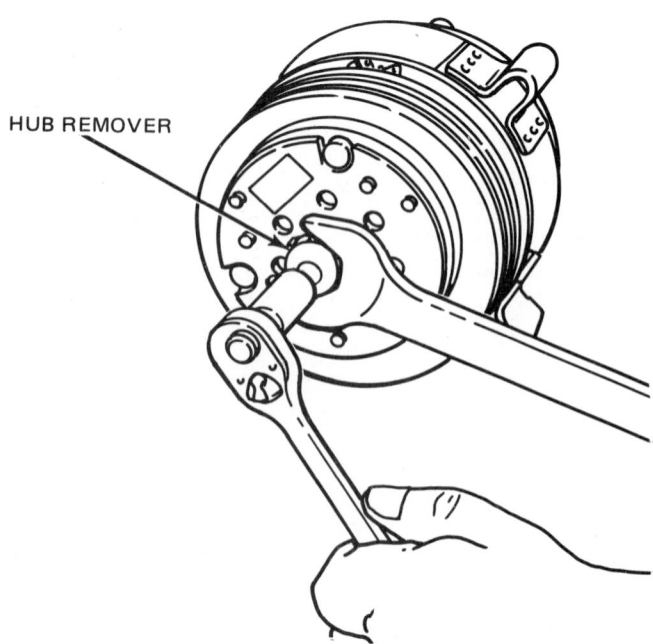

Fig. 9-34 Use hub remover tool to remove clutch hub.

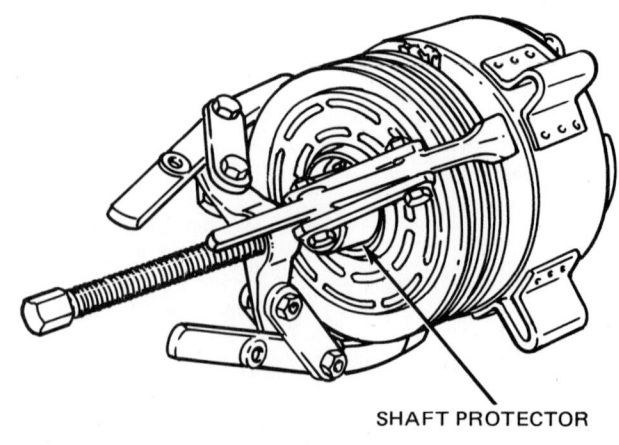

Fig. 9-35 Use shaft protector and pulley remover to remove clutch pulley.

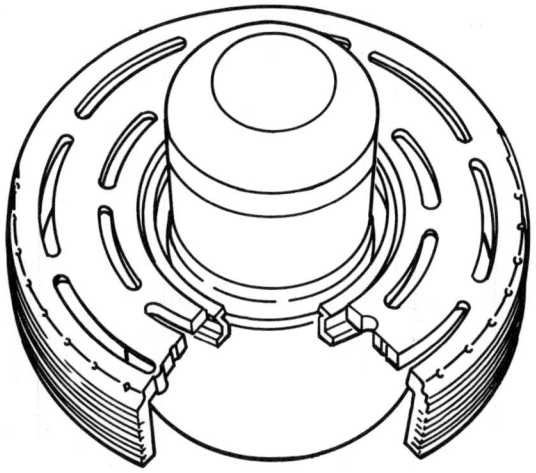

Fig. 9-36 Place pulley on clutch pulley support.

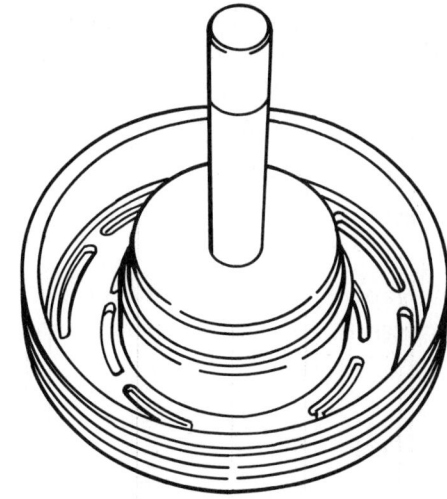

Fig. 9-37 Seat bearing in pulley using tool.

3. Turn the pulley over, flat side atop a clean board.
4. Position the new bearing in the bearing bore of the pulley and use the pulley bearing replacer to seat the bearing, figure 9-37. Be sure that the bearing and bore are aligned.
5. Stake the new bearing. Use a blunt drift or punch at three equally spaced places inside the bore. Do not use the same places that were used to retain the old bearing.

Replace Pulley Assembly

1. Install the field coil. The slots of the coil should fit over the housing lugs. The electrical connector should be toward the top of the compressor.
2. Install the pulley and bearing assembly on the front of the compressor. If properly aligned, the assembly should slide on. If difficult, use pulley replacer and tap lightly with a plastic hammer. *Do not use unnecessary force.*
3. Apply a drop of thread lock to the threads of the pulley retainer nut.
4. Install the pulley retainer nut and tighten to 65-70 ft-lb (88-94 N·m) using spanner and torque wrenches.

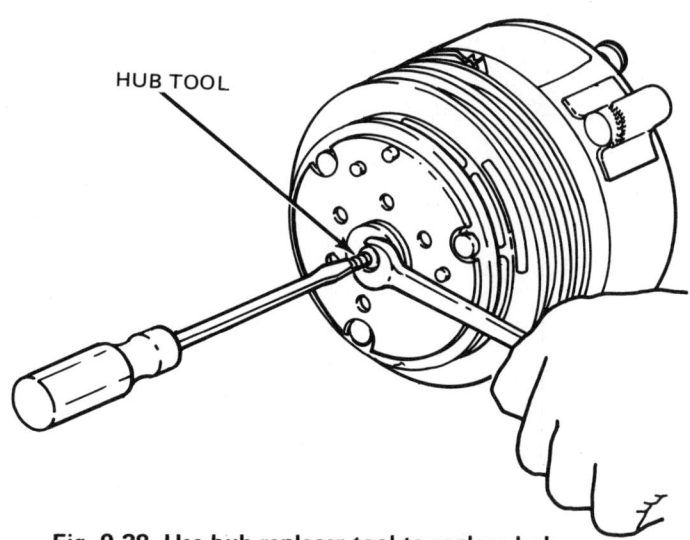

Fig. 9-38 Use hub replacer tool to replace hub.

Chapter Nine, Compressor Repair

5. Being sure that the key is aligned with the keyway of the clutch hub, install the hub and shim(s) onto the compressor shaft. Use the hub replacer, figure 9-38. Do not drive the hub onto the shaft as compressor damage will result.
6. Install the nut and tighten to 10-14 ft-lb (14-18 N·m).
7. Check the air gap at three equally spaced intervals around the pulley. Record the measurements.
8. Rotate the compressor pulley one-half turn (180°) and repeat step 7. The smallest air gap permitted is between 0.021 in (0.53 mm) and 0.036 in (0.91 mm). If greater or less than these specifications, add or remove shims (step 5) to bring air gap into specifications.

Remove Seal

1. Remove the clutch and coil as previously outlined.
2. Remove the key from the compressor shaft.
3. Carefully pry the dust shield from the compressor, using a small screwdriver, figure 9-39. Take care not to damage the end of the compressor housing.
4. Remove the seal snap ring retainer, using the internal snap ring pliers.
5. Clean the inside of the seal cavity to prevent entry of foreign material when the seal is removed.
6. Insert the shaft seal seat tool and engage the seal. Tighten the outer sleeve to expand the tool in the seal seat, figure 9-40.

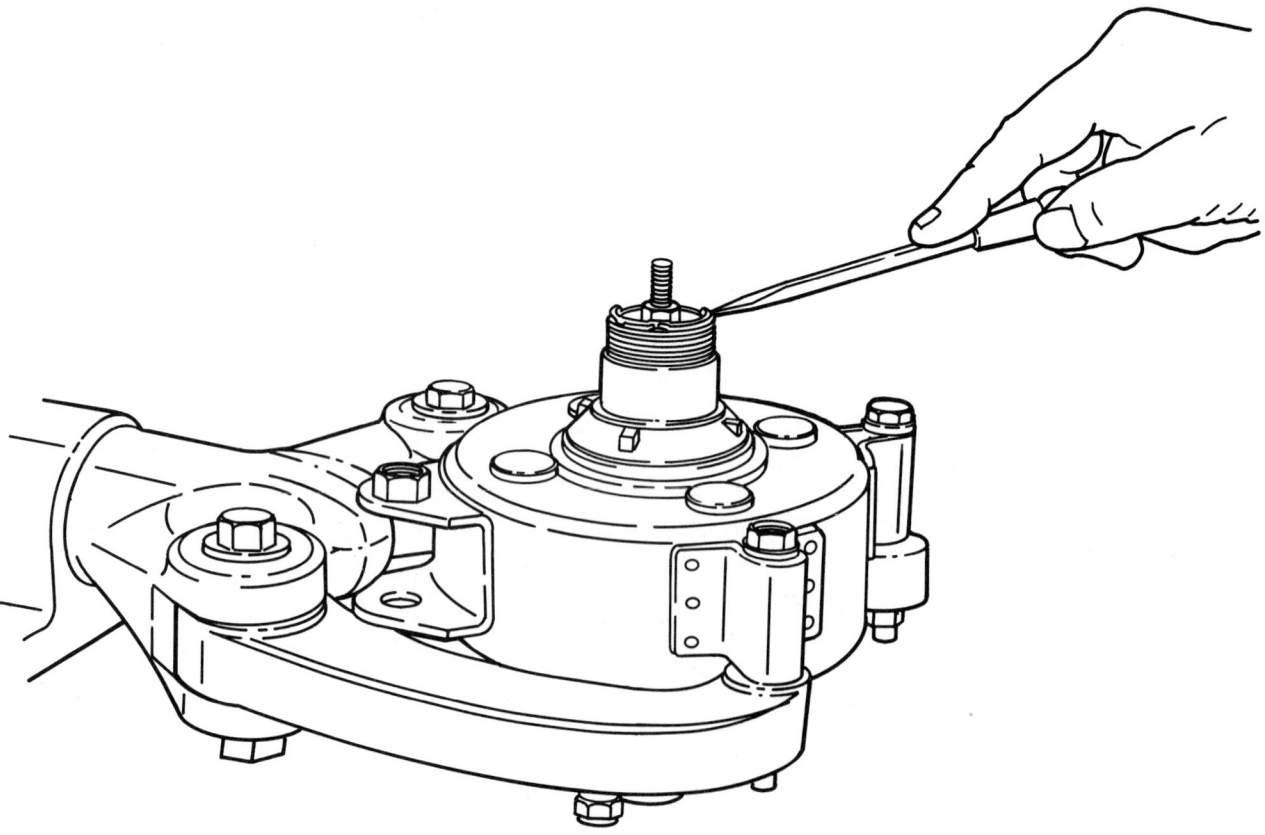

Fig. 9-39 Use screwdriver to pry dust shield from seal cavity.

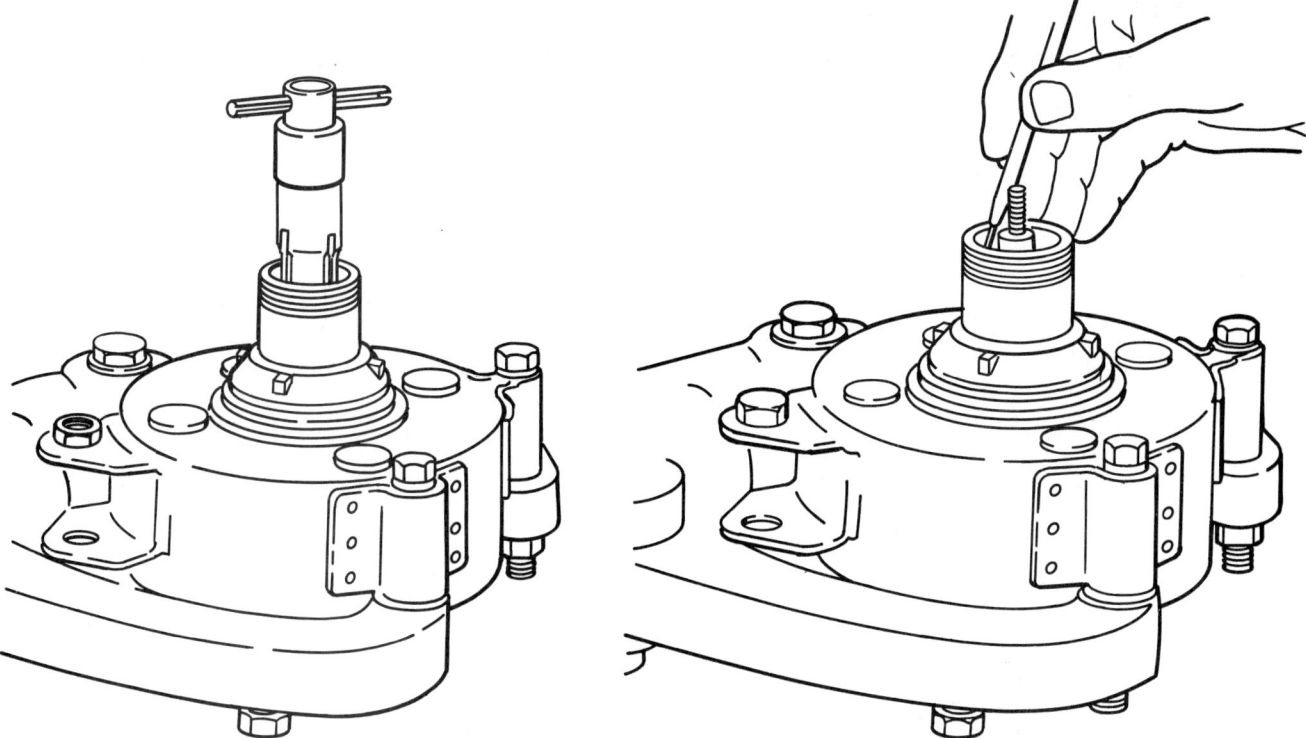

Fig. 9-40 Insert shaft seal seat tool into seal cavity.

Fig. 9-41 Remove O-ring using O-ring remover tool.

7. Pull on the tool, while rotating it clockwise (cw), to remove the seal seat.
8. Use the O-ring remover and remove the O-ring, figure 9-41.
9. Insert the seal assembly tool into the compressor. While forcing the tool downward, rotate it counterclockwise (ccw) to engage the tangs of the seal, figure 9-42.
10. Pull the seal from the compressor and remove the seal from the tool.
11. Check the inside of the compressor to insure that all surfaces are free of nicks and burrs.

Install Seal

1. Coat the O-ring liberally with clean refrigeration oil and insert it into the cavity, using the O-ring installer, O-ring sleeve, and O-ring guide.
2. With the O-ring in place, remove the tools from the cavity.
3. Coat the shaft seal liberally with clean refrigeration oil and carefully engage the seal with the seal remover/replacer tool, figure 9-43.
4. Carefully place the seal over the shaft and, while rotating it, slide the seal down the shaft until the assembly engages the flats and is in place.
5. Rotate the tool to disengage it from the seal. Remove the tool from the cavity.
6. Coat the seal seat liberally with clean refrigeration oil and engage the seal seat with the remover/replacer tool, figure 9-44.
7. Carefully insert the seal seat onto the compressor shaft with a clockwise (cw) rotation. Take care not to disturb the O-ring installed in step 1.

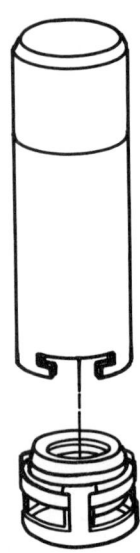

Fig. 9-42 Insert seal on remover/replacer tool.

8. Disengage the tool from the seal seat and remove the tool.
9. Using snap ring pliers, install the snap ring.
10. Place the compressor in a horizontal position and install the pressure test fitting.
11. Pressurize the compressor with Refrigerant 12 to 50 psig (344.75 kPa).
12. Leak test as outlined in Chapter Seven. If the shaft seal leaks, install the shaft nut and rotate the compressor shaft several turns by hand. Recheck for leaks.
13. Remove the nut. Release pressure and remove the test fitting.
14. Install the dust shield.
15. Replace the clutch and coil as previously outlined.

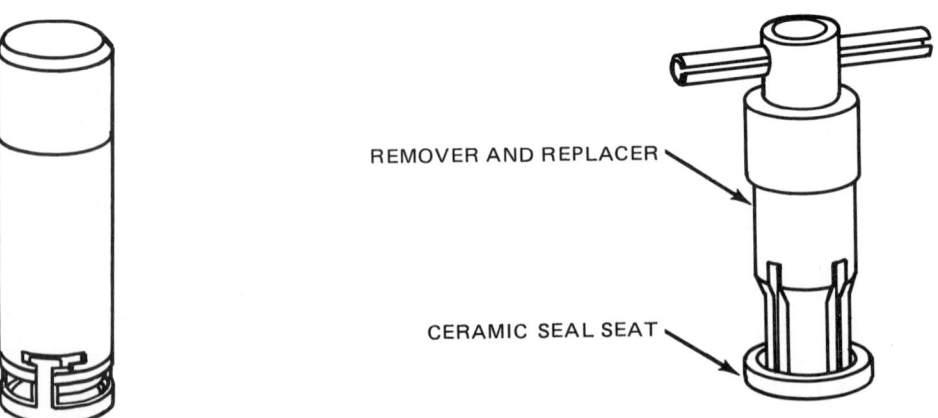

Fig. 9-43 Engage seal with remover/replacer tool.

Fig. 9-44 Engage seal seat with remover/replacer tool.

SERVICE PROCEDURE 5:

REPLACING THE COMPRESSOR SHAFT OIL SEAL (YORK AND TECUMSEH COMPRESSORS)

This procedure can be followed when it is necessary to replace the compressor shaft oil seal. If the seal area can be serviced on the car, it is not necessary to remove the compressor from its mountings. If the engine fan or radiator clearance makes it impossible to remove the clutch for seal service, the compressor must be removed from the car.

PROCEDURE

Prepare the Compressor for Service

1. Isolate the compressor or purge system of refrigerant.
2. Using a 1/2-inch socket, remove the 7/16-inch Nyloc bolt from the compressor crankshaft at the clutch hub.
3. Using a 5/8-inch NC bolt, remove the clutch rotor. This bolt is inserted into the clutch hub at the point where the 7/16-inch Nyloc bolt was removed, figure 9-45.
4a. If the fields of a stationary field clutch are mounted on the seal plate, remove the three retaining bolts and remove the fields.
4b. If the rotating fields and brushes are mounted on the seal plate, remove the brushes. Take care not to break the soft carbon brushes.
5. Clean the seal plate and all adjoining surfaces.
6. Remove the Woodruff key, figure 9-46.

Remove the Seal Assembly

1. Remove the six (or remaining three) capscrews from the seal plate.
2. Gently pry the seal plate loose. Be careful not to nick or mar the crankcase mating surface or the compressor crankshaft, figure 9-47.

Fig. 9-45 Using a 5/8-inch NC bolt to remove the clutch pulley from the York compressor.

Fig. 9-46 Removing the Woodruff key before servicing the seal assembly.

150 Chapter Nine, Compressor Repair

Fig 9-47 Remove the capscrews and then remove the seal plate.

Fig. 9-48 Carefully remove the shaft seal assembly. Take care not to damage mating surfaces.

3. Remove the seal nose assembly from the crankshaft by prying behind the seal. Be careful not to nick or mar the crankshaft, figure 9-48.

4. With a razor blade, remove all gasket material from the crankcase mating surface.

Install the New Seal Assembly

1. Soak the new seal and all gaskets in clean refrigeration oil for a few minutes. Apply ample oil to the crankshaft and mating parts.

2. Remove the carbon nose end from the shaft seal and slide the shaft seal on the crankshaft. If drive pins are located in the shaft shoulder, line up the notches in the shaft seal spring holder to engage. *If the new seal does not have notches, remove the drive pins.*

3. Install the seal nose, figure 9-49. Flush the assembly with clean refrigeration oil.

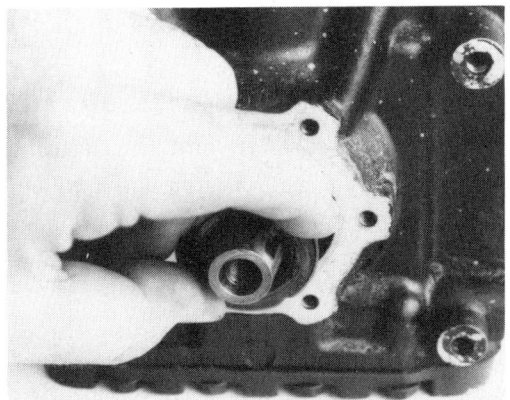

Fig. 9-49 Coat the new seal assembly with clean refrigeration oil and carefully slide the assembly onto the compressor crankshaft.

Install the New Seal Plate

1. Use clean refrigeration oil to flush the seal plate and seal nose to remove any foreign particles.

2. *York Compressor:* Place the new seal plate and gasket(s) over the crankshaft; then move the seal back to the final operating position. Insert the original three (or six) capscrews and adjust them until they are fingertight.

   Tecumseh Compressor: Place the new seal plate and O-ring over the crankshaft and move the seal back to the final operating position. Insert the original three (or six) capscrews and tighten them until they are fingertight.

3. Rotate the compressor crankshaft to insure that there is no binding due to misalignment.

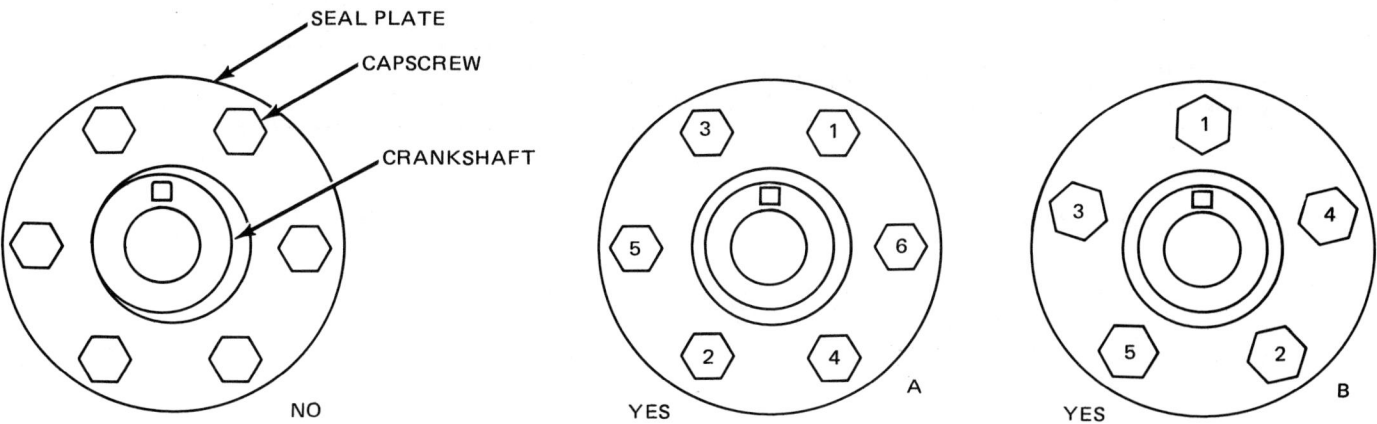

Fig. 9-50 Before attempting to torque the capscrews in the seal plate, be sure that the plate is not off-center to the crankshaft as illustrated on the left. Note an almost even air gap between the seal plate and the crankshaft on the right. Torque the capscrews according to the sequence shown: A for six capscrew seal plate, and B for five capscrew seal plate.

4. Check that there is an even clearance between the crankshaft and the seal plate all around.
5. Tighten all capscrews evenly to a torque of 10–12 ft-lb (13.6–16.3 N·m). Tighten the capscrews in a diagonally opposite sequence, figure 9-50.

Return the Compressor to Service

1. Replace the clutch field or brush assembly.
2. Replace the Woodruff key in the crankshaft.
3. Replace the clutch rotor and 5/16-inch Nyloc bolt.

SERVICE PROCEDURE 6:

REPLACING THE COMPRESSOR SHAFT OIL SEAL (CHRYSLER AIR-TEMP)

This procedure can be used when it is necessary to replace the compressor shaft oil seal on a Chrysler Air-Temp unit. In general, the seal can be replaced without removing the compressor.

PROCEDURE

Prepare the Compressor for Service

NOTE: If the compressor is equipped with both high- and low-side service valves, the compressor can be isolated. If the compressor is not equipped with high- and low-side service valves, the system must be purged of refrigerant.

1. Using a 1/2-inch socket, remove the 7/16-inch bolt from the crankshaft. The bolt is located at the clutch hub.
2. Using a 5/8-inch NF or NC bolt, remove the clutch rotor. This bolt is inserted into the clutch hub at the point where the 7/16-inch bolt was removed.
3. If the clutch is equipped with stationary fields, locate the three screws holding it to the seal housing. Remove the screws and the fields. If the unit is equipped with rotating fields, carefully remove the brush set by removing the two screws holding the set to the seal housing.
4. Clean the seal plate and all adjacent surfaces.

Remove the Old Seal Assembly

1. Remove the Woodruff key from the crankshaft.
2. Remove the bearing housing bolts.
3. Remove the bearing housing by inserting two screwdrivers in the slots provided and prying the housing from the crankcase, figure 9-51.
4. Remove the bearing housing O-ring gasket and discard it.
5. Remove the stationary seat and gasket assembly from the bearing housing and discard it.
6. Remove the shaft seal assembly from the crankshaft, using a small screwdriver. Discard this assembly. Take care not to nick or scratch the crankshaft.
7. Clean all foreign material from the bearing housing and crankshaft.
8. It may be necessary to polish these surfaces liberally with clean refrigeration oil.

Install New Seal Assembly

1. Lubricate the crankshaft, the bearing housing and all adjacent parts with clean refrigeration oil.
2. Dip the stationary seat and gasket assembly into clean refrigeration oil for a few minutes.
3. Install the stationary seat and gasket assembly into the bearing housing. Insure that it is fully seated. Do not damage the seal surface.
4. Place the bearing housing O-ring in the groove provided.

5. Dip the seal assembly into clean refrigeration oil for a few minutes.
6. Slide the seal assembly on the compressor crankshaft. Insure that the carbon nose of the seal assembly is facing outward.
7. Install the crankshaft bearing housing, with the seal and O-ring in place, on the crankcase body. Replace the capscrews and draw them in uniformly.
8. Tighten the bearing housing capscrews to a torque of 10–13 ft-lb (13.6–17.6 N·m).
9. Replace the Woodruff key. Replace the brush or field assembly.
10. Replace the clutch assembly and the 5/16-inch retaining bolt.

Fig. 9-51 Removing the crankshaft bearing housing.

SERVICE PROCEDURE 7:

SERVICING THE DELCO AIR FOUR-CYLINDER COMPRESSOR

This service procedure is given in two parts: Part I for clutch service and Part II for seal service. Either service may be performed on the car if there is sufficient room. This procedure, however, assumes that the compressor has been removed from the vehicle.

PROCEDURE, PART I

CLUTCH SERVICE

Removing the Clutch Plate and Hub Assembly

1. Using the clutch hub holding tool and a 9/16-inch thinwall socket, remove the retaining nut from the compressor shaft.
2. Using the clutch plate and hub assembly remover tool, remove the clutch plate and hub assembly.
3. If the shaft key is not removed in step 2, remove the shaft key.

Clutch Rotor-Bearing and Coil-Pulley Rim Removal

1. Mark the location of the clutch coil terminals to insure proper reassembly.
2. Remove the rotor and bearing assembly retaining ring using the snap ring pliers, figure 9-52.
3. Install the rotor bearing and puller guide over the end of the compressor shaft, figure 9-53. *The guide should seat on the front head of the compressor.*
4. Using a puller, remove the clutch rotor and assembly parts, figure 9-54.

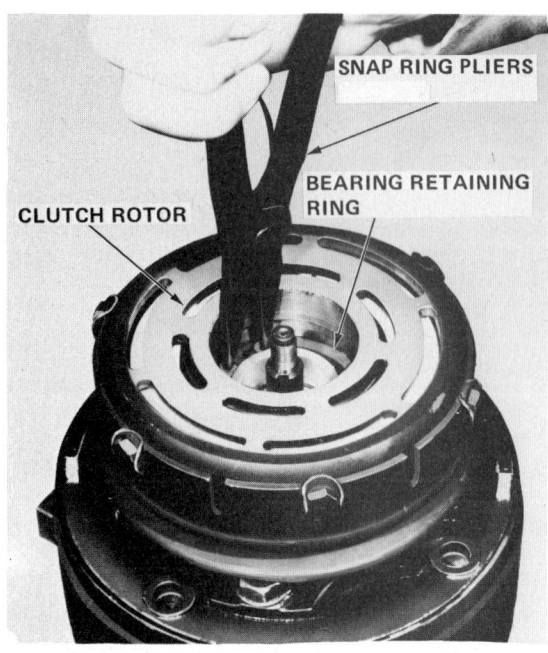

Fig. 9-52 Removing the bearing retaining ring.

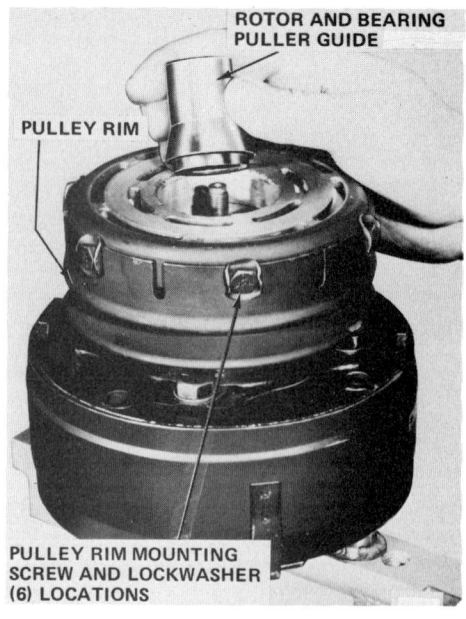

Fig. 9-53 Positioning the rotor and bearing puller guide.

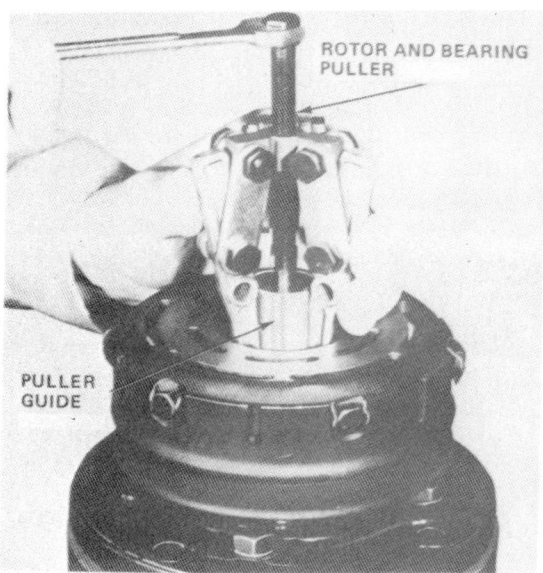

Fig. 9-54 Removing the clutch rotor.

Fig. 9-55 Bending the locking tabs to allow removal of the capscrews.

Fig. 9-56 Separating the pulley rim from the rotor. The clutch coil is found in this assembly.

Split the Clutch Rotor-Bearing and Coil-Pulley Rim

1. Using a cold chisel and hammer, bend the tabs of the six pulley rim mounting screw lockwashers flat, figure 9-55.
2. Using a 7/16-inch 6-point box wrench, loosen and remove all six screws.
3. Separate the pulley rim from the rotor, figure 9-56.

Replacing the Bearing

1. Place the rotor and bearing assembly, split side down, atop two soft wood blocks, figure 9-57.

156 Chapter Nine, Compressor Repair

2. Using the appropriate tool, with hammer, drive the bearing from the rotor, figure 9-58. The bearing may also be removed with an arbor press.
3. Turn the rotor over with the frictional surface resting on a block of soft wood.
4. Using the appropriate tool, with hammer, drive the bearing into the rotor. To insure the alignment of the bearing outer surface into the rotor inner surface, the use of an arbor press, figure 9-59, is recommended.

Fig. 9-57 Place the rotor atop two soft wood blocks.

Fig. 9-58 Driving the old bearing from the rotor.

Fig. 9-59 Pressing the new bearing into the rotor.

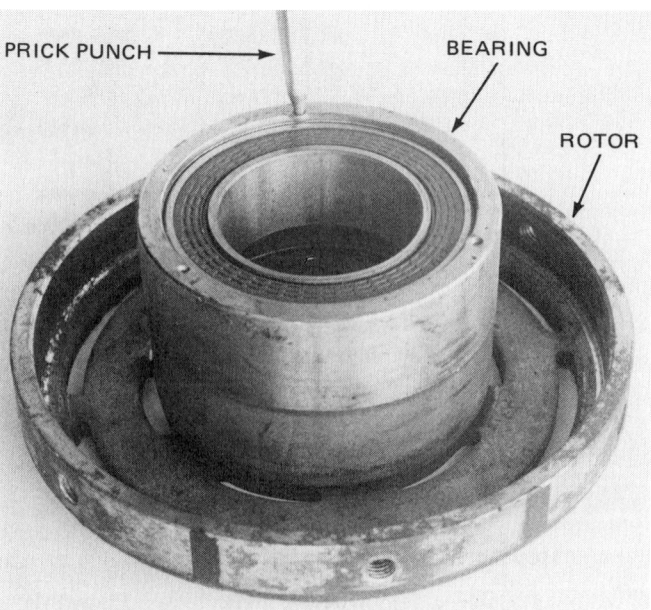

Fig. 9-60 Using a prick punch to stake the bearing into the rotor.

Fig. 9-61 Bend the tabs against the capscrews to prevent loosening during use.

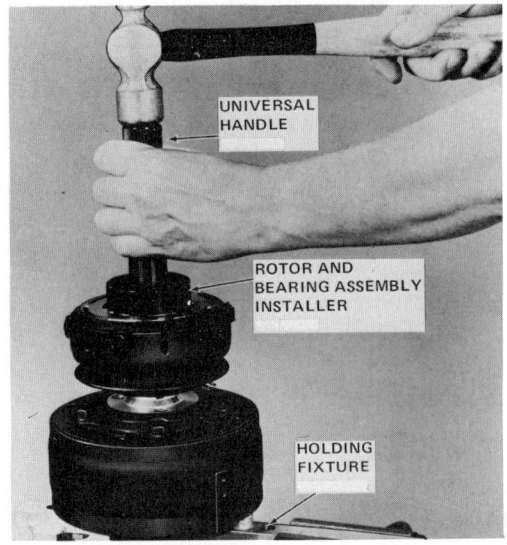

Fig. 9-62 Using the rotor and bearing assembly installer.

5. After the bearing is seated in the rotor, use a prick punch to stake it in place, figure 9-60.

Reassemble the Clutch Rotor-Bearing and Coil-Pulley Rim

1. With the coil in place, join the pulley rim to the rotor.
2. Replace and/or tighten the six retaining screws using a 7/16-inch 6-point box wrench.
3. Using a cold chisel and hammer, bend the tabs of the six mounting screw lockwashers up against a flat of each of the screws (one tab for each screw), figure 9-61.

Fig. 9-63 Key, inserted into the keyway of the hub, should protrude 3/16 inch (4.7 mm).

Replace the Clutch Rotor-Bearing and Coil-Pulley Rim

1. Position the assembly on the front head of the compressor.
2. Using the rotor assembly installer with a universal handle, figure 9-62, drive the assembly into place. *Before the assembly is fully seated, insure that the coil terminals are in the proper location and the three protrusions on the rear of the coil housing align with the locator holes in the front head.*
3. Install the retainer ring, using snap ring pliers.

Replace the Clutch Plate and Hub Assembly

1. Clean the frictional surfaces of the clutch plate and rotor, if necessary.
2. Insert the key into the slot (keyway) of the hub. *Do not insert the key into the compressor crankshaft slot (keyway).*

   NOTE: The key should protrude about 3/16 inch (0.187 5 in or 4.7 mm) below the hub, figure 9-63.

158 Chapter Nine, Compressor Repair

3. Place the clutch plate and hub assembly onto the compressor shaft by matching the key of the hub to the keyway of the shaft.
4. Using a clutch plate and hub installer, press this part on the crankshaft. *Do not hammer this part into position.*
5. Use a nonmagnetic feeler gauge to insure an air gap of 0.020 to 0.040 inch (0.508 to 1.016 mm) between the frictional surfaces.
6. Replace the shaft nut and torque to 8–12 ft-lb (10.8–16.3 N·m).

PROCEDURE, PART II

SEAL SERVICE

Remove the Old Seal

1. Using a 9/16-inch thinwall socket wrench and clutch hub holding tool, remove the shaft nut, figure 9-64.
2. Using a clutch hub and drive plate puller, remove this part, figure 9-65.
3. Remove the shaft seal seat retainer ring using the snap ring pliers.
4. Remove the seal seat using a shaft seal seat remover.
5. Using the shaft seal remover, remove the shaft seal, figure 9-66.
6. Using an O-ring remover (a wire with a hook on the end), remove the shaft seal seat O-ring. *Take care not to scratch the mating surfaces.*

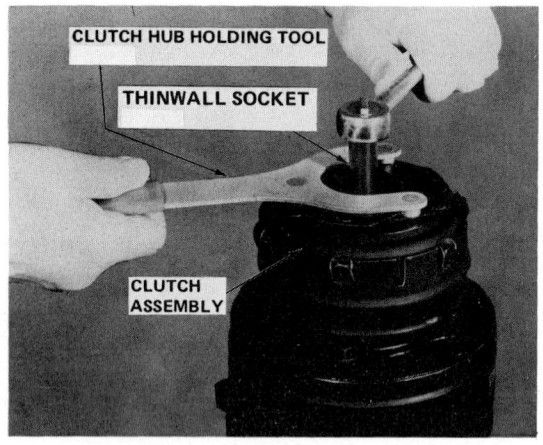

Fig. 9-64 Removing the shaft locknut.

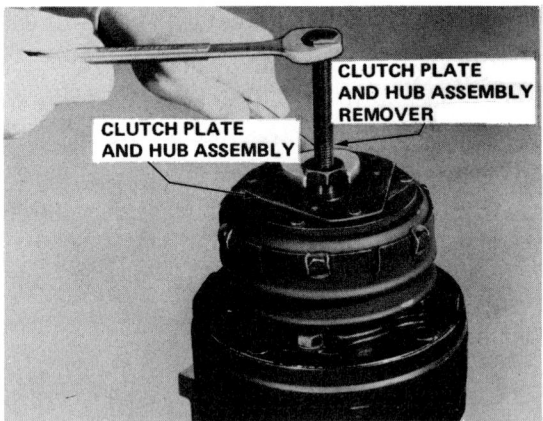

Fig. 9-65 Removing the hub and drive plate assembly.

Install the New Seal

1. Insure that the inner bore of the compressor is free of all foreign matter. Flush the area with clean refrigeration oil.
2. Place the seal seat O-ring on the installer tool and slide the O-ring into place, figure 9-67. Remove the tool.
3. Coat the shaft seal liberally with refrigeration oil and place it on the shaft seal installer tool. Slide the shaft into place in the bore. Rotate the seal clockwise until it seats on the flats provided. Rotate the tool counterclockwise and remove it.

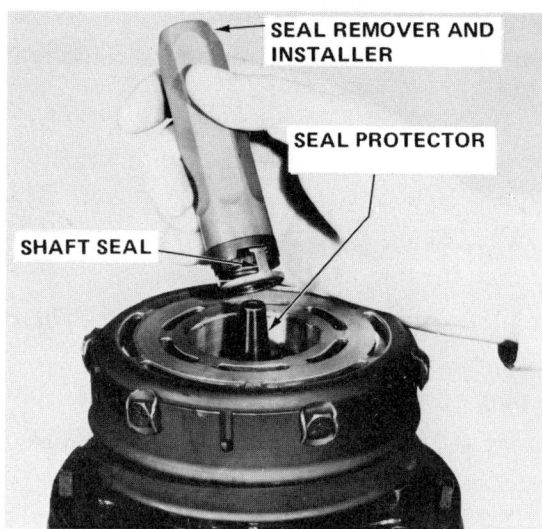

Fig. 9-66 Removing the shaft seal assembly.

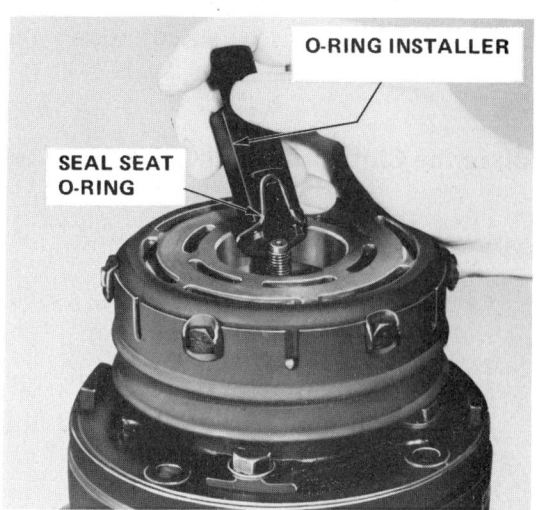

Fig. 9-67 Installing the seal seat O-ring.

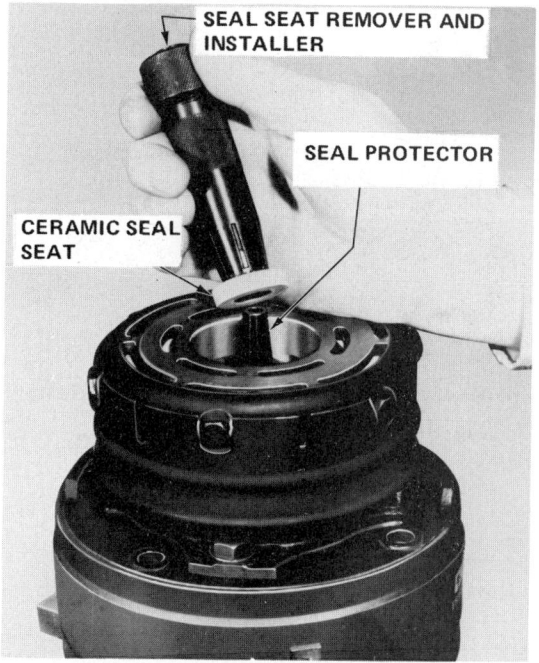

Fig. 9-68 Installing the shaft seal seat.

4. Place the shaft seal seat on the remover/installer tool, figure 9-68. Slide the shaft seal seat into position and remove the tool.

5. Install the shaft seal seat snap ring. Note that the beveled edge of the snap ring must face the outside of the compressor.

6. Before replacing the clutch hub and drive plate, the seal should be checked for leaks.

Leak Test the Shaft Seal

1. With the test fitting in place, connect the manifold and gauge set to the test ports.

2. Tap a can of refrigerant and purge the lines of air. Open the high- and low-side manifold hand valves to allow the refrigerant pressure to enter the compressor.

3. With a leak detector, check the shaft seal area for escaping refrigerant.

4. If a small leak is detected, rotate the crankshaft a few turns to seat the seal; then recheck the seal area for leaks.

Replace the Clutch Hub and Drive Plate Assembly

1. Place the drive key into the clutch plate keyway, figure 9-69. About 3/16 inch (4.8 mm) of the key should be allowed to protrude over the end of the keyway.

2. Align the key with the keyways of the drive plate and compressor crankshaft. Then slide the drive plate into position.

3. Using a hub and drive plate installer, press this part on the crankshaft.

4. A clearance of 0.030 inch ±0.010 in (0.76 mm ± 0.25 mm) should exist between the drive plate and the rotor.

5. Replace the shaft nut.

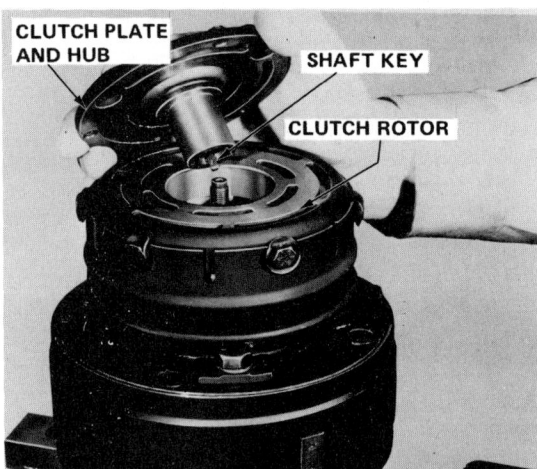

Fig. 9-69 Drive plate key installed.

SERVICE PROCEDURE 8:

SERVICING THE DELCO AIR SIX-CYLINDER COMPRESSOR (A-6)

Special service tools are required to service this compressor clutch. They are available from several sources, such as Robinair and Kent Moore. The following service procedure is based on the use of the proper service tools, and assumes that the compressor has been removed from the car.

PROCEDURE

Hub and Drive Plate Removal

1. Mount the compressor in a holding fixture and secure the fixture in a vise.
2. Using a drive plate holding tool and the 9/16-in thinwall socket, remove the locknut from the shaft.
3. Using the snap ring pliers, remove the clutch hub retaining ring. Remove the spacer under the ring.
4. Remove the hub and drive plate with the hub and drive plate remover tool, figure 9-70.

Pulley and Bearing Assembly Removal

1. Using the snap ring pliers, remove the pulley and bearing snap ring retainer, figure 9-71.
2. Place a puller pilot over the crankshaft. Using a pulley puller, remove the pulley, figure 9-72.
   NOTE: The puller pilot must be in place. Placing the puller against the crankshaft will damage the internal assembly.

Fig. 9-70 Removing the hub and drive plate assembly.

Fig. 9-71 Removing the pulley retaining ring.

162 Chapter Nine, Compressor Repair

Fig. 9-72 Removing the pulley.

Fig. 9-73 Removing the coil housing retainer ring.

3. If the pulley bearing is to be replaced, use a sharp tool, such as a small screwdriver, to remove the wire retaining ring.
4. From the rear of the pulley, press or drive the bearing out.

Coil Housing Assembly

1. Scribe the location of the coil housing with relation to the compressor body to insure proper alignment during reassembly.
2. Using snap ring pliers, remove the coil housing retainer ring, figure 9-73.
3. Lift off the coil housing assembly.

Remove the Old Seal

1. Remove the shaft seal seat retainer ring using internal snap ring pliers, figure 9-74.
2. Remove the seal seat using a shaft seal seat remover, figure 9-75. (Use the appropriate tool.)

Fig. 9-74 Removing the shaft seal retainer.

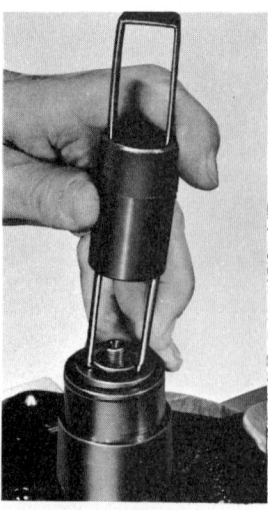

Fig. 9-75 Removing the seal seat.

Fig. 9-76 Removing the shaft seal assembly.

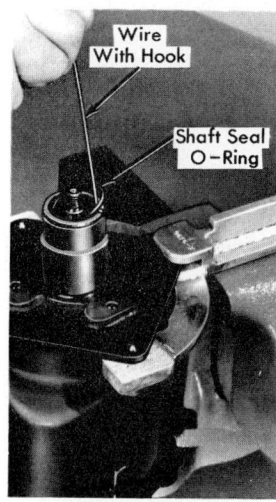

Fig. 9-77 Removing the seal seat O-ring.

3. Using the shaft seal remover, remove the shaft seal, figure 9-76.

4. Using an O-ring remover (a wire with a hook on the end), remove the shaft seal seat O-ring, figure 9-77. *Take care not to scratch the mating surfaces.*

Install the New Seal

1. Insure that the inner bore of the compressor is free of all foreign matter. Flush the area with clean refrigeration oil.

2. Wet the seal seat O-ring with refrigerant oil and place it on the seal installer tool; slide the O-ring into place; then, remove the tool.

3. Coat the shaft seal liberally with refrigeration oil and place it on the shaft seal installer tool. Slide the shaft seal into place in the bore. Rotate the seal clockwise until it seats on the flats provided. Rotate the tool counterclockwise and remove it.

4. Wet the shaft seal seat with refrigerant oil and place it on the remover/installer tool. Slide the shaft seal seat into position and remove the tool.

5. Install the shaft seal seat snap ring. Note that the beveled edge of the snap ring must face the outside of the compressor.

6. Before replacing the clutch hub and drive plate, the seal should be checked for leaks.

Replace the Coil Housing

1. Note the original position of the coil housing by the scribe marks.
2. Slip the coil housing into place.
3. Replace the snap ring to secure the housing.

Replace the Pulley and the Bearing Assembly

1. Press the new bearing into the pulley, figure 9-78, and replace the wire retaining ring (if bearing replacement is necessary).

164 Chapter Nine, Compressor Repair

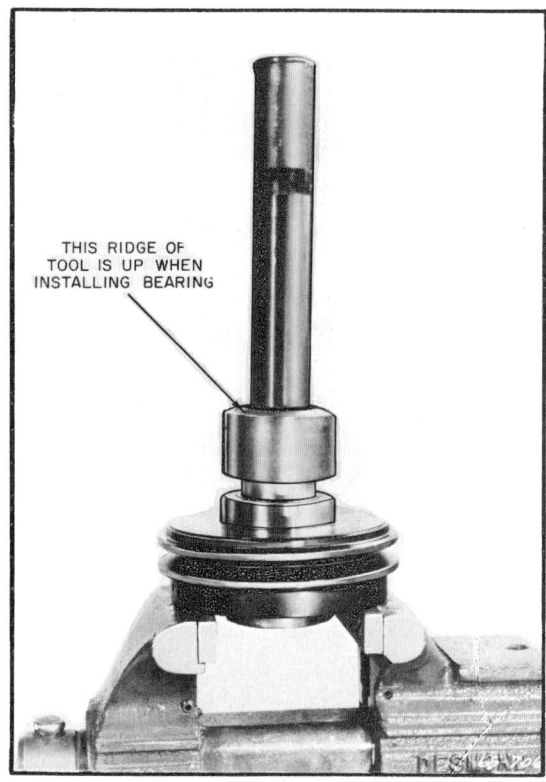

Fig. 9-78 Installing the pulley and drive plate bearing.

Fig. 9-79 Installing the pulley and drive plate on the compressor.

Fig. 9-80 Drive plate key installed in keyway.

2. Using the proper tool, figure 9-79, press or drive the pulley and bearing assembly on the compressor front head.

3. Install the retainer snap ring.

Replace the Clutch Hub and Drive Plate Assembly

1. Place the drive key into the crankshaft keyway, figure 9-80. About 3/16 inch (4.8 mm) of the key should be allowed to protrude over the end of the keyway.

2. Align the key with the keyways of the drive plate and compressor crankshaft. Then slide the drive plate into position.

   NOTE: Take care not to force the drive key into the shaft seal. Occasional rotation of the drive plate during assembly insures that it is seated properly.

3. Using a hub and drive plate installer, press this part on the crankshaft, figure 9-81. (Refer to the note following step 2 of this procedure.)

4. A clearance of 0.030 inch ±0.010 in (0.76 mm ± 0.25 mm) should exist between the drive plate and rotor, figure 9-82.

5. Replace the spacer and clutch hub retainer ring. The retainer ring is installed using the snap ring plier.

6. Replace the shaft nut and torque to specifications, as applicable.

Fig. 9-81 Installing the drive plate.

Fig. 9-82 Checking the air gap.

SERVICE PROCEDURE 9:

SERVICING THE DELCO AIR DA-6 COMPRESSOR

This service procedure is given in six parts. Part I for Clutch Service, Part II for Compressor Shaft Seal Service, Part III for Rear Head Service, Part IV for Front Head Service, Part V for Compressor Cylinder and Shaft Assembly, and Part VI for Center Cylinder Seal.

PROCEDURE, PART I

CLUTCH SERVICE

Remove Clutch

1. Clamp the compressor into an appropriate holding fixture.
2. Hold the clutch hub with the clutch hub holding tool and remove the shaft nut, figure 9-83.
3. Use the clutch plate and hub installer/remover tool to remove the clutch hub, figure 9-84.
4. Remove the shaft key and set aside for reassembly.
5. Use the snap ring pliers to remove the rotor snap ring, figure 9-85.
6. Use the pulley rotor and bearing guide over the compressor shaft and insert the puller in the rotor slots to remove the rotor, figure 9-86.

Remove Clutch Coil

1. Mark the clutch coil terminal location on the compressor front head for ease in reassembly.
2. Install the puller pilot on the front head.
3. Install the puller and tighten the forcing screw against the pilot to remove the clutch coil, figure 9-87.

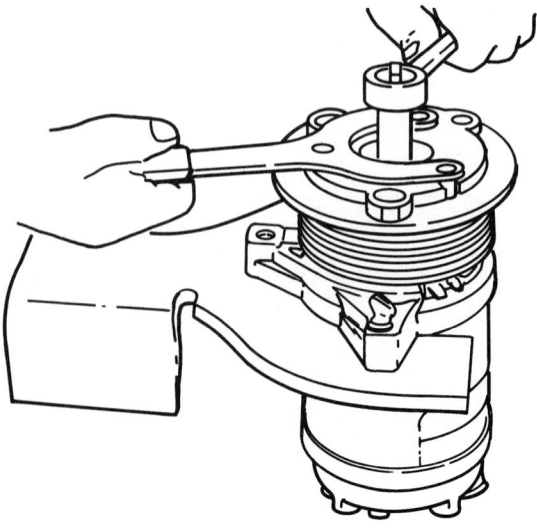

Fig. 9-83 Remove the shaft nut while holding the clutch hub.

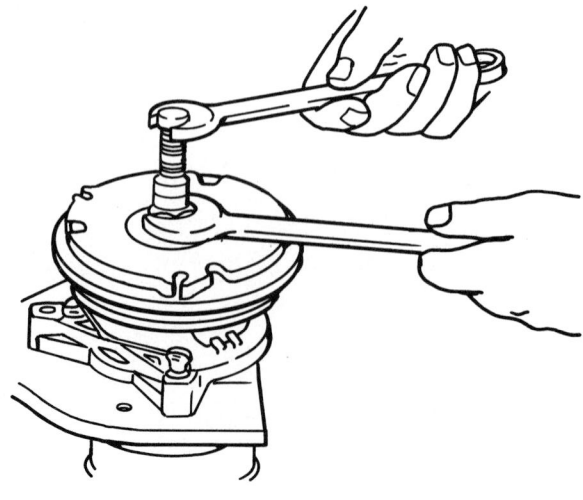

Fig. 9-84 Remove the clutch hub.

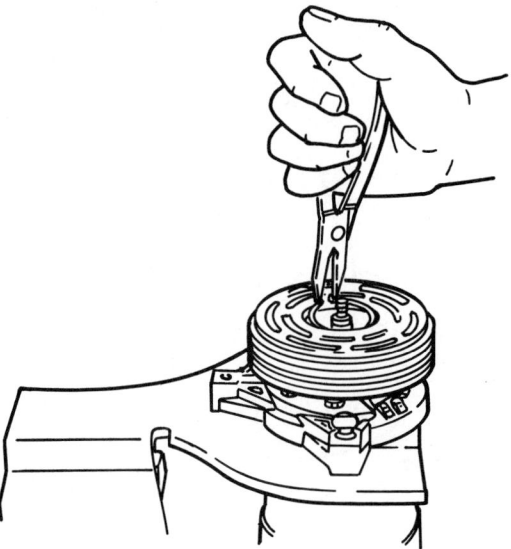

Fig. 9-85 Use snap ring pliers to remove the snap ring.

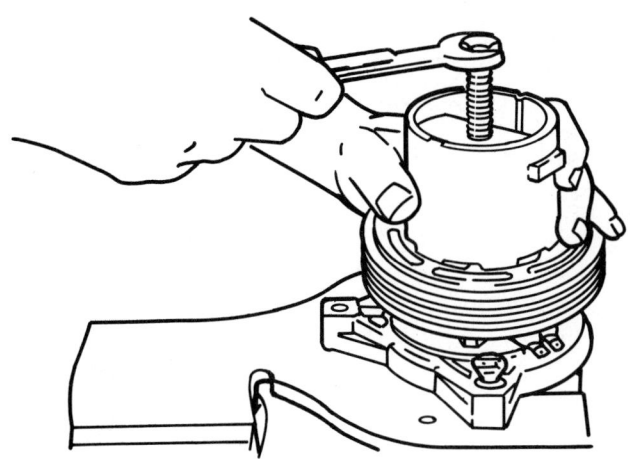

Fig. 9-86 Remove the rotor using the rotor remover tool.

Replace Bearing

1. Attach the rotor and bearing puller tool (less forcing screw) to the rotor. Place the puller atop a solid flat surface, figure 9-88.
2. With the rotor bearing remover tool and universal handle, drive the bearing out of the rotor hub.
3. Remove the rotor and bearing puller tool from the rotor.
4. Place the rotor on the support block, figure 9-89, to support the rotor during bearing installation.
5. Align the bearing with the hub bore. Using the puller and bearing installer tool, drive the bearing fully into the hub.

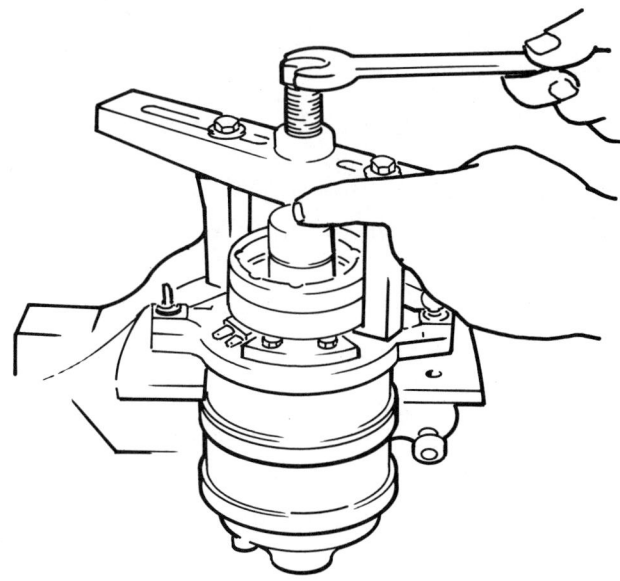

Fig. 9-87 Remove the clutch coil.

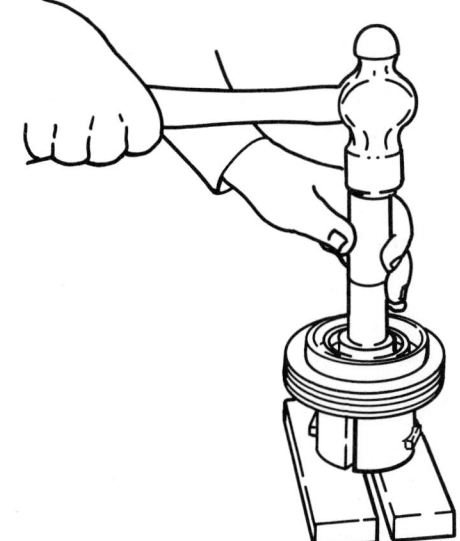

Fig. 9-88 Place the puller atop a solid flat surface and, using the rotor bearing remover tool, drive the bearing out of the rotor.

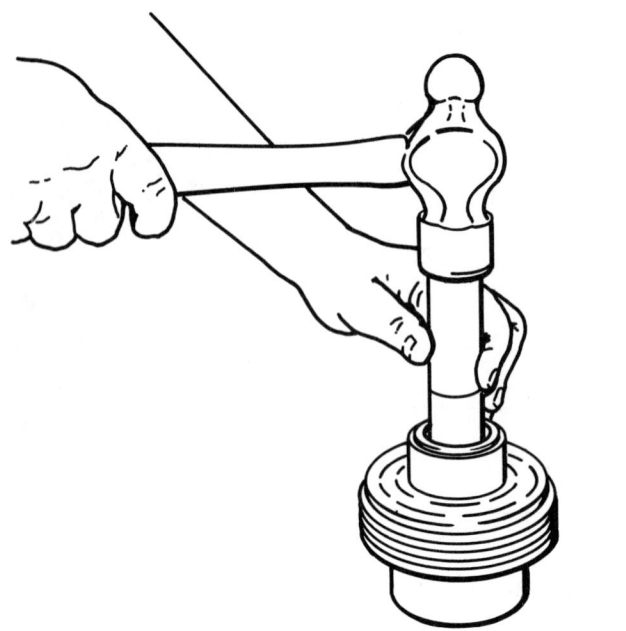

Fig. 9-89 Place the rotor on the support block and, using the bearing installer tool, drive the bearing fully into the rotor.

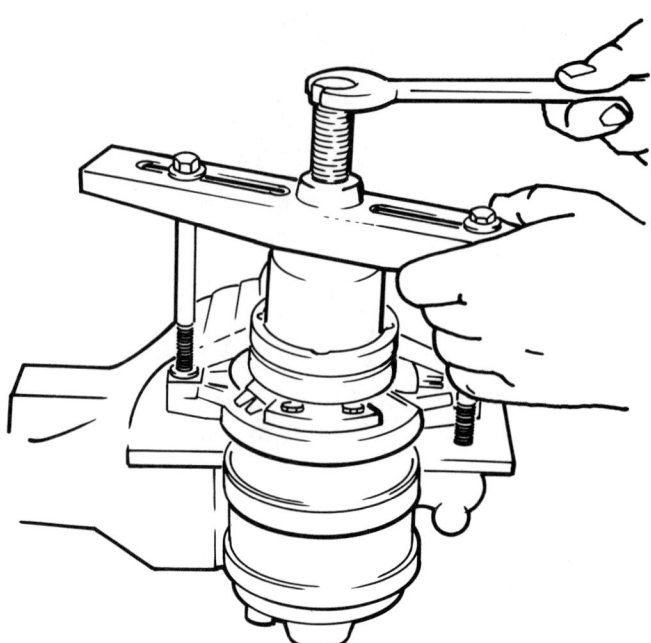

Fig. 9-90 Assemble the clutch coil installer.

6. Position the bearing staking guide and staking pin tool in the hub bore.
7. Strike the staking pin with a hammer. Form three stakes 120° apart. The staked metal should not touch the outer race of the bearing. *Take care not to damage the bearing during staking procedure.*
8. Remove the staking tools and support block.

Replace Clutch Coil

1. Place the clutch coil on the front head of the compressor. Note the location of the electrical terminals as marked during removal of the coil.
2. Assemble the clutch coil installer, puller crossbar, and bolts atop the clutch coil, as shown in figure 9-90.
3. Turn the forcing screw of the crossbar to force the clutch coil onto the front head of the compressor. Make sure that the clutch coil and clutch coil installer tool remain *in-line* during this procedure.
4. After the clutch coil is fully seated, use a 1/8-inch punch and stake the front head at 120° intervals to hold the coil in proper position.

Replace Clutch

1. Position the rotor and bearing assembly on the front head.
2. Assemble the puller pilot, crossbar and bolts atop the rotor and bearing assembly, as shown in figure 9-91.
3. Tighten the forcing screw to force the rotor and bearing assembly onto the compressor front head. Make sure that the assembly stays *in-line* during this procedure.
4. Use the snap ring pliers to install the rotor and bearing assembly retainer snap ring.

5. Install the shaft key into the hub key groove. The key should protrude about 1/8 inch (3.2 mm) out of the keyway.

6. Align the shaft key with the shaft keyway and position the clutch plate and hub assembly onto the compressor shaft.

7. Install the drive plate installer and bearing onto the clutch plate and hub assembly, figure 9-92. The forcing tip of the installer must be flat or the end of the shaft/axial plate assembly will be damaged.

8. Using wrenches, as shown, force the clutch plate and hub assembly onto the compressor shaft. Remove the tool from time to time to insure that the key is still in place in the keyway. The key should be even with or slightly above the clutch hub when the hub is fully seated.

9. Using nonmagnetic feeler gauges, check the air gap. The air gap should be between 0.015 in (0.38 mm) and 0.025 in (0.64 mm).

10. Install the shaft nut and torque it to 8-16 ft-lb (11-22 N·m).

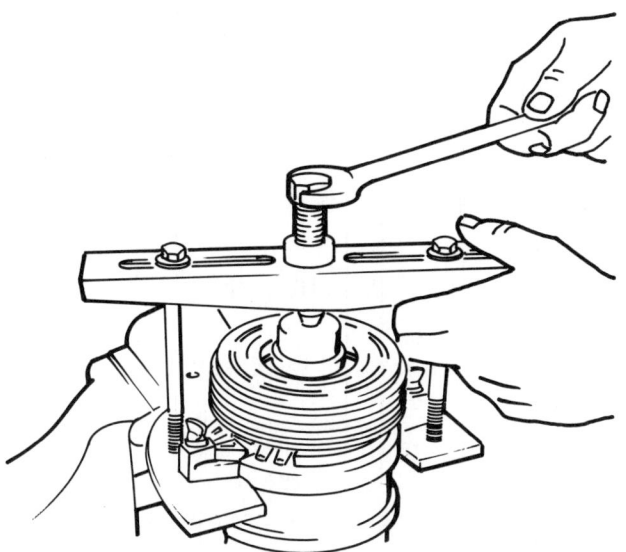

Fig. 9-91 Assemble the puller pilot, crossbar, and bolts atop the rotor and bearing assembly.

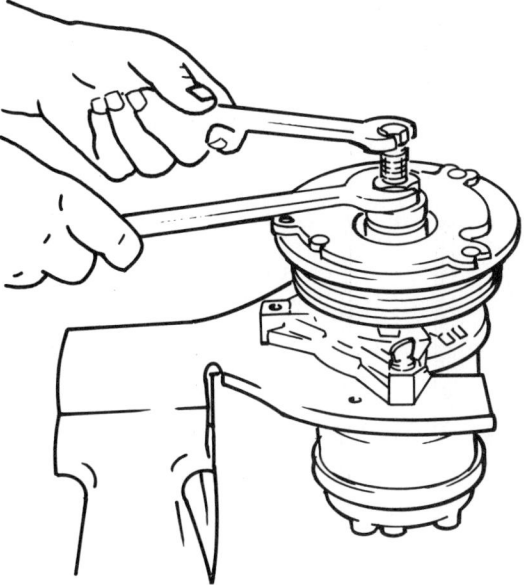

Fig. 9-92 Install the clutch plate and hub assembly.

PROCEDURE, PART II

COMPRESSOR SHAFT SEAL SERVICE

Remove the Old Seal

1. Using a 9/16-inch thinwall socket wrench and clutch hub holding tool, remove the shaft nut.

2. Using snap ring pliers, remove the clutch hub retainer ring.

3. Remove the spacer under the retainer ring.

4. Using a clutch hub and drive plate puller, remove this part.

5. Remove the shaft seal seat retainer ring using internal snap ring pliers, figure 9-93.

6. Remove the seal seat using a shaft seal seat remover, figure 9-94. (Use the appropriate tool.)

Fig. 9-93 Removing the shaft seal retainer.

Fig. 9-94 Removing the seal seat.

7. Using the shaft seal remover, remove the shaft seal, figure 9-95.
8. Using an O-ring remover (a wire with a hook on the end), remove the shaft seal seat O-ring, figure 9-96. *Take care not to scratch the mating surfaces.*

Install the New Seal

1. Insure that the inner bore of the compressor is free of all foreign matter. Flush the area with clean refrigeration oil.
2. Wet the seal seat O-ring with refrigerant oil and place it on the seal installer tool; slide the O-ring into place; then, remove the tool.
3. Coat the shaft seal liberally with refrigeration oil and place it on the shaft seal installer tool, figure 9-97. Slide the shaft seal into place in the bore. Rotate the seal clockwise until it seats on the flats provided. Rotate the tool counterclockwise and remove it.

Fig. 9-95 Removing the shaft seal assembly.

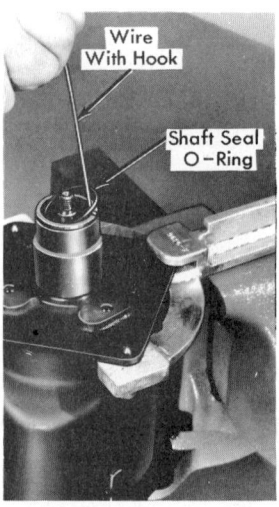

Fig. 9-96 Removing the seal seat O-ring.

Fig. 9-98 Drive plate key installed in keyway.

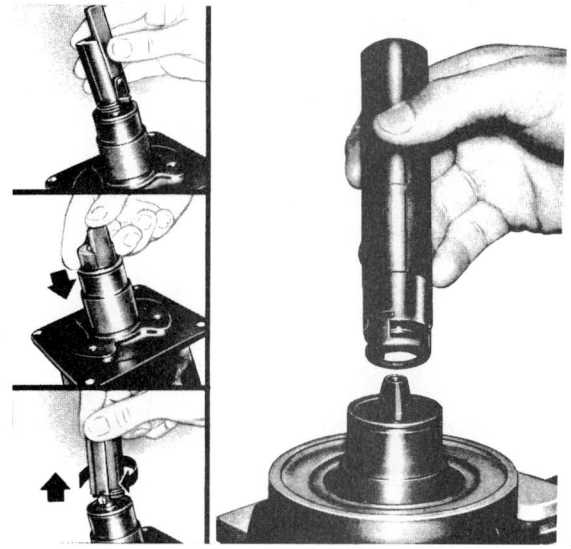

Fig. 9-97 Installing the seal seat O-ring and the shaft seal.

4. Wet the shaft seal seat with refrigerant oil and place it on the remover/installer tool. Slide the shaft seal seat into position and remove the tool.

5. Install the shaft seal seat snap ring. Note that the beveled edge of the snap ring must face the outside of the compressor.

6. Before replacing the clutch hub and drive plate, the seal should be checked for leaks.

Replace the Clutch Hub and Drive Plate Assembly

1. Place the drive key into the crankshaft keyway, figure 9-98. About 3/16 inch (4.8 mm) of the key should be allowed to protrude over the end of the keyway.

2. Align the keys with the keyways of the drive plate and compressor crankshaft. Then slide the drive plate into position.

3. Using a hub and drive plate installer, press this part on the crankshaft.

4. A clearance of 0.030 inch ± 0.010 in (0.76 mm ± 0.25 mm) should exist between the drive plate and the rotor.

PROCEDURE, PART III

REAR HEAD SERVICE

Remove Head

1. Drain the oil from the compressor into a graduated container. Note the quantity drained and discard oil.

2. Remove the clutch and coil assembly as outlined in Part I of this service procedure.

3. Mark the location and note the alignment of the front head, cylinder assembly, and rear head, figure 9-99. This is important to insure proper reassembly.

4. Remove the six compressor through bolts and gaskets. Discard the gaskets.

5. With a plastic hammer and wooden block, tap around the edge of the rear head to disengage it from the cylinder assembly, figure 9-100.

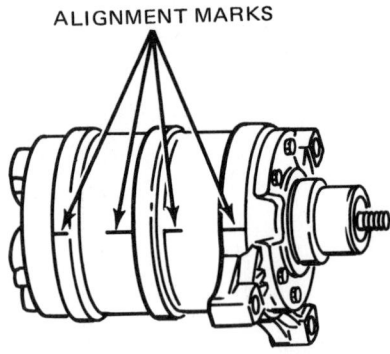

Fig. 9-99 Mark the location of the front head, cylinder assembly, and rear head to insure proper reassembly.

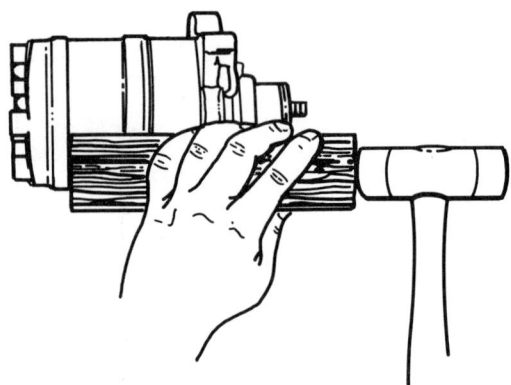

Fig. 9-100 Disengage the rear head from the cylinder assembly.

6. Separate the rear head, head gasket, valve plates and O-ring. Discard the gasket and O-ring.
7. Inspect the head and valve plates. Discard any that are found to be defective.

Replace Head

1. Secure the front head and cylinder assembly in the holding fixture, figure 9-101.
2. Install two guide pins in the front head and cylinder assembly, as shown in figure 9-102. Insert the guide pins with the small diameter end *up* as shown.
3. Liberally lubricate a new O-ring with clean refrigeration oil. Install the O-ring in the rear cylinder O-ring groove.
4. Install the suction reed valve plate over the guide pins.
5. Install the discharge valve plate over the guide pins. Check for proper position of the valve plates.
6. Install the rear head gasket over the guide pins. Be sure that it is in the proper position.
7. Carefully install the rear head over the guide pins. The alignment mark on the rear head should match the alignment mark on the cylinder assembly.
8. Using both hands, press down on the rear head to force it over the O-ring. Recheck alignment marks.
9. Remove the compressor from the holding fixture and place it on the workbench.
10. Install new through bolt gaskets on the six through bolts.
11. Install four bolts into the compressor. After all four bolts have been threaded into the rear head, remove the two guide pins.
12. Install the other two through bolts and alternately torque all six to 72-84 in-lb (8-10 N·m).
13. Replace the same quantity of oil as was removed. Use only 525 viscosity clean refrigeration oil.
14. Replace the clutch and coil assembly as outlined in Part I.

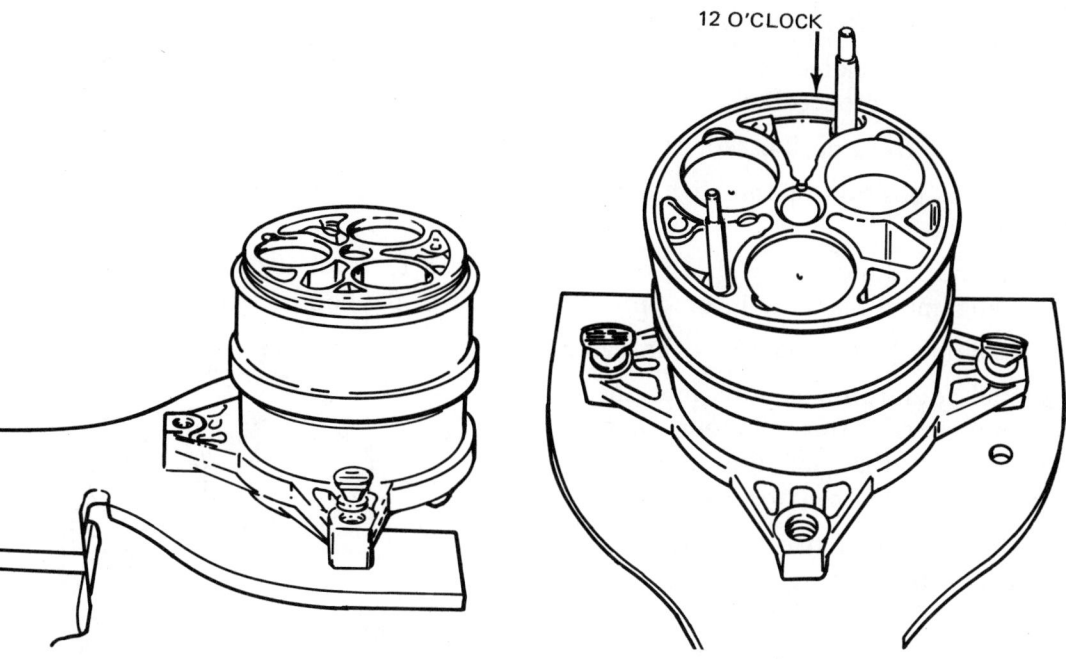

Fig. 9-101 Secure the front head and cylinder assembly in the holding fixture.

Fig. 9-102 Install two guide pins in the front head and cylinder assembly.

PROCEDURE, PART IV

FRONT HEAD SERVICE

Remove Head

1. Drain the compressor oil into a graduated container. Note the quantity of oil removed and discard the oil.
2. Remove the clutch and coil assembly as outlined in Part I.
3. Remove the compressor shaft seal assembly as outlined in Part II.
4. Mark the location and note the alignment of the front head, cylinder assembly, and rear head, figure 9-99. This step is important to insure proper reassembly.
5. Remove the six through bolts and discard washers.
6. Using a plastic hammer, tap the front head to disengage it from the cylinder assembly.
7. Remove the front head, valve plates, O-ring, and head gasket. Discard the O-ring and head gasket.
8. Inspect the head and valve plates. Discard any that are found to be defective.

Replace Head

1. Rest the rear head and cylinder assembly on the support block, figure 9-103.
2. Install two guide pins into the rear head and cylinder assembly. Insert the guide pins with the small diameter *down* as shown.
3. Liberally lubricate the new O-ring with clean refrigeration oil and install the O-ring in the front cylinder O-ring groove.

4. Install the suction reed valve plate over the guide pins.
5. Install the discharge valve plate over the guide pins. Check for proper position of valve plates before proceeding.
6. Install the front head gasket over the guide pins.
7. Note the position of the alignment marks and carefully install the front head over the guide pins.
8. Using both hands, press down on the front head to force it over the O-ring. Recheck the alignment marks to insure proper alignment of the compressor assembly.
9. Install new gaskets on all six through bolts.
10. Install four through bolts into the compressor. After all four bolts have been threaded into the rear head, remove the two guide pins.
11. Install the other two through bolts and alternately torque all six bolts to 72–84 in-lb (8-10 N·m).
12. Install the new shaft seal as outlined in Part II.
13. Replace the same quantity of oil as was removed. Use only clean 525 viscosity refrigeration oil.
14. Replace the clutch and coil assembly as outlined in Part I.

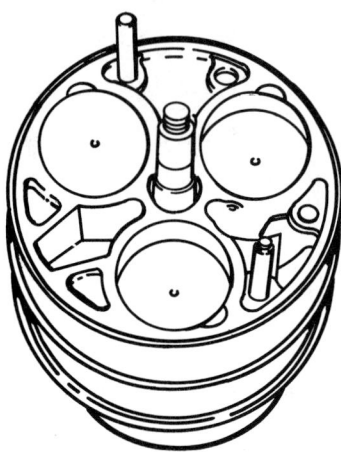

Fig. 9-103 Rest rear head and cylinder assembly on support block.

PROCEDURE, PART V

COMPRESSOR CYLINDER AND SHAFT ASSEMBLY

Remove Assembly

1. Follow steps 1 through 6 of Part III, *Remove Head*, to remove the rear head assembly.
2. Follow steps 3, 5, and 6 of Part IV, *Remove Head*, to remove the front head assembly.

Replace Assembly

1. Set rear head on support block and insert two guide pins, figure 9-104. Install the rear head gasket in the proper position.
2. Install the rear discharge valve plate over the guide pins. Check for proper positioning of the valve plate.
3. Install the rear suction valve plate over the guide pins. Check to insure the proper positioning of the valve plates.
4. Lubricate the rear head O-ring liberally with clean refrigeration oil and install the O-ring in the rear cylinder O-ring groove.
5. Carefully lower the cylinder assembly over the guide pins to the rear head.
6. Using both hands, press the cylinder and shaft assembly down into the rear head.
7. Follow steps 3 through 14 of Part IV, *Replace Head*, to replace the front head assemblies.

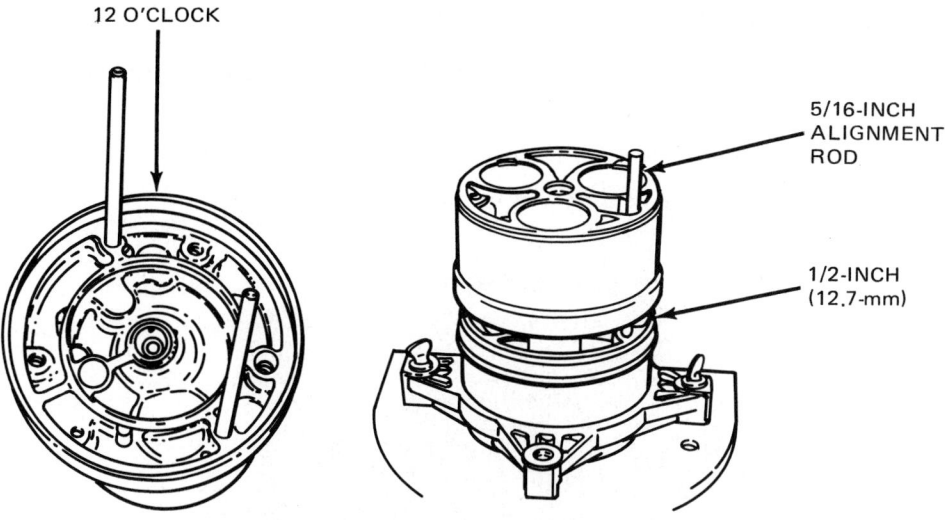

Fig. 9-104 Set rear head on support block with two guide pins.

Fig. 9-105 Separate the two cylinder halves no more than 1/2 inch (12.7 mm).

PROCEDURE, PART VI

CENTER CYLINDER SEAL

Remove Seal

1. Follow steps 1 through 6 of Part III, *Remove Head*, to remove the rear head assembly.
2. Follow steps 3, 5, and 6 of Part IV, *Remove Head*, to remove the front head assembly.
3. Using a wooden block and plastic hammer, figure 9-105, tap around the rear cylinder half to separate the two cylinder sections. Do not separate the sections more than one-half inch (12.7 mm).
   NOTE: Depending on the position of the pistons, one may be pulled out of the cylinder bore when the halves are separated. Make no attempt at this time to reinsert the piston.
4. Remove and discard the center cylinder assembly O-ring.
5. Check to be sure that the small O-ring between the two cylinder halves is in place. It may stick to the front half or be in the rear half recess. It need not be replaced unless it is missing.

Replace Seal

1. Secure the front head in the holding fixture, figure 9-106.
2. Carefully insert the cylinder and shaft assembly into the front head, shaft end *down*.
3. Lubricate the center O-ring with clean refrigeration oil and position it at the center cylinder O-ring groove.
4. With the discharge crossover O-ring in place (see step 5), insert a piece of 5/16-inch drill rod through the discharge crossover passage in both cylinder halves. This will insure proper alignment.
5. Using both hands, carefully press the cylinder halves together.

6. Remove the drill rod.
7. Reassemble the rear head, valve plates, gasket, and O-ring, following the procedures given in Part III, *Replace Head*.
8. Install the clutch coil as outlined in Part I, *Replace Clutch Coil*.
9. Install the clutch assembly as outlined in Part I, *Replace Clutch*.

Fig. 9-106 Secure the front head in the holding fixture.

SERVICE PROCEDURE 10:

SERVICING THE DELCO AIR V-5 COMPRESSOR

The Delco Air V-5 compressor requires special service tools for repairs. Like the DA-6 compressor, the V-5 compressor internal assembly is not serviceable.

This service procedure is given in five parts. Part I, Clutch Service, Part II, Compressor Shaft Seal Service, Part III, Rear Head Service, Part IV, Front Head Service, and Part V, Control Valve Service.

PROCEDURE, PART I

CLUTCH SERVICE

Remove Clutch

1. Clamp the compressor into an appropriate holding fixture.
2. Hold the clutch hub with the clutch hub holding tool and remove the shaft nut, figure 9-107.
3. Use the clutch plate and hub installer/remover tool to remove the clutch hub, figure 9-108.
4. Remove the shaft key and set aside for reassembly.
5. Use the snap ring pliers to remove the rotor snap ring, figure 9-109.
6. Use the pulley rotor and bearing guide over the compressor shaft and insert the puller in the rotor slots to remove the rotor, figure 9-110.

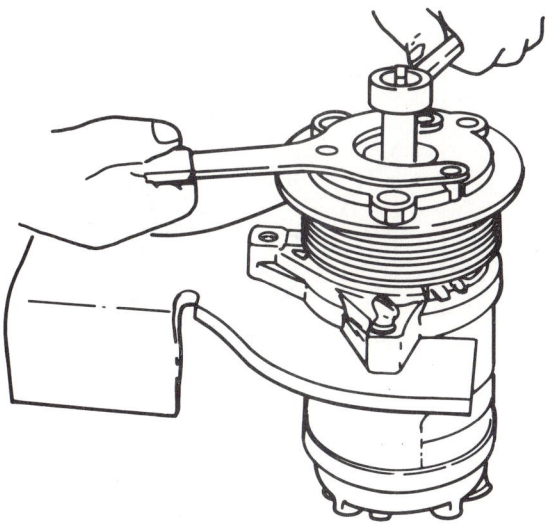

Fig. 9-107 Remove the shaft nut while holding the clutch hub.

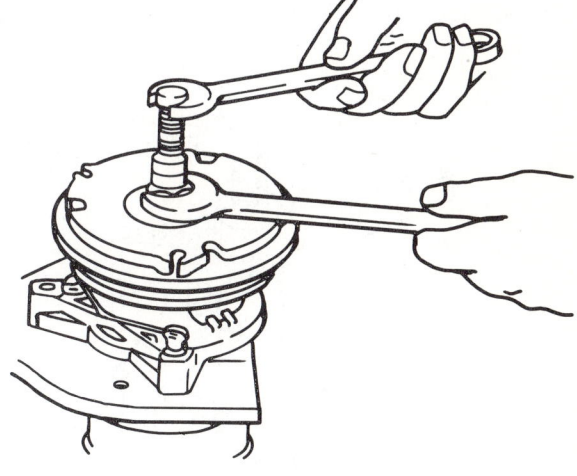

Fig. 9-108 Remove the clutch hub.

Remove Clutch Coil

1. Mark the clutch coil terminal location on the compressor front head for ease in reassembly.

Chapter Nine, Compressor Repair

2. Install the puller pilot on the front head.
3. Install the puller and tighten the forcing screw against the pilot to remove the clutch coil, figure 9-111.

Fig. 9-109 Use snap ring pliers to remove the snap ring.

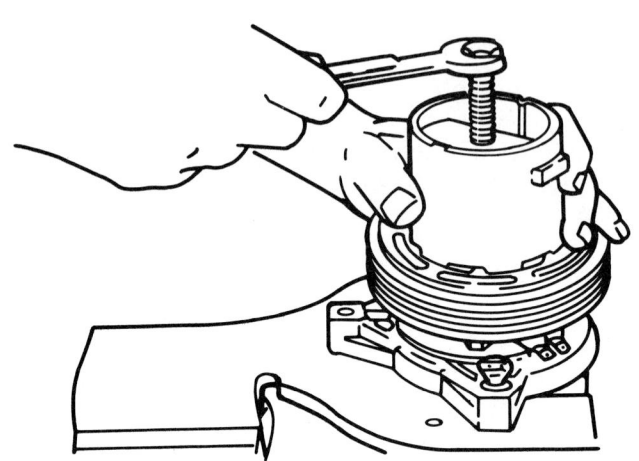

Fig. 9-110 Remove the rotor using the rotor remover tool.

Replace Bearing

1. Attach the rotor and bearing puller tool (less forcing screw) to the rotor. Place the puller atop a solid flat surface, figure 9-112.
2. With the rotor bearing remover tool and universal handle, drive the bearing out of the rotor hub.
3. Remove the rotor and bearing puller tool from the rotor.

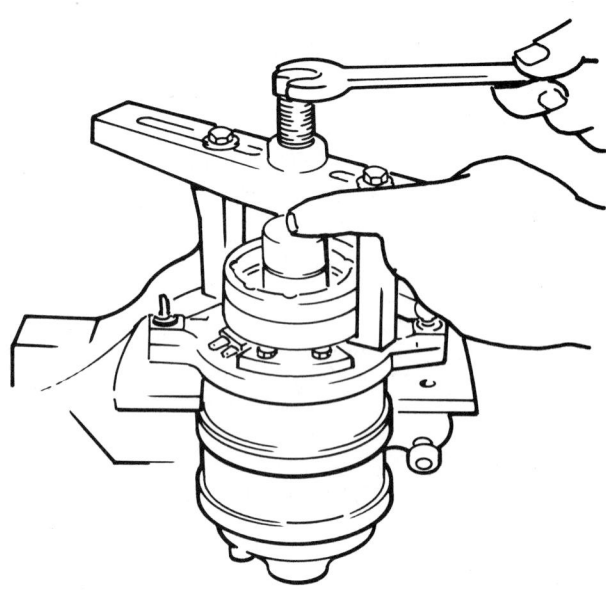

Fig. 9-111 Remove the clutch coil.

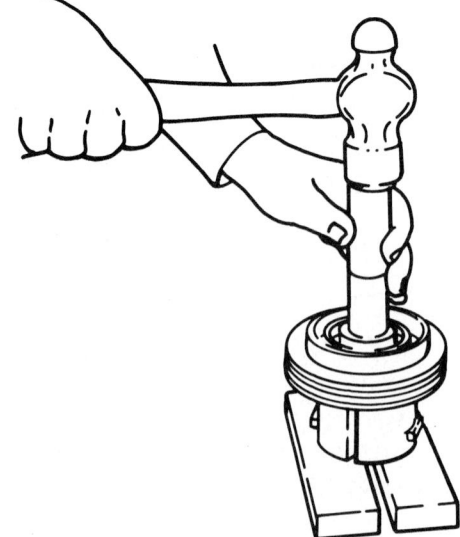

Fig. 9-112 Place the puller atop a solid flat surface and, using the rotor bearing remover tool, drive the bearing out of the rotor.

4. Place the rotor on the support block, figure 9-113, to support the rotor during bearing installation.

5. Align the bearing with the hub bore. Using the puller and bearing installer tool, drive the bearing fully into the hub.

6. Position the bearing staking guide and staking pin tool, figure 9-114, in the hub bore.

7. Strike the staking pin with a hammer. Form three stakes 120° apart. The staked metal should not touch the outer race of the bearing. *Take care not to damage the bearing during staking procedure.*

8. Remove staking tools and support block.

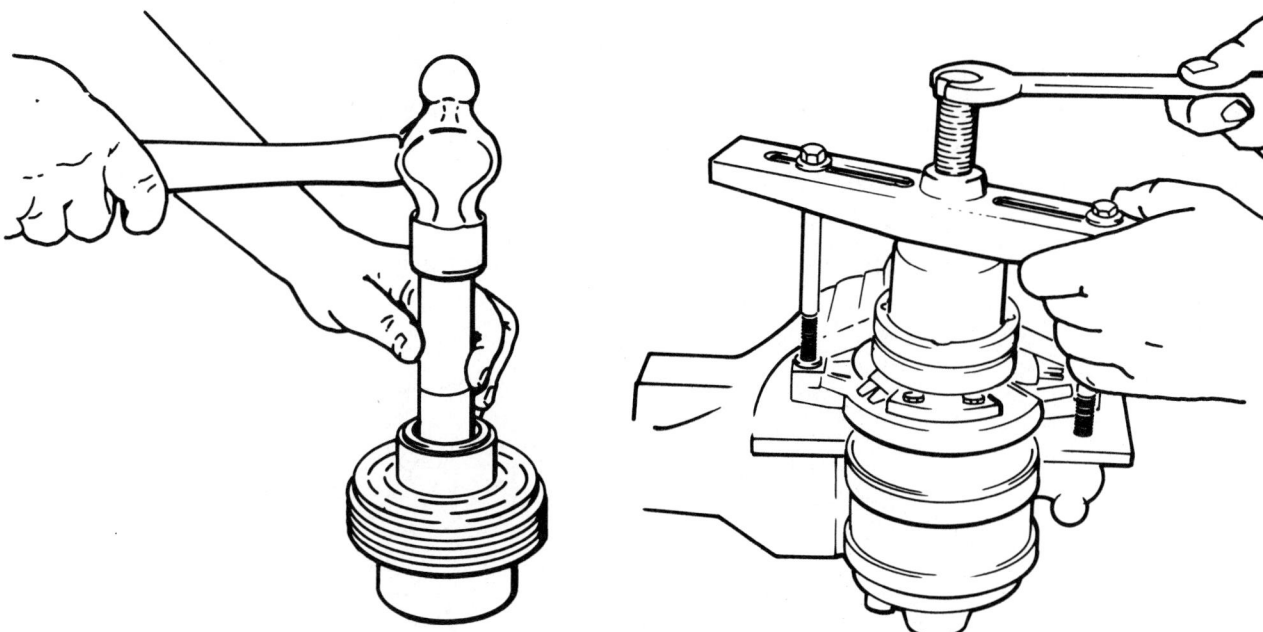

Fig. 9-113 Place the rotor on the support block and, using the bearing installer tool, drive the bearing fully into the rotor.

Fig. 9-114 Assemble the clutch coil installer.

Replace Clutch Coil

1. Place the clutch coil on the front head of the compressor. Note the location of the electrical terminals as marked during removal of the coil.

2. Assemble the clutch coil installer, puller crossbar, and bolts atop the clutch coil, as shown in figure 9-114.

3. Turn the forcing screw of the crossbar to force the clutch coil onto the front head of the compressor. Make sure that the clutch coil and clutch coil installer tool remain *in-line* during this procedure.

4. After the clutch coil is fully seated, use a 1/8-inch punch and stake the front head at 120° intervals to hold the coil in proper position.

Replace Clutch

1. Position the rotor and bearing assembly on the front head.

2. Assemble the puller pilot, crossbar and bolts atop the rotor and bearing assembly, as shown in figure 9-115.

3. Tighten the forcing screw to force the rotor and bearing assembly onto the compressor front head. Make sure that the assembly stays *in-line* during this procedure.

4. Use the snap ring pliers to install the rotor and bearing assembly retainer snap ring.

5. Install the shaft key into the hub key groove. The key should protrude about 1/8 inch (3.2 mm) out of the keyway.

6. Align the shaft key with the shaft keyway and position the clutch plate and hub assembly onto the compressor shaft.

7. Install the drive plate installer and bearing onto the clutch plate and hub assembly, figure 9-116. The forcing tip of the installer must be flat or the end of the shaft/axial plate assembly will be damaged.

8. Using wrenches, as shown, force the clutch plate and hub assembly onto the compressor shaft. Remove the tool from time-to-time to insure that the key is still in place in the keyway. The key should be even with or slightly above the clutch hub when the hub is fully seated.

9. Using nonmagnetic feeler gauges, check the air gap. The air gap should be between 0.015 in (0.38 mm) and 0.025 in (0.64 mm).

10. Install the shaft nut and torque it to 8-16 ft-lb (11-22 N·m).

Fig. 9-115 Assemble the puller pilot, crossbar, and bolts atop the rotor and bearing assembly.

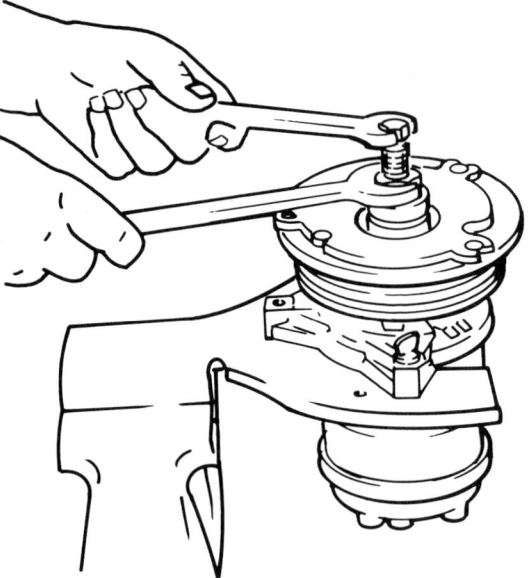

Fig. 9-116 Install the clutch plate and hub assembly.

PROCEDURE, PART II

COMPRESSOR SHAFT SEAL SERVICE

Remove Seal

1. Clamp the compressor into an appropriate holding fixture.

2. Hold the clutch hub with the clutch hub holding tool and remove the shaft nut, figure 9-117.

3. Use the clutch plate and hub installer/remover tool to remove the clutch hub, figure 9-118.

Service Procedure Ten   181

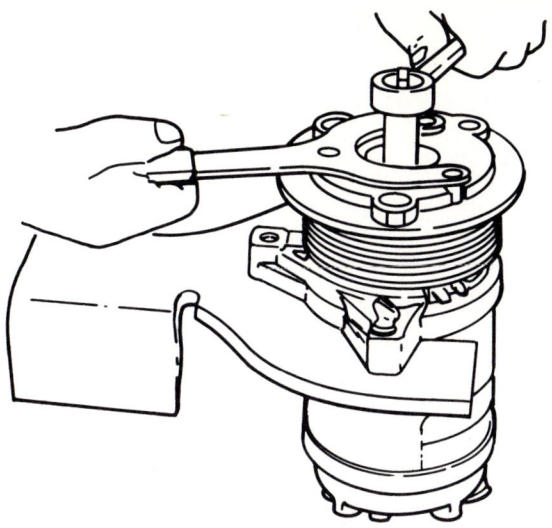

Fig. 9-117 Remove the shaft nut while holding the clutch hub.

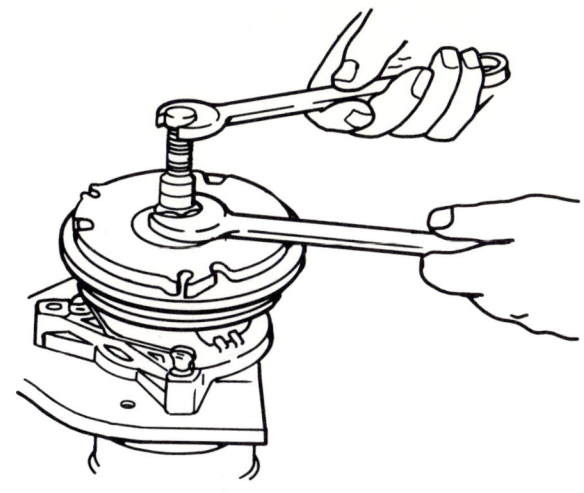

Fig. 9-118 Remove the clutch hub.

4. Remove the shaft key and set aside for reassembly.
5. Clean the inside of the seal cavity to prevent any dirt or foreign matter from entering the compressor when the seal is removed.
6. Engage the knurled tangs of the seal seat remover and installer tool into the seal by turning the tool clockwise (cw).
7. With a rotary motion, remove the seal from the cavity, figure 9-119.
8. Remove the O-ring from the seal cavity using the O-ring remover tool.
9. Clean and check the seal cavity for nicks and/or burrs.

Replace Seal

1. Lubricate the new O-ring with clean refrigeration oil and attach it to the O-ring installer.
2. Install the O-ring into the seal cavity. The lower recess is for the O-ring seal.
3. Rotate the tool to seat the O-ring into its recess and remove the installer tool.
4. Lubricate the new seal with clean refrigeration oil and attach it to the seal remover/installer tool.
5. Install the seal protector, figure 9-120, in the seal and place over the compressor shaft.
6. Push seal into place with a rotary motion.
7. Using snap ring pliers, install the new snap ring to retain the seal. Use the sleeve from the remover/installer to press on the snap ring until it snaps into its groove.
8. With a clean, lint-free cloth, remove the excess oil from the seal cavity.
9. Install the shaft key into the hub key groove. The key should protrude about 1/8 inch (3.2 mm) out of the keyway.
10. Align the shaft key with the shaft keyway and position the clutch plate and hub assembly onto the compressor shaft.

182 Chapter Nine, Compressor Repair

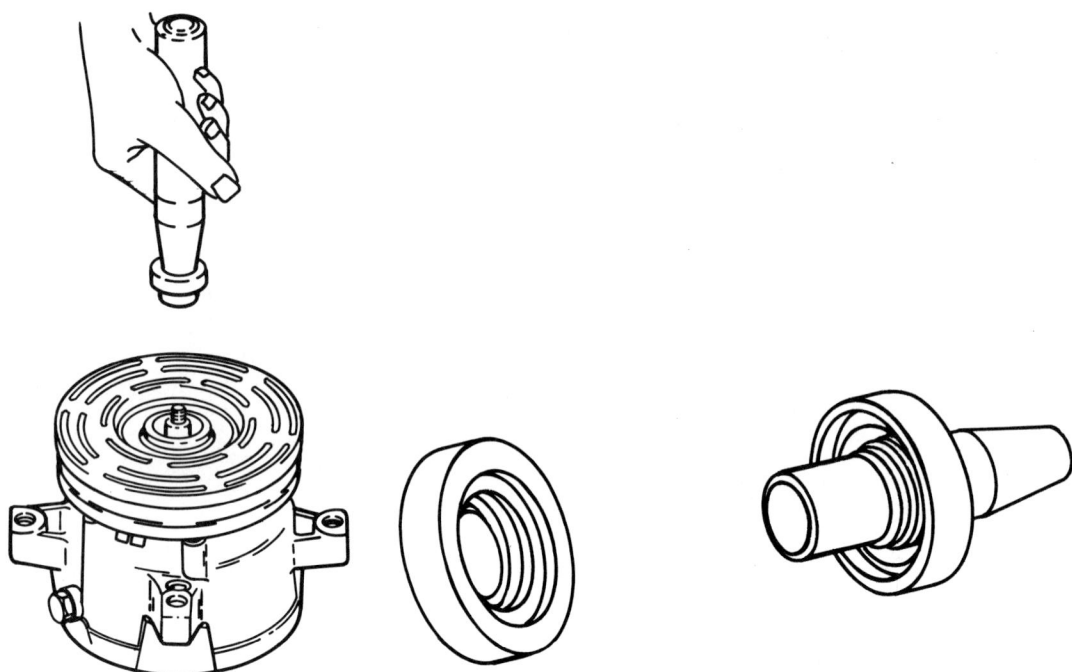

Fig. 9-119 With a rotary motion, remove the seal.

Fig. 9-120 Install the seal protector in the seal.

11. Install the drive plate installer and bearing onto the clutch plate and hub assembly, figure 9-116. The forcing tip of the installer must be flat or the end of the shaft/axial plate assembly will be damaged.

12. Using wrenches, as shown, force the clutch plate and hub assembly onto the compressor shaft. Remove the tool from time to time to insure that the key is still in place in the keyway. The key should be even with or slightly above the clutch hub when the hub is fully seated.

13. Using nonmagnetic feeler gauges, check the air gap. The air gap should be between 0.015 in (0.38 mm) and 0.025 in (0.64 mm).

14. Install the shaft nut and torque it to 8-16 ft-lb (11-22N m).

PROCEDURE, PART III

REAR HEAD SERVICE

Remove Head

1. Drain the oil from the compressor into a graduated container. Note the quantity drained and discard oil.

2. Remove the clutch and coil assembly as outlined in Part I of this service procedure.

3. Mark the location and note the alignment of the front head, cylinder assembly, and rear head, figure 9-121. This is important to insure proper reassembly.

4. Remove the six compressor through bolts and gaskets. Discard the gaskets.

5. With a plastic hammer and wooden block, tap around the edge of the rear head to disengage it from the cylinder assembly, figure 9-122.

6. Separate the rear head, head gasket, valve plates and O-ring. Discard the gasket and O-ring.

7. Inspect the head and valve plates. Discard any that are found to be defective.

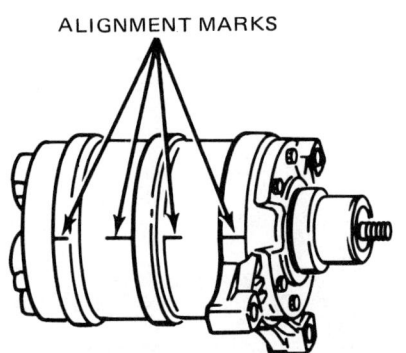

Fig. 9-121 Mark the location of the front head, cylinder assembly, and rear head to insure proper reassembly.

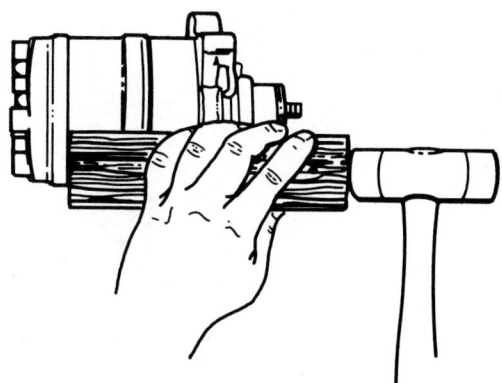

Fig. 9-122 Disengage the rear head from the cylinder assembly.

Replace Head

1. Place the rear head on a clean, flat surface with the control valve facing at 6 o'clock position, figure 9-123.

2. Insert the guide pins in the mounting holes at 5 and 11 o'clock positions, small end facing *down*.

3. Install the discharge valve plate over the guide pins.
   NOTE: The elongated hole should be at the upper left (11 o'clock) guide pin, figure 9-124.

4. Install the suction valve plate over the guide pins. (See note for step 3.)

5. Remove the 5 o'clock guide pin before proceeding.

6. Lubricate the new O-ring with clean refrigeration oil and install it in the cylinder O-ring groove.

7. Carefully install the front head and cylinder assembly over the guide pin.
   NOTE: Locate the relief boss for the compressor guide pin at the 6 o'clock position.

8. Using both hands, press the front head and cylinder assembly down and into the rear head.

9. Add the new gaskets to the six through bolts. Install five bolts into the assembly.

10. Insure that three or four through bolts are securely screwed into the rear head. Then, remove the 11 o'clock guide pin.

11. Insert the other through bolt and torque all bolts to 72-84 in-lb (8-10 N·n).

12. Leak check the assembly. Attach the pressure testing connector and pressurize the compressor to 50 psig (344.8 kPa) with Refrigerant 12. Check the front and rear O-rings, shaft seal, and through bolt gaskets.

13. Depressurize the compressor and remove the testing connector.

Fig. 9-123 Place the rear head on a flat surface with control valve facing 6 o'clock.

Fig. 9-124 Insert assembly guide pin at 11 o'clock.

Replace Clutch Coil

1. Place the clutch coil on the front head of the compressor. Note the location of the electrical terminals as marked during removal of the coil.

2. Assemble the clutch coil installer, puller crossbar, and bolts atop the clutch coil, as shown in figure 9-125.

3. Turn the forcing screw of the crossbar to force the clutch coil onto the front head of the compressor. Make sure that the clutch coil and clutch coil installer tool remain *in-line* during this procedure.

4. After the clutch foil is fully seated, use a 1/8-inch punch and stake the front head at 120° intervals to hold the coil in proper position.

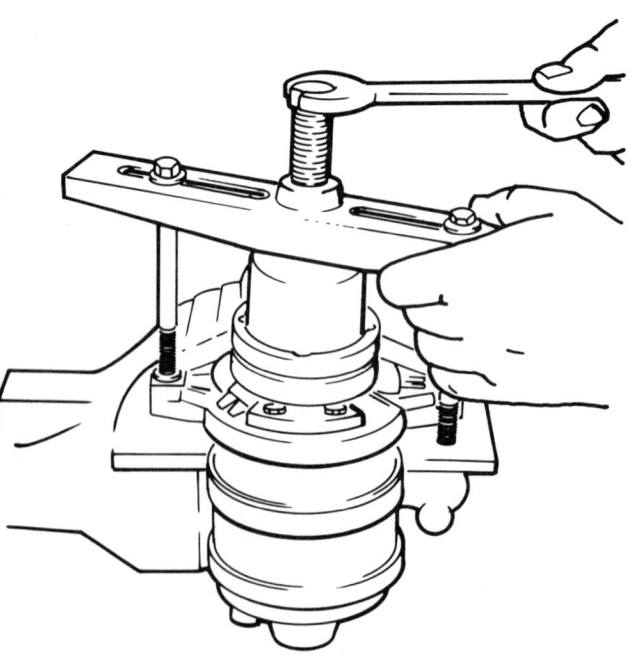

Fig. 9-125 Assemble the clutch coil installer.

Replace Clutch

1. Position the rotor and bearing assembly on the front head.

2. Assemble the puller pilot, crossbar and bolts atop the rotor and bearing assembly, as shown in figure 9-115.

3. Tighten the forcing screw to force the rotor and bearing assembly onto the compressor front head. Make sure that the assembly stays *in-line* during this procedure.

4. Use the snap ring pliers to install the rotor and bearing assembly retainer snap ring (see figure 9-109).

5. Install the shaft key into the hub key groove. The key should protrude about 1/8 inch (3.2 mm) out of the keyway.

6. Align the shaft key with the shaft keyway and position the clutch plate and hub assembly onto the compressor shaft.

7. Install the drive plate installer and bearing onto the clutch plate and hub assembly, figure 9-116. The forcing tip of the installer must be flat or the end of the shaft/axial plate assembly will be damaged.

8. Using wrenches, as shown, force the clutch plate and hub assembly onto the compressor shaft. Remove the tool from time to time to insure that the key is still in place in the keyway. The key should be even with or slightly above the clutch hub when the hub is fully seated.

9. Using nonmagnetic feeler gauges, check the air gap. The air gap should be between 0.015 in (0.38 mm) and 0.025 in (0.64 mm).

10. Install the shaft nut and torque it to 8-16 ft-lb (11-22 N m).

PROCEDURE, PART IV

FRONT HEAD SERVICE

Remove Head

1. Drain the compressor oil into a graduated container. Note the quantity of oil removed and discard the oil.

2. Remove the clutch and coil assembly as outlined in Part I.

3. Remove the seal assembly following the procedures given in this service procedure, Part II, *Remove Seal*, steps 1 through 9.

4. Mark the location and note the alignment of the front head, cylinder assembly, and rear head, figure 9-121. This step is important to insure proper reassembly.

5. Remove the six through bolts and discard washers.

6. Using a plastic hammer, tap the front head to disengage it from the cylinder assembly.

7. Remove the front head, valve plates, O-ring, and head gasket. Discard the O-ring and head gasket.

8. Inspect the head and valve plates. Discard any that are found to be defective.

Replace Head

1. Place the rear head and cylinder assembly on the support ring tool with the control valve facing 6 o'clock.

2. Install an assembly guide pin at 11 o'clock, small end *down*, figure 9-124.

3. Lubricate the new O-ring with clean refrigeration oil and place it in the cylinder O-ring groove.
4. Install the thrust washer(s) and bearing in the same order as removed.
5. Carefully install the front head over the guide pin.
6. Using both hands, press the front head assembly down over the O-ring on the cylinder assembly.
7. Add the new gaskets to the six through bolts. Install five bolts into the assembly.
8. Insure that three or four bolts are securely screwed into the rear head. Then, remove the 11 o'clock guide pin.
9. Insert the other through bolt and torque all bolts to 72-84 in-lb (8-10 N·m).
10. Follow the procedures outlined in this service procedure, Part II, *Replace Seal*, steps 1 through 8, to replace the seal assembly.
11. Follow the procedures outlined in this service procedure, Part III, *Replace Head*.

PROCEDURE, PART V

CONTROL VALVE SERVICE

Remove Valve

1. Use snap ring pliers to remove the control valve retaining ring.
2. Remove the control valve assembly.

Install Valve

1. Lubricate O-ring(s) with clean refrigeration oil.
2. Use thumb pressure to push the control valve into the compressor.
3. Use the snap ring pliers to install the snap ring. Be sure that the snap ring is properly seated in the ring groove.

GLOSSARY

Absolute Pressure: pressure measured from absolute zero instead of normal atmospheric pressure.

Absolute Temperature: temperature measured on the Rankine and Kelvin thermometers calibrated from absolute zero. The freezing point of water on the Rankine Scale is 492°R (273°K).

Absolute Zero: the complete absence of heat, believed to be −459.67°F (−273.15°C). This is shown as 0° on the Rankine and Kelvin temperature scales.

A/C: abbreviation for air conditioning or air conditioner.

Accumulator: a tank located in the tailpipe to receive the refrigerant that leaves the evaporator. This device is constructed to insure that no liquid refrigerant enters the compressor.

Accumulator-Dehydrator: an accumulator that includes a desiccant. See "Accumulator" and "Desiccant."

Air Conditioner: a device used in the control of the temperature, humidity, cleanness, and movement of air.

Air Conditioning: the control of the temperature, humidity, cleanness, and movement of air.

Air Door: a door in the duct system that controls the flow of air in the air conditioner and/or heater.

Air Inlet Valve: a movable door in the plenum blower assembly that permits the selection of outside air or inside air for both heating and cooling systems.

Air Outlet Valve: a movable door in the plenum blower assembly that directs airflow into the heater core or into the ductwork that leads to the evaporator.

Ambient Air: air surrounding an object.

Ambient Air Temperature: see "Ambient Temperature."

Ambient Compressor Switch: an electrical switch that energizes the compressor clutch when the outside air temperature is 47°F (8.3°C), or above. Similarly, the switch turns off the compressor when the air temperature drops below 32°F (0°C).

Ambient Sensor: a thermistor used in automatic temperature control units to sense ambient temperature. Also see "Thermistor."

Ambient Switch: a switch used to control compressor operation by turning it on or off. The switch is regulated by ambient temperature.

Ambient Temperature: temperature of the surrounding air. In air-conditioning work, this term refers to the outside air temperature.

Amplifier: a device used in automatic temperature control units to provide an output voltage that is in proportion to the input voltage from the sensors.

Antifreeze: a commercially available additive solution used to increase the boiling temperature and reduce the freezing temperature of engine coolant. A solution of 50% water and 50% antifreeze is suggested for year-round protection.

Aspirator: a device that uses suction to move air, accomplished by a differential in air pressure.

A.T.C.: abbreviation for automatic temperature control.

Atmosphere: air.

Atmospheric Pressure: air pressure at a given altitude. At sea level, atmospheric pressure is 14.696 psia (101.329 kPa absolute).

Automatic: a self-regulating system or device which adjusts to variables of a predetermined condition.

Automatic Control: a thermostatic dial on the instrument panel that can be set at a comfortable temperature level to control the flow of air automatically.

Automatic Temperature Control: the name of an air-conditioner control system designed to maintain an in-car temperature and humidity level automatically at a preset level or condition.

Auxiliary Seal: a seal mounted outside the seal housing to prevent refrigeration oil from entering the clutch assembly.

Back Idler: a pulley that tightens the drive belt; the pulley rides on the back or flat side of the belt.

Back Seat (Service Valve): turning the valve stem to the left (ccw) as far as possible back seats the valve. The valve outlet to the system is open and the service port is closed.

Bellows: an accordion-type chamber which expands or contracts with temperature changes to create a mechanical controlling action such as in a thermostatic expansion valve.

Belt: see "V-belt," "V-groove belt," "Serpentine belt."

Belt Dressing: a prepared spray solution formulated for use on automotive belts to reduce or eliminate belt noise. Not recommended for serpentine belts.

Bimetallic: two dissimilar metals fused together; these metals expand (or contract) at different temperatures to cause a bending effect. Bimetallic elements are used in temperature sensing controls.

Bimetallic Thermostat: a thermostat that uses bimetallic strips instead of a bellows for making or breaking contact points.

Bleeding: slowly releasing pressure in the air-conditioning system by drawing off some liquid or gas.

Blower Circuit: all of the electrical components required for blower speed control.

Blower Fan: see "Squirrel-Cage Blower" or "Fan."

Blower Motor: see "Motor."

Blower Relay: an electrical device used to control the function or speed of a blower motor.

Blower Switch: a dash-mounted device that allows the operator to turn the blower motor on/off and/or control its speed.

Boiling Point: the temperature at which a liquid changes to a vapor.

Bowden Cable: a wire cable inside a metal or rubber housing used to regulate a valve or control from a remote place.

British Thermal Unit (Btu): a measure of heat energy; one Btu is the amount of heat necessary to raise one pound of water one degree Fahrenheit.

Btu: abbreviation for British thermal unit.

Calorie: the smallest measure of heat energy. One calorie is the amount of heat energy required to raise one gram of water one degree Celsius. There are 252 calories in one Btu.

Can Tap: a device used to pierce, dispense, and seal small cans of refrigerant.

Capacity: refrigeration produced, measured in tons or Btu per hour.

Capillary: a small tube with a calibrated length and inside diameter used as a metering device.

Capillary Attraction: the ability of tubular bodies to draw up a fluid.

Capillary Tube: a tube with a calibrated inside diameter and length used to control the flow of refrigerant. In automotive air-conditioning systems, the tube connecting the remote bulb to the expansion valve or to the thermostat is called the capillary tube.

CCFOT: abbreviation for cycling clutch fixed orifice tube.

CCOT: abbreviation for cycling clutch orifice tube.

Celsius: a metric temperature scale using the freezing point of water as zero. The boiling point of water is 100°C (212°F English).

Centigrade: a term often used to indicate "Celsius." A term not used in the SI metric system. See "Celsius."

CFM: also cfm. Abbreviation for cubic feet per minute.

Change of State: rearrangement of the molecular structure of matter as it changes between any two of the three physical states: solid, liquid, or gas.

Charge: a specific amount of refrigerant or oil by volume or weight.

Charging: the act of placing a charge of refrigerant or oil into the air-conditioning system.

Charging Hose: a hose with a small diameter constructed to withstand high pressures; the hose is located between the unit and the manifold set.

Charging Station: a unit containing a manifold and gauge set, charging cylinder, vacuum pump, and leak detector. This unit is used to service air conditioners.

Check Valve: a device located in the liquid line or inlet to the drier. The valve prevents liquid refrigerant from flowing the opposite way when the unit is shut off.

Check Valve Relay: an electrical switch to control a solenoid-operated check valve.

CID: abbreviation for cubic-inch displacement.

Clean: see "Purge" and "Flush."

Clutch: a coupling device which transfers torque from a driving to a driven member when desired.

Clutch Armature: that part of the clutch attached to the compressor crankshaft that is pulled in when engaged.

Clutch Coil: see "Clutch Field."

Clutch Field: consists of many windings of wire and is fastened to the front of the compressor. Current applied to the field sets up a magnetic field that pulls the armature in to engage the clutch.

Clutch Plate: see "Clutch Armature."

Clutch Rotor: that portion of the clutch in which the belt rides. The rotor is freewheeling until the clutch is engaged. On some clutches the field is found in the rotor and the electrical connection is made by the use of brushes.

Cold: the absence of heat.

Comb: see "Condenser Comb."

Combination Valve: used on some Ford car lines, an H-valve having a suction throttling valve and expansion valve combined.

Comfort: a pleasing and enjoyable environment; the removal of excessive heat, moisture, dust, and pollen from the air.

Compound Gauge: a gauge that registers both pressure and vacuum (above and below atmospheric pressure); used on the low side of the systems.

Compressor: a component of the refrigeration system that pumps refrigerant and increases the pressure of the refrigerant vapor.

Compressor Discharge Pressure Switch: a pressure-operated electrical switch that opens the compressor clutch circuit during high-pressure conditions.

Compressor Displacement: a value obtained by multiplying the displacement of the compressor cylinder or cylinders by a given r/min, usually the average engine speed of 30 mph, or 1 750 r/min.

Compressor Protection Switch: an electrical switch installed in the rear head of some compressors to stop the compressor in the event of a loss of refrigerant.

Compressor Shaft Seal: an assembly consisting of springs, snap rings, O-rings, shaft seal, seal sets, and gasket. The shaft seal is mounted on the compressor crankshaft and permits the shaft to be turned without a loss of refrigerant or oil.

Condensate: water taken from the air; the water forms on the exterior surface of the evaporator.

Condensation: the process of changing a vapor to a liquid.

Condenser: the component of a refrigeration system in which refrigerant vapor is changed to a liquid by the removal of heat.

Condenser Comb: a comb-like device used to straighten the fins on the evaporator or condenser.

Condenser Temperature: the temperature at which compressed gas in the condenser changes from a gas to a liquid.

Condensing Pressure: head pressure as read from the gauge at the high-side service valve; the pressure from the discharge side of the compressor to the condenser.

Conditioned Air: air that is cool, dry, and clean.

Conduction: the transmission of heat through a solid.

Conduction of Heat: the ability of a substance to conduct heat.

Contaminants: anything other than refrigerant and refrigeration oil in the system.

Control Head: the master controls (such as temperature and fan speed) which the driver uses to select the desired system condition.

Convection: the transfer of heat by the circulation of a vapor or liquid.

Coolant: water or a mixture of water and antifreeze used in the cooling system to carry away unwanted engine heat.

Coolant Recovery Tank: see "Expansion Tank."

Cooling System: all of the components that are required to remove heat from the engine. These include the engine water jackets, water pump, radiator, thermostat, pressure cap, and connecting hoses.

Core: the coolant passages and fins of a radiator or heater found between the two header tanks.

Corrosion: the decomposition of metal; caused by a chemical action, usually acid.

Crankcase: see "Sump."

Crankshaft: that part of a reciprocating compressor on which the wobble plate or connecting rods are attached to provide for an up-down or to-fro piston action.

Crankshaft Seal: see "Compressor Crankshaft Seal."

Cubic-inch Displacement: the cylinder volume of a compressor as the piston moves from the bottom of its stroke to the top of its stroke, in cubic inches.

Cutoff Switch: an electrical switch which is pressure or temperature operated. The switch is used to interrupt the compressor clutch circuit during certain low- or high-pressure conditions.

Cycling Clutch Fixed Orifice Tube: an air-conditioning system having a fixed orifice tube (expansion tube) in which the air temperature is controlled by starting and stopping the compressor with a thermostat or pressure control. See "CCFOT."

Cycling Clutch System: an air-conditioning system in which the air temperature is controlled by starting and stopping the compressor with a thermostat or pressure control.

Cylinder: a circular tubelike opening in a compressor block or casting in which the piston moves up and down or back and forth; a circular drum used to store refrigerant.

Declutching Fan: an engine cooling fan mounted on the water pump. A temperature sensitive device is provided to govern or limit terminal speed.

Defrost Door: a small door within the duct system to divert a portion of the delivery air to the windshield.

Dehumidify: to remove water vapor from the air.

Deice Switch: a switch used to control the compressor operation to prevent evaporator freezeup.

Delay Relay: see "Time-delay relay."

Density: the weight or mass of a gas, liquid, or solid.

Depressurize: see "Discharge."

Desiccant: a drying agent used in refrigeration systems to remove excess moisture.

Design Working Pressure: the maximum allowable working pressure for which a specific system component is designed to work safely.

Dew Point: the point where air becomes 100% saturated with moisture at a given temperature.

Diagnosis: the procedure followed to locate the cause of a malfunction.

Diaphragm: a rubber-like piston or bellows assembly which divides the inner and outer chambers of back-pressure-regulated air-conditioning control devices.

Dichlorodifluoromethane: see "Refrigerant 12."

Diode: an electrical check valve. Current flows only in one direction through a diode.

Discharge: bleeding some or all of the refrigerant from a system by opening a valve or connection and permitting the refrigerant to escape slowly.

Discharge Air: conditioned air as it passes through the outlets and enters the passenger compartment.

Discharge Line: connects the compressor outlet to the condenser inlet.

Discharge Pressure: pressure of the refrigerant being discharged from the compressor; also known as the high-side pressure.

Discharge Pressure Switch: see "Compressor Discharge Pressure Switch."

Discharge Side: that portion of the refrigeration system under high pressure, extending from the compressor outlet to the thermostatic expansion valve inlet.

Discharge Valve: see "High-Side Service Valve."

Displacement: in automotive air conditioning, this term refers to the compressor stroke X-bore.

Downflow Radiator: a radiator in which the coolant flow is from the top tank to the bottom tank, as opposed to a "Crossflow Radiator."

Drier: a device containing desiccant; a drier is placed in the liquid line to absorb moisture in the system.

Drip Pan: a shallow pan, located under the evaporator core, used to catch condensation. A drain hose is fastened to the drip pan and extends to the outside to carry off the condensate.

Drive Pulley: a pulley attached to the crankshaft of an automobile; this pulley drives the compressor clutch pulley through the use of a belt or belts.

Duct: a tube or passage used to provide a means to transfer air or liquid from one point or place to another.

EEVIR: abbreviation for evaporator equalizer valves-in-receiver; see "Valves-in-Receiver."

Electromagnet: a temporary magnet created by passing electrical current through a coil of wire. A clutch coil is a good example of an electromagnet.

Electromagnetic Field: the magnetic force created by an electromagnet.

Electronic Leak Detector: an electrically (ac or dc) powered leak detector that emits an audible and/or visual signal when its sensor is passed over a refrigerant leak.

Engine Idle Compensator: a thermostatically controlled device on the carburetor which prevents stalling during prolonged hot weather periods while the air conditioner is operated.

Engine Thermal Switch: an electrical switch designed to delay the operation of the system in cool weather to allow time for the engine coolant to warm up.

EPR: see "Evaporator Pressure Regulator."

Equalizer Line: a small-bore line used to provide a balance of pressure from one point to another, as in a thermostatic expansion valve.

ETR: see "Evaporator Temperature Regulator."

Evacuate: to create a vacuum within a system to remove all trace of air and moisture.

Evaporation: the process of changing from a liquid to a vapor.

Evaporator: the component of an air-conditioning system that conditions the air.

Evaporator Control Valve: can refer to any of the several types of evaporator suction pressure control valves or devices that are used to regulate the evaporator temperature by controlling the evaporator pressure.

Evaporator Core: the tube and fin assembly located inside the evaporator housing. The refrigerant fluid picks up heat in the evaporator core when it changes into a vapor.

Evaporator Equalizer Valves-in-Receiver: see "Valves-in-Receiver."

Evaporator Housing: the cabinet, or case, that contains the evaporator core. Often, the diverter doors, duct outlets, and blower mounting arrangement are found on the housing.

Evaporator Pressure Regulator: a back-pressure-regulated temperature control device used by Chrysler products.

Evaporator Temperature Regulator: a temperature-regulated device used by Chrysler Air-Temp to control the evaporator pressure.

Expansion: the increase in volume of a gas or a liquid as it becomes heated.

Expansion Tank: an auxiliary tank, usually connected to the inlet tank or a radiator, which provides additional storage space for heated coolant. Often called a coolant recovery tank.

Expansion Tube: a metering device, used at the inlet of some evaporators, to control the flow of liquid refrigerant into the evaporator core.

Expansion Valve: see "Thermostatic Expansion Valve."

External Equalizer: see "Equalizer Line."

Fahrenheit: an English thermometer scale using 32° as the freezing point of water, and the boiling point of water as 212°F.

Fan: a device having two or more blades attached to the shaft of a motor. The fan is mounted in the evaporator and causes air to pass over the evaporator. A fan is also a device having four or more blades, mounted on the water pump, which cause air to pass through the radiator and condenser.

Feeler Gauge: see "Nonmagnetic Feeler Gauge."

Field: a coil with many turns of wire located behind the clutch rotor. Current passing through this coil sets up a magnetic field and causes the clutch to engage.

Field Coil: see "Clutch Field" or "Electromagnet."

Filter: a device used with the drier or as a separate unit to remove foreign material from the refrigerant.

Filter Drier: a device having a filter to remove foreign material from the refrigerant and a desiccant to remove moisture from the refrigerant.

Fin Comb: see "Condenser Comb."

Fins: thin metal strips in an evaporator, condenser, or radiator found around the tubes to aid in heat transfer.

Fixed Orifice Tube: a refrigerant metering device, used at the inlet of evaporators, to control the flow of liquid refrigerant allowed to enter the evaporator. See "FOT."

Flare: a flange or cone-shaped end applied to a piece of tubing to provide a means of fastening to a fitting.

Flash Gas: gas resulting from the instantaneous evaporation of refrigerant in a pressure-reducing device such as an expansion valve or a fixed orifice tube.

Flooding: a condition caused by too much liquid refrigerant being metered into the evaporator.

Fluid: a liquid, free of gas or vapor.

Fluorocarbon: pertains to a group of refrigerants; R-12, for example, is a fluorocarbon.

Flush: to remove solid particles such as metal flakes or dirt. Refrigerant passages are purged with refrigerant.

Foaming: the formation of a froth of oil and refrigerant due to the rapid boiling out of the refrigerant dissolved in the oil when the pressure is suddenly reduced.

FOT: abbreviation for fixed orifice tube. See "Fixed Orifice Tube."

Freeze Plug: see "Core Plug."

Freeze Protection: controlling evaporator temperature so that moisture on its surface does not freeze and block the airflow.

Freezeup. failure of a unit to operate properly due to the formation of ice at the expansion valve.

Freezing Point: the temperature at which a given liquid solidifies. Water freezes at 32°F (0°C); this value is its freezing point.

Front Idler: a groove pulley used in automotive air conditioning as a means of tightening the drive belt. The belt rides in the pulley groove(s).

Front Seat: closing of the compressor service valves by turning them as far as possible in the clockwise direction.

Front Seating: closing off the line leaving the compressor open to the service port fitting. This allows service to the compressor without purging the entire system. *Never* operate the system with the valves front seated.

Frosting Back: the appearance of frost on the tailpipe and suction line extending back as far as the compressor.

Functional Test: see "Performance Test."

Fuse: an electrical device used to protect a circuit against accidental overload or unit malfunction.

Fusible Link: a type of fuse made of a special wire which melts to open a circuit when current draw is excessive.

Gas: a vapor having no particles or droplets of liquid.

Gasket: a thin layer of material or composition that is placed between two machined surfaces to provide a leakproof seal between them.

Gauge Manifold: see "Manifold."

Gauge Set: two or more instruments attached to a manifold and used for measuring or testing pressure.

Halide Leak Detector: a device consisting of a tank of acetylene gas, a stove, chimney, and search hose used to detect leaks by visual means.

Halogen Leak Detector: see "Electronic Leak Detector."

Head: that part of a compressor that covers the valve plates and separates the high side from the low side.

Head Pressure: pressure of the refrigerant from the discharge reed valve through the lines and condenser to the expansion valve orifice.

Heat: energy; any temperature above absolute zero.

Heat Exchanger: an apparatus in which heat is transferred from one fluid to another, on the principle that heat moves to an object with less heat.

Heat Intensity: the measurement of heat concentration with a thermometer.

Heat of Respiration: the heat given off by ripening vegetables or fruits in the conversion of starches and sugars.

Heat Quantity: the amount of heat as measured on a thermometer. See "British Thermal Unit."

Heat Radiation: the transmission of heat from one substance to another while passing through, but not heating, intervening substances.

Heat Transmission: any flow of heat.

Heater Core: a water-to-air heat exchanger which provides heat for the passenger compartment.

Heater Hose: rubber or composition lines used to move heated coolant to the heater and back to the cooling system.

Heater Valve: a manual or automatic valve in the heater hose used to open (start) or close (stop) coolant flow to the heater core.

Hg: chemical symbol for mercury (used to identify a vacuum).

High Head: a term used when the head (high-side) pressure of the system is excessive.

High Heat Load: refers to the maximum amount of heat that can be absorbed by R-12 as it passes through the evaporator.

High-load Condition: those instances when the air conditioner must operate continuously at its maximum capacity to provide the cool air required.

High-pressure Control: see "High-pressure Cutoff Switch."

High-pressure Cutoff Switch: an electrical switch that is activated by a predetermined high pressure. The switch opens a circuit during high-pressure periods.

High-pressure Lines: the lines from the compressor outlet to the expansion valve inlet; these lines carry high-pressure liquid and gas.

High-pressure Relief Valve: a mechanical device designed so that it releases the extreme high pressures of the system to the atmosphere.

High-pressure Switch: see "High-pressure Cutoff Switch."

High-pressure Vapor Line: see "Discharge Line."

High Side: see "Discharge Side."

High-side Pressure: see "Discharge Pressure."

High-side Service Valve: a device located on the discharge side of the compressor; this valve permits the service technician to check the high-side pressures and perform other necessary operations.

High Suction: the low-side pressure is higher than normal due to a malfunction of the system.

High Vacuum: a vacuum below 500 microns (0.009 6 psia or 0.66 kPa).

High-vacuum Pump: a two-stage vacuum pump that has the capability of pulling below 500 microns (0.009 6 psia or 0.66 kPa). Many vacuum pumps can pull to 25 microns (0.005 psia or 0.003 kPa).

Hot Gas: the condition of the refrigerant as it leaves the compressor until it gives up its heat and condenses.

Humidity: see "Moisture."

H-Valve: an expansion valve with all parts contained within used on some Chrysler and Ford car lines.

Hydrochloric Acid: a corrosive acid produced when water and R-12 are mixed as within an automotive air-conditioning system.

Ice Melting Capacity: refrigerant equal to the latent heat of fusion of a stated weight of ice at 144 Btu per pound.

ID: also id. Abbreviation for inside diameter.

Ideal Humidity: a relative humidity of 45% to 50%.

Ideal Temperature: temperature from 68° to 72°F (20° to 22.2°C).

Idler: a pulley device that keeps the belt whip out of the drive belt of an automotive air conditioner. The idler is used as a means of tightening the belt.

Idler Eccentric: a device used with the idler pulley as a means of tightening the belt.

In-car Sensor: a thermistor used in automatic temperature control units for sensing the in-car temperature. Also, see "Thermistor."

Inches of Mercury: an English unit of measure when referring to a vacuum; abbreviated inHg.

In-duct Sensor: a thermistor used in automatic temperature control units for sensing the in-duct return air temperature. Also, see "Thermistor."

Inside Diameter: the measure across the inside walls of a tube or pipe at its widest point.

Insulate: to isolate or seal off with a nonconductor.

Insulation Tape: tape (either rubber or cork) that is used to wrap refrigeration hoses and lines to prevent condensate drip.

In-vehicle Sensor: see "In-car Sensor."

Junction: a point where two or more components, such as electrical wires or vacuum hoses, are joined.

Junction Block: a device on which two or more junctions may be found.

Kilopascal: a unit of measure in the metric system. One kilopascal is equal to 0.145 pound per square inch (psi) in the English system.

Kilopascal Absolute: see "kPa Absolute."

Kinetic: refers to motion.

kPa: abbreviation for kilopascal.

kPa Absolute: a metric unit of measure for pressure measured from absolute zero.

kPa Gauge: a metric unit of measure for pressure measured from atmospheric or sea-level pressure.

Latent Heat: the amount of heat required to cause a change of state of a substance without changing its temperature.

Latent Heat of Condensation: the quantity of heat given off while changing a substance from a vapor to a liquid.

Latent Heat of Evaporation: the quantity of heat required to change a liquid into a vapor without raising the temperature of the vapor above that of the original liquid.

Latent Heat of Fusion: the amount of heat that must be removed from a liquid to cause it to change to a solid without causing a change of temperature.

Latent Heat of Vaporization: see "Latent Heat of Evaporation."

Leak Detector: see "Halide Leak Detector" or "Halogen Leak Detector."

Liquid: a column of fluid without gas pockets or solids.

Liquid Line: the line connecting the drier outlet with the expansion valve inlet. The line from the condenser outlet to the drier inlet is sometimes called a liquid line.

Liter: a metric unit of measure. One liter is equal to 0.264 2 gallon in the English system.

Load: the required rate of heat removed in a given time.

Low-head Pressure: the high-side pressure is lower than normal due to a malfunction of the system.

Low Pressure: usually refers to system pressure below normal; less than expected for a given condition.

Low-pressure Control: see "Low-pressure Cutoff Switch."

Low-pressure Cutoff Switch: an electrical switch that is activated by a predetermined low pressure. This switch opens a circuit during certain low-pressure periods.

Low-pressure Line: see "Suction Line."

Low-pressure Side: see "Suction Side."

Low-pressure Switch: see "Low-pressure Cutoff Switch."

Low-pressure Vapor Line: see "Suction Line."

Low Side: see "Suction Side."

Low-side Service Valve: a device located on the suction side of the compressor which allows the service technician to check low-side pressures or perform other necessary service operations.

Low-suction Pressure: pressure lower than normal in the suction side of the system due to a malfunction of the unit.

Lubricant: a lubricating material such as grease or oil; see "Refrigeration Oil."

Magnetic Clutch: a coupling device used to turn the compressor on and off electrically.

Manifold: a device equipped with a hand shutoff valve. Gauges are connected to the manifold for use in system testing and servicing.

Manifold Gauge: a calibrated instrument used to measure pressures in the system.

Manifold Gauge Set: a manifold complete with gauges and charging hoses.

Melting Point: the temperature above which a material cannot exist as a solid at a given pressure.

Mercury: see "Hg."

Metering Device: any device that meters or regulates the flow of a liquid or vapor. See "Thermostatic Expansion Valve," "Fixed Orifice Tube," and "Expansion Tube."

Mineral Spirits: a petroleum distillate that is suitable for use as a solvent.

Mobil Gel: a trade name. See "Desiccant."

Mobil Sorbead: a drying agent. See "Desiccant."

Modulated Vacuum: a vacuum signal that is regulated to a particular level. See "Vacuum."

Moisture: droplets of water in the air; humidity, dampness or wetness.

Molecular Sieve: a drying agent. See "Desiccant."

Motor: an electrical device which produces a continuous turning motion. A motor is used to propel a fan blade or a blower wheel.

Mount and Drive: pulleys, mounting plates, belts, and fittings necessary to mount a compressor and clutch assembly on an engine.

Muffler: a hollow tubular device used in the discharge line of some air conditioners to minimize the compressor noise transmitted to the inside of the car. Some units use a muffler on the low side as well.

Nichrome Wire: wire made of an alloy of nickel (Ni) and chromium (Cr) that withstands high temperatures. Used for dropping resistors in blower speed controls.

Nonmagnetic Feeler Gauge: thin strip(s) of metal of calibrated thickness made of nonferrous metals to check air gap of components that may have a magnetic field.

OD: also, od. Abbreviation for outside diameter.

Oil: an organic chemical used as a lubricant. A specially formulated oil is used in air-conditioning systems.

Oil Bleed Line: an external line that usually bypasses an expansion valve, evaporator pressure regulator, or bypass valve to insure positive oil return to the compressor at high compressor speeds and under a low charge or clogged system condition.

Oil Bleed Passage: internal orifice that bypasses an expansion valve, evaporator pressure regulator, or bypass valve to insure a positive oil return to the compressor.

Oil Injection Cylinder: a special cylinder that may be used to inject a measured amount of refrigeration oil into the system.

Oil Injector: see "Oil Injection Cylinder."

Operational Test: see "Performance Test."

Orifice Tube: see "Expansion Tube" or "Fixed Orifice Tube."

O-ring: a synthetic rubber gasket with a round (O-shaped) cross section.

Outside Diameter: the measure across the outside walls of a tube or pipe at its widest point.

Overcharge: indicates that too much refrigerant or refrigeration oil is added to the system.

Parts per Million: the unit used to measure the amount of moisture in refrigerant. The maximum (desirable) moisture content is ten parts of moisture to one million parts of refrigerant, or 10 ppm.

Performance Test: readings of the temperature and pressure under controlled conditions to determine if an air-conditioning system is operating at full efficiency.

Pickup Tube: a tube extending from the outlet of the receiver almost to the bottom of the tank to insure that 100% liquid is supplied to the liquid line or metering device.

Pilot-operated Evaporator Pressure Regulator: an EPR valve that is regulated by an internal pilot valve pressure.

Piston: a cylindrical part that moves up and down or back and forth in a compressor cylinder.

POASTV: see "Positive Absolute Suction Throttling Valve."

POA Valve: see "Positive Absolute Suction Throttling Valve."

POEPR: the abbreviation for pilot-operated evaporator pressure regulator.

Positive Absolute Suction Throttling Valve: a suction throttling valve used by Delco Air. This valve has a bronze bellows under a nearly perfect vacuum which is not affected by atmospheric pressure.

Pounds Per Square Inch Absolute: pressure which is not compensated or adjusted for altitude or other variables.

Power Servo: a servo unit used in automatic temperature control which is operated by a vacuum or an electrical signal.

PPM: also, ppm. Abbreviation for "Parts Per Million."

Pressure: force per unit of area; the pressure of refrigerant is measured in pounds per square inch.

Pressure Cap: a radiator cap which increases the pressure of the cooling system and allows higher operating temperatures.

Pressure Drop: the difference in pressure between any two points; a pressure drop may be caused by a restriction or friction.

Pressure Line: although all refrigerant lines are under pressure, the term "pressure line" refers to the discharge line. See "Discharge Line."

Pressure Switch: an electrical switch that is actuated by a predetermined low or high pressure. A pressure switch is generally used for system protection.

Pressure Tester: a device used to pressure test the cooling system and pressure cap to insure that the systems are not leaking under pressure.

Primary Seal: a seal between the compressor shaft seal and the shaft to prevent the leakage of refrigerant and oil.

Programmer: that part of an automatic temperature control system that controls the blower speed, air mix doors, and vacuum diaphragms.

Propane: a flammable gas used in the halide leak detector.

Psi: abbreviation for pounds per square inch.

Psia: abbreviation for pounds per square inch absolute.

Psig: abbreviation for pounds per square inch gauge.

Pulley: a flat wheel with a V-groove machined around the outer edge; when attached to the drive and driven members, the pulley provides a means of driving the compressor.

Pump: the compressor. Also refers to the vacuum pump.

Pumpdown: see "Evacuate."

Purge: to remove moisture and/or air from a system or a component by flushing with a dry gas refrigerant to remove all refrigerant from a system.

Quick Coupler: a coupler that allows hoses to be quickly connected and/or disconnected. Most shop air hoses, for example, are equipped with quick couplers.

R-12: abbreviation for Refrigerant 12.

Radial Compressor: a space-saving compressor used on small cars.

Radiation: the transfer of heat without heating the medium through which it is transmitted.

Radiator: a coolant to air heat exchanger. The device that removes heat from coolant passing through it.

Radiator Cap: see "Pressure Cap."

Radiator Core: see "Core."

Radiator Hose: rubber or synthetic tubes used to carry coolant from the engine to the radiator and from the radiator to the engine.

Radiator Pressure Cap: see "Pressure Cap."

Radiator Pressure Test: see "Pressure Test."

Ram Air: air that is forced through the radiator and condenser coils by the movement of the vehicle or the action of the fan.

Receiver: a container for the storage of liquid refrigerant.

Receiver/Dehydrator: a combination container for the storage of liquid refrigerant and a desiccant.

Receiver/Drier: see "Receiver/Dehydrator."

Reciprocating Compressor: an air-conditioning compressor in which the pistons move up and down or back and forth.

Red Dye Trace Solution: the dye shows the exact location of a leak in the air-conditioning system by depositing a colored film around the leak.

Reed Valves: thin leaves of steel located in the valve plate of automotive compressors; these leaves act as suction and discharge valves. The suction valve is located on the bottom of the valve plate and the discharge valve is on top.

Refrigerant: the chemical compound used in a refrigeration system to produce the desired cooling.

Refrigerant 12: the refrigerant used in automotive air conditioners, as well as other air-conditioning and refrigeration systems. The chemical name of Refrigerant 12 is dichlorodifluoromethane. The chemical symbol is CCl_2F_2.

Refrigeration: the removal of heat by mechanical means.

Refrigeration Cycle: the complete cycle of the refrigerant back to the starting point, evidenced by temperature and pressure changes.

Refrigeration Oil: highly refined oil free from all contaminants, such as sulfur, moisture, and tars.

Relative Humidity: the actual moisture content of the air in relation to the total moisture that the air can hold at a given temperature.

Relay: an electrical switch device that is activated by a low-current source and controls a high-current device.

Remote Bulb: a sensing device connected to the expansion valve by a capillary tube. This device senses the tailpipe temperature and transmits pressure to the expansion valve for its proper operation.

Remote Sensing Bulb: see "Remote Bulb."

Resistance: the property of a substance that impedes current and results in the dissipation of power in the form of heat.

Resistor: a voltage dropping device, usually wire wound, which provides a means of controlling fan speeds.

Restriction: a blockage in the air-conditioning system caused by a pinched or crimped line, foreign matter, or moisture freezeup.

Restrictor: an insert fitting or device used to control the flow of refrigerant or refrigeration oil.

Revolutions Per Minute: the number of times a moving member rotates through 360° in one minute.

Rheostat: a wire-wound variable resistor used to control blower motor speeds.

R/min: also, r/min. Abbreviation for revolutions per minute.

Room Temperature: with reference to the temperature range of 68°F (20°C) to 72°F (22.2°C).

Rotary Vacuum Valve: that part of a vacuum control that is used to divert a vacuum signal for operation of doors, switches, and/or valves.

Rotor: the rotating or freewheeling portion of a clutch; the belt sides on the rotor.

RPM: also, rpm. Abbreviation for "Revolutions Per Minute."

Safety Glasses: eyeglasses with shatterproof lenses worn for eye protection.

Safety Goggles: goggles worn over eyeglasses for eye protection.

Saturated Desiccant: a desiccant that contains all of the moisture it can hold at a given temperature.

Saturated Drier: see "Saturated Desiccant."

Saturated Point: the point at which matter must change state at any given temperature and pressure.

Saturated Temperature: the boiling point of a refrigerant at a particular pressure.

Saturated Vapor: saturation indicates that the space holds as much vapor as possible. No further vaporization is possible at this particular temperature.

Schrader Valve: a spring-loaded valve similar to a tire valve. The Schrader valve is located inside the service valve fitting and is used on some control devices to hold refrigerant in the system. Special adapters must be used with the gauge hose to allow access to the system.

Screen: a metal mesh located in the receiver, expansion valve, and compressor inlet to prevent particles of dirt from circulating through the system.

Sending Unit: that part of a temperature or pressure warning device that triggers or transmits a warning signal to the dash gauge or lamps.

Sensible Heat: heat that causes a change in the temperature of a substance, but does not change the state of the substance.

Sensor: a temperature-sensitive unit such as a remote bulb or thermistor. See "Remote Bulb" and "Thermistor."

Serpentine: curving or winding.

Serpentine Belt: a flat or V-groove belt that winds through all of the engine accessories to drive them off the crankshaft pulley.

Service Port: fitting found on the service valves and some control devices; the manifold set hoses are connected to this fitting.

Service Valve: see "High-side (Low-side) Service Valve."

Shaft Seal: see "Compressor Shaft Seal."

Short Cycling: can be caused by poor air circulation or a maladjusted thermostat. The unit runs for very short periods.

Sight Glass: a window in the liquid line or in the top of the drier; this window is used to observe the liquid refrigerant flow.

Silica Gel: a drying agent used in many automotive air conditioners because of its ability to absorb large quantities of water.

Slugging: the return of liquid refrigerant or oil to the compressor.

Solenoid Valve: an electromagnetic valve controlled remotely by electrically energizing and deenergizing a coil.

Solid: a state of matter that is not liquid and is not a gas or vapor.

Sorbead: a desiccant.

Specific Heat: the quantity of heat required to change one pound of a substance by one degree Fahrenheit.

Specifications: service information and procedures provided by the manufacturer that must be followed in order for the system to operate properly.

Squirrel Cage: a blower case designed for use with the squirrel-cage blower.

Squirrel-Cage Blower: a blower wheel designed to provide a large volume of air with a minimum of noise. The blower is more compact than the fan and air can be directed more efficiently.

Stethoscope: an instrument used to convey sounds of the engine to the ear of the technician.

Strainer: see "Screen."

Stroke: the distance a piston travels from its lowest point to its highest point.

STV: see "Suction Throttling Valve."

Subcooler: a section of liquid line used to insure that only liquid refrigerant is delivered to the expansion valve. This line may be a part of the condenser or may be placed in the drip pan of the evaporator.

Substance: any form of matter.

Suction Line: the line connecting the evaporator outlet to the compressor inlet.

Suction Line Regulator: see "Suction Throttling Valve" or "Evaporator Pressure Regulator."

Suction Pressure: compressor inlet pressure. Reflects the pressure of the system on the low side.

Suction Service Valve: see "Low-side Service Valve."

Suction Side: that portion of the refrigeration system under low pressure; the suction side extends from the expansion device to the compressor inlet.

Suction Throttling Valve: a back-pressure-regulated device that prevents the freezeup of the evaporator core.

Suction Throttling Valve-POA: see "Positive Absolute Suction Throttling Valve."

Sump: the bottom part of the compressor that contains oil for lubrication of the moving parts of the compressor. Not all compressors have a sump.

Sun Load: heat intensity and/or light intensity produced by the sun.

Sun-load sensor: a device that senses heat and/or light intensity. See "Photovoltaic Diode."

Super Heat: adding heat intensity to a gas after the complete evaporation of a liquid.

Superheated Vapor: vapor at a temperature higher than its boiling point for a given pressure.

Superheat Switch: an electrical switch activated by an abnormal temperature-pressure condition (a superheated vapor); used for system protection.

Swash Plate Compressor: a compressor in which the pistons are driven by an offset (swash) plate affixed to the main shaft, such as the Delco Air six-cylinder compressor.

Sweeping: see "Purge."

System: all of the components and lines that make up an air-conditioning system.

Tailpipe: the outlet pipe from the evaporator to the compressor. See "Suction Line."

Tank: see "Header Tank" and "Expansion Tank."

Temperature: heat intensity measured on a thermometer.

Temperature Gauge: a dash-mounted device that indicates engine temperature.

Temperature Indicator: see "Temperature Gauge." May also be COLD and HOT lamps to warn of overcooling or overheating of engine coolant.

TEV: abbreviation for thermostatic expansion valve.

Thermal: of, caused by, or pertaining to heat.

Thermal Delay Fuse: a device used with the "Compressor Protection Switch" which heats and blows a fuse to stop compressor action during abnormal operation.

Thermal Fuse: a temperature-sensitive fuse link designed so that it melts at a certain temperature and opens a circuit.

Thermal Limiter: an electrical or mechanical device used to control the intensity or quantity of heat.

Thermistor: a temperature-sensing resistor that has the ability to change values with changing temperature.

Thermostat: a device used to cycle the clutch to control the rate of refrigerant flow as a means of temperature control. The driver has control over the temperature desired.

Thermostatic Clutch Control: see "Thermostat."

Thermostatic Expansion Valve: the component of a refrigeration system that regulates the rate of flow of refrigerant into the evaporator as governed by the action of the remote bulb sensing tailpipe temperatures.

Thermostatic Switch: see "Thermostat."

Throttling Valve: see "Suction Throttling Valve" and "Evaporator Pressure Regulator."

Time-delay Relay: an electrical switch device that provides a time delay before closing (or opening).

Ton of Refrigeration: the effect of melting one ton of ice in 24 hours. One ton equals cooling 12 000 Btu per hour.

Total Heat Load: The amount of heat to be removed or added, based on all conditions.

Trace: a colored dye (suitable for use in a refrigeration system) introduced to the system to detect leaks.

Transducer: a vacuum valve used to transfer the electrical signal from the amplifier into a vacuum signal. This vacuum signal regulates the power servo unit in automatic temperature control units.

Trunk Unit: an automotive air-conditioning evaporator that mounts in the trunk compartment and is ducted through the package tray.

TXV: abbreviation for thermostatic expansion valve.

Undercharge: a system that is short of refrigerant; this condition results in improper cooling.

Vacuum: any pressure below atmospheric pressure.

Vacuum Check Relay: a mechanical air-operated device that checks (closes off) a vacuum line to a pot whenever the manifold vacuum pressure falls below the applied vacuum pressure.

Vacuum Check Valve: an air-operated mechanical device that checks (closes) a vacuum line to the vacuum reserve tank whenever the manifold vacuum pressure falls below the reserve vacuum pressure.

Vacuum Hose: see "Vacuum Line."

Vacuum Line: a rubber tube used to transmit a vacuum reading from one to another.

Vacuum Motor: a device designed to provide mechanical control by the use of a vacuum.

Vacuum Pot: see "Vacuum Motor."

Vacuum Power Unit: a device for operating the doors and valves of an air conditioner using a vacuum as a source of power.

Vacuum Programmer: a device with a bleed valve which changes vacuum pressure by bleeding more or less air thereby controlling the vacuum signal.

Vacuum Pump: a mechanical device used to evacuate the refrigeration system to rid it of excess moisture and air.

Vacuum Reserve Tank: a container that is used to store reserve (engine) vacuum pressure.

Vacuum Tank: see "Vacuum Reserve Tank."

Valve Plate: a plate containing suction and/or discharge valves located under the compressor heads.

Valves-in-receiver (VIR): an assembly containing the expansion valve, suction throttling valve, desiccant, and receiver.

Vapor: see "Gas."

Vapor Lines: lines that are used to carry refrigerant gas or vapor.

Variable Displacement: to change the displacement of a compressor by changing the stroke of the piston(s).

V-belt: a rubber-like continuous loop placed between the engine crankshaft pulley and accessories to transfer rotary motion of the crankshaft to the accessories.

Ventilation: the act of supplying fresh air to an enclosed space, such as the inside of an automobile.

Venturi: a tubelike device that contains a restriction to create a negative pressure.

V-Groove Belt: see "Serpentine Belt."

VIR: abbreviation for "valves-in-receiver."

Viscosity: the thickness of a liquid or its resistance to flow.

Volatile Liquid: a liquid that evaporates readily to become a vapor.

V-pulley: used in automotive applications to drive the accessories, such as a water pump, generator, alternator, power steering, and air-conditioner compressor.

Water Control Valve: a mechanically operated or vacuum-operated shutoff valve that stops the flow of hot water to the heater.

Water Pump: a device, usually belt driven, that provides a means of circulating coolant through the engine and cooling system.

Water Valve: see "Water Control Valve."

Wobble Plate Compressor: see "Swash Plate Compressor."

Woodruff Key: an index key that prevents a pulley from turning on a shaft.

INDEX

A

Absolute cold, 3
Accumulator, 23–24
    cycling clutch FOT system, system diagnosis, 64–65
Actuator, water valve, 54–55
Air conditioning
    basic system, 10–12
    compressors and, 12–22
        design of, 12–14
        drives, 14–15
        electromagnetic clutch, 21–22
        function of, 12
        piston type, 15–19
        reciprocating, 15–19
        variable displacement, 20–21
        York vane rotary, 19–20
Air movement, body comfort and, 5
Ambient
    air, 1
    temperature, 1
Aspirator, 53
Automatic temperature controls, 46–55
    aspirator, 53
    blower, 50
    brake booster vacuum switch, 54
    clutch control, 50
    clutch diode, 50
    control panel and, 48–49
    coolant temperature sensor, 53–54
    electronic, 48
    heater delay switch, 54
    high pressure switch, 52
    high-side switch, 51
    in-car temperature sensor, 53
    low-side switch, 52
    lower pressure switch, 52
    mode actuator, 54
    outside temperature sensor, 52
    power module, 50
    power steering cutoff switch, 54
    pressure cycling switch, 52
    programmer and, 49–50
    sensors, 48
    sunload sensor, 52
    throttle position sensor, 54
    vehicle speed sensor, 54
    water valve actuator, 54–55
Axial plate, 13–14

B

Blower motor, 31, 50
Body comfort, 4–5
    conditions which affect, 5
Brake booster vacuum switch, 54

C

CCFOT (fixed orifice tube), 28
CCOT (orifice tube), 28
Charging the system, 98–101
Clutch
    control, 50
    diode, 50
Cold, defined, 3
Combination valves, 29–30, 38–39
Combo valve, 29–30
Compressor
    system diagnosis, 61
    volumetric test procedure on, 103–104
Compressor repair
    Delco, 161–65
        air,
            DA-6, 166–76
            V-5, 177–86
        four cylinder, 154–60
        six cylinder, 161–65
    Nippondenso, 129–35
        ten-cylinder, 136–38
    safety and, 128
    Sankyo, 139–44
    shaft oil seal, 149–51
    Tecumseh, 144–48
Compressors, 12–22
    design of, 12–14
    drives, 14–15
    electromagnetic clutch, 21–22
    function of, 12
    piston type, 15–19
    reciprocating, 15–19
    variable displacement, 20–21
    York vane rotary, 19–20
Condensation, latent heat of, 2
Condensers, 31–32
    cycling clutch, system diagnosis, 62
Conduction, defined, 1
Control panel, 48–49
Controls, 33–42
    master, 39
    regulators,
        evaporator pressure, 33–35
        suction pressure, 33
    relay,
        ambient, 41
        electrovacuum, 41
        time-delay, 41
    switch,
        compressor discharge pressure, 40–41
        pressure cutoff, 40
        superheat, 42
    thermostat, 40
    valves,
        combination, 38–39

in-receiver (VIR), 36–38
suction throttling, 35–36
thermostatic vacuum, 41–42
Convection
   body comfort and, 4
   defined, 1
Coolant temperature sensor, 53–54
Crankshaft, compressor, 13
Cycling clutch
   diagnosis of, 71–76
   fixed orifice tube (CCFOT), 28
   orifice tube (CCOT), 28
   system, 43, 44

D
Dehydrator cycling clutch, system diagnosis, 63
Delco
   compressor repair,
      air,
         DA-6, 166–76
         V-5, 177–86
      four cylinder, 154–60
      six cylinder, 161–65
Desiccant, receiver/drier and, 22
Diagnosis. *See* system diagnosis.
Drives, 14–15
Dye
   adding to system, 94–95
   leak detection with, 82

E
EEVIR. *See* evaporator equalizer valves-in-receiver.
Electromagnetic clutch, compressors and, 21–22
Electronic leak detectors, 82–83, 91
Electronic temperature control systems, 48, 49
Electrovacuum relay (EVR), 41
English temperature pressure chart, 57
EPR. *See* evaporator pressure regulator.
Equalizers, thermostatic expansion valve and, 27
Evacuating the system, 93
Evaporation, body comfort and, 4–5
Evaporator, 30–31
Evaporator equalizer valves-in-receiver (EEVIR), 28
Evaporator pressure regulator (EPR), 33–35, 44
EVR. *See* electrovacuum relay.
Expansion tube, 28

F
Filter, receiver/drier and, 22
Fittings, refrigerant, servicing, 107–10
Fixed orifice tube (FOT), testing and/or replacing, 116–19
Fusion, latent heat of, 2

G
Gauges
   calibration and scales, 79–80
   high-side, servicing, 79
   low-side, servicing, 78–79
   third, servicing, 80

H
Halide leak detector, 81, 91
Halogen electronic leak detection method, 91
Hand shutoff valve, servicing, 84–85
Heat
   body comfort and, 4–5
   defined, 1, 3
   types of, 1–3
Heater delay switch, 54
High-side
   gauge, servicing, 79
   temperature switch, 51
Hoses, 32
   refrigerant, servicing, 107–10
   servicing, 80
Humidity, body comfort and, 5

I
In-car temperature sensor, 53
In-receiver valve (VIR), 36–38

K
Kelvin scale, 3

L
Latent heat, 1–2
   of condensation, 2
   of fusion, 2
   of vaporization, 1
Leak detection, 81–83, 89–92
Liquid
   saturated, 1
   subcooled, 1
Low-side
   gauge, servicing, 78–79
   temperature switch, 52

M
Master control, 39
Moisture removal, 85–86
Motors, blower, 31

N
Nippondenso
   compressor repair, 129–35
      ten-cylinder, 136–38

O
Oil level, compressor, checking and, 120–27
Orifice tube
   fixed, 28
   system diagnosis, 68
Outside temperature sensor, 52

P
Pickup tube, receiver/drier and, 22–23
Piston type compressor, 15–19
   action, 19
   applications of, 16, 18–19

Index

POASTV. *See* positive operated suction throttling valve.
Positive displacement pump, 24
Positive operated suction throttling valve (POASTV), 28
Power module, 50
Power steering cutoff switch, 54
Pressure chart, English temperature, 57
Pressure cycle switch, 52
Programmer, 49–50
Purging the system, 96–97

R
R-12, 5–6
    temperature and pressure relationship of, 6–7
Radiation
    body comfort and, 4
    defined, 1
Receiver/drier components, 22–23
Reciprocating compressors, 15–19
    action, 19
    applications of, 16, 18–19
Refrigerant, 5–8
    defined, 5
    handling, 5, 6
    safety precautions for, 7–8
    temperature and pressure relationship of, 6–7
Refrigeration
    cycle, 8–9
    oil, 8
Regulators
    evaporator pressure, 33–35
    suction pressure, 33
Relays
    ambient, 41
    electrovacuum, 41
    time-delay, 41
Repair
    Compressor. *See* compressor repair.
    compressor,
        isolating from system, 102
        oil level and, 120–27
        performing a volumetric test on, 103–104
    fixed orifice tube, 116–19
    performance testing and, 105–106
    refrigerant, hose and fittings, 107–10
    valves-in-receiver (VIR),
        rebuilding, 112–15
        testing performance and, 111
Rotating field clutch, 21–22

S
Safety, system service and, 77
Sankyo, compressor repair, 139–44
Saturated liquid, 1
Schrader valve, servicing, 83
Sensible heat, 1
Sensors, 48
    coolant temperature, 53–54
    in-car temperature, 53
    outside temperature, 52
    sunload, 52
    throttle position, 54
    vehicle speed, 54
Serpentine drive, 15
Servicing. *See* system service.
Shaft oil seal, repair, 149–51
Sight glass, receiver/drier and, 23
Soap solution, leak detection with, 81–82, 91
Specific heat, 2–3
Speed sensor, 54
Stationary clutch field, 21
Strainer, receiver/drier and, 23
STV. *See* suction throttling valve.
Subcooled liquid, 1
Suction, pressure regulator, 33
Suction,
    accumulator, 24
    pressure regulator, 33
    throttling valve (STV), 29, 35–36
    system, 44, 45
Sunload sensor, 52
Superheat switch, 42
Swash plate, 13–14
Switches
    brake booster vacuum, 54
    compressor discharge pressure, 40–41
    heater delay, 54
    high-side temperature, 51
    low-side temperature, 52
    power steering cutoff, 54
    pressure cutoff, 40
    pressure cycle, 52
    superheat, 42
System
    charging, 98–101
    evacuating, 93
    purging, 96–97
System diagnosis
    accumulator, cycling clutch FOT system, 64–65
    compressor, 61
    condenser-cycling clutch, 62
    cycling clutch TXV or FOT system, 71–76
    dehydrator cycling clutch, 63
    orifice tube, cycling clutch for system, 68
    thermostat, cycling clutch TXV or FOT system, 69–70
    thermostatic expansion valve, cycling clutch TXV system, 66–67
System service
    charging the system, 98–101
    compressor,
        checking oil level, 120–27
        isolating from system, 102
        volumetric test procedure, 103–104
    fixed orifice tube (FOT), testing and/or replacing, 116–19
    gauge set, 78–80
    leak detectors and, 81–83
    leak testing the system, 89–92
    manifold, 77–78
    procedure,
        adding dye to system, 94–95
        evacuating the system, 93

manifold and gauge, connecting into system, 87–88
purging the system, 96–97
refrigerant, hoses and fittings, 107–10
safety and, 77
system performance testing, 105–106
valves, 83–86
valves-in-receiver (VIR), rebuilding, 112–15
testing performance of, 111
Systems, types of, 43–45

T

Tecumseh, compressor repair, 144–48
Temperature
    automatic controls, 46–55
        See also automatic temperature controls.
    body comfort and, 5
    coolant sensor, 53–54
    in-car sensor, 53
    outside, sensor, 52
Temperature switch
    high-side, 51
    low-side, 52
Thermal heat, 2–3
Thermostat
    control, 40
    diagnosis of, 69–70
Thermostatic expansion valve, 24–27, 28–29
    as a control device, 26–27
    cycling clutch TXV system, system diagnosis, 66–67
    equalizers and, 27
    operation of, 24–26
Third gauge, servicing, 80
Throttle position sensor, 54
Trace solution, adding to system, 94–95

Troubleshooting
    insufficient cooling, 59
    no cooling, 59–60
    noisy compressor, 58
    noisy system, 57–58
    system cools intermittently, 58–59
TXV. *See* thermostatic expansion valve.

V

Vacuum, water boiling point in a, 85
Valves
    combination, 29–30, 38–39
    servicing, 83–86
    suction throttling, 29, 35–36
    thermostatic vacuum, 41–42
    types of, 30
    valves-in-receiver, 28–29
Valves-in-receiver (VIR), 28–29, 36–38
    rebuilding, 112–15
    system, 45
    testing performance of, 111
Vaporization, latent heat of, 1
Variable displacement compressor, 20–21
Vehicle speed sensor, 54
VIR. *See* valves-in-receiver.

W

Water
    boiling point in a vacuum, 85
    valve actuator, 54–55
Wobble plate, 13–14

Y

York vane rotary compressor, 19–20